Russian Energy and Foreign Relations

This book examines Russia's new assertiveness and the role of energy as a key factor in shaping the country's behavior in international relations, and in building political and economic power domestically, since the 1990s.

Energy transformed Russia's fortunes after its decline during the 1990s. The wealth generated from energy exports sparked economic recovery and political stabilization, and has significantly contributed to Russia's assertiveness as a great power. Energy has been a key factor in shaping Russia's foreign relations in both the Eurasian and global context. This development raises a host of questions for both Russia and the West about the stability of the Russian economy, how Russia will use the power it gains from its energy wealth, and how the West should react to Russia's new-found political weight.

Given that energy is likely to remain at the top of the global political agenda for some time to come, and Russia's role as a key energy supplier to Europe is unlikely to diminish soon, this book sheds light on one of the key security concerns of the twenty-first century: Where is Russia headed and how does energy affect the changing dynamics of Russia's relations with Europe, the US, and the Asia-Pacific region.

This book will be of interest to students of Russian politics, energy security, international relations, and foreign policy in general.

Jeronim Perovic is a senior researcher at the Institute of History at the University of Basel and a visiting scholar at the Center for Security Studies at ETH Zurich. **Robert W. Orttung** is a visiting scholar at the Center for Security Studies at ETH Zurich and a senior fellow at the Jefferson Institute. **Andreas Wenger** is professor of international security policy and director of the Center for Security Studies at ETH Zurich.

CSS Studies in security and international relations
Series Editors: Andreas Wenger and Victor Mauer
Center for Security Studies, ETH Zurich

The *CSS Studies in Security and International Relations* examine historical and contemporary aspects of security and conflict. The series provides a forum for new research based upon an expanded conception of security and will include monographs by the Center's research staff and associated academic partners.

War Plans and Alliances in the Cold War
Threat perceptions in the East and West
Edited by Vojtech Mastny, Sven Holtsmark, and Andreas Wenger

Transforming NATO in the Cold War
Challenges beyond deterrence in the 1960s
Edited by Andreas Wenger, Christian Nuenlist, and Anna Locher

US Foreign Policy and the War on Drugs
Displacing the cocaine and heroin industry
Cornelius Friesendorf

Cyber-Security and Threat Politics
US efforts to secure the information age
Myriam Dunn Cavelty

Securing 'the Homeland'
Critical infrastructure, risk and (in)security
Edited by Myriam Dunn Cavelty and Kristian Søby Kristensen

Origins of the European Security System
The Helsinki process revisited 1965–75
Edited by Andreas Wenger, Vojtech Mastny, and Christian Nuenlist

Russian Energy Power and Foreign Relations
Implications for conflict and cooperation
Edited by Jeronim Perovic, Robert W. Orttung, and Andreas Wenger

Russian Energy Power and Foreign Relations

Implications for conflict and cooperation

Edited by Jeronim Perovic,
Robert W. Orttung, and Andreas Wenger

LONDON AND NEW YORK

First published 2009
by Routledge
2 Park Square, Milton Park, Abingdon, Oxon OX14 4RN

Simultaneously published in the USA and Canada
by Routledge
270 Madison Ave, New York, NY 10016

Routledge is an imprint of the Taylor & Francis Group, an informa business

Transferred to Digital Printing 2010

© 2009 Selection and editorial material, Jeronim Perovic, Robert W. Orttung, and Andreas Wenger; individual chapters, the contributors

Typeset in Times by Wearset Ltd, Boldon, Tyne and Wear

All rights reserved. No part of this book may be reprinted or reproduced or utilized in any form or by any electronic, mechanical, or other means, now known or hereafter invented, including photocopying and recording, or in any information storage or retrieval system, without permission in writing from the publishers.

British Library Cataloguing in Publication Data
A catalogue record for this book is available from the British Library

Library of Congress Cataloging in Publication Data
A catalog record for this book has been requested

ISBN10: 0-415-48438-3 (hbk)
ISBN10: 0-415-58599-6 (pbk)
ISBN10: 0-203-88009-9 (ebk)

ISBN13: 978-0-415-48438-1 (hbk)
ISBN13: 978-0-415-58599-6 (pbk)
ISBN13: 978-0-203-88009-8 (ebk)

We dedicate this book to our wives, Franca, Susan, and Astrid

Contents

List of illustrations	ix
List of contributors	xi
Acknowledgments	xiii
List of abbreviations	xv

1 Introduction: Russian energy power, domestic and
international dimensions   1
JERONIM PEROVIC

PART I
The domestic dimension of Russian energy   21

2 The sustainability of Russia's energy power: implications
for the Russian economy   23
PHILIP HANSON

3 Energy and state–society relations: socio-political aspects of
Russia's energy wealth   51
ROBERT W. ORTTUNG

4 Developing Russia's oil and gas industry: what role for
the state?   71
HEIKO PLEINES

PART II
Russia's role in international energy markets   87

5 Russia's key customer: Europe   89
STACY CLOSSON

viii Contents

6   Russia's role in the Eurasian energy market: seeking control
    in the face of growing challenges   109
    JULIA NANAY

7   Russia's future customers: Asia and beyond   132
    NINA POUSSENKOVA

PART III
International policies toward Russia   155

8   European perspectives for managing dependence   157
    PAMI AALTO

9   US energy policy and the former Soviet Union: parallel
    tracks   181
    PETER RUTLAND

10 Chinese perspectives on Russian oil and gas   201
    INDRA ØVERLAND AND KYRRE ELVENES BRÆKHUS

PART IV
Conclusion   223

11 Russia's energy power: implications for Europe and for
    transatlantic cooperation   225
    ANDREAS WENGER

    Index   245

Illustrations

Figures

2.1	Per capita gross national income in 2006 as a percentage of US GNI for selected countries	25
2.2	Annual average rates of GDP growth, 2000–5, among selected middle-income countries	25
2.3	Some indicators of Russian dependence on oil and gas	27
2.4	Year-on-year (yoy) percentage changes in average prices and volumes of Russian oil exports, 1999–2006	34
2.5	Projected production, import, and domestic consumption of major fuels, 2005–30	36
2.6	Production, import, domestic consumption, and exports of gas, 2005–30	37
3.1	World oil prices, 1989–2007	55
3.2	Freedom House political rights scores for Russia	56
4.1	There should be no foreign investment in this sector of the economy!	73
4.2	Share of state-owned companies in oil and gas production	75
4.3	Russia's five biggest oil companies	76
7.1	Key players in Russia's east, 2000–7	139

Maps

1.1	Russian oil pipelines	4
1.2	Russian gas pipelines	5
6.1	Caspian oil pipelines	113
6.2	Caspian gas pipelines	113
7.1	East Siberia and the Russian Far East	133

Tables

2.1	Science, technology, and communications in Russia and other BRICs, early 2000s	30

2.2	Total domestic energy supply per unit of GDP in 2005: selected countries	38
3.1	Political leaders with powerful corporate positions at the end of Putin's second presidential term	64
5.1	Natural gas supplies in 1982 and 1990	92
7.1	Estimated distributions of total initial oil and gas reserves by region	134
7.2	Maximum oil and gas production levels in Eastern Siberia and the Far East	135
8.1	The role of gas imports from Russia among EU member states	164
8.2	Challenges and options for European energy security society	169
9.1	US trade with Russia, 1995–2006	186
9.2	US trade with Russia, 2005–7	186
10.1	China's top 12 sources of crude oil, 2001–6	204

Contributors

Pami Aalto is Jean Monnet Professor and Director of the Jean Monnet Centre of Excellence at the University of Tampere, Finland. He is also member of the Eurasia Energy Group at the Aleksanteri Institute, University of Helsinki.

Kyrre Elvenes Brækhus is a Chinese government scholar at Tsinghua University in Beijing and a part-time senior analyst at Arreon Carbon, a firm that originates and purchases carbon credits in the Chinese market. He also writes for the Economist Intelligence Unit.

Stacy Closson is a Trans-Atlantic Post-Doctoral Fellow for International Relations and Security (TAPIR).

Philip Hanson is an Associate Fellow of the Russia and Eurasia Programme of Chatham House (the Royal Institute of International Affairs) in London. He is also Emeritus Professor of the Political Economy of Russia and Eastern Europe at the University of Birmingham.

Julia Nanay is a Senior Director at PFC Energy, a consultancy in Washington, DC heading the Russia and Caspian Service and regional consulting activities.

Robert W. Orttung is a visiting scholar at the Center for Security Studies at ETH Zurich and a senior fellow at the Jefferson Institute in Washington, DC.

Indra Øverland is Head of the Energy Programme at the Norwegian Institute of International Affairs and Associate Professor at the University of Tromsø (part-time).

Jeronim Perovic is a senior researcher at the Institute of History at the University of Basel and a visiting scholar at the Center for Security Studies at ETH Zurich.

Heiko Pleines is Head of the Department of Politics and Economics at the Research Centre for East European Studies and lecturer in Comparative Politics and European Studies at the University of Bremen.

Nina Poussenkova is a senior researcher at the Institute of World Economy and International Relations and a scholar-in-residence at the Carnegie Moscow Center.

Peter Rutland is Professor of Government at Wesleyan University.

Andreas Wenger is Professor of International Security Policy and Director of the Center for Security Studies at ETH Zurich.

Acknowledgments

Understanding Russia's development over the past decade requires taking into consideration the role of energy: Russia is the world's leading exporter of natural gas and trails only Saudi Arabia in oil exports. High world energy prices naturally have a profound effect on the performance of Russia's economy, which grew by over 6 percent during each of the past eight years. Oil money filled the coffers of the state and private companies alike, bringing back confidence to a country that in the 1990s accepted Western financial assistance. But how sustainable is Russia's economic growth, based to a large extent on the sale of oil and gas? What are the repercussions of Russia's new wealth for domestic developments, and how does it affect Russia's behavior in foreign political and economic affairs? How should the West deal with a country that has, under the leadership of President Vladimir Putin and his successor Dmitry Medvedev, become increasingly assertive? This book seeks to provide answers to these questions.

We believe that the processes inside Russia as well as the behavior of Russia abroad can only be understood if viewed in a comprehensive manner. Accordingly, contributions in this book look at both domestic and international dimensions of Russian energy power. In addition, the contributors view Russian energy relations from two different perspectives by looking at Russian energy policies toward key international markets and analyzing the energy policies of Europe, the US, and China toward Russia. The combination of these different aspects makes this book unique.

The research was originally undertaken for a conference titled "Energy Security and Russia–EU Relations." This event, which took place on 10 March 2007 at ETH Zurich, was organized by the Center for Security Studies at ETH Zurich and co-sponsored by the Swiss National Science Foundation and the Russian Foundation for Basic Research. The three editors then focused on the conceptualization of a book and selected the most appropriate papers from among the contributions prepared for the conference. Revised papers were then presented on 26–27 October 2007 at the follow-up conference "Energy and the Transformation of International Relations: Global Perspectives and the Role of Russia." The conference took place at ETH Zurich and was financed through a generous grant from the German Marshall Fund of the United States. Based on discussions during the conference, the contributors revised their chapters once again.

Acknowledgments

We would particularly like to thank the participants of the two conferences who provided useful comments to the authors in preparing the resultant chapters. They were Margarita Balmaceda, Elena Merle-Beral, Michael Bradshaw, Stefan Brem, Christian Cleutinx, Michael Da Costa, Stefan Dörig, Monica Enfield, Matteo Fachinotti, Bassam Fattouh, John Gault, Roland Götz, Tim Guld, Mikkal Herberg, Graeme Herd, Jan Kalicki, Sergei S. Kolchin, Viacheslav Kulagin, Ivan Kurilla, Tanvi Madan, Andrei Makarychev, Silvia Mathis, Tatiana Mitrova, Andrew Monaghan, Liliana Proskuriakova, John Roberts, Oliver Schelske, Peter Sparding, Roger Tissot, Bill Tompson, Michael E. Webber, and Peter Zweifel.

We would like to thank Christopher Findlay for his editorial help and Frank Haydon for creating the maps and arranging the various tables and graphs. We are also grateful to Jennifer Gassmann and Silvia Azzouzi for excellent logistical help for the two conferences in Zurich. Despite the support of colleagues, the editors remain solely responsible for any errors in the text.

Jeronim Perovic, Robert W. Orttung, and Andreas Wenger
Zurich, Basel, and Washington

Abbreviations

ACG	Azeri–Chirag–Guneshli
AIOC	Azerbaijan International Operating Company
APR	Asia Pacific Region
BAM	Baikal–Amur Mainline
bcm	billion cubic meters
bcm/y	billion cubic meters per year
b/d	barrels per day
bn	billion
BOFIT	Bank of Finland Institute for Economies in Transition
BP	British Petroleum
BPS	Baltic Pipeline System
BRIC	Brazil, Russia, India, and China
BTC	Baku–Tbilisi–Ceyhan
CAC	Central Asia-Center
CEE	Central and Eastern Europe
CEO	Chief Executive Officer
CEPS	Centre for European Policy Studies
CERA	Cambridge Energy Research Associates
CFSP	Common Foreign and Security Policy
CIS	Commonwealth of Independent States
CMEA	Council for Mutual Economic Assistance
CNODC	China National Oil and Gas Exploration and Development Corporation
CNOOC	China National Offshore Oil Corporation
CNPC	China National Petroleum Corporation
CPC	Caspian Pipeline Consortium
CPI	Consumer Price Index
CRS	Congressional Research Service
EBRD	European Bank for Reconstruction and Development
EC	European Commission
ECT	Energy Charter Treaty
EEA	European Economic Area
EEC	European Economic Community

EIA	Energy Information Administration
ESPO	East Siberia–Pacific Ocean
EU	European Union
FDI	Foreign Direct Investment
FSB	Federal Security Service
GDP	Gross Domestic Product
GNI	Gross National Income
GUEU	Georgia–Ukraine–European Union
IEA	International Energy Agency
IEF	International Energy Forum
IGA	Inter-Governmental Agreement
IMF	International Monetary Fund
IOC	International Oil Company
IPO	Initial Public Offerings
IR	International Relations
IT	Information Technology
JV	Joint Venture
kcm	thousand cubic meters
KGB	Committee on State Security
KMG	KazMunaiGaz
KNOC	Korea National Oil Corporation
LNG	Liquefied Natural Gas
mbd	million barrels per day
mcm	million cubic meters
MEMR	Ministry of Energy and Mineral Resources
MERT	Ministry of Economic Development and Trade
MIC	Military–Industrial Commission
Minpromenergo	Ministry of Industry and Energy
mmt	million metric tons
mn	million
mn/y	million per year
MNR	Ministry of Natural Resources
mt	million tons
mt/y	million tons per year
NAIRIT	National Association and Development of IT
NATO	North Atlantic Treaty Organization
NGO	Non-Governmental Organization
NICO	Naftiran Intertrade Company
NOC	National Oil Company
NTI	Nuclear Threat Initiative
OECD	Organization for Economic Cooperation and Development
ONGC	Oil and Natural Gas Corporation
OPEC	Organization of Petroleum Exporting Countries
OPIC	Overseas Private Investment Corporation
pa	per annum

PCA	Partnership and Cooperation Agreement
PPP	Purchasing Power Parity
PSA	Production Sharing Agreement
PWR	Pressurized Water Reactor
R&D	Research and Development
RF	Russian Federation
RFE/RL	Radio Free Europe/Radio Liberty
RUE	RosUkrEnergo
RZD	Russian Railways
SCO	Shanghai Cooperation Organisation
SCP	South Caucasus Pipeline
SIDANCO	Siberian–Far Eastern Oil Company
Sinopec	China Petroleum and Chemical Corporation
SOCAR	State Oil Company of Azerbaijan Republic
SODECO	Sakhalin Oil Development Corporation
SPO	Secondary Public Offerings
sq km	square kilometer
TAPI	Turkmenistan–Afghanistan–Pakistan–India
tcm	trillion cubic meters
TCO	TengizChevroil
TCP	Trans-Caspian Pipeline
tn	trillion
TNK	Tyumen Oil Company
toe	tons of oil equivalent
TPAO	Turkish Petroleum Corporation
UES	United Energy Systems of Russia
UK	United Kingdom
UNCTAD	United Nations Conference on Trade and Development
UNESCO	United Nations Educational, Scientific, and Cultural Organization
US	United States
USA	United States of America
USSR	Union of Soviet Socialist Republics
VLCC	Very Large Crude Carrier
WTO	World Trade Organization
yoy	year-on-year

1 Introduction
Russian energy power, domestic and international dimensions

Jeronim Perovic

Concerns over secure energy supplies are high on the global political agenda. Because global demand for oil and gas is expected to grow faster than supply, the energy market is generally tight and prices are generally high. These developments have dramatically increased the awareness among Western energy consumers of their precarious dependency on those countries that produce and export fossil fuels. In the larger European context, Russia stands out as the single most important energy supplier. The European Union (EU) imports nearly a third of its oil and almost half of its natural gas from Russia – although the level of dependency differs greatly among the EU member states. Some of Russia's post-Soviet neighbors, as well as the non-EU members in the Western Balkans and Turkey, are also heavily dependent on Russian energy. Russia is important for Eurasia's energy flows, as the bulk of the gas and oil transported from the energy-rich Caspian states still passes through Russian pipelines.

Conversely, the high oil price environment of the past five years has also had a large impact on Russia's development. The massive new wealth generated from oil and gas exports has helped Russia to recover from its steep decline during the 1990s. Economic growth has gone hand in hand with political stabilization and has improved the lives of many Russian citizens. Thanks to earnings from energy sales, Russia not only repaid its foreign debts to the Paris Club, but also accumulated massive financial reserves. This new wealth marks a very significant development, since it means that Russia feels it is no longer beholden to the West and can pursue a more "independent" foreign policy line. This attitude has been reflected in sometimes sharp Russian rhetoric over energy export diversification from Europe to Asia or the suggestion to build a "gas cartel" with other major gas producers. It is also seen at the level of public diplomacy, where Russian leaders are striking more aggressive tones, or in Moscow's announcement that it plans to increase military spending substantially, including the modernization of its nuclear forces.

Russia's rise as an energy power has stirred up a level of controversy in the transatlantic debate on Russia and in the Russian–Western dialog that has not been seen since the days of the Cold War. During the Cold War, the US frequently criticized its Western European allies for seeking to foster energy ties with the Soviet Union and claimed that the inflow of foreign currency generated from energy sales would help the Kremlin's efforts to modernize its military. A major and repeated controversy between Washington and its Western European allies with regard to Soviet energy concerned efforts to have gas supplies delivered via pipeline. The US government feared that increased European dependence on Soviet gas supplies would weaken the political resolve of Europe, and would cause countries to submit to political pressures under threat of gas supplies being cut off.[1]

The threat of a cut-off or reduction in energy supplies was prominently discussed against the background of a potential energy crisis in the Soviet Union. In 1977, for instance, the CIA published three famous reports on the prospects for Soviet oil production and trade, predicting that the Soviet Union would soon run out of oil and become dependent on imports within a decade. These reports implied that, should an energy crisis occur, it would affect oil and gas exports to Western Europe, as Moscow would likely prefer supplying its allies in Eastern Europe or cutting gas exports altogether in order to offset a domestic decline in oil production.[2]

Unlike their US counterparts, the Europeans were in general much less alarmist and considered energy relations with the Soviet Union a strictly commercial issue. Especially against the background of the 1973 oil crisis, when OPEC decided to stop shipping oil to the US and some of its allies because of their support of Israel in the Yom Kippur War, some Western European countries – West Germany in particular – opted to establish closer relations with the Soviet Union in order to lessen dependency on energy imports from the Middle East.[3]

The motives on the part of the Soviet leadership to increase energy sales to Western Europe were less clear at the time. The Soviets perceived energy exports as a way to increase much-needed earnings in hard currency and as a diplomatic strategy vis-à-vis the West. Nevertheless, there was ambivalence in the Kremlin with regard to the potential benefits of selling more energy to the West. This concern became especially evident in the negotiations preceding the 1981 decision to build the Urengoi gas pipeline. This pipeline was the first major East–West gas link directly connecting the gigantic Urengoi gas field in West Siberia to Germany and Western Europe. While some in the Kremlin favored this project as a means of driving a wedge between Western Europeans and North Americans, others argued that the pipeline would in fact strengthen the "enemy" and make the Soviet Union dangerously dependent on a single source for its foreign currency earnings.[4]

The Cold War is over, yet the issues and questions that have been raised in connection with Russia's rise as an energy power are strikingly similar to those discussed in the past. Energy sales still account for the biggest part of Russia's hard-currency earnings, and Europe is still Russia's largest trading partner. Hence, Russia's leadership recognizes that a major challenge for Russia is to diversify its economy, which means developing the non-energy sector. Russia also strives to diversify the geography of its energy exports by building up a customer base in East Asia. As in the past, however, the Russian leadership is divided over these goals, and there are diverging opinions on the benefits and downsides of Russian energy policies.

As in the past, there is still widespread concern on the part of Russia's energy customers that there might soon be shortfalls in Russian supplies to Europe caused by under-investment in the exploration and development of new oil and gas fields and by a potential redirection of energy flows away from Europe; this time, not to the former Soviet Union's Eastern European allies, but to China and other new consumers in the Asia-Pacific region.

Finally, perceptions still vary greatly regarding Russia's role and intentions. While Russia claims to pursue strictly economic interests in its energy policy, many outsiders – especially in the US – maintain that Russia is using energy supplies to Europe as a political tool. Some even claim that Russia is using energy provisions as part of a bargain to tie its neighbors and European partners into its orbit – just as the Soviet Union did when it sought to strengthen control over its Eastern European allies via the building of oil and gas pipelines. While the US is generally much more concerned about the political use of energy than the Europeans, some European governments also view dependency on Russia very negatively.

This book sheds light on one of the most controversial issues in the debate on global energy security: the role of Russia as an energy power. Unlike other analyses of Russian energy, this book provides a comprehensive view that includes the role of Russian energy in its numerous manifestations.[5] It covers foreign and domestic dimensions of Russia's energy wealth and looks at the country's energy power from various perspectives: After a thorough analysis of Russian policies toward international markets, this book also considers the views of Europe, the US, and China on Russia. China did not play any significant part in the Soviet Union's energy policy after the worsening of Sino-Soviet relations beginning in the late 1950s, but has in recent years emerged as the largest potential customer of Russian energy in the east. Finally, this book will also examine how Europe and the US should together react to an increasingly assertive Russia.

By way of introducing the topic of Russian energy power, this introductory chapter provides an overview of Russia's energy potential and reviews the main themes of the book before summarizing the individual chapters.

Russia's energy potential

Russia's energy potential is vast. Russia ranks among the world's leading countries in terms of reserves, production, and consumption in all the major categories of global primary energy sources: oil, natural gas, and coal.

According to BP estimates, Russia in 2006 held some 6.6 percent of proven global oil reserves, which made it rank sixth among the world's leading oil nations. Russia produced over 12 percent of the world's total oil, which made it the second largest oil producer after Saudi Arabia. Russia controls around a third of global natural gas reserves and is also the world's largest gas producer. The

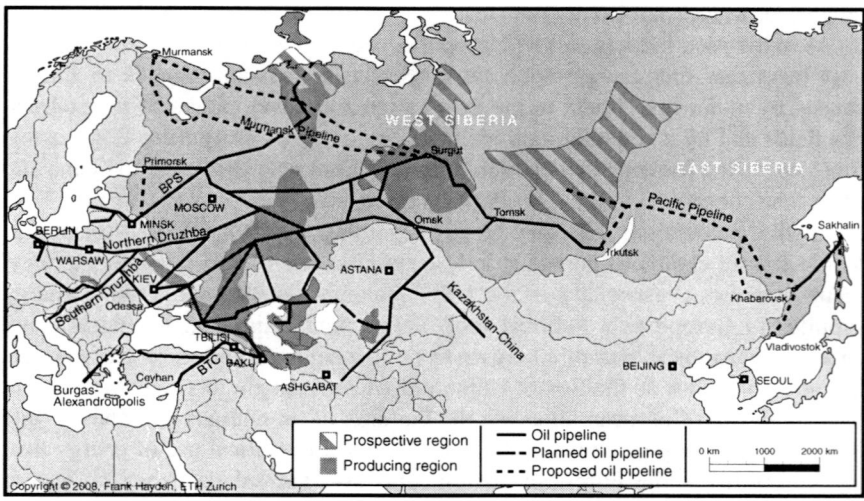

Map 1.1 Russian oil pipelines.

country has the second largest coal reserves after the US. Russia is the fourth largest producer of electric power, has the fifth largest hydroelectric capacity, and ranks fifth in terms of nuclear power production.[6]

Even if we are to assume that Russia's existing oil reserves, according to BP estimates, will be depleted in about 22 years at current production rates, the country holds gas reserves that will last for another 78 years, at least.[7] Coal will last for many more decades and other energy sources (especially hydro and biomass) are massive, but still largely untapped. Russia's Energy Strategy to 2020, which was adopted in 2003, suggests that as much as 30 percent of the country's energy needs could be met using alternative sources, if these were developed to their full potential. Russia currently gets only about 3.5 percent of its energy supply from renewable sources, including its numerous hydroelectric dams.[8]

Also, observers expect that East Siberia, the Far East, and Russia's polar region could contain massive amounts of oil and gas. According to an estimate by TNK-BP, East Siberia has proven oil reserves of about seven billion barrels, but since only 5 percent of the oil-producing zones have been explored so far, the reserves could well be 75 billion barrels. This would be equal to the current proven reserves for the entire country or a quarter of the reserves of Saudi Arabia.[9]

Russia is important for global energy security because of its role as a supplier of fossil fuels. Russia has emerged as the single most important supplier of oil and gas to Europe. According to European Commission (EC) figures, 27 percent of EU oil consumption and 24 percent of gas consumption are covered by imports from Russia. As far as EU imports are concerned, 30 percent of its oil and 44 percent of its gas come from Russia.[10] Some of Russia's post-Soviet

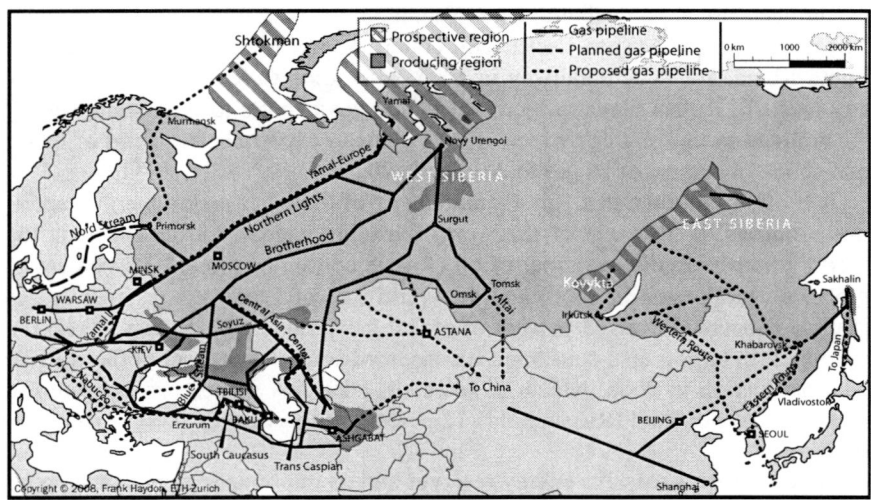

Map 1.2 Russian gas pipelines.

neighbors (i.e. Ukraine, Belarus, Armenia, and Moldova) as well as other non-EU states (especially the Western Balkan countries and Turkey) are also heavily dependent on Russian oil and gas supplies.

In addition to oil and gas, Russia exports significant quantities of electricity to Finland, Poland, and Turkey, as well as to some of the post-Soviet states and China. There is a large potential for increasing exports to Europe if Russia and the EU manage to synchronize their energy grids.[11] Russia is also a major exporter of coal. Sixty percent of Russian coal exports are destined for Europe and the CIS states. Russian coal was responsible for almost 12 percent of EU coal consumption in 2005.[12] Furthermore, a few European states are very dependent on imports from Russia: Russian coal accounts for half of the UK's and around 20 percent of Germany's domestic coal consumption.[13] Russia produces 6 percent of the world's uranium and supplies around a third of Europe's uranium needs.[14]

Russia is the most important channel for Eurasian energy flows headed for Europe and the most significant consumer of gas from Kazakhstan, Uzbekistan, and Turkmenistan. Despite Russia's continuing importance as a transit and consumer country, some of the Caspian oil and gas directed westwards now circumvents Russian territory via newly constructed pipelines from Azerbaijan via Georgia to Turkey. Additionally, small amounts of Turkmen gas flow to Iran by pipeline, and some of Kazakhstan's oil is shipped to China via a new pipeline. By 2009, more Central Asian gas will be shipped to China via a planned pipeline from Turkmenistan.

Russia also seeks to become a key player on the Asian oil and gas markets. Plans are underway to explore and develop East Siberian oil and gas fields and to build a network of oil and gas pipelines in the East. Sakhalin Island's oil and gas projects are already able to supply some oil to Asia, while exports of liquefied natural gas (LNG) to Pacific rim countries, including the US, Japan, and South Korea, are to be underway in 2008. According to Russia's Energy Strategy to 2020, Russia plans to increase oil and gas exports to Asia significantly. As outlined in this strategy paper, Russia plans to export about a third of its oil and about 15 percent of its gas to Asia by 2020.[15]

It is often forgotten that Russia, unlike any of the other major energy exporting countries, is also one of the world's leading energy consumers. It is the world's fourth largest consumer of oil (Russia consumed around 3.3 percent of global oil production in 2006) and the world's second largest consumer of gas (Russia consumed over 15 percent of global gas production). Russia is also the world's fifth largest coal consumer; it consumed some 3.6 percent of the world's coal production in 2006, which is, however, relatively modest, if compared to its huge coal potential (Russia holds 17 percent of the world's total proven coal reserves).[16]

Given Russia's massive energy reserves and its importance as both a supplier and consumer of energy, the question, ultimately, is not whether Russia will remain relevant for global energy security, but how Russia will use its enormous energy potential. Both the domestic trajectories and the way Russia develops its relations to the outside world will influence the role that Russia will play as a supplier of energy to Europe and the world.

Domestic dimensions of Russian energy

Tsar Alexander III was famous for his saying that Russia had only two true allies – her army and her navy. During the presidency of Vladimir Putin, Russia's true allies appeared to be oil and gas. In fact, the earnings generated from the sales from these two commodities are gigantic.

In February 1999, the price for a barrel of Urals oil dropped to US$9. By the end of June 2008, a barrel of Urals was traded at over US$130 on the international spot market.[17] Russia produced around six million barrels of crude oil per day in 1996, around a third of which it exported. In 2006, it produced nearly ten million barrels, around half of which it exported (if petroleum products are added). The increase in oil production, exports, and prices has meant a massive increase in financial return: In the first three months of 1999, when oil prices were low and the country's oil production still crumbling, revenues from oil exports totaled some US$2 billion. In 2007, Russia earned that much in crude exports in less than a week.[18] Almost half of Russia's total export earnings in 2007 were oil-related.[19]

The accumulation of new wealth from energy sales has had a large impact on Russia's domestic development, with ambiguous results, however. In terms of the national economy, the high oil prices have contributed to annual Russian GDP growth of over six percent on average since 1999 and filled the coffers of Russian energy companies and the state alike. These oil windfalls have helped to form a middle class and reduce poverty; and yet, Russia has also shown signs of a rentier state, with increasingly authoritarian elites focused on taking a share of hydrocarbon revenues rather than promoting long-term sustainable development and economic diversification away from Russia's reliance on the energy sector. In the area of domestic politics, high oil prices have helped to stabilize the political system, but have coincided with a marked turn away from democracy and civil liberties. The high oil prices have not caused this turn, but they have certainly made it easier for the political rulers to implement policies aimed at repressing the nascent Russian civil society and the development of a political opposition.

There are two major challenges involved for Russia's energy sector and its internal developments. One is whether Russia will actually manage to keep energy production at sufficient levels to meet growing foreign and domestic demand. There have been prominent voices – in both Russia and the West – warning that Russia will not be in a position to maintain oil exports and increase gas supplies to Europe, meet growing domestic demand, and at the same time also ship oil and gas to Asia, given that most of its current oil and gas are extracted from declining fields. According to this view, it is the shortage in investment in exploration and development that will soon create serious bottlenecks.[20]

These developments are all the more troubling since many experts believe that the re-nationalization of the energy sector is having a negative impact on Russia's oil and gas output, and economic growth in general.[21] Because most of the new oil and gas is located in hard-to-access regions in Russia's north and off-shore, developing these fields requires huge financial investments up front. Russia has now managed to bring its "strategic" fields under the control of state-owned companies and has re-nationalized large parts of its energy sector. For both technical and financial reasons, it is essential for Russia's state companies to cooperate with foreign companies in order to develop difficult and capital-intensive projects in Russia's harsh northern territories. However, international and private Russian companies are reluctant to invest in risky and expensive projects without tax incentives and other contractual inducements to do so.

A second challenge involves the potential negative effects of high oil rents on Russia's domestic development and the distortion of Russia's economy in favor of the raw material sector. According to the World Bank, the oil and gas sector in 2006 accounted for 20 percent of Russia's GDP, yet the sector generated over 60 percent of the country's export earnings and 30 percent of all its foreign direct investment.[22] The importance of the raw material sector has even been growing in recent years: According to data from Russia's Federal Statistics Service, mineral products accounted for 42.4 percent of Russian total exports in 1995, but for 65.7 percent in 2006. Together with metals and timber, raw materials in 2006 had a share of 85.3 percent in Russia's exports.[23]

The oil and gas sector employs only about 2 percent of the working population. However, many more profit directly and indirectly from this sector, and the vested interests in oil and gas are enormous. Some of the windfall profits are retained by the companies themselves, and a part of this money is reinvested in company projects. The larger part is collected by the state in the form of taxes, duties, and fees. One way to absorb excessive liquidity is through state funds. In 2004, Russia set up an oil stabilization fund, which by January 2008 had accumulated over US$156.81 billion.[24] At the same time, the state also built up foreign exchange reserves and accumulated over US$474 billion by the end of 2007, making Russia the world's third largest holder of such reserves after China and Japan.[25]

These funds absorb only one part of oil and gas revenues, however. Another part of state-collected revenues is redistributed through informal channels and benefits a large array of auxiliary funds, projects, and individual companies and officials.[26] Energy has provided the Russian state with the means to pay pensions and fund infrastructure and social development projects. On the other hand, it has also led to an increase in corruption and bad governance. In fact, a major dilemma for the Russian authorities is to decide how to spend the money generated from oil without risking inflation or an increase in corruption.

The Russian government has declared diversification of the economy one of its priorities. However, not only has the raw materials sector grown faster than the other sectors, but imports have grown quickly against a more slowly developing domestic industry. Accordingly, some experts consider Russia to be suffering from the symptoms of "Dutch Disease": A report by the Austrian National Bank shows that from early 2002 to early 2006, Russian imports from the EU-25 grew significantly faster than domestic production in nearly all product categories.[27] The government is seeking to promote the non-energy sector and has made efforts in this respect (e.g. by promoting the IT sector, the aviation industry, etc.); but economic forecasts indicate that Russia still has a very long way to go to achieve a more diversified economic structure.[28]

In sum, energy has provided the fuel for Russia's economic growth and has helped to stabilize Russia after the political chaos and economic turmoil of the 1990s. But the price of this stabilization has been a decline of democracy and an economic development that disproportionately favors the raw materials sector. Russia's stability is very much linked to the ability of the ruling elite to redistribute rents in a way so as to accommodate the various conflicting interests in Russian society. At least indirectly, Russia's stability is tied to a well-functioning domestic and international energy market and stable prices. An energy crisis inside Russia or major disruptions on the international energy markets would ultimately test Russia's precarious political stability. The challenge for Russia will be to reform the energy sector to ensure that Russia makes the most effective use of its energy potential and manages the rents from energy wealth in a way that is best for the country's long-term political, economic, and social development.

International dimensions of Russian energy

Russia's ruling elite considers energy to be the engine of economic growth and the basis for the country's claim to great-power status in international relations. Russia is not an "energy superpower," as some suggest; compared to leading

Western economies, Russia is still a relatively weak power with a gross domestic product per capita only about a quarter of that of the US in real terms. However, the country's importance as Eurasia's leading energy power, combined with its seat on the UN Security Council and its huge arsenal of nuclear weapons, make it a key regional player with global ambitions. While Russia sees new opportunities opening up on the international markets due to its energy potential, the outside world is watching Russia's foreign expansion with concern.

Russia's neighbors in particular are feeling Moscow's increasing pressure. Moscow has intermittently shut down gas supplies to some of its post-Soviet neighbors in order to secure higher energy prices. When Russia shut down gas deliveries to Ukraine in January 2006, there were immediate supply shortages for a number of European countries, reminding them how dependent they are on Russian energy. This action damaged Russia's reputation as a reliable supplier of energy to Europe and led to calls in Europe to diversify away from Russia.

Russia's role as a reliable energy supplier also suffered when the Kremlin began to renationalize the oil sector and reestablish control over all of the country's larger "strategic" oil and gas fields. Especially during the second term of Putin's presidency, a number of production sharing agreements (PSAs) and joint ventures with foreign companies were called off, concessions and licenses to private Russian companies were retracted, and there were cases of outright expropriations.

These actions earned Russia bad press in the West. The price dispute between Gazprom and Ukraine, for instance, has been portrayed in Western media as a politically motivated action and "punishment" from the Kremlin for the country's "Orange Revolution" of 2004.[29] The building of a gas pipeline under the Baltic Sea directly connecting Russia and Germany or the conclusion of long-term agreements between state monopolist Gazprom and key European countries are often seen as part of a larger "divide and conquer" policy aimed at undermining efforts by EU members to pursue a common European energy policy.[30] Russia's declared goal of entering the Asian energy market is frequently depicted as an attempt to play off East against West. Some argue that Russia might redirect already scarce energy to Asia, mostly to China, thus leaving less for Europe.[31]

Russians, however, have a different perspective and accuse the West of getting Russian intentions wrong.[32] They deny using energy as a political lever and argue that their actions are driven purely by business interests as they seek to secure the highest possible return for their energy sales. In the case of Ukraine and Belarus, which are important transit states for Russian energy to Europe, Russia argues that building new pipelines circumventing these two states will make supplies from Russia to Europe more secure. Russia also points out that raising the prices for Russian gas shipped to Ukraine and other post-Soviet states to world market levels is a healthy development, as it stops the subsidization of these economies with cheap Russian energy.

Russia has also a different view on relations with Europe, arguing that it is working hard to meet European needs and hopes to have the right to work in European markets. State-controlled Gazprom's strategy of building new export pipelines backed by long-term contracts seeks to ensure maximum security of demand so as to guarantee that investments in new gas production capacity will be profitable. Thus, Gazprom seeks to secure its sales before it has the gas available to actually fill the pipelines. As Gazprom CEO Aleksei Miller likes to declare, gas will not be produced until it is sold.[33] From Russia's point of view, attempts by the EU to introduce legislation that would make it more difficult for foreign companies to enter Europe's downstream market are against Gazprom's interest, and Russia has been reacting angrily to such proposals.

At the heart of the current Russia–EU energy debate are different views on the issue of "reciprocity." From the point of view of Brussels, if Russian energy companies are allowed into the EU energy market, then EU companies should be allowed to enter the Russian energy market, especially the oil and gas supply market, which is monopolized by two state-controlled monopolies, Gazprom and Transneft. In this context, Europeans want Russia to ratify the Energy Charter Treaty, which would not only enhance transparency, but also pave the way for a reform of Russia's energy sector.

Russia, however, does not subscribe to the EU line of reasoning. Russian Energy Minister Viktor Khristenko has suggested that European companies were in fact investing more in Russia than Russian companies were in the EU, batting down arguments that Moscow has more limits on foreign investment in Russia than the EU has at home.[34] Russia reacted particularly angrily when the EC came forward with a proposal in summer 2007 that aims to break up big utilities that control power supply, generation, and transmission; this is directed at some of Europe's own big energy companies, but would also effectively bar foreign companies such as Gazprom from controlling European networks unless they play by the same rules as EU companies and their home country has an agreement with Brussels. Stanislav Tsygankov, Gazprom's director for international relations, warned the participants at the annual EU–Russia energy conference in May 2008 that the EC's proposal would lead to "instability and unpredictability" across the energy sector.[35]

There are also contradictory views regarding Russia's intentions to diversify to Asia. The Russian government and Gazprom plan to develop the eastern direction of their energy strategy and have made their diversification plans known to the Europeans. Russia insists, though, that it does not intend to redirect gas destined for Europe to Asia since it plans to develop new fields in East Siberia and the Far East in order to make enough gas available for the Asian market. Even if pipelines are constructed that tie Asia to the fields in Western Siberia (a region that has traditionally supplied the European market), the key issue is – according to Russia – not politics, but the price that Russia's customers in the West and East are ready to pay. Just as the Europeans want a more diversified supply structure, the Russians want to avoid being dependent on only one customer capable of buying its energy.

Assessments of Russia's energy policy differ not only between Russia and the West, but also between individual Western countries. The US, which does not import any significant amount of energy from Russia, has been much more outspoken than Europe. US Secretary Condoleezza Rice, for example, noted on 22 October 2007 that

> We respect Russia's interests, but no interest is served if Russia uses its great wealth, its oil and gas wealth, as a political weapon, or (...) if it treats its independent neighbors as part of some old sphere of influence.[36]

While European governments and the EU have in general been more careful in criticizing Russia, given their dependence on Russian energy supplies, some European governments have nevertheless been very critical of Russia. The Polish government, for instance, has been one of the most anti-Russian in its rhetoric and has repeatedly called on the EU to reduce its dependence on energy imports from Russia. The German government, on the other hand, has been the prime example of a European country actively seeking to foster dependencies with Russia; backed by then-chancellor Gerhard Schröder, Germany and Gazprom in 2005 agreed on the construction of the Nord Stream gas pipeline, which will run under the Baltic Sea, connecting the countries directly.

In another part of the world, most East Asian governments see the rise of Russia as an opportunity to secure energy from the still-to-be-developed fields of East Siberia and the Far East. They are not so much concerned about the potential geopolitical consequences of Russia's rise, but are more annoyed about the reluctance and slow pace at which Russia and its companies have gone about the development of new oil and gas fields and the building of a transportation infrastructure in the East.

So far, the rows in European–Russian relations are not reflected at the general level of business cooperation. Nevertheless, Russia's sometimes harsh rhetoric and a number of its foreign policy actions, especially the shutting down of pipelines to its neighbors in order to achieve higher prices, have tarnished Russia's image as a stable supplier of energy to Europe and created considerable political tensions. The challenge for Russia and its energy partners is thus to manage relations in such a way as to make sure not to undermine the stability of the system, which could potentially hurt the interests of all parties involved. Nurturing the energy dialog and communicating in a more transparent way would be a first step toward deepening mutual understanding and doing away with negative perceptions and prejudices that have been lingering since the Cold War era.

Organization and overview of the book

The chapters collected in this book present a variety of perspectives on Russian energy. The book is divided into four parts. Part I analyzes the role of energy for Russia's domestic economic, political, and social dynamics. Part II considers Russia's role in three key markets: Europe, the Caspian region, and Asia. Part III turns the perspective around and looks at the energy policies of Europe, the US, and China toward Russia. Part IV then draws some conclusions for European and US cooperation with Russia in the area of energy.

The first chapter in Part I of this book is Philip Hanson's contribution entitled "The sustainability of Russia's energy power: implications for the Russian economy." At the center of his chapter is the question of whether Russia's rapid growth in prosperity and international influence, fueled in recent years by oil and gas, is likely to continue. Hanson presents a cautious examination of the prospects for Russia as an "energy power," arguing that the economic gains that have accrued to Russia from its energy exports in recent years are far from secure. For Europe, the consequences are stark: while Russia might not cut off gas flows in a political dispute, it may simply not produce enough energy to meet Europe's expanding needs.

Poorly defined policies and excessive state intervention hamper the prospects for oil and gas production, in Hanson's view. Since 2003, oil production growth has slowed dramatically as Russia's leaders increased the tax burden on the industry and expanded the state's direct ownership of oil assets, often acting unpredictably. The Russian authorities project very slow growth (less than 1 percent a year) in both oil and gas output to 2030, but are dangerously confident that hydrocarbon prices will remain high and other producers' output growth will also be sluggish. To maintain or slightly increase oil and gas exports, Russia expects to:

- increase coal and nuclear production rapidly as a substitute for gas in the domestic energy balance;
- continue its control over Central Asian export flows and the monopoly transit profits they produce; and
- curb domestic energy usage by raising domestic prices for both gas and electricity.

Hanson argues that there can be no certainty that these goals will be achieved in the long term. Moreover, Hanson points to a number of problems in the Russian economy that might become acute if the price of oil falls. Most importantly, besides energy and metals exports, no sectors of the Russian economy are internationally competitive. The working-age population is declining. Additionally, spare capacity, a source of growth during the recent output recovery, is more or less used up. Domestic income and demand growth remain high, but inflation has re-emerged as a problem, and the state relaxed its fiscal prudence as Putin's presidential term came to an end.

The next chapter is Robert Orttung's "Energy and state-society relations: socio-political aspects of Russia's energy wealth." Orttung examines the link between Russia's energy wealth and its political development. Is it a coincidence that Russia's political system has become more authoritarian and more corrupt with rising oil prices? Orttung points out that there is no direct causal link between the extent of Russia's oil wealth and the level of democracy in the political system; the retreat from democracy and civic liberties started well before the prices of oil began to grow in about 2003. However, the massive new rent generated from the sale of energy has provided political leaders in Russia with the necessary resources to exert the kind of control over society and opposition groups that they want.

Orttung argues that the small group of people who control the levers of the Russian state have extensive coercive and financial resources at their disposal to subdue any form of political or popular opposition to their rule. Given their tight hold on power, Russia's rulers are in a position to distribute energy sector rents to make sure the various political actors remain loyal to them. The system that Putin created is thus based on an expensive arrangement of rent distribution, as it ties different elite groups to the state to guarantee the stability of the system. Orttung does not see this kind of stability to be sustainable in the long run, however. The system is extremely inflexible and vulnerable, since it depends on continuing high prices in the international commodities market. Putin's political system works well for extracting profits from the Russian energy sector and has benefited from the recent high prices, but its rigid centralization of power and expansion of state control over society is not suited for a country that hopes to compete in a dynamic and globalized world economy.

In the final chapter of this introductory section, Heiko Pleines investigates the impact of increasing state involvement in Russia's oil and gas industry. In his chapter "Developing Russia's oil and gas industry: what role for the state?," Pleines is concerned with the much-disputed question of how state ownership in the energy sector affects the efficiency of energy company operations. Against the background of the re-nationalization trends under Putin, the author looks into key areas, such as the treatment of foreign investors, the state's methods for increasing ownership in the energy industry, state programs to develop the energy industry, including the promotion of domestic processing, and plans for the reform of broader market regulation.

Pleines argues that the share of state ownership in the economy as such is not the problem – as, for example, the case of Norway shows. What is important for the performance and efficiency of companies – regardless of their ownership – is whether they are able to compete in a market environment. Pleines concludes that empirical evidence from Russia indicates that so far, private companies are performing better under market conditions than state-owned companies. However, the key problem is that the situation in Russia is characterized by a high degree of insecurity regarding property rights and the legal environment, which promotes inefficient behavior of private as well as state-owned companies. These problems arise because the role of the state in the energy sector is still to a large degree determined by politics rather than by economic rationale.

Part II of the book examines Russia's role in the international energy markets. Stacy Closson's chapter "Russia's key customer: Europe" provides an overview of Russian–European energy relations and discusses the main trends and problems in bilateral relations. Based on an analysis of Russian views and concerns with regard to Europe, the author seeks to arrive at a more balanced view of Russia's energy role in Europe that questions some of the conventional wisdom in the Western press, which portrays Russia as a threat.

Closson argues that as alarming as recent developments concerning the shut-off of gas to European customers and expanded Russian business operations in Europe may be, the warnings of an encroaching Russian energy giant do not consider the strong inter-dependency between Russia and Europe. Europe needs Russia's oil and gas, but Russia is also dependent on Europe, which is by far Russia's most important trading partner and its main source of foreign-currency earnings. Given the fact that Russia's energy export infrastructure is still almost exclusively oriented toward the European market, Russia has only limited leverage with regard to Europe. However, because of Europe's inaction, Closson explains, Russia was able to turn a seemingly disadvantageous position to its advantage, creating the appearance that Europe was dependent on Russia. Beyond this appearance, Russia has a very strong interest to remain Europe's key supplier of energy and to be perceived as a reliable partner. While a more confrontational scenario cannot be excluded for the future, Russia is more likely to pursue the middle ground in seeking solutions with its European partners over reciprocity and critical issues in European–Russian relations. Instead of engaging the whole of Europe via Brussels, Russia is more likely to follow a strategy of strengthening bilateral alliances – such as ties with Germany, Austria, or the southeastern European states – thus creating "circles of influence."

In her chapter on "Russia's role in the Eurasian energy market: seeking control in the face of growing challenges," Julia Nanay analyzes the dynamics in Eurasia's evolving energy market and the role of Russia. The author examines the complex energy geopolitics that dictate Russia's relations with the three major energy-producing and energy-exporting countries of the Caspian: Azerbaijan, Kazakhstan, and Turkmenistan. The chapter examines the transformation of the relationship of these three countries with Russia from the time they gained their independence in the early 1990s up to the era of Vladimir Putin and also assesses prospects for the future.

The growing involvement of foreign investors from the US, Europe and, more recently, China has helped transform the business landscape in the region and brought with it a whole host of geopolitical opportunities and tensions. Despite these geopolitical changes, however, Russia is still very important, since the oil and gas export networks, particularly from Central Asia, remain oriented toward the north. Russia continues to provide the revenue lifeline for both Kazakhstan and Turkmenistan, which depend heavily on Russia for access to paying markets. So far, only Azerbaijan, which sits on the western side of the Caspian close to Turkey, has been able to break its energy links to Russia with one of the West's most successful infrastructure projects in the region, the Baku–Tbilisi–Ceyhan (BTC) pipeline. Against the background of high oil prices and the energy security concerns of the US and Europe, which seek direct access to Caspian energy, Russia has been pursuing an active energy diplomacy by working diligently to court the regional leaders and their state-owned companies in its determination to head off the next big challenge to its hegemony, namely the diversion of Central Asian gas away from routes through Russia. Although Russia's efforts to maintain control have been fairly successful under Putin, the situation remains extremely fluid. While Russia will certainly maintain an influential role, the next four years will determine the extent to which the West can hope to access more Caspian oil and gas directly, and in what volumes.

Nina Poussenkova looks at Russia's eastern energy strategy in her chapter "Russia's future customers: Asia and beyond." The diversification of energy exports to Asia by developing the depressed East Siberia and Far East regions is considered a national security matter of highest priority for Russia. Poussenkova analyzes the challenges, opportunities, and implications involved in creating a major new petroleum province in the east and the prospects for energy relations with China, Japan, South Korea, and other countries along the Pacific Ocean.

The author is pessimistic about any quick success in this endeavor, which requires not only massive new financial investments in the exploration and development of new fields, but also overcoming a psychological blockade in establishing stronger relations with East Asian countries, particularly China. Russia and China have long claimed to be strategic partners, yet Russia fears becoming a "resource hinterland" for China. This apprehension seems to be a main reason why none of the pipeline projects that have been under discussion between Russia and China since the mid-1990s have so far been realized. To construct these pipelines, Russia will need to work with foreign partners in order to bring in the necessary funds and technical skills required to succeed in developing the fields in this harsh region. Despite this need, the Russian state, through its state-controlled companies Gazprom and Rosneft, has in recent years focused more on gaining control over existing projects than on expanding cooperation with foreign partners. Despite these problems, however, Poussenkova believes that Russia will eventually succeed in developing its eastern territories and enter the Asian market, because it has a strong interest in doing so. Russia clearly is afraid that without any tangible progress, existing economic, social, and demographic problems in Eastern Siberia and the Far East will get worse, threatening Russia's national security and territorial integrity.

Part III examines international policies toward Russia. The first chapter in this part is by Pami Aalto, who examines "European perspectives on managing dependence." The chapter analyzes how the EU and individual European countries view their energy relations with Russia. It includes case studies of the energy strategies of three selected European countries – Germany, the United Kingdom, and Poland – in order to illustrate the difficulties of the EU in formulating a common energy policy vis-à-vis Russia.

The main obstacle to a common EU energy policy, Aalto argues, is that interdependencies between individual European countries and Russia have evolved differently over time. While EU efforts to formulate an energy policy toward Russia date back to the early 1990s, individual EU member countries have their own particular history of relations with Russia, often reaching back much farther in time. The main tension between the EU and its member states relates to their respective approaches to the implementation of market principles and enhanced competition in the energy sector, security of supply, and sustainable energy policies seeking to reduce dependence on fossil fuels. While the EU has sought to institutionalize its policies in each of these areas, the individual European states approach them selectively, depending on their particular set of interests. The author sees little likelihood that overall EU policy and the policies of its individual members will converge in the near future. While the European–Russian energy trade is unlikely to shrink in terms of the volumes of oil, gas, and coal shipped from east to west, one is likely to see a more regionalized energy landscape as regards relations to Russia. Due to the construction of new pipelines connecting Russia to Europe in the north and in the south, the Central and Eastern European countries will lose importance, while the northern and southeastern European regions will become more important. Another likely trend is a more diversified trade base between Europe and Russia. On top of trade in fossil fuels, cooperation in the area of efficiency and renewables as well as enhanced collaboration in the electricity sector are promising new fields of mutual engagement and could form the foundation of a future common European–Russian energy policy agenda.

The second chapter in Part III is concerned with the US perspective on Russian energy. In his contribution, "US energy policy and the former Soviet Union: parallel tracks," Peter Rutland analyzes US policies toward Russia in the context of the changes after 1991. While the US is not dependent on Russian energy supplies and trade volumes between the two countries are marginal, Russian energy is important to Washington in terms of larger strategic considerations. The US is concerned about Russia's domestic developments and how Russia will use energy supplies to influence Europe and its former Soviet neighbors. Russia's increasingly assertive foreign policy and its willingness to use energy as a way to achieve political goals have heightened these concerns.

Energy has played a very modest role in US–Russia relations, as only a small number of projects involving US companies inside Russia have been successfully realized since 1991. Nevertheless, Washington has followed energy dynamics in the former Soviet Union closely and has conducted an active energy diplomacy that has been – and still is – based on the following premise:

- Russia should open up to foreign investment in its energy sector, since Russia needs Western capital and technology to successfully develop its oil and gas reserves;
- ideally, Western companies would have majority control in these projects, since such management would enable them to control the speed at which the new fields will come on stream;
- at the same time, the US believes that it is in the West's best interest to assist new producing countries outside Russia and to build alternative export routes to bring their oil to world markets without transiting Russia. Direct links to the outside world will help these countries to become economically independent from Russia, since they would be less vulnerable to Russian pressure.

Rutland states that in the various phases of US–Russia relations since 1991, but especially under Putin, Russian policy has been opposed to these US interests.

Today, the Russian state seeks to control all major energy projects in the country. Also, Russia is today much more active in seeking to block or delay the construction of alternative export pipelines. At the same time, Russia is also successfully promoting its own pipeline projects to Europe. Overall, Rutland criticizes US energy policy toward the former Soviet Union and Russia, since it was based on the false hope of a quick transformation toward a liberal Western-oriented market.

The last chapter in this part looks at "Chinese perspectives on Russian oil and gas," written by Indra Øverland and Kyrre Brækhus. Their chapter explores Chinese interests in Russian energy and analyzes the views of Beijing with regard to the emergence of Russia as an energy supplier to Asia. So far, China receives only very modest oil supplies from Russia via rail, but these volumes could increase substantially should Russia develop new fields in East Siberia and implement planned oil and gas pipeline projects connecting these fields with the Chinese market.

Øverland and Brækhus argue that the basic energy relationship between China and Russia is based on a convergence of interests between Russian natural resource abundance and Chinese market demand. Beijing views Moscow as a key partner, and as the only great power that is not in some way aligned against it. The advantage of geographic proximity provides China with a direct overland link to resources rather than the vulnerable overseas routes to the Middle East and Africa. Thus, Russian supplies carry a unique strategic significance for Beijing, which lacks a powerful blue-water navy. Nevertheless, the authors also see numerous sources of tension in the bilateral relationship. From the Chinese point of view, the most disturbing issues are the slow speed at which Russia is proceeding in the development of new fields and pipeline construction, the unpredictability of Russian decision-making, murky rules with regard to access for Chinese companies in the exploration and development of oil and gas fields in Russia, latent rivalry in Central Asia, and attempts by Moscow to play off China and Japan against each other. For China, one way to establish stable and more predictable relations is to empower the Shanghai Cooperation Organisation (SCO), which Beijing views as an important tool for institutionalizing its relationship and securing access to Russian oil and gas.

In the final part of the book, Andreas Wenger draws some conclusions for the West's relations toward Russia. In his chapter "Russia's energy power: implications for Europe and for transatlantic cooperation," Wenger examines the interests of Russia and the West and determines where there is possible common ground for cooperation. He looks in particular into Russian–European relations and also seeks to understand how Russian energy power affects, if at all, transatlantic cooperation.

Notes

1 For an overview and summary of the literature on the subject, see: Jonathan Stern, "Gas Pipeline Co-Operation Between Political Adversaries: Examples from

18 *J. Perovic*

Europe," Report Submission to Korea foundation Project Energy and Environmental Cooperation in the Korean Peninsula, Chatham House Paper, January 2005, www.chathamhouse.org.uk/files/3222_jsjan05.pdf (accessed 29 January 2008).
2 Thane Gustafson, *Crisis Amid Plenty: The Politics of Soviet Energy Under Brezhnev and Gorbachev* (Princeton: Princeton University Press, 1989), 28f.
3 For an overview, see: Sanam S. Haghighi, *Energy Security: The External Legal Relations of the European Union with Major Oil- and Gas-Supplying Countries* (Portland: Hart, 2007), especially 37–64.
4 Thane Gustafson, *Soviet Negotiating Strategy: The East–West Gas Pipeline Deal, 1980–1984* (Santa Monica: RAND, 1985).
5 There is a large body of literature that examines the situation of the Russian energy industry. These books range from classics such as Gustafson's *Crisis Amid Plenty* to more recent treatments, such as David Lane, ed., *The Political Economy of Russian Oil* (Lanham: Rowman & Littlefield, 1999); John D. Grace, *Russian Oil Supply: Performance and Prospects* (Oxford: Oxford University Press, 2005); Jonathan Stern, *The Future of Russian Gas and Gazprom* (Oxford: Oxford University Press, 2005); Michael Ellman, ed., *Russia's Oil and Gas: Bonanza or Curse?* (London: Anthem Press, 2006); and Marshal Goldman, *Petrostate: Putin, Power and the New Russia* (New York: Oxford University Press, 2008). Other important books and articles on Russian energy are cited in this chapter.
6 All figures from: British Petroleum (BP), *Statistical Review of World Energy 2007* (London: BP, 2007); the review can be downloaded at www.bp.com/productlanding.do?categoryId=6848&contentId=7033471 (accessed 13 December 2007).
7 BP, *Statistical Review of World Energy 2007*, 6; 22.
8 Ministry of Industry and Energy (Minpromenergo), *Energeticheskaia strategiia Rossii na period do 2020 goda*, approved as decree no. 1234-r by the Russian government on 28 August 2003, www.minprom.gov.ru/docs/strateg/1/ (accessed 13 December 2007); see also: Elena Duraeva, "Erneuerbare Energien in Russland: Nutzung durch internationale Kooperation," *Osteuropa* 54, Heft 9–10 (October 2004): 152–60.
9 Greg Walters, "Russian Oil Companies Push East for New Growth," *Dow Jones Newswires*, 16 May 2007, www.rigzone.com/news/article.asp?a_id=45234 (accessed 8 August 2007).
10 European Commission (EC), *The European Union and Russia: Close Neighbours, Global Players, Strategic Partners* (Brussels: European Commission External Relations, October 2007), 13, http://ec.europa.eu/external_relations/library/publications/34_eu_russia.pdf (accessed 23 December 2007).
11 For an overview, see: Energy Information Administration (EIA), *Russia Country Analysis Brief* (Washington, DC: Department of Energy, Energy Information Administration, April 2007, www.eia.doe.gov/emeu/cabs/Russia/Full.html (accessed 17 December 2007).
12 Andris Piebalgs, "EU–Russia Energy Cooperation," Speech at the International Energy Week, Moscow, 23 October 2007, 2, available from the EC's website at http://ec.europa.eu/energy/index_en.html (accessed 7 January 2008).
13 Nigel Yaxley, "British and European Imports of Russian Coal," CoalImp Association of UK Coal Importers, www.coalimp.org.uk/resources/Coaltrans+Russia+18–06–07.pdf (accessed 18 December 2007).
14 "Russia: Uranium Mining and Milling Overview," The Nuclear Threat Initiative (NTI), February 2001, www.nti.org/db/nisprofs/russia/fissmat/minemill/overview.htm (accessed 18 December 2007).
15 MPE RF, *Energeticheskaia strategiia Rossii na period do 2020 goda*.
16 All figures from: BP, *Statistical Review of World Energy 2007*.
17 EIA, "World Crude Oil Prices," http://tonto.eia.doe.gov/dnav/pet/hist/wepcuralsw.htm (accessed 7 July 2008).

18 Clifford Gaddy, "U.S.–Russia Economic Relationship: Implications of the Yukos Affair," Testimony before the House of Financial Services Subcommittee on Domestic and International Monetary Policy, Trade and Technology, Washington, DC, 17 October 2007.
19 In the period January–September 2007, some 49 percent of Russia's export earnings were oil-related: Bank of Finland, *Russia BOFIT Weekly*, no. 43 (October 2007).
20 For example: Alan Riley and Frank Umbach, "Out of Gas: Looming Russian Gas Deficits Demand Readjustment of European Energy Policy," *Internationale Politik – Global Edition* 8 (Spring 2007): 83–90; Vladimir Milov, Leonard Coburn, and Igor Danchenko, "Russia's Energy Policy 1992–2005," *Eurasian Geography and Economics* 47, no. 3 (2006): 285–313.
21 For example: Michael McFaul and Kathryn Stoner-Weiss, "The Myth of the Authoritarian Model: How Putin's Crackdown Holds Russia Back," *Foreign Affairs* 87, no. 1 (2008): 68–84.
22 World Bank, *Russian Economic Report*, no. 13 (Washington, DC: The World Bank, December 2006), http://ns.worldbank.org.ru/files/rer/RER_13_eng.pdf (accessed 25 September 2007).
23 Federal State Statistics Service, "Commodity Structure of Exports of the Russian Federation," www.gks.ru/free_doc/2007/b07_12/25–08.htm (accessed 7 July 2008).
24 "Russia Oil Fund Rises to $156.8 bln on Jan 1," *Reuters*, 9 January 2008, http://uk.reuters.com/article/oilRpt/idUKL0971670520080109 (accessed 23 January 2008).
25 "Russia's Gold, Foreign Exchange Reserves Grew by $7.8bn," *Kommersant*, 10 January 2008, www.kommersant.com/p-11893/Gold_exchange_reserves/ (accessed 23 January 2008).
26 The Brookings Institution, *The Russian Federation*, The Brookings Foreign Policy Studies Energy Security Series (Washington, DC: The Brookings Institution, October 2006), 8, www.3.brookings.edu/fp/research/energy/2006russia.pdf (accessed 17 December 2007).
27 Stephan Barisitz and Simon Erik Ollus, "The Russian Non-Fuel Sector: Signs of the Dutch Disease? Evidence from EU-25 Import Competition," in *Focus on European Economic Integration*, 1/2007 (Oesterreichische Nationalbank, CEEC Research Platform, 2007), 150–66, www.oenb.at/de/img/feei_2007_1_barisits_ollus_tcm14–58444.pdf (accessed 21 December 2007).
28 For an overview, see: Ellmann, *Russia's Oil and Gas*.
29 For example: Adrian Blomfield, "Putin Sends a Shiver Through Europe," *Telegraph.co.uk*, 2 January 2006, www.telegraph.co.uk/news/main.jhtml?xml=/news/2006/01/02/wruss02.xml&sSheet=/portal/2006/01/02/ixportaltop.html (accessed 4 January 2008).
30 For example: Ariel Cohen, "Europe's Strategic Dependence on Russian Energy," *Backgrounder*, no. 2083 (Washington, DC: The Heritage Foundation, 2007), www.heritage.org/Research/Europe/upload/bg_2083.pdf (accessed 4 January 2008).
31 For example: Andrew Kramer, "Gazprom Reaps the Benefit of Friends in the Kremlin," *New York Times*, 23 September 2006, www.nytimes.com/2006/09/23/business/worldbusiness/23sakhalin.html (accessed 4 January 2008).
32 See, for example, Vladimir Putin, "Transcript of Press Conference with the Russian and Foreign Media, Round Hall," The Kremlin, Moscow, 1 February 2007, www.kremlin.ru/eng/speeches/2007/02/01/1309_type82915type82917_117600.shtml.
33 Aleksei Miller, "Gazprom – Strategy for the Energy Sector Leadership," Speech at the Annual Shareholders Meeting, Moscow, 30 June 2006, www.gazprom.ru/eng/articles/article20334.shtml (accessed 28 January 2008).
34 "Russia and EU Ignore Access Row," *Upstreamonline.com*, 16 October 2007, www.upstreamonline.com/live/article142431.ece (accessed 18 October 2007).

35 Cited from: "A Warning to Europe from Gazprom," *New York Times*, 21 May 2008, www.nytimes.com/2008/05/21/business/worldbusiness/21gazprom.html (accessed 7 July 2008).
36 Condoleezza Rice, "Opening Remarks at the Office of the Historian's Conference on U.S.–Soviet Relations in the Era of Détente, 1969–1976," Washington, DC, 22 October 2007, www.state.gov/secretary/rm/2007/10/93788.htm (accessed 4 January 2008).

Part I
The domestic dimension of Russian energy

2 The sustainability of Russia's energy power
Implications for the Russian economy

Philip Hanson[1]

In early 2008, Russian economic policymakers were taking a rather complacent view of Russia's future. In the "innovation" scenario espoused by the Ministry of Economic Development and Trade (MERT), Russia's economic growth over the period to 2020 would average more than 6 percent a year.[2] Russian oil and gas production would continue to increase throughout that period – albeit slowly. Meanwhile, an earlier draft government document had assumed that world oil prices would stay in a high range, and everybody else's output of hydrocarbons would "stabilize."[3]

This chapter will show that in fact Russia's prospects as an "energy power" are less secure than this optimistic view assumes. The Pollyanna perspective is espoused in public by Russia's Ministry of Industry and Energy (Minpromenergo) and MERT. They might just possibly turn out to be right. But more caution would be in order. To begin with, there is the risk of a sustained and substantial fall in the oil price. This is something that Russian officials, like many analysts and business people around the world, now disregard; but it is unwise to rule it out for the next 23 years. Moreover, there are good reasons to doubt the ability of Russia's oil and gas producers to sustain output growth. Innovation and diversification in the non-hydrocarbon economy are promised, but the promises are not convincing.

Doom and gloom are not inevitable. Rather, a sober assessment points not to collapse, but to slowing growth. Recent levels of investment in the energy sector have been inadequate. Increased state control in the sector does not augur well for competition and dynamism in oil and gas. And Russia's overall economic growth will slow down unless there is a large and sustained increase in investment and more openness to competition, both within hydrocarbons and in the economy at large.

The first section of the chapter describes, in broad outline, the starting point: where the Russian economy stands in comparison with other economies and how it has recently been performing. The second section is an assessment of the extent and nature of Russian economic dependence on oil and gas. The third section is a review of the diversification of the Russian economy, both as a result of activity through the market and as a project for state policymakers. Then there is a section on energy-sector prospects to 2030 in the light of official Russian-government assessments and projections. The final section before the conclusions is concerned with Russian economic prospects more broadly. In the light of the possible scenarios for oil and gas, what can we reasonably expect for the Russian economy overall? The conclusions suggest some implications for Europe's energy security.

Russia's economic performance since 1998

Russia is now, in World Bank terminology, an upper-middle-income country. Its recent economic development has been unquestionably a success story. Since the financial crisis of 1998, the Russian economy has grown rapidly, while prudent macro-economic management has made the state financially robust and minimally indebted to the outside world.

Russia's per capita gross national income is still far below those of the richest countries, but it is at the same time a multiple of those of the truly poor countries. That middle-income category is one in which one would normally expect to see rapid, catch-up growth over the very long term: on average, that is, over 20 or more years. Middle-income countries have the potential to absorb new technology from more advanced countries and, largely by that means, to reduce the gap between themselves and the rich world. This potential is all the greater if, like Russia, they have reasonably good education systems.

This generally promising diagnosis holds up even though Russian society exhibits a high degree of inequality: between average incomes in different regions, between town and country, and overall between households. Most measures show Russian inequality across all households to be rather high, and more akin to the degree of inequality found in Latin America than to that found in Europe. On the other hand, several measures show some decline in inequality between the late 1990s and the early 2000s.[4] And it can be estimated that the proportion of the population living in poverty was in the order of 12 percent in 2006.[5] In the mid-1990s, it had been as high as 40 percent. In other words, recent Russian prosperity really has "trickled down".

Figure 2.1 puts Russia's development level in perspective, placing its per capita gross national income (GNI), measured at purchasing power parity,[6] alongside those of a number of other countries, all measured as a percentage of the US figure.

On this measure, Russia's development level is above that of Brazil, China, India, or Turkey and roughly on a par with Mexico and South Africa. At the same time, Russia now lags well behind Estonia, though the latter was only a little ahead of the Russian Federation when both were parts of the USSR.

Middle-income countries may have the potential for rapid long-term growth, but by no means all of them achieve it. Argentina, notoriously, has stagnated for much of the past half-century. So far, Russia looks to be doing rather well. In comparison with a selection of other middle-income countries, Russia was growing rapidly in the first half of the present decade. Indeed, it has grown rapidly over the whole period 1998–2007. Figure 2.2 presents some comparative medium-term growth figures.

Recently, then, Russia has been progressing substantially faster than Mexico or South Africa, at a rate not so very different from India or Turkey, but decidedly

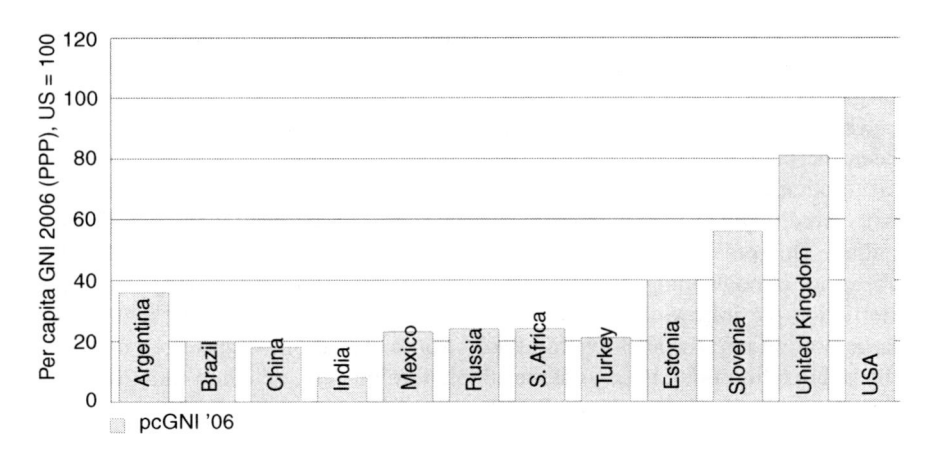

Figure 2.1 Per capita gross national income in 2006 as a percentage of US GNI for selected countries (based on US dollars at purchasing power parity).

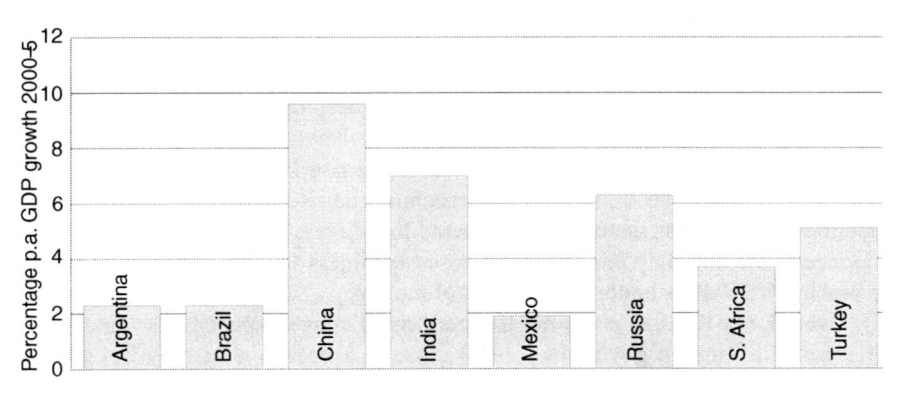

Figure 2.2 Annual average rates of GDP growth, 2000–5, among selected middle-income countries.

less fast than that of China. However, Russia had one significant initial advantage over these other countries: it has been recovering from a prolonged fall in output (1989–98, with a brief remission in 1997). Its nine most recent years of strong growth, therefore, contain a recovery component. The size and duration of this recovery effect cannot be reliably gauged. Still, the fact of its existence means that some slowdown is likely in the future unless other sources of growth become stronger.

The Russian economic recovery was triggered by an enforced devaluation of the ruble in 1998 and then picked up by a strong rise in oil prices. Most analysts agree that these two recovery elements had been fully used up at least by some point in 2006.[7] Usable spare capacity was down to something like a normal level, and the real effective exchange rate (the ruble's exchange rate against a trade-weighted basket of currencies, adjusted for inflation in all the countries concerned) was at least back to the level it had reached before the August 1998 financial crisis.

One impressive feature of Russian economic performance since 1998 has been the restraint shown in macro-economic management. The Russian monetary authorities have only the most limited instruments for managing interest rates, credit, and exchange rates, and most of the burden has fallen on budgetary policy. This policy, under Finance Minister Aleksei Kudrin, has been directed above all at controlling spending so as to maintain a budgetary surplus, and at sterilizing the inflow of petro-dollars, principally (from 2003) by channeling a large portion into the stabilization fund.[8] Some of that inflow has been used, via the stabilization fund, to pay off the state's foreign debt, which in mid-2007 was down to a minuscule 4 percent of GDP.

Thanks to this macro-economic prudence on the part of Russia's policymakers, the inflation rate was slowly brought down into single figures in 2006. The prospect of elections (however controlled by the leadership) in late 2007 to early 2008 generated pressures for higher state spending that even Kudrin was unable to withstand; federal budget spending was increased by 37 percent in 2007 and, not surprisingly, inflation rose again. Now Kudrin is proposing much more restrictive spending plans for 2008–11, to push back against inflation.[9] Kudrin's earlier success in fighting inflation was achieved despite the country experiencing very rapidly rising export revenues. There has, however, been another benign influence helping to contain inflation: the strong rise in the demand for money. This new demand has come close to matching the rise in money supply. Rapid economic growth has increased the demand for money; meanwhile, growing confidence in the currency has led to increased readiness to hold rubles, with rubles replacing US dollars in domestic stocks of money.

Overall, the Russian economy has performed above expectations – including those of the Russian government – for close to a decade. Not only has growth been strong and inflation mostly contained, but, as was noted above, economic benefits have trickled down more than is often suggested. A middle class of professionals, managers, and owners of small businesses is emerging. Its numbers may currently stand at about 25 million, or slightly under a fifth of the whole population. That middle class shows little interest in challenging the authority of the political elite; it is preoccupied with making and spending money. Rapidly rising expectations have been driving a consumer boom exemplified by the brisk development of shopping malls and car dealerships. Clearly, the growth has been oil-driven, but that does not make it any less real; nor does it necessarily imply, by itself, that rapid growth in Russia is not sustainable.

Energy dependence[10]

The contemporary Russian economy is heavily dependent on oil and gas exports. Russia is far from being a standard petro-state, however; it is not a "hole-in-the-ground" economy, even though the natural resource sector is the main segment of the economy that is internationally competitive.

Oil and gas exports have not been driving Russian growth directly. That is to say that the rise in production, in real terms (that is, adjusted for inflation), in these sectors has not been a major component of the increase in real GDP. That is hardly surprising. Output of gas has been almost stagnant; oil production growth was fast in 1999–2004 but has since slowed; and the oil and gas industries employ fewer people than the Russian railways: less than 2 percent of the employed workforce. What has driven growth is the rise in revenues of these industries, chiefly derived from their sales to Europe at rapidly rising prices. Those revenues feed the state budget (some, but not all, of this financial inflow being withdrawn from circulation in the stabilization fund), personal incomes, and company profits.

The importance of exports in all this can be illustrated in the case of gas. In 2006, 24 percent of gas output was exported outside the CIS, almost all of it to Europe, yet non-CIS-export receipts accounted for more than half of Gazprom's revenue.[11] The Russian state's revenues depend heavily on oil and gas production (Figure 2.3), which make up a quarter of the country's GDP, three-fifths of its exports, and half of the federal budget, respectively.

It is mainly through their effect on incomes and spending, therefore, that oil and gas prices affect the levels of Russian overall economic activity. The demands for inputs into oil and gas production also play a part, but only a modest part; much equipment is imported. Input–output analysis of the supply links between industries shows that other input demands from the hydrocarbons sector tend to

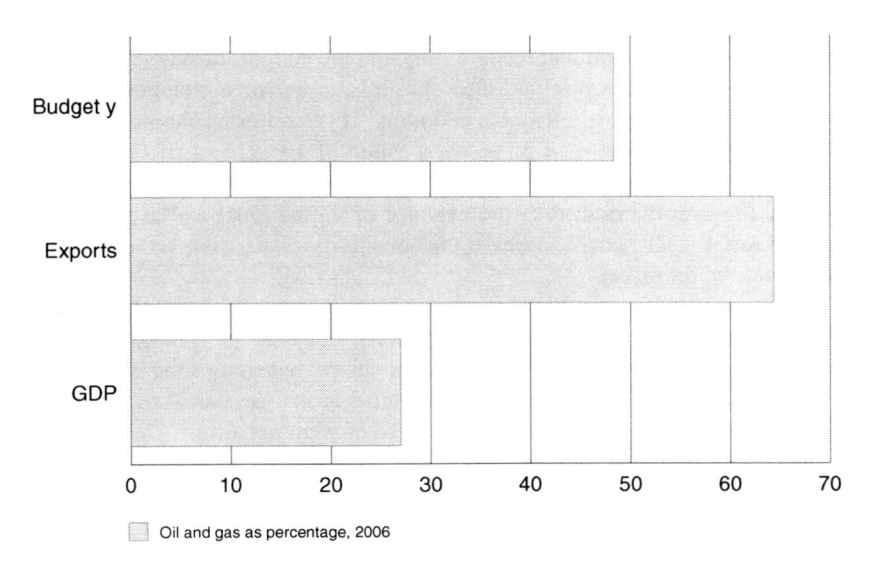

Figure 2.3 Some indicators of Russian dependence on oil and gas (in percent).

be on Russian services rather than Russian goods production.[12] In any case, the overall effect of a change in the oil price, acting mainly through incomes and spending, is substantial. The Bank of Finland Institute for Economies in Transition (BOFIT) estimates that a sustained $10 rise in the oil price boosts Russian GDP by about 2 percent.[13]

This effect does not come solely from crude oil exports. The crude oil price affects the prices of oil products, and the pricing formulae for natural gas in the long-term supply contracts on which Gazprom operates are in turn based on crude-oil and oil-product prices. Therefore, the revenue from hydrocarbons as a whole is geared toward the oil price, albeit with varying lags for different parts of that revenue. About two-thirds of oil export revenue, at mid-2007 prices and under 2007 rules, goes into the government's stabilization fund (*stabfond*); that leaves a substantial part of hydrocarbons (crude oil plus oil products plus natural gas) export revenue not being sterilized through the stabilization fund – overall, about three-fifths in the first half of 2007.[14] Some of that non-sterilized revenue, mainly from oil products and gas, was taxed; but if it did not go into the *stabfond*, it was tax revenue that could feed government spending.

From the beginning of 2008, the treatment of hydrocarbons export revenue was to be changed. The tax base for what had been the *stabfond* was extended from the mineral extraction tax and export duties on crude oil only to cover oil products and gas as well. The *stabfond* itself was to be replaced by three funds: a reserve fund, invested in low-risk foreign-government securities; a fund for national welfare, invested in higher-yield assets such as foreign equities; and an explicit "oil and gas subsidy" to the federal budget. The reserve fund was to be initially 10 percent of GDP. The oil and gas subsidy was to be set for three years at a time in the rolling three-year budget process that started in 2007 – and the government aimed to limit that subsidy in the course of the budget process. But there is no binding rule on the division between the national welfare fund and the budget subsidy.

This new arrangement could alter the linkage between changes in the world oil price and the domestic Russian economy. If the oil price should rise at a time when the reserve fund is at or above a value of 10 percent of GDP, the additional revenue would no longer automatically be sterilized. Political pressure to transfer more to the budget at the expense of the national welfare fund may be hard to resist. That would increase the sensitivity of Russian GDP, or inflation, or both to the oil price.

In autumn 2007, one other change was looming on the foreign-currency-inflow front. Imports were rising faster than exports, not only in volume terms, but in aggregate value, lowering the surplus in the current account of the balance of payments. Russia's MERT offered three alternative growth scenarios to the year 2020, in two of which the trade surplus disappeared or went negative.[15] Other projections converge on a trade surplus (and therefore a current account surplus) that disappears by 2012. That was already the direction of change in 2007. Thus, the inflow of funds through the current account of the balance of payments was expected to decline, if not disappear altogether, in the medium term. So much the better, as far as inflation control is concerned.

However, the net private-sector flow of capital – a net outflow through 2004 – has recently turned into a net inflow, with signs of further growth to come. That could mean that Russia continues to receive a net inflow of currency overall. The difference would be that this new capital-account inflow would not be sterilized by a device comparable to the *stabfond*, which operates specifically on oil revenue. Inflation might be imported through a different, and less controlled, channel.

Economic diversification away from energy dependence

What of the performance of the Russian non-energy economy? Diversification of the economy remains an objective of Russian policy, even at a time when complacency about the country's "energy power" is the rule. There has indeed been some diversification – a good deal of it done at the grass-roots level by firms, not the state. The main weakness of the non-natural-resource segment of the Russian economy, however, is a serious one. Its international competitiveness is low.

Industry as a whole, including oil, gas, metals, and other extractive industries, accounts for around two-fifths of GDP when oil and gas distribution are classified as part of industry.[16] About half of this total is manufacturing, and manufacturing growth since 1998 has been slightly below overall GDP growth – in other words, quite robust. However, only a very small part of Russian industry produces goods for export. Oil, gas, and metals have accounted recently for around 80 percent of merchandise exports. As far as tradable goods are concerned, Russian manufacturers engage mainly in making import substitutes. Typically, they slot into lower-quality segments of the market for their product-range, avoiding head-on competition with imports.

This weakness is apparent from the trade statistics. These show Russia as being, in some respects, the least competitive of the large emerging-market countries. Julian Cooper[17] has analyzed the exports of Russia, Brazil, China, India, and Turkey at three-digit level (broken down, that is, into product-groups, roughly corresponding to what would commonly be defined as industrial branches). He asks where, among medium- and high-technology fields, there are signs of competitive advantage (defined as having a share in world exports of that product group greater than the country's share in exports overall). He found, from the data for 2004, the following areas of strength: for China, computer equipment, telecoms equipment, rotating electric plants, and furniture; for Brazil, agricultural machinery, tractors, aircraft, and internal combustion engines; for Turkey, tractors and passenger cars; for India and Russia, nothing. It is true that if internationally comparable data on weapons sales were available, Russia would show some competitive strength in arms sales; but Cooper notes signs of weakening performance even there.

If Russia is to diversify its economy successfully, it will need to acquire areas of export competitiveness outside the natural resource sector. Among the prerequisites for this are effective investment in research and development (R&D), in information technology (IT), and in education and training. Table 2.1 shows a

Table 2.1 Science, technology, and communications in Russia and other BRICs, early 2000s

	Units	Russia	Brazil	China	India
R&D spending 2002	$ bn	14.7	13.1[a]	72.0	20.8[a]
	%GDP	1.3	1.0[a]	1.2	0.7[a]
IT spending 2004	%GDP	3.3	6.3	4.4	3.8
Internet users 2004	per 10,000	1,110	1,218	723	324
Broadband subscribers 2004	per 10,000	9	124	165	6
Hi-tech exports 2004	$ bn	3.4	5.5	161.6	2.8
As % manufacturing exports		9	12	30	5

Source: Julian Cooper, *Russia as a BRIC: Only a Dream?*, European Research Working Paper series, no. 13 (Birmingham: The University of Birmingham European Research Institute, July 2006), Table 3, www.eri.bham.ac.uk/research/working_papers/WP13Cooper.pdf (accessed 9 September 2008).

Note
a 2000.

number of selected measures of inputs and results, in this connection, for Russia in comparison with Brazil, India, and China.

The service sector, including financial services, has been booming. A large part of services output cannot be exported or imported. That means that neither export nor import competition is a problem. It is possible, therefore, for a large sector to develop and thrive in which productivity is rather low by international standards. This was for a long time the situation in Japan. At the same time, the Japanese also had highly competitive export industries; apart from the natural resource sector, Russia does not.

In both manufacturing and services, however, domestic competition can be provided by foreign firms entering the Russian market. That has been happening on a substantial scale recently. The fact that foreign firms now play major roles in Russian banking (about 20 percent of assets),[18] real estate (including retail development), retailing, brewing, confectionery, and car assembly gives some indication of lines of business that are dynamic and attractive – even if the indigenous Russian firms in those industries are, for the most part, not capable of competing abroad. This roster of industries that are both attractive and open to foreign direct investment is extending to construction as the state begins to develop a major infrastructure program involving public-private partnerships.[19]

Another clue to identifying the branches of the economy that are developing strongly is the launching of initial public offerings (IPOs) of shares on Western stock markets. These confirm the pattern suggested above. In the first nine months of 2007, at least 16 Russian IPOs and three secondary public offerings (SPOs) were arranged in the West, mainly on the London Stock Exchange. In total, they raised over $26 billion. Of the 19 offerings, five were by retail and consumer-goods businesses, four by banks, and three by real estate firms. By far the largest amount of money raised was by banks, with a total of $17.6 billion.[20]

In fact, the bulk of the money raised in this way by banks was raised by state-controlled (i.e. majority-state-owned) banks. This situation indicates one rather unusual feature of current Russian development: the state is trying to be an active developer of businesses in whatever the Kremlin classifies as "strategic" activities. Officially, "strategic" lines of production are the 39 (mostly defense-related) listed in legislation that is pending on the subject, plus fossil fuel and mineral deposits above certain sizes that will be specified in a long-delayed revision of the subsoil law. Unofficially, Russian policymakers are seeking to ensure state dominance in several other industries, including banking.[21]

Few analysts expect this leading role for the state to be good for the economy. But at least the approach is pragmatic. The policymakers, aware that they need foreign technology and finance, allow for and encourage Western participation even in "strategic" sectors, provided it is not accompanied by control. Thus, Boeing has a joint venture with titanium producer VSMPO-Avisma, and Italy's Finmeccanica holds a 25 percent share in the plane-maker Sukhoi.

Two major industries within the natural resource sector are overwhelmingly privately controlled and developing strongly: coal and metals. Russia is the world's fifth largest producer and third largest exporter of coal, and investment in the industry has been rising fast without much state involvement.[22] Within the metals industry, both steel and non-ferrous metals firms are unquestionably strong. Aluminum, steel, and nickel firms, with strong market power inside Russia and export capabilities, have been turning themselves into international companies. Oleg Deripaska's UC Rusal is, at the time of writing, the world's largest aluminum producer, with smelters and other plants on several continents. Severstal and other leading steel producers have been buying foreign companies, including in the US, and are also becoming global businesses. The only hydrocarbons-based companies with much international reach beyond the CIS are Gazprom and Lukoil. Gazprom has invested in downstream distribution assets in Europe. Lukoil has bought into oil-products distribution in both Europe and the US.

Some of these leading firms have also been moving into new industries in Russia and thus diversifying by becoming conglomerates. Deripaska, again, is building a stake in car-making;[23] Aleksei Mordashov, the main owner of Severstal, has gained control of the leading generating-equipment producer, Silovye mashiny,[24] and is also well-established in timber-processing.[25] Of course, acquiring an existing company does not create new capacity, and therefore, does not by itself alter the structure of the economy. However, these acquisitions are one means by which investment funds are channeled from one industry to another. Furthermore, they are associated with plans to expand the target business.

It can be useful to think of a national economy as the sum of the economic activity that is conducted within its borders *plus* the economic activity in other countries of companies controlled by firms based within the nation in question.[26] In this sense, Russian business is expanding – mainly, it has to be said, in the metals sector – even faster than Russian GDP indicates. This outward foreign direct investment often incorporates more advanced processing – notably in the steel industry – so that a Russian company can be moving up the value-added chain even if it is doing so outside Russia's borders.

All of these developments are the result of private initiative operating through the market. The Russian state, under Putin's leadership, has been pursuing diversification in a quite different fashion. It is working through state-controlled development of industries that are relics of the old Soviet military-industrial sector. One of these, the nuclear industry, will be discussed in the next section, as it is a component of the energy sector itself. The others are aerospace, shipbuilding, weapons production, and nanotechnology. In each of these, a state-controlled holding company has been created that will group together the enterprises of the sector, while leaving at least some of those enterprises partly privately-owned and open (at the discretion of Russian policy-makers) to alliances with foreign firms. These alliances could take the form of joint ventures (separate from the Russian parent company, such as Boeing has with titanium producer VSMPO-Avisma) or minority foreign stake-holdings, such as Finmeccanica has in Sukhoi. This approach is meant to encourage the inflow of foreign technology and capital without surrendering control.

The state holding companies that have been created to promote the development of supposedly more "advanced" lines of production are Rosatom, for the civil and military nuclear industry; Rostekhnologii, primarily for defense-related production and including the state company Rosoboroneksport, but also including the AvtoVAZ car works; Nanotekhnologii, whose name is self-explanatory; the United Aircraft Company, for aircraft production; and the United Shipbuilding Company. All were created in their present form in 2006–7, and all are designed to bring together research and development units – chiefly from what remains (in Russia) of the empire of the Soviet Military-Industrial Commission (MIC). MIC was supposed to coordinate the activities of units that came under a number of military–industrial branch ministries.

The resources to be allocated to this network of research and production units are not easy to assess. Some will generate substantial own revenue: Rostekhnologii from arms sales, for example. Most, if not all, will get substantial allocations from the budget. The scale of this is hard to assess. Planned federal-budget spending on civilian science and technology, including space and electronics, is officially given as 119.1 billion rubles for 2008, while the budget overview document lists only 26.8 billion rubles for strictly military programs.[27] Together, these outlays amount to only about 0.4 percent of projected GDP in 2008.

The order of magnitude is lower than, but not radically different from, an independent calculation of budget spending in 2006 "to support innovation" by the National Association and Development of IT (NAIRIT, in its Russian acronym): 188.4 billion rubles.[28] Notably, NAIRIT has reckoned that 56 percent of this amount never reached the projects for which it was intended. These funds, according to Olga Uskova of NAIRIT, found their way to companies associated with the officials involved. There is no obvious reason why things should improve.

In short, the Russian economy amounts to a great deal more than a petro-state, but the prospects of the non-natural-resource sector are far from assured. In the following, we will consider the prospects of the energy sector, and in particular its future capacity to meet Europe's rising demand for oil and gas.

Russia's future energy export capacity

Much Western discussion of Russian energy supply has focused on the reliability of Russian oil and gas supplies to Europe, and on Moscow's possible use of energy supply for foreign-policy ends. My aim in this section is to discuss the European concerns in the context of broader Russian policies. Russian energy policy is about Russia's domestic production and consumption of energy as well as about exports. It will help us to put European "energy security" concerns in perspective if we consider Russian worries about energy supply and demand as well.

Russia's concerns should be seen against the background of the growth slow-down that has already taken place in the volume of oil exports, as illustrated in Figure 2.4. Largely because of state policy – limited export pipeline capacity (which is state-controlled), increased taxation, and the re-nationalization of a large chunk of the industry – an export growth that had been dynamic has turned sluggish. The state's re-acquisition of major hydrocarbons assets – most notably of Yukos, Sibneft, Kovykta, and Sakhalin-2 – is the best-known part of this story. But it is not the whole of it. Taxation and the control of pipelines have also played a part.

Meanwhile, both output and export volumes of natural gas have grown slowly, at best, since the Soviet era. The gas industry never experienced the burst of rapid growth that the oil industry experienced under predominantly private control in 1999–2004. One of the ironies of Russian energy policy is that the policymakers are now looking to the coal industry – still privately owned and still dynamic – to help bail the rest of the energy sector out of difficulties, now that the state has asserted control over oil as well as gas.

The brisk and selective overview of Russia's energy policies and prospects that follows is based in part on the 2003 Energy Strategy[29] and an early draft of the successor strategy to 2030.[30] The analysis of these documents will be supplemented by estimates from independent studies. The energy strategy documents provide a picture of official Russian expectations about the sector and of at least some of the policies to be pursued toward it. They are obliged to be optimistic. But they are also obliged to identify the problems to be overcome – and in doing so, they largely confirm the critiques of independent analysts.

The 2007 draft strategy, like the existing one, does not envisage rapid growth of primary fuel output.[31] Both oil and gas output are projected, even in the "favorable" scenario, as growing at an average annual rate of less than 1 percent between 2005 and 2030.

34   P. Hanson

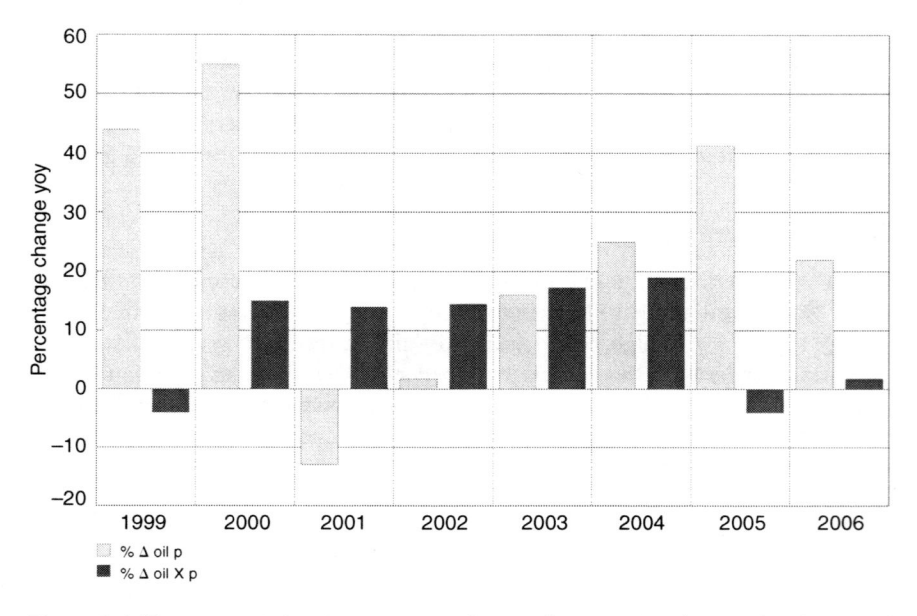

Figure 2.4 Year-on-year (yoy) percentage changes in average prices and volumes of Russian oil exports, 1999–2006.

The draft 2030 strategy set out a "favorable" and a "conservative" scenario for the period 2005–30, with a breakdown of production, consumption, imports, and exports by major type of fuel for five-year intervals (2010, 2015, 2020, etc.). It also reviewed major policy issues and options, and made recommendations for policy. The authors of the draft see the energy sector as continuing to be a major driver of Russian economic growth to 2030.

They make one important assumption, common to both their scenarios, about the future: that a period of "stabilization" of hydrocarbons extraction levels is looming in the next few years, both in Russia and in the world as a whole. Consequently, they project average annual prices for Urals crude oil as mostly rising over the period – to $75 a barrel in 2030 in the conservative scenario and to $85 in the favorable scenario. (The draft was written before the oil price went above $100 a barrel, so these projections no longer look so "optimistic"; they nonetheless embody an assumption that the nominal oil price would remain in a historically high range.) They do not consider the possibility of a sustained and significant fall in oil prices during the next 23 years. The Russian planners, therefore, view with equanimity the prospect of a quarter of a century of slow growth in Russian hydrocarbons output. In effect, they predict that production of oil and gas will grow, but only sluggishly, yet do not anticipate that such a trend will do their national economy any harm, since they believe that everybody else's output growth will be sluggish, too, and that oil and gas prices will stay high. In projecting slow rates of output growth for their two main energy

The sustainability of Russia's energy power 35

exports, oil and gas, the authors have not departed radically from the view taken in the existing strategy document covering the period to 2020. They simply extend this slow growth further forward.

Even this generally optimistic document, however, points to major problems. The authors note that in 2000–5, developments diverged considerably from the earlier document's projections for that period. On the positive side, output of the "fuel-energy sector" rose somewhat more than planned. Furthermore, domestic energy-intensity of production fell more than planned. The authors estimate, however, that 75–80 percent of the reduction in energy-intensity is the result of structural change in the economy, notably the expansion of services relative to industry.

The negative developments noted for 2000–5 are serious. Most striking of all is the shortfall in investment. Compared with the "requirements" of the existing strategy, actual fixed investment in oil extraction was only 85 percent of the projected total, investment in gas extraction was just under 50 percent, and investment in electricity was 54 percent. Moreover, the figures for investment in oil extraction show an unwelcome development over time. If the current-price annual figures given in the draft are deflated by the average-annual producer-price index, real investment in oil extraction rises at a healthy rate in 2003 (up 23 percent over 2002) and then falls year by year through 2005. In that year, it was down to 63 percent of the 2003 total. The Yukos effect is clear. This slump in investment can be compared with the situation in coal mining, where the state has so far stayed well out of the way: in this sector, investment rose by 50 percent between 2005 and 2006.[32]

The authors of the draft 2030 strategy note that the investment climate in hydrocarbons and electricity needs to be improved, tax rates reduced, and electricity and gas prices liberalized rapidly – and that clear decisions must be made soon on all these matters if investors are to have the incentives and the funds to invest more and if domestic energy-users are to have the incentives to improve energy-efficiency. The draft identifies as serious problems the absence of clear rules for the state's intervention in the sector and for dealings with international oil companies. Western analysts will endorse all of these suggestions; the question is whether Russian politicians will.

In comparison with the existing strategy, the new draft tilts the growth rate of hydrocarbons to 2020 up very slightly. But that growth remains modest in both scenarios. In both the conservative and the favorable variant, the output of each major fuel increases in each five-year period. But whether the projected levels of domestic consumption and exports can be reached depends on a continuing, rapid improvement in energy efficiency. In the favorable scenario, GDP growth is mostly between 6 and 7 percent per annum. This is the scenario that is put forward as the basis for policy. In the conservative scenario, growth is between 5 and 6 percent a year.

The aim in general is an increase in domestic energy usage of no more than around one third (35 percent) of the rate of economic growth. Meanwhile, increased imports (predominantly of gas from Central Asia) help bridge the gap between slow production growth of major fuels (0.8 percent pa 2005–30 for oil and 0.9 percent for gas in the favorable scenario), on the one hand, and rates of total domestic energy consumption growth that slow over the period, but do not fall below 1 percent a year (in the favorable scenario) on the other. The favorable scenario is illustrated in Figure 2.5. For each year, the column on the left represents the total domestic output of oil, gas, coal, hydro-electricity, and nuclear power, added up in millions of tons of "standard fuel"; the diminutive middle column represents energy imports (in practice, just Central Asian gas), and the right-hand column shows the total available supply, i.e. output plus imports. The two lines trace the projected evolution of total domestic usage and of exports.

Also helping to balance the energy books are a relatively rapid growth of coal and nuclear energy, and their substitution for gas in Russian electricity generation. This development was a feature of the strategy to 2020. One modification in the new draft strategy to 2030 is that the hugely ambitious growth hitherto projected for nuclear power (4.7 percent a year in 2005–20) is eased down to 3.7 percent for the period 2005–20 in the new draft. This reduction is a tacit acknowledgement that the massive nuclear plant-building program will not meet its original 2020 targets. Coal output is now projected as growing at 2.4 percent pa from 2005–30 in the favorable scenario, and at 1.3 percent pa in the conservative scenario – both well above the best official expectations for oil and gas. Coal

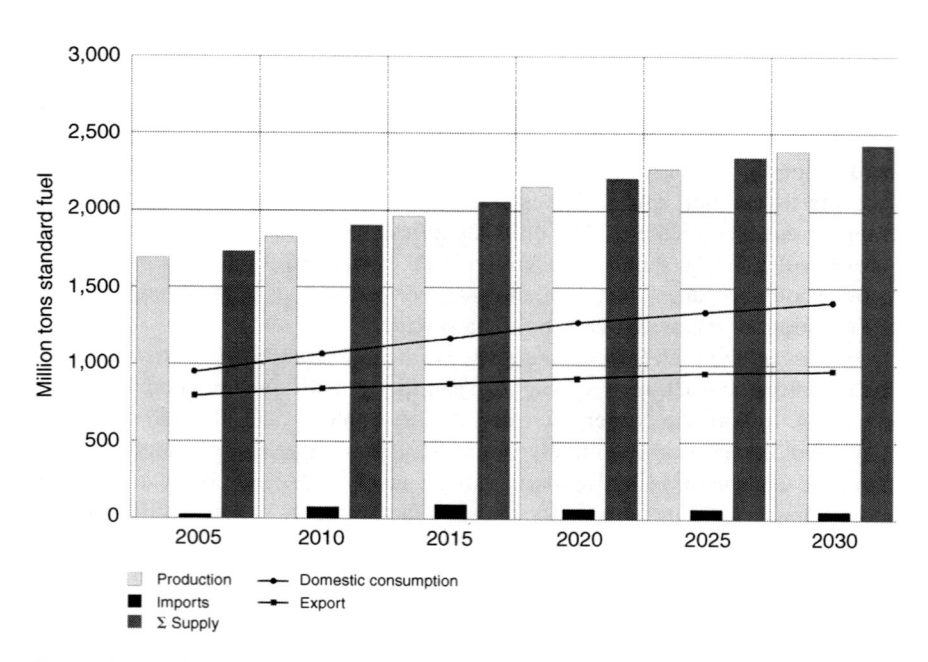

Figure 2.5 Projected production, import, and domestic consumption of major fuels, 2005–30 (million tons of standard fuel, favorable scenario).

exports are projected to develop across an approximately flat trajectory, so that domestic usage of coal rises faster even than output; along with nuclear power, coal is substituted for gas in electricity generation, freeing gas supplies for export.

The role of gas imports from Central Asia is, on the face of it, modest. They peak at 79 bcm, or close to 10 percent of Russian production, in 2015 in the favorable scenario. But they are treated as a key balancing item. In the favorable scenario, they are reduced after 2015, falling to 37 bcm in 2030. In the conservative scenario, however, domestic gas consumption grows only slightly more slowly than in the favorable variant, while Russian gas production rises at only 0.5 percent a year on average; in this scenario, imports from Central Asia are kept at 70 bcm pa from 2010 to 2030. The projected evolution of gas production, imports, domestic usage, and exports is shown in Figure 2.6.

The Russian energy planners therefore treat Central Asian gas supplies as a freely-adjustable balancing item. This is a high-handed approach to the supply agreements with Turkmenistan and Kazakhstan. Perhaps Central Asian policy-makers will feel they can count on Russia missing its own production targets, and therefore, continuing to need 70 bcm pa of their gas through 2030. If not, the message contained in this draft will strengthen their interest in other pipeline routes.

Export volume would grow slowly even in the favorable scenario. From 2005 to 2030, total oil exports rise at 0.6 percent pa to 403 mt pa; gas exports rise at an annual rate of 1.1 percent to 275 bcm. However, there is a half-hidden message

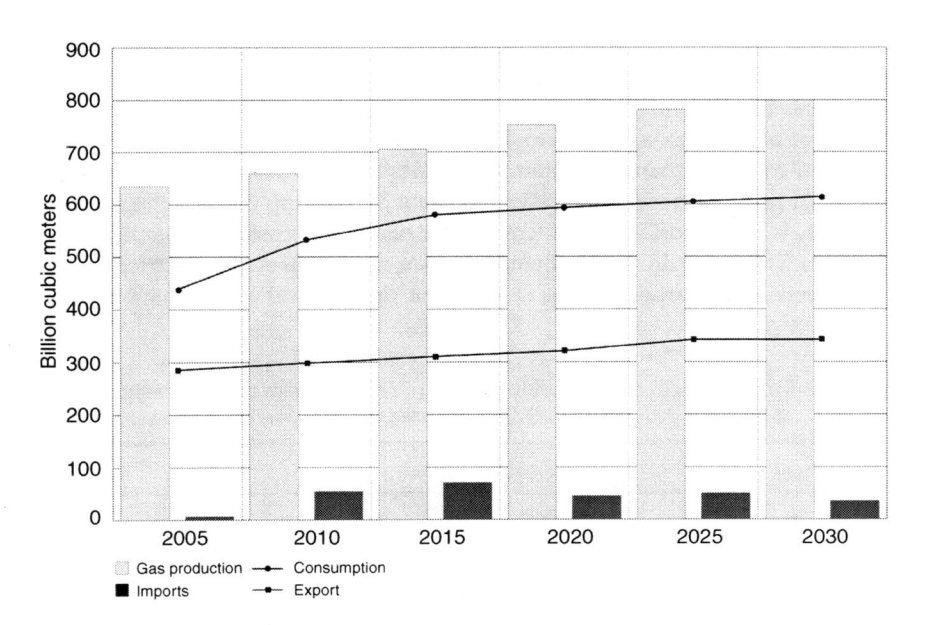

Figure 2.6 Production, import, domestic consumption, and exports of gas, 2005–30 (bcm, favorable scenario).

here that is worrying so far as Europe is concerned. The modest growth projected for total exports is completely made up of gas exports projected for China and the Asia-Pacific Basin under the (separate) Eastern Gas Program. The latter would be 78 bcm in 2030.[33] In other words, if the figures in these two separate documents are brought together (and they ought to be compatible if national energy planning is internally consistent), the total projected gas exports to Europe plus Turkey plus the other CIS states would be lower in 2030 than in 2005.

Which parts of these official projections are robust and which are implausible? Certainly, continued energy-saving in the domestic economy is plausible. Between 1998 and 2005, primary energy consumption rose at an average rate of 1.5 percent pa, while GDP rose at an average annual rate of 6.7 percent.[34] Moreover, Russian energy usage per unit of GDP is still high by international standards, as Table 2.2 shows. Canada is singled out for comparison on grounds of climatic similarity.

It will, however, be more difficult in the future to keep up the recent rate of improvement in energy usage. We noted above that the authors of the 2030 energy strategy attributed at least three-quarters of the recent Russian reduction of energy-intensity to structural change in the economy rather than to improved energy usage in existing lines of production. Much of the sectoral change in the economy toward less energy-intensive activities, like services, has already happened; output growth by increased usage of previously spare capacity has probably reached its limits; and the working-age population is now starting to decline, increasing the pressure to substitute capital and energy for labor. Therefore, given output growth, domestic energy usage, though declining relative to GDP, may be higher than projected.

Raising domestic gas prices substantially and relatively soon would certainly help curb domestic usage. The planned rises in gas and electricity tariffs are not trivial. The Federal Tariff Service calculated in September 2007 that meeting the target of raising gas prices to Russian industrial users enough to equalize Gazprom's rate of return on export and domestic industrial sales would entail a three-fold price increase in the latter. The date for meeting this target, scheduled for 2011, is not far off.[35] Price increases for residential customers would follow in 2013. There would be an immediate knock-on effect on electricity costs and prices. The main doubt has to be about the political determination of the

Table 2.2 Total domestic energy supply per unit of GDP in 2005: selected countries (tons of oil equivalent per $1,000 of GDP based on 2000 purchasing power parity)

Country/region	Energy/GDP
Canada	0.27
Russia	0.47
OECD	0.18
World	0.21

Source: International Energy Agency (IEA), *Key World Energy Statistics 2007* (Paris: IEA, 2007), 48–57.

Russian leadership to push this through. Certainly these price increases would be unpopular with consumers.

There is also some merit in the planners' objective of bringing coal to the rescue. Not only is this a widely-perceived way forward around the world, but, as has been noted already, the Russian coal-mining industry is so far largely outside state control and is exhibiting strong growth of output and investment. But plans for Gazprom to take control of a joint venture with one of the largest coal companies, SUEK, could be the start of state intervention, with its usual deadening effects.

The greatest doubts arise over the projected output levels of oil and gas. Notoriously, Russian oil output growth has slowed dramatically since 2004, as state control of the industry has increased.[36] Some other authoritative projections are even more pessimistic than those of the Russian government. The International Energy Agency (IEA) judged in mid-2007 that Russian oil output would probably stop rising in 2010. The IEA baseline scenario rests on a 3 percent pa fall in output from existing fields in the period 2007–10, with some offsetting development of new fields: Sakhalin-1, Sakhalin-2, and Lukoil's Timan-Pechora. The IEA puts Russian crude oil output at 10.6 mbd in 2010, and at 10.5 mbd in 2012. What happens after 2012 will depend on the rate at which East Siberian fields are developed.[37] The very large shortfalls in investment in gas and electricity in 2000–5, and in oil after 2003, were noted by the authors of the 2030 strategy (see above).

A slowdown in Russian hydrocarbons output, or an outright fall, would not be surprising. In 1998–2004, Yukos, Sibneft, and TNK (the last of these forming a joint venture with BP in 2003) rapidly increased crude oil production by improving management and technology at existing fields, in part by using the skills of Western oilfield services companies like Schlumberger. What they and most other oil companies did not do was to invest heavily in exploration and development of new fields.[38] As established fields peak and decline, output growth is expected to slow. In the case of the gas industry, unofficial projections even predict falling output by 2010 unless major new fields in Yamal are developed more quickly than many expect.

At present, some 70 percent of Russian electricity is generated from gas, accounting for a substantial part of the 68 percent or so of Russian gas production that is consumed domestically. The planned shift to coal and nuclear in fueling power stations is one of the ways in which Russian policymakers hope to cope with sluggish gas production.

The plans for nuclear power are therefore an important part of the strategy. They contribute (in both the 2020 and the 2030 strategies) to an outcome in which electricity generation outpaces the growth of hydrocarbons output. There are at present 31 reactors at ten power stations, with an installed capacity of 23.2 GW. Of these, 15 are pressurized water reactors (PWRs), 15 are "channel-type" (Chernobyl-type), and one is a fast breeder reactor.[39] In his 26 April 2007 address to the Russian parliament,[40] President Putin referred to a program under which 26 nuclear reactors were to be built in 12 years. These plans are in line with the 2020 Strategy, according to which nuclear generation is to increase from

131 billion kWh in 2000 to 230–300 billion kWh in 2020, raising the nuclear share of electricity output from about 16 percent in 2003 to 23 percent in 2020, with almost a third of European Russia's electricity (32 percent) coming from nuclear power in 2020.[41] That is a very ambitious program indeed. It is scaled down somewhat in the draft 2030 strategy, where "accelerated construction of nuclear reactors" comes only after 2015, and the preliminary target for 2030 is for nuclear plants to provide 25–30 percent of all electricity generated – not much of an increase, as a proportion of the total, over the earlier target for 2020.

It may well be that even the slightly modified nuclear program is over-ambitious. Independent estimates for each of the seven electricity-system regions of Russia show the nuclear percentage share of electricity generation falling between 2008 and 2011: from 25 to 22 in the Center; 33 to 28 in the North-West; 6 to 5 in the South; 2 to 1 in the Urals, and 14 to 13 in the Middle Volga; no estimates for Siberia and the (Russian) Far East are given.[42] It is true that declines between 2008 and 2011 are not, as a matter of logic, incompatible with increases between 2003 and 2020 or between 2005 and 2030. It is unlikely, however, that, given the time needed to build and start up nuclear power stations, the projections are compatible in practice.

The new nuclear power stations are to be PWRs – basically the same system as the one mainly used in the West – rather than channel-type reactors. Both strategy documents make it clear that the Russian nuclear industry is to aim at being technologically and commercially competitive internationally. Recent announcements about the state holding company Atomenergoprom (to come into existence in 2008) indicate that it will span fuel and plant production as well as exports and will cover the civilian nuclear market.[43] It is questionable whether it can deliver the rapid growth of Russian nuclear capacity called for by energy planners in a timely and safe manner.[44]

What are the implications for Russian oil and gas exports? We have already seen the volume growth of Russian oil exports slow dramatically, as Figure 2.4 illustrates. We also know that these oil and gas exports matter enormously to the Russian economy – see Figure 2.3. The share of the hydrocarbons sector in GDP and budget shown in Figure 2.3 stems primarily from oil and gas exports because of the low prices for output delivered to the home market. Those exports are overwhelmingly to Europe. This suggests that Russia is unlikely to seek deliberately to curtail oil or gas exports to Europe for foreign-policy reasons, short of an acute crisis in relations. The risk to revenues and to business reputation would be very great. The greater problem for Europe, almost certainly, is Russia's future capacity to deliver more.

In 2006, 44 percent of Russian oil production and about a quarter of gas production went to non-CIS countries.[45] Russian policymakers have the following options for maintaining and increasing hydrocarbons exports to non-CIS countries, so long as output growth remains slow:

- Further reduce the already modest deliveries to CIS countries.[46]
- Obtain more gas from Central Asia for delivery to Europe.

- Reduce domestic hydrocarbons consumption by raising domestic prices.
- Reduce domestic hydrocarbons consumption by substituting coal, nuclear, hydro, and alternative energy sources for oil and gas in electricity generation.
- Increase domestic energy-efficiency by means other than raising domestic energy prices.

The strategy documents have most to say on the last two options. Gazprom's part in implementing them in practice looks unhelpful. For a start, it seeks control of a number of electricity generating companies in the course of the divestment of generating capacity by the state electricity monopoly, UES. The reform of the electricity industry was meant to introduce private capital and competition into generation, not to foster absorption by a state-controlled gas monopolist that may control up to 30 percent of electricity generation.[47] Gazprom would have an incentive to assist in raising energy efficiency in generation, but the incentive would be stronger in a firm that had less monopoly power and more demanding shareholders.

Gazprom also seeks control – in the form of a 50 percent + 1 share stake in a joint venture – of SUEK, the leading coal producer (which also owns some power stations). The Federal Anti-Monopoly Service opposes this, but is not expected to be able to defeat Gazprom. Western banks are happy to lend to Gazprom, and it could probably contribute substantially to financing the development of the coal industry, and thus facilitating the substitution of coal for gas in power stations. On the other hand, managing this development by direct Gazprom control may not be too promising. The Ministry of Economic Development and Trade, as well as the Federal Anti-Monopoly Service, has expressed concern about the project.[48]

Gazprom's own gas production (it accounts for around 85 percent of the Russian total) is approximately flat. Its plans for raising supplies up to about 2012 rest on a growth of output from Russian independent producers (including oil companies) and the acquisition at favorable prices of growing amounts of Central Asian gas – which for the time being lacks other means of reaching rich markets. Meanwhile, Gazprom is also buying its way into Russian projects that others have brought close to fruition (Sakhalin Energy, Itera's field at Beregovoe), using state muscle to encourage the original owners to sell Gazprom a controlling stake.

On the other hand, Gazprom is not so much involved in upstream development of its own. Its $20.1 billion investment program for 2007 includes $6.4 billion for acquisitions, against $3.9 billion for development of major fields. Its 2006 capital spending on gas extraction was about $4.2 billion, and total capital spending on hydrocarbons extraction, processing, and transport was about $15 billion.[49] Gazprom says it needs to spend R11.5 trillion ($460 billion at the late-2007 exchange rate of 25 rubles to the US dollar) on gas development through 2030.[50] That works out to about $20 billion a year on average – well above present levels. So long as oil and gas prices stay high, and if Gazprom can focus its spending more on its core business, that enhanced capital spending can probably be financed. But the capital spending is an input. How much trust can be placed in Gazprom's achieving the planned output is another matter.

The long-term increase in gas supply would occur mainly in East Siberia and the Russian Far East. Sakhalin apart, the bulk of likely reserves in this area have yet to be properly explored and proved up. Output in the region was 8 bcm in 2006, and the Eastern Gas Program (Gazprom's version of which has been adopted by the government) aims to raise this to 27.4 bcm by 2010 and 108.3 bcm by 2020.[51] Having wrestled the giant Kovykta gas field in East Siberia away from TNK-BP on the pretext that TNK-BP had produced less from it than their license terms required, Gazprom does not plan to start production there before 2017.[52] The odds would seem to suggest that Gazprom, even if it spends the money, will not deliver the promised output in the time in which it has pledged to do so. Vladimir Milov, a former deputy energy minister of Russia, considers it likely that Russian gas production will fall in 2008–15 unless some $4–5 billion a year is invested in developing fields in Yamal; at present, he says, the rate of spending is only about $1 billion a year.[53]

Control of Central Asian oil and gas supplies is one option for maintaining non-CIS exports for which the present Russian system is well-suited. The 12 May 2007 pipeline deal between Russia, Turkmenistan, and Kazakhstan, finalized on 20 December 2007, is a sign of progress in that direction. It locks Turkmenistan into supplying increasing amounts of gas through Russia.[54] Gazprom had been expecting to buy gas from Central Asia at around $130–150 per kcm and sell it on to Europe at about $240, but in early 2008 it was forced to concede "European" prices for Turkmen gas. At the same time, the new Turkmen leader appears to have forgone the option of by-passing Russia by delivering gas through a Transcaspian pipeline (yet to be built) via Azerbaijan, Georgia, and Turkey. It is likely that the prospects of Russian political support and Russian up-front financing for the new pipeline (northwards along the eastern side of the Caspian) tipped the balance.[55]

What are the prospects for Russia at least maintaining oil and gas supplies to Europe, given the slow hydrocarbons output growth anticipated in Moscow? EU-25 gas consumption rose at 2.3 percent pa in 2000–5,[56] and will very likely continue to rise, though perhaps more slowly. So the slow projected growth of Russian gas production, on the face of it, appears to be a problem for Europe.

One source of concern that can probably be discounted for the next few years is Moscow's talk of switching gas deliveries eastwards. There are indeed plans for deliveries to China and the Pacific Rim; and liquefied natural gas (LNG) from Sakhalin is already being contracted to Japan and Mexico. But these developments are, first, mostly some way ahead and, second, dependent on the development of gas fields in East Siberia and the Russian Far East; they would not imply a diversion of existing West Siberian sources of supply to Europe. Indeed, the Russians are building the Nord Stream pipeline under the Baltic, adding pipeline capacity to Europe. Also, Gazprom has retreated from plans for future gas supply from the (yet to be developed) Shtokman field to be transported as LNG to the east coast of the US; instead, it now plans to add Shtokman gas to pipeline supplies to Europe in the first phase of the project, with only part of the output going into LNG in the second phase.

As far as other policies for maintaining or expanding exports to Europe are concerned, the picture is mixed. There will probably be some success in further constraining deliveries to Western CIS countries, if only because of the price rises that have been negotiated. There seems also to be considerable success in tapping more Central Asian gas at bargain prices (though these will probably rise over time) for transmission to Europe by Gazprom. The prospects for releasing more oil and (especially) gas for export by constraining domestic consumption – through fuel substitution, raising domestic prices, and promoting greater energy efficiency – are less clear. There are genuine political constraints on raising domestic gas and electricity prices, both to industrial users and to households. In the electricity industry itself, the aim of Anatoly Chubais' liberalization program is to separate generating assets from distribution, privatize them, and sell them, thus raising funds for the repair and improvement of the industry's infrastructure. Electricity production assets will be attractive to private investors, including foreign investors, as long as electricity charges to commercial users are freed by 2011; more precisely, the success of the plan – which is not yet legislated – depends on investors being confident that it will be realized. Obviously, these price increases will provoke resistance. They may be delayed. That would constrain Russia's gas export potential in two ways: it would keep domestic incentives to curb energy consumption weak and it would restrict the investment funds available to Gazprom.

How much investment is needed is impossible to say. For gas and electricity, the figures bandied about, some of which have already been mentioned, come from interested parties. In the case of oil, where less sensitive policy issues are at stake, the numbers may be a little more trustworthy. Leonid Fedun, a vice-president of Lukoil, says that an investment of $300 billion in the oil industry over the next eight to nine years is needed to prevent output falling.[57] That, at an annual rate, is around one-third more than the total fixed investment in the whole "fuel-energy sector" in 2006.[58]

In the medium term, Gazprom plans to buy and trade increasing amounts of gas produced by independent gas producers (including oil companies). Its control of the trunk pipeline system, and of all storage and processing of gas, however, has been brutally leveraged to get control of non-Gazprom gas and to prevent other Russian producers benefiting from export prices. That stifles the incentive for independents to increase gas output in the first place. Top-down management of fuel substitution might be quite effective, but a lot depends on the very ambitious nuclear program.

There is not enough hard evidence for quantifying probable outcomes through 2010, let alone 2020 or 2030. This review of the issues should, however, provide guidance regarding the key developments to monitor. A plausible scenario would be one in which oil production continues to be sluggish; gas production falls, initially because developments at Yamal are behind schedule and then because developments of the Shtokman and East Siberian fields also are delayed; the raising of domestic gas and electricity prices is deferred so that domestic energy-intensity declines more slowly than planned; the nuclear building program also falls behind schedule; and the buoyant growth of the coal industry eases off as state involvement in it grows. In such a scenario, Russia's hydrocarbons exports might well contract in volume, posing acute difficulties for Europe. A quite separate danger, and one that is primarily a danger for Russia itself, would be a large and sustained fall in the oil price, curbing state spending and slowing Russian growth more generally. (The federal budget would be protected for a time by drawing on the reserve fund, but that would not suffice against a fall below $40 a barrel that lasted for more than a year.) Both these developments, however, could spur policy reconsiderations that would be constructive.

Damaging delays in the development of major oil and gas projects could induce policymakers to reconsider their priorities. What is the acceptable cost, in terms of lost export earnings, of preserving political control of the oil industry? The new law on foreign investment in strategic sectors, which nominally went into effect on 7 May 2008, does not clarify prospects as much as might have been expected. It sets a 10 percent ceiling on future foreign acquisitions of stakes in companies developing fields with more than 70 mt of oil or 50 bcm of gas, but allows exceptions to be made in particular cases, at Russian government discretion. However, the mechanism for considering such applications has not been set up as of mid-2008, so foreign investment plans in the sector are likely to be put on hold, and it remains to be seen how the exceptions policy might work in practice.[59] Possibly, the political leadership will decide that more openness to foreign capital and technology is needed, and that openness in turn requires more acceptance of large foreign stakeholdings[60] in major fields as well as clearer and more stable rules for foreign investment in oil and gas.

A period of sustained low oil prices could, as many liberal commentators hope, force the political elite to turn back to market reforms. High oil prices have fostered a complacent belief that Russia can do pretty well for itself without further reform. From the liberal critics' point of view, it could be helpful if that complacency were challenged.

If Europe and the US went into recession and growth in China slowed significantly, a sustained fall in oil prices would be possible. A more likely scenario is one in which world oil prices remain in a historically high range while Russian hydrocarbons production contracts, and while moves to constrain domestic energy usage are minimal and export volumes stall or drop. In such a case, some degree of re-opening of "strategic" natural resource deposits to large-scale Western participation would be possible. Meanwhile, European governments would have to pursue more actively the quest for alternative sources of energy supplies.

Long-term implications of "energy power" for the Russian economy

Whatever the restrictions on its capacity to increase oil and gas exports, the Russian economy will, for some years at least, develop on the back of those exports. Does that mean it is threatened by the "natural resource curse"?

If metals (steel, nickel, aluminum, and gold, in particular) are added, Russian export dependence on raw-material-based industries rises to around 80 percent. The success of these industries as exporters has had obvious benefits for the country, such as rising revenues that are used to fund investment; rising state funding of social benefits and pensions; and a greatly increased claim on the wider world's attention. But it also has drawbacks. Russian hydrocarbons and metals exports are not highly processed. This might not matter if research-based production in other sectors were flourishing, which could open the way for sustained long-run growth when oil prices fall – or merely stop growing. But that is not the case. As we have noted, a detailed study of product groups shows that Russia is weaker as an exporter of medium and high-technology products than Brazil, China, or Turkey.[61]

Russia is in no position to compete with low-wage Asian producers of manufactured goods. It might perhaps, as the Putin leadership plans, build on past strengths in military-related high-technology areas like aerospace, but it has not yet done so. Worse, domestic industrial output that competes with imports has been growing less strongly than the corresponding imports.[62] This suggests that the so-called "Dutch disease" may be infecting Russia: growth in natural-resource exports pushes up the exchange rate, making other parts of the economy less competitive than they would otherwise have been, whether as sources of exports or of import-substitutes.

The Dutch disease may not be as detrimental as its reputation would suggest. The Dutch have made a pretty good recovery from it. It deserves serious consideration nonetheless. It is one of a family of ailments that some economists have grouped together and labeled the "natural resource curse". The empirical basis for this phenomenon is the relatively slow growth in the late twentieth century of countries that at the start of a 20- or 30-year period of observations had a high ratio of natural-resource exports to GDP, even when adjustment was made for other influences.[63] One version of the curse is that wealthy and powerful natural resource companies, whether privately-owned or state-owned, provide a setting in which corruption can flourish; the economy can easily come under the sway of politicians who live off the (relatively) easy pickings of these industries. That may or may not be a widely developed phenomenon, but it certainly fits contemporary Russia. That does not augur well either for economic diversification or for good government in the future.

I have argued that Russia is a good deal more than a petro-state. The oil and gas sectors employ only a tiny fraction of its workforce, and do not lever up wages in other sectors. It has a dynamic services sector and a manufacturing sector that at least provides a wide range of import-substitutes, even if it is not competitive as a producer of exports. Some diversification has been taking place. Still, Russian economic growth is sensitive to the oil price; dynamism in non-energy tradables is lacking; and there are some symptoms of the Dutch disease. On top of that, the country has weakened its own hydrocarbons sector by increasing state control of the oil industry; and it faces a declining labor force and the end of recovery growth as previously under-used capacity is used up, as well as a rising real exchange rate that harms competitiveness. Fixed investment has been modest for a catching-up, middle-income country; it rose sharply in 2007, but mainly (on a preliminary assessment) because of rising capital spending by state-controlled companies. State-managed investment is unlikely to be effective in offsetting the influences favoring a slowdown.

I do not subscribe to the melodramatic view that the Russian economy is about to implode because of an overload of state control. But I do consider, on balance, that Russian growth is likely to slow over the next few years. It seems also to be the case that, even as a supplier of oil and gas to the rest of the world, Russia will at best show only slow growth. The same prospect, however, is in the offing for other major oil and gas producers as well. Somewhat slower growth than recently registered seems likely.

Conclusions

For the EU, the principal concern is gas supplies. These come to Europe mainly through pipelines, and sourcing is rather rigid. Sources of supply for oil can be diversified much more readily. The same is true for coal, of which Russia is a major supplier for the UK, Germany, Finland, Greece, Spain, and Romania.[64]

The present energy-supply situation between Russia and the EU is not quite one of mutually assured dependence. It is true that Moscow needs the money and the European states need the oil and gas. However, the bargaining positions are not symmetrical. In the critical gas market, Russia has an entrenched, state-owned monopoly exporter: Gazprom. Effectively, the Russian side is a single negotiating unit. On the EU side, various companies and governments act separately. National dependence on Russian gas as a share of total gas usage ranges from about 2 percent in the UK through something of the order of 40 percent in Germany[65] to 100 percent or close to 100 percent in several eastern members of the EU, including Finland. The incentives to solidarity are weak.

The desirable arrangements on the EU side, so far as gas is concerned, are well-rehearsed (*The Economist* rehearses them once a month): more LNG terminals to facilitate gas supply from further afield; more inter-connecting links in the European pipeline network to allow more switching around of supplies from different sources; determined implementation of the European Commission's Competition Directorate program to break up European energy monopolies like Ruhrgas, Gaz de France, and Eni (natural partners for Gazprom); and more convergence on a common EU energy policy. These would weaken Russia's market power. Supporters of energy market liberalization, however, cannot count on rapid progress toward it – if indeed there is any progress at all.

Brussels has made a great deal of the Russian state's refusal to ratify the Energy Charter Treaty (ECT), including the Transit Protocol attached to it. Ratifying this would commit Russia to opening up access to its pipelines on an equal, competitive footing, to all comers. There is no practical gain to be expected from pursuing this campaign. Russia, like the US and Middle Eastern oil exporters, has no wish to ratify the ECT. Not only have the Russian authorities said so, but they have moved to entrench Gazprom's export monopoly in law – a move that is diametrically opposed to the ECT.

Vladimir Milov has argued persuasively that it is in Russia's long-term interest to promote a comprehensive agreement with the EU on conditions of energy supply. Such an agreement would lay down principles, for example, in regard to transit arrangements, and provide for recourse to the law to resolve disputes.[66] This would avoid both the discriminatory nature of the ECT[67] and the unstable arrangements inherent in Russia's present bilateral transit arrangements.

Meanwhile, the real worry is not so much Russian use of energy leverage, but Russia's doubtful capacity to increase, or even maintain, its oil and gas supplies to Europe. That depends primarily on internal Russian developments: on the rapidity with which remaining major gas fields in Western Siberia are developed; on some recovery of momentum in an oil industry rendered sluggish by high taxation and increased state control; on the continued cornering of Central Asian gas by Russia; and on the Russian state's ability to push through a real liberalization of the electricity industry and to impose increased gas and electricity prices on Russian commercial customers.

The bottom line for Europe is that it will probably need to supplement Russian oil and gas supplies with supplies from elsewhere – not for the sake of preserving its "energy security" against a state that wants to play political games with hydrocarbon supplies, but to insure itself against that state's difficulties in providing those supplies.

Notes

1 The author is indebted to the editors, to other project members, and to two anonymous reviewers for helpful corrections and comments.
2 Ministry of Economic Development and Trade (MERT), *Kontseptsiia dolgosrochnogo sotsial'no-ekonomicheskogo razvitiia Rossiiskoi Federatsii* (Moscow: MERT, March 2008).
3 Ministry of Industry and Energy (Minpromenergo), Institut energeticheskoi strategii, *Kontseptsiia energeticheskoi strategii Rossii na period do 2030g.* (proekt) (Moscow: Minpromenergo, 2007), especially Tables 3.1 and 3.2.
4 Nick Manning, "Effects of Transformation on Inequality in Russia," in *The Transformation of State Socialism. System Change, Capitalism or Something Else?*, ed. David Lane (Basingstoke: Palgrave Macmillan, 2007), 161–79.
5 Author's calculation from official Russian (Rosstat) data at www.gks.ru/free_doc/2007/b07_11/07–09.htm (accessed 17 December 2007). Rosstat has stopped calculating a minimum income level since the end of 2004. I have taken the income distribution data from the source above and used the fourth-quarter 2004 "living minimum" figure adjusted for consumer-price inflation in 2005 and 2006 to arrive at this estimate.
6 That is, at an exchange rate adjusted for differences in price levels, and not simply the prevailing exchange rate.
7 For example: L. Grigoriev, "Investitsionnyi protsess: nakoplennye problemy i interesy," *Voprosy ekonomiki*, no. 4 (2008): 44–61.
8 An inflow of money into a country is "sterilized" if it is withdrawn from the domestic circulation of money so as not to generate inflationary pressure.
9 Ol'ga Kuvshinova, Nadezhda Ivanitskaia, and Dmitrii Kaz'min, "Konservativnost' protiv infliatsii," *Vedomosti*, 18 June 2008.

10 The first part of this section of the paper overlaps with a section of Philip Hanson, "The Russian Economic Puzzle: Going Forwards, Backwards or Sideways?," *International Affairs* 83, no. 5 (2007): 869–89.
11 Output data from Rosstat; export volumes from Russian Customs data (www.customs.ru); revenue share quoted from Gazprom sources in *Vedomosti*, 26 June 2007.
12 Yasushi Nakamura, "Economy-Wide Influences of the Russian Oil Boom: A National Accounting Matrix Approach," in *Dependent on Oil and Gas: Russia's Integration into the World Economy*, ed. Shinichiro Tabata (Sapporo: Slavic Research Center, Hokkaido University, 2006), 31–51.
13 Simon-Erik Ollus, "Natural Resources – a Blessing or a Curse?," in *New Conditions for Growth in Russia*, BOFIT Online, no. 7, ed. Seija Lainela, Simon-Erik Ollus, Jauko Rautava, Heli Simola, Pekka Sutela, and Merja Tekoniemi (Helsinki: Bank of Finland, 2007), 4–11.
14 Author's calculation from Central Bank of Russia estimates of the balance of payments, www.cbr.ru/statistics/credit_statistics/print.asp?file=bal_of_payments_est.htm (accessed 15 August 2007).
15 *Vedomosti*, 13 June 2007.
16 Tabata, *Dependent on Oil and Gas*.
17 Julian Cooper, "Can Russia Compete in the Global Economy?," *Eurasian Geography and Economics* 47, no. 4 (2006): 407–26, here 412.
18 Derived from Central Bank of Russia, *Biulleten' bankovskoi statistiki*, no. 6 (2007).
19 Neil Buckley, "Fixing Holes in the Road," *Financial Times*, "Investing in Russia" supplement, 2 October 2007, 3.
20 Derived from *Deutsche UFG Economics*, 28 September 2007, 10 and *Financial Times*, 28 September 2007.
21 At present, state-controlled banks probably account for somewhat over half of all bank assets. The Russian government, in its November 2006 bilateral deal with the US on the terms of Russian accession to the World Trade Organization, secured a compromise under which Russia reserved the right to block further foreign acquisition of banks in Russia if the foreign asset-share ever exceeded 50 percent. See: Juliet Johnson, "The US–Russian WTO Agreement on Financial Services," in *Russia and the WTO: A Progress Report*, NBR Special Report no. 12 (Seattle: The National Bureau of Asian Research, 2007).
22 Andrew Monaghan, *Stakhanov to the Rescue? Russian Coal and the Troubled Emergence of a Russian Energy Strategy*, Russian Series 07/34 (Shrivenham: Defence Academy of the United Kingdom, Advanced Research and Assessment Group, November 2007).
23 *Vedomosti*, 29 September 2007.
24 *Vedomosti*, 13 September 2007.
25 *Vedomosti*, 20 December 2007.
26 From one point of view, this approach entails double counting, since it does not net out the activity of foreign-owned firms within the nation in question. But the resilience and command over resources of the nation's companies depends in part on what they do abroad, while some of its factor income also comes from foreign firms operating within its borders.
27 Ministry of Finance, *Main Results and Trends of Budget Policy 2008–2010* (Moscow: Ministry of Finance, 2007), 38, 43, www.1.minfin.ru/budref_eng/budpolres08–10.doc (accessed 18 December 2007).
28 *Vedomosti*, 31 October 2007.
29 Minpromenergo, *Energeticheskaia strategiia Rossii na period do 2020 goda*, approved as decree no. 1234-r by the Russian government on 28 August 2003, www.minprom.gov.ru/docs/strateg/1/ (accessed 7 July 2008).

30 Minpromenergo, *Kontseptsiia energeticheskoi strategii Rossii na period do 2030g.*
31 Here and subsequently, "primary fuel" means the sum of all power generated from oil, gas, coal, nuclear, and hydroelectric energy. It excludes biofuels, peat, solar, and wind and wave power – on which the strategy has rather little to say. The Russian practice is to sum these in units of *uslovnoe toplivo*. I use here the tons of oil equivalent (toe) measure that is more familiar in the West. This difference of unit does not affect shares of different fuels in the energy balance or growth rates of production or usage. It should be noted that the Minpromenergo draft energy strategy to 2030 is being re-worked at the time of writing.
32 Monaghan, *Stakhanov to the Rescue?*, 13.
33 For the Eastern Gas Program, see "Vostochnaia gazovaia programma – utverzhdena!," *Minpromenergo News*, 7 September 2007, www.minprom.gov.ru/activity/energy/news/329 (accessed 15 October 2007).
34 Derived from British Petroleum (BP), *Statistical Review of World Energy 2006* (London: BP, 2006) and Troika Dialog, *Russia Economic Monthly*, March 2007.
35 *Vedomosti*, 7 September 2007.
36 On the rise of Rosneft, the state-controlled national champion in the oil industry, see Nina Poussenkova, "Lord of the Rigs: Rosneft as a Mirror of Russia's Evolution," paper written for "The Changing Role of National Oil Companies in International Energy Markets," a project jointly sponsored by the Japan Petroleum Energy Center and the James A. Baker III Institute for Public Policy, Rice University, Houston, March 2007.
37 See *Vedomosti*, 10 July 2007 for a discussion of these projections by Russian analysts.
38 My guess is that this reflected their lack of confidence (well-founded, it turned out) in their property rights in the longer term. Lukoil – private, but much better connected politically – was engaged in more development of new fields. See Isabel Gorst, "Lukoil: Russia's Largest Oil Company," paper written for "The Changing Role of National Oil Companies in International Energy Markets," a project jointly sponsored by the Japan Petroleum Energy Center and the James A. Baker III Institute for Public Policy, Rice University, Houston, March 2007: the author notes on page 3 that Lukoil boss Vagit Alekperov spends 80 percent of his working time monitoring developments in the Kremlin.
39 www.minatom.ru/News/Main/view?id=44653&idChannel=681 (accessed 22 May 2007); the reference to Chernobyl is by me; to be fair, the RBMK-1000 channel-type reactors have been retrofitted with stronger safety controls.
40 www.kremlin.ru/appears/2007/04/26/1156_type63372type82634_125401.shtml (accessed 23 May 2007).
41 These percentage values are from the text of the 2020 *Strategy*. The numbers given in Chart 13 of the document show a range of percentage shares.
42 Brokerkreditserviz estimates cited in *Vedomosti*, 5 September 2007.
43 *Vedomosti*, 28 April 2007.
44 Atomenergoprom will report to Rosatom, the state body with overall responsibility for both civil and military nuclear programs. That body, in its turn, is also to be converted into a corporation (see: *Oxford Analytica Daily Brief*, 5 October 2007, www.OxAn.com). These reorganizations may well make sense in the long run, but they will probably complicate the running of the nuclear program in the shorter term.
45 Rosstat for production figures and Russian Customs Service (www.customs.ru) for trade volumes. However, the customs data appear not to identify gas that transits Russia (mainly from Central Asia) to Western CIS and Europe as imported, so other sources are needed to get a precise fix on the re-export of non-Russian gas.
46 In early 2008, Gazprom was planning both to expand the volume of gas delivered to non-CIS states from about 151 bcm in 2007 to 163 bcm in 2008 (this would be partly a rebound after an unusually mild weather in 2007) and to reduce deliveries to "the

50   P. Hanson

CIS and Baltics" (*sic*) from currently 55 to 50 bcm. See: Irina Malkova, "Gazprom narashchivaet eksportnuiu vyruchku," *Vedomosti*, 18 June 2008.
47 *Vedomosti*, 12 March 2007.
48 Ibid.
49 www.gazprom.ru/documents/presentation_29.06.2007_Ananenkov.pdf (accessed 8 October 2007), at slide 33, with rubles converted to US dollars at the average 2006 exchange rate of R27.2 = $1.
50 *Vedomosti* 10 September 2007.
51 "Vostochnaia gazovaia programma – utverzhdena!" and *Vedomosti*, 10 September 2007.
52 Ibid.
53 Interview, "Temnaia energiia," *Vedomosti*, 17 March 2008.
54 *Oxford Analytica Daily Brief*, 14 May 2007.
55 However, an apparently very well-informed Russian source tells me (private communication, October 2007) that Turkmenistan has subsequently indicated continued interest in the Nabucco project, and that Russia can object, but cannot block the building of a Transcaspian pipeline.
56 BP, *Statistical Review of World Energy*.
57 Catherine Belton, "Warning on Output Levels," *Financial Times*, "Investing in Russia" supplement, 2 October 2007, 4.
58 This is a back-of-an-envelope calculation. Rosstat gives fuel-energy-sector fixed investment in 2006 as 13.9 percent of total fixed investment, and gives the latter as 17.9 percent of GDP (in rubles). Converting the GDP figure to dollars at the exchange rate produces a figure of $986 billion, so fuel-energy-sector fixed investment in 2006 was, at the exchange rate, of the order of $24.5 billion.
59 See Laura Brank, Daria Litvinova, and Kevin Withane, "The Strategic Sectors Law and Its Impact on Foreign Investment in Russia," Chadbourne & Parke LLP, *CIS Legal Newswire*, 15 June 2008.
60 Not necessarily controlling stakes, but substantially more than the 20 percent or so that seems in practice to be the current informal limit.
61 Cooper, "Can Russia Compete in the Global Economy?"
62 Simon-Erik Ollus and Stephan Barisitz, *The Russian Non-Fuel Sector: Signs of Dutch Disease? Evidence from EU-25 Import Competition*, BOFIT Online, no. 2 (Helsinki: Bank of Finland, 2007).
63 See notably Jeffrey D. Sachs and Andrew Warner, "The Curse of Natural Resources," *European Economic Review* 45, nos 4–6 (2001): 827–38.
64 Monaghan, *Stakhanov to the Rescue?*
65 The importance of this should not be exaggerated, however. Less than 10 percent of German electricity is generated from gas – much less than for the UK or for Russia itself.
66 Vladimir Milov, "Russia–EU Energy Dialog: Filling a Vacuum," *Russia in Global Affairs* 5, no. 4 (2007): 132–43.
67 The ECT exempts inter-state deliveries within the EU from its Transit Protocol.

3 Energy and state–society relations
Socio-political aspects of Russia's energy wealth

Robert W. Orttung

At the end of President Vladimir Putin's second term, Russians viewed their political system through the prism of what they perceived to be the state weakness and chaos of the 1990s. When the Soviet Union collapsed, Russian citizens were left without many of the supports that they had become used to during the Soviet era. Having lost the guarantees of a basic standard of living and free health care, they were left on their own in a vicious new capitalist system. They watched their economy plummet, as gross domestic product dropped 43.3 percent between 1991 and 1998.[1] Powerful oligarchs grabbed the most lucrative assets of the state in rigged auctions that favored insiders. As the apparent loser in the Cold War, Russia saw its international standing drop from being one of two superpowers to that of mere regional power. Only the dramatic financial collapse of 1998 was finally able to shake up the old system enough to set the country on a course for economic growth. Russia's economy began to recover in 1999.

As he rose to power at the end of 1999, Putin was able to take advantage of this rising economic tide and used it to help restore Russian political prestige. He re-established Russian pride by apparently erasing one of the most embarrassing legacies of the 1990s, the loss of Chechnya and the defeat of the Russian military at the hands of a small rebel alliance. Putin used brutal force to reassert Russian control over the breakaway republic. He then went on to restore the power of the state that had been hollowed out at the end of the Soviet era and under his predecessor Boris Yeltsin. Putin restored Russian citizens' pride in their leaders and themselves.

After winning the presidential elections at the beginning of 2000, Putin created a political system that is in many ways unique to Russian history: it combines some czarist and Soviet practices, achievements from the eras of Mikhail Gorbachev and Yeltsin, and new features. Russia is much more open to foreign influence than it was during the Soviet period. Most Russian citizens are free to travel, and Russians have access to the internet, which provides unfettered information, debate, and some ability to organize online. With the end of official state planning for the economy and the occurrence of high oil and gas prices, Russian citizens are now better off economically than ever before. Consumer goods are widely available, giving the average person a sense of well-being.

These feelings permeate Russian society even though only a small elite actually controls the distribution of the oil rents. In contrast to the upheavals of the 1990s, Putin has been able to create a feeling of stability in the political system that has made him enormously popular with his constituents.

However, these accomplishments have been accompanied by a systematic assault on democracy and civil liberties. During his eight years in office, Putin returned some of the Soviet-style approaches to ruling Russia, particularly the centralization of power. In a new twist, however, he has carved out a strong autonomous role for the security services. During the Soviet era, the Committee on State Security (KGB) was a powerful organization, but it was subordinate to the Communist Party of the Soviet Union, which is gone now. While there may be pluralism at the top of Russia's political system among a variety of clans, the Federal Security Service (FSB), the KGB's successor, ensures control further down. The public has little ability to exercise oversight over the government, and corruption is rampant. While the system is apparently stable in the short term, it lacks the basis for long-term institutionalization.

Putin's Russia provides a powerful case study of democratization and its setbacks against the global background of political and economic change. Most scholars and practitioners have given up on the idea, fashionable in the early 1990s, that transitions to democracy are inevitable.[2] Instead, as an alternative, some have returned to Samuel Huntington's idea of sequencing, arguing that the imposition of order is a necessary precondition for building democracy.[3] The central tenet of this approach is the need to build institutions and then allow greater participation to assert public control over them. However, it is clear that Russia's path is not heading in the direction of building political institutions, developing a stable economy, and then allowing democracy. The negative repercussions of the Russian state's immoderate power are too large for this path to be successful, especially when the factor of energy profits is built in. A key problem is that the centralized state had stimulated extensive corruption, which means that much of Russia's energy wealth is not collected by the state, but by bureaucrats, middlemen, and others interested in personal gain.

This chapter seeks to tease out the relationship between energy and politics in Russia. While there is an important connection between Russia's energy wealth and its political development, the causal arrow does not simply go in one direction, with the presence of oil wealth leading to authoritarianism and corruption. Instead, oil is a facilitator for tendencies that were already present in the system. Authoritarianism reappeared in Russia in the mid-1990s, well before the price of oil began to increase. The resources generated by the rise in energy prices did not initiate Putin's shift toward authoritarianism, but they have supported it. High energy profits act as an enabler, allowing political leaders to exert the kind of control over society that they desire.

The relationship between energy wealth and the political system is dynamic. Russia's energy wealth provides resources that its political elites can use in their efforts to control property and financial resources in society. Likewise, though, the nature of the political system has an impact on the development of Russia's energy wealth. Increasing state control over the energy sector shapes the way Russia's resources are being managed and developed. The energy industry is becoming less efficient as the state asserts control over it.

This chapter proceeds along the following lines. First, it lays out the complex and dynamic relationship between Russia's energy wealth and the political system. Second, it examines how Russia's leaders have used energy resources to build up the state's coercive capacity. Finally, it explains how the state managers use energy rents to maintain the loyalty of the political elite and the population. The conclusion argues that the concentration of power, repression of independent groups among the population, weak administrative capacity of the state, and expensive reliance on payoffs to maintain loyalty undermine Russia's political stability over the long term.

Energy wealth and Russia's political system

The link between Russia's energy wealth and its political system is not a direct causal relationship in which the presence of energy wealth leads straight to the establishment of a corrupt, authoritarian regime. There were already plenty of problems with Russian democracy in the 1990s that undermined the democratic transition even before oil prices began to rise sharply in 2003. The high oil prices, however, contributed to these problems.

After the collapse of the Soviet Union, Russia's state capacity was extremely weak, but reformers set aside efforts to address this problem in order to deal with day-to-day survival. As a result, throughout the 1990s, the Russian state lacked the coherence to play an effective role in Russia's developing economic system.[4] To implement his painful economic reforms at the end of 1991, Yeltsin relied on his personal authority by serving simultaneously as president and prime minister.[5] By April 1992, the Russian parliament was strongly opposed to Yeltsin's plans, paving the way for a destructive struggle between the executive and legislative branches, culminating in the president's use of tanks to shut down the parliament and pave the way for new elections in December 2003. In the wake of these obviously undemocratic moves, the newly established Russian government began to privatize some of the key energy assets that it had inherited from the Soviet era. In particular, it sold off most of the country's oil industry to private investors. Typically, the men who purchased these assets were able to use their inside connections to acquire the property at a fraction of its real value.[6] The oligarchs then engaged in a process of asset stripping in which they were able to privatize much of Russia's wealth. With the economy reeling, between 1993 and 1998, Russia ran a budget deficit of approximately 9 percent of GDP, and Yeltsin's popularity dropped to record lows.[7] In order to ensure that the Communists did not come to power on a wave of popular discontent in the 1996 Russian presidential elections, the media voluntarily sacrificed its independence and backed Yeltsin, even covering up the fact that he had had a disabling heart attack before the voting was complete. The health of democracy was no better at the sub-national level. Although they were elected directly by their constituents, Russia's governors began to assert power for themselves and frequently operated in violation of federal laws.[8] In many cases, they behaved as mini-dictators within their own regions.

Following the tank assault on the parliament, the tainted 1996 presidential elections, and the growing insubordination in the regions, Russian democracy was under considerable strain by the mid-1990s, long before energy prices began to rise. When Putin came to power as acting president at the beginning of 2000, he and his allies first strengthened the capacities of the state that they inherited from the Yeltsin era to make it an effective actor within the Russian political arena. They systematically set about attacking the power and wealth of the governors and oligarchs and were successful in bringing them into line. In addition, they eliminated what remained of Russia's pluralistic press, squashed civil society groups, exerted extensive control over the electoral process, and brought the judiciary into line to provide necessary decisions in political cases.[9] Putin's policies at this stage were not a function of high energy prices, because the prices had not started to rise quickly when he took these steps.

Having reasserted state power during the first three years of Putin's term, Russia's leaders then focused on bringing energy sector assets under their own control. The logic was simple: "Whoever controls oil, controls the country. And therefore, whoever controls the country inevitably tries to gain control over oil," according to Konstantin Simonov, the president of the Center for the Russian Political Situation.[10] Putin and his team argued that the owners who had acquired their wealth in the 1990s had done so illegitimately. Since Putin's group controlled the capacities of the state, they were able to use its coercive potential to reverse the earlier deals and assert their own influence over the assets of the energy sector. Their actions meant undoing some of the key privatizations of the Yeltsin era, such as the creation of the Yukos and Sibneft oil companies, and revising some of the concessions made to foreign energy companies working in Russia, as in the cases of the Sakhalin off-shore projects and the giant Kovykta gas field in Siberia.[11] Between 2003 and 2007, the Russian state was able to reassert its majority ownership of Gazprom and renationalize approximately half of Russia's oil industry. It also grabbed direct majority control over the most important oil and gas fields that were being developed by foreign energy companies.

This brief overview of recent Russian history shows that energy rents were not the main factor driving political events. Rather, Putin was reacting to his perception of the 1990s and working to correct what he considered to be some of the mistakes of that era. In fact, the shift away from democratic governance began long before energy prices started their dizzying assent in 2003. As Figures 3.1 and 3.2 show, the decline in Russian democracy, as measured by the level of political freedoms according to the Freedom House publication *Freedom in the World*, started in 1997 when oil prices were actually dropping. These data clearly show that energy rents are not the main driver pushing Russia toward authoritarianism. To understand the evolution of the Russian political system, it is necessary to look at a wide variety of factors. However, despite the lack of a direct causal link, there is a strong correlation between rising energy prices and Putin's expanding use of authoritarian methods. In this sense, the high oil prices have facilitated the existing predilection away from political freedom.

Figures 3.1 and 3.2 illustrate this correlation clearly: as the price of oil rose in the first decade of the twenty-first century, the level of political freedom in Russia deteriorated. The Freedom House scale ranks political systems from 1 to 7, with 1 being the most free and 7 being the least free. During the 1990s, oil and natural gas prices were relatively low and did not provide a large source of income that Yeltsin's administration could use to buy political support. The Yeltsin era was also a time when there was a relatively pluralistic media, which, for example, felt free to criticize important Kremlin initiatives, such as fighting the Chechen War. There were also opportunities for civil society groups to organize and for opposition political parties to form and operate. Of course, all was not well during this era. As noted above, the Kremlin used force against the opposition, the media failed to provide accurate coverage of the 1996 elections, corruption was rampant, and the Yeltsin administration sold off valuable energy assets in rigged auctions to a few well-connected individuals. In contrast to that time, during Putin's two terms in office, energy prices rose constantly, providing the Kremlin with extensive resources and giving ordinary citizens a general sense that their standard of living was increasing. These resources have

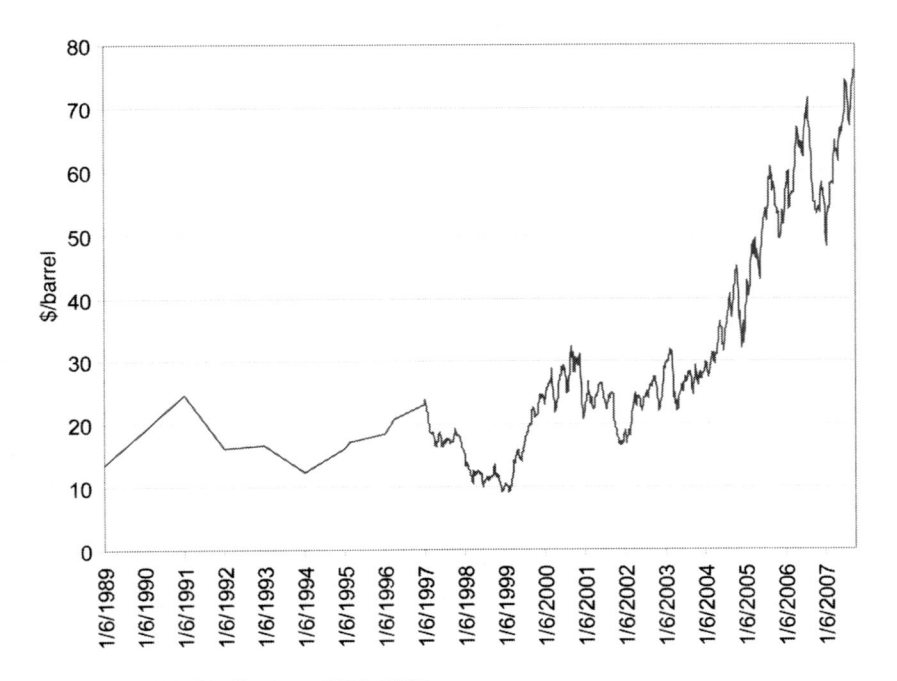

Figure 3.1 World oil prices, 1989–2007.

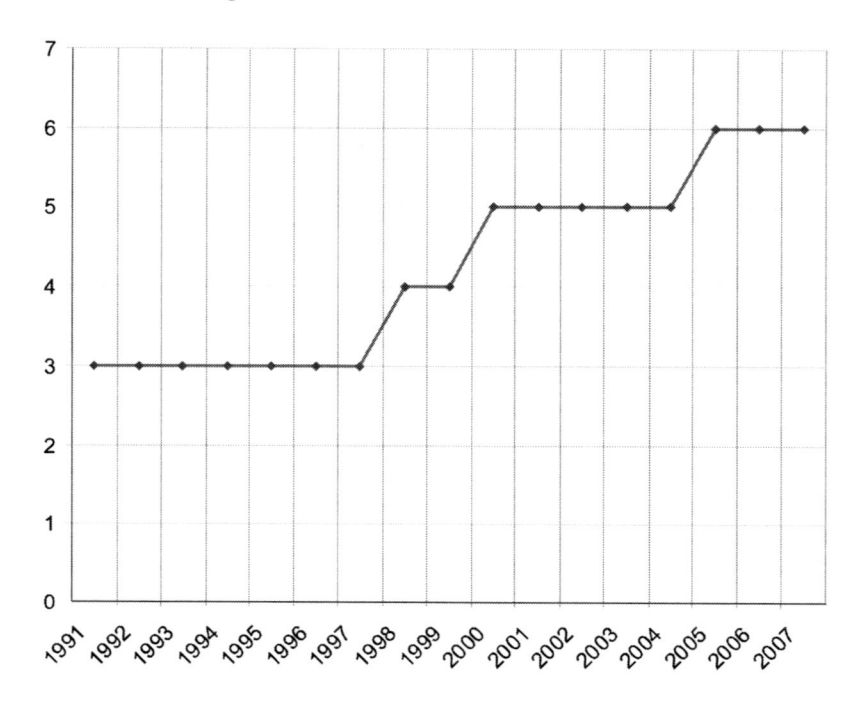

Figure 3.2 Freedom House political rights scores for Russia.

Note
According to the Freedom House measures, 1–2 represent consolidated democracies, while 6–7 represent consolidated authoritarian regimes.

helped make it possible for Putin to eliminate many of the political freedoms that Russians had gained in the 1990s.

The Russian case generally does confirm the key conclusions of the resource curse literature. For example, Michael L. Ross found that "oil does hurt democracy" in a wide variety of geographic locations.[12] However, the Russian case shows that oil was not the main factor in undermining Russian democracy, though it contributed to the regime's ability to impose a non-democratic system. Putin eliminated the political rights of Russian citizens for a variety of reasons, and the presence of oil wealth was only one of many factors.[13]

Philip Hanson's chapter in this volume provides evidence that Russia is suffering from some of the economic consequences predicted by the resource curse literature. However, while Russia does seem to be suffering from the resource curse, the country has managed to avoid some of the negative political-economic consequences anticipated by the resource curse literature. This literature suggests, for example, that when governments derive sufficient revenue from oil and gas, they reduce the tax burden on the population and thereby reduce the population's demand for accountability in government actions. A political elite that is growing rich from energy revenue does not depend on extracting resources from society and therefore can assume that society will not be motivated to take a major interest in influencing its policies. Russian reality tells a different story. Since the collapse of the Soviet Union, the Russian state has learned to tax much better than it had in the past and tax revenue has increased markedly.[14] Given its growing tax burden, one would expect the Russian population to demand greater accountability. However, the population has been generally passive toward the state.

Energy resources converted to extensive coercive capacity

It is in the area of political consequences from high energy wealth that the resource curse and rentier state literature has the best fit with Russian conditions.[15] This literature argues that resource wealth allows states to spend more on internal security and repress the democratic desires of the population.[16] It also claims that energy income allows the government to block the formation of groups that are independent of the state and that might demand the political rights required to impose an alternative set of policies. In addition to building up coercive capacity, the literature shows that the elites can use energy income and subsidies to buy the quiescence of the masses. This section measures the Russian experience against these expectations by examining the Russian state's growing coercive capacities, the suppression of autonomous group formation, and the use of energy subsidies.

Increased repressive capacities

By the end of his second term, the Putin administration had invested heavily in increased repressive capacities, which allowed him and his allies extensive control over Russia's political and economic life. Putin has drawn extensively on his KGB background to expand the power and reach of the secret police throughout Russian society. Under President Putin's system of government, a small group of elites controlled the key positions in Russian policymaking. Analysts typically identified four men as being the most powerful: Deputy heads of the Presidential Administration Igor Sechin and Viktor Ivanov, FSB head Nikolai Patrushev, and First Deputy Prime Minister Sergei Ivanov.[17] More than half of the Kremlin's senior bureaucrats came from the power ministries, which include the FSB and other agencies that wield coercive power, according to sociologist Olga Kryshtanovskaya.[18] When it gained leadership over the newly-created National Anti-Terrorism Committee in 2006, the FSB secured the ability to give orders to all other agencies, formally augmenting its already large informal power.[19]

The Kremlin exercised extensive oversight over the Russian political system and left essentially no room for spontaneity. The December 2007 parliamentary elections handed an overwhelming majority of the seats to pro-government parties, with only a token Communist opposition allowed representation in a body that has little real power. At the end of his constitutionally-defined two terms in office, Putin selected Dmitry Medvedev as his successor and then deployed extensive state resources to guarantee his election in March 2008.

Putin announced that he would stay in power as prime minister and presumably continues to guide the country from this post. These actions render the constitution's provision that Russia's leader will stay in power for eight years meaningless. The Russian authorities have applied their extensive coercive capacity to keep down political protests of all types. Urban protest rallies in St. Petersburg and Moscow held in 2006 and 2007, dubbed "Marches of Those Who Disagree," typically ended in a confrontation with the OMON special purpose police squad. In the regions beyond Moscow and St. Petersburg, local authorities prevented opposition presidential candidates from making public appearances or trying to reach out to their constituents even though they were likely to win only meager support. Since 2004, the Russian president has appointed governors across the country, meaning that they serve at his pleasure and effectively can be removed at any time if the Kremlin leadership so decides.

The FSB has gained extensive control over Russia's business community, pushing out most of the Yeltsin-era oligarchs who might have caused Putin problems. These rich businessmen who were willing to use their money to finance opposition activities included Boris Berezovsky, Vladimir Gusinsky, and Mikhail Khodorkovsky. Berezovsky and Gusinsky left Russia for a life in exile, and Khodorkovsky was sentenced to eight years in a Siberian prison in 2005.

The destruction of Yukos and the subsequent purchase of its assets by the state-owned Rosneft launched the beginning of an effort by Putin and his colleagues to regain control over energy industry assets in Russia. Of course, there may have been many reasons for the attack on Yukos, since Khodorkovsky was at the time of his arrest seeking a foreign buyer for a stake in the company and had also discussed plans to build a private oil pipeline to China that would have been outside the control of the Russian oil pipeline monopoly Transneft. Khodorkovsky was also active in the political opposition and had publicly accused Putin's government of corruption. Although Khodorkovsky had shadowy beginnings and relied on unsavory business practices early in his career, at the time that Putin decided to prosecute Yukos, it was one of the most transparent and dynamic companies operating in Russia. The ultimate result of the case was to transfer Yukos assets to state control. Additionally, in 2005, Gazprom paid $13 billion to acquire Sibneft, an oil company that had been privatized in the 1990s to Roman Abramovich and Berezovsky. Abramovich, who unlike Khodorkovsky retained warm relations with the Kremlin, was well compensated for handing over these assets.

Beyond the state purchase of these assets, the FSB has placed its members at key points throughout the Russian business sector, and the government has continued to bring businesses under its control. Among the energy industry leaders with a FSB background in 2008 were Igor Sechin, the chairman of the board of the Rosneft oil company, the state-owned company that in 2008 was the second largest in Russia. In September 2006, he appointed the son of FSB Director Nikolai Patrushev as his personal advisor.[20] In October 2007, another Putin ally with an intelligence background, Nikolai Tokarev, took over the oil pipeline monopoly Transneft. Earlier, Tokarev had been the head of Zarubezhneft, the state-owned overseas oil developer, whose biggest project was in Vietnam. FSB affiliates also hold key posts in Gazprom and head other key industries. Outside the energy sector, one prominent example is Sergei Chemezov, the general director of Russia's arms exporting monopoly, which in 2005 bought AvtoVAZ, Russia's largest carmaker. Additionally, in May 2007, the Kremlin created the United Aviation Corporation, which unites all the major aircraft manufacturers in one company headed by First Deputy Prime Minister Sergei Ivanov, a former defense minister. Two months later, in July 2007, the Kremlin created the United Shipbuilding Company, which brought together the country's military and civilian shipbuilders, under Deputy Prime Minister Sergei Naryshkin.[21]

Suppressing independent group formation

In addition to greatly expanding its coercive capacity, the Putin administration has taken action to exert extensive control over Russian society and prevent it from taking any autonomous actions to hold the state accountable. In terms of sheer capacity, Russian society has great potential to influence key policy decisions, since the population is highly educated, well linked by a variety of personal and professional networks, and increasingly connected and informed through the internet, where there are a variety of news and blogging sites making it possible to build communities that are interested in particular issues. Approximately one-fifth to one-quarter of the population now belongs to the middle class (though estimates vary on the actual size), and this class could potentially play a role in Russian politics. However, Russian society is far from living up to its potential in terms of political organization and the ability to influence governmental policy-making processes.[22] The EBRD 2007 Transition report shows that Russia is an outlier among former Communist countries, with much less democracy than one would expect from the size of its middle class.[23] In part, the problem stems from the fact that a large part of the middle class is employed by the state and the large state-run corporations, and that its wealth is not dependent on entrepreneurship.[24] Accordingly, the middle class is not free to advocate own policy solutions independently.

Since his first months in office upon becoming president, Putin has systematically attacked media freedom in Russia as a way of reducing the ability of society to mobilize. Russia's energy wealth, and particularly the natural gas monopoly Gazprom, played a major role in this effort. In carrying out this crackdown, Putin initially brought the three main television networks under control, since they are by far the most popular source of information for members of the Russian population. Subsequently, he extended his influence over Russian radio stations and the leading newspapers. At the end of Putin's second term, the only remaining non-government-controlled news sources were a few small-circulation newspapers and a handful of internet sites.

Russia's energy wealth was a key factor in the state's ability to crack down on the media. Rather than nationalizing media companies and controlling them directly, the state used Gazprom money, or capital connected to the gas monopoly's subsidiary companies, to exert its influence. Gazprom-media was able to take over NTV, Russia's first private national network and one that had been critical of government policies, because the previous owner, oligarch Vladimir Gusinsky, had borrowed heavily from Gazprom to keep his business afloat. When the Kremlin grew tired of the broadcaster's criticism and replaced the management and journalists with more compliant alternatives, it asserted that the takeover was a "business decision" rather than an act of political censorship. Gazprom and its affiliates now hold a large media empire that, besides NTV, includes radio station Ekho Moskvy, the newspapers *Izvestiia* and *Kommersant*, and the news website www.gazeta.ru. While these outlets remain critical of some Kremlin policies, Gazprom can use its ownership position to direct analysis away from taboo topics that the Kremlin does not want aired in the media.

That there are limitations on the freedom of speech in Russia is not surprising, since the country has a long history of censorship and the general trend for oil-rich countries is to have unfree media.[25] On the one hand, rulers need to have accurate sources of information in order to make appropriate policy decisions and to understand the popular reaction to their decisions. On the other, allowing the free publication of information could undermine their regime. Accordingly, rulers in non-democratic countries have to decide where to draw the line between gathering information and preventing the free circulation of this information within society. Under Putin, the Russian authorities have consistently pursued a policy based on the assumption that less public information serves their interests best.

With the media firmly in hand, the Putin administration has gone to extensive lengths to suppress the formation of independent groups among the population. At the beginning of 2006, Putin signed a new law on non-governmental organizations (NGOs) that imposes extensive new registration and reporting requirements on them.[26] While the legislation was not political in itself, meeting its requirements made many of Russia's groups vulnerable to the authorities because the reporting requirements were so onerous and complicated that bureaucrats would always be able to find errors if they wanted to prosecute a particular group.

Russian groups lack autonomous sources of funding from inside Russian society. There is no tradition of individual or corporate donations to NGOs or tax incentives to encourage such support. The government only provides funding to groups whose political agenda it supports or to apolitical charity groups, such as those that work with orphans. Businesses take their cues from the state in making their contributions. As a result, many Russian groups interested in human rights, public-sector transparency, and other causes that might evoke government opposition received their funding from foreign sources because there was no domestic alternative. The government has particularly cracked down on this kind of funding, citing the desire to reduce the ability of foreign donors to influence Russian society. Liudmila Alekseeva, head of the Moscow Helsinki Group, described the 2006 NGO law as a "strangling cord for civil society, with the foreign NGOs the first to go."[27]

After the destruction of Yukos, the business community remained cowed and unwilling to put up a united front. There were a variety of business organizations that bring together the most powerful businesses, but these associations fell under the power of the Kremlin and have little ability to influence state policy.[28] The fact that the Russian courts sentenced Yukos leader Khodorkovsky to a significant jail term sent a strong message to other business leaders not to engage in the political process or try to oppose Kremlin policies.

Political parties are also weak and do not perform the functions that they ordinarily carry out in democratic societies. In fact, they have been replaced by regional political machines and oligarchic financial-industrial groups.[29] Rather than combining and articulating grievances from among the population and developing new leaders, the most important parties in Russia are created by the elites to serve elite interests.

The general suppression of all civil society organizations made it very hard for energy-sector watchdog groups to establish themselves and organize efforts to monitor the flow of money generated from resource sales in Russia. International efforts, such as the Extractive Industries Transparency Initiative, have not had much luck setting up programs in Russia, though they have set up websites for Azerbaijan and Kazakhstan.[30] Theoretically, it is possible to build up a variety of public–private coalitions among social groups, journalists, think tanks, and concerned public officials to track the flow of energy rents, but under prevailing conditions, these groups have made little actual progress.[31] There are some public policy institutes that provide critical analysis of Russian energy policies either as their main purpose or as part of their broader analyses. Examples include: Vladimir Milov's Institute of Energy Policy (www.energypolicy.ru), the Institute on Problems of Globalization, and Indem. However, these think tanks are primarily focused on influencing various groups within the elite and do not devote much effort to themes that would be of broader interest to society, such as how oil profits are distributed within the context of government social policy or what influences the price of gasoline at the pump. These think tanks rarely, if ever, work to assemble a coalition of social forces that could seek to influence the country's energy policies. In the conditions of Putin's Russia, working to assemble such a coalition would be fraught with danger.

The Russian government's destruction of the relatively transparent Yukos sent a signal to other companies not to operate in such an open manner. Additionally, the government has shut off attempts to shed more light on practices at Gazprom. Hermitage Capital's William Browder, who worked assiduously to open up the company, faced the cancellation of his Russian visa in 2005 apparently because of his efforts in this area. Such efforts to increase corporate transparency make a difference.[32] In two cases of corporate governance abuse, researchers found that Hermitage was able to gain relief in one case by bringing it to the attention of the international media. In the other case, Hermitage had no interest and the share dilution went through unchecked.[33]

Energy subsidies to the population

A further prediction from the resource curse literature is that high oil and gas revenues allow states to spend more money on direct subsidies to the population, thereby reducing demands for democratization. Again, Russia meets these expectations as the government continues to provide heavy subsidies for energy prices.

However, in this area, Putin's policies have not been as straightforward as they are regarding the use of coercive capacities and group suppression. In fact, in many areas, Putin's team has cut the level of subsidies to the population. Under the Soviet system, the state had held energy costs to residences and factories artificially low, and consumers did not pay anywhere near their true cost. After the collapse of the Soviet Union, Russia created a competitive market for oil products, but natural gas, which is much more important to the Russian economy, remained heavily subsidized. During Putin's first term, these subsidies were greatly reduced as prices rose and customers were forced to pay in cash rather than through barter exchanges.[34] While the Russian government has reduced some of the subsidies, it has not eliminated them entirely. Rather, the Kremlin continued to manipulate such subsidies for political purposes, and progress toward bringing domestic energy prices up to international levels slowed considerably as Putin's second term came to an end and the political elite began to consider how to ensure that they would remain in power when Putin left the presidency. Natural gas prices on the domestic market rose from $10 to $50/kcm in the five years before 2007, though this price was much less than the approximately $250 that European customers were then being charged for the same amount of gas.[35] As Putin and the people around him sought to maintain their hold on power, the authorities postponed any price increases until well after the 2008 presidential elections in order to preserve Putin's high personal ratings in public opinion and to avoid making politically-unpopular demands on the population.[36] In 2006, 75 percent of Russia's end-user domestic energy consumption was purchased at regulated prices, so subsidies remain extensive.[37] The artificially low prices mean that domestic demand for energy is growing. Since this energy is bought at sub-market prices, it is not used efficiently, limiting Russia's ability to export greater supplies of natural gas and increasing its contributions to global greenhouse gas emissions.

The electricity sector presents an interesting case in this regard, because it is moving counter to other trends in the Russian energy sector. Unlike the gas and oil sectors, where Putin has increased state control, liberal reforms to break up and privatize the former electricity monopoly were moving forward in 2007.[38] However, the reformers put off raising electricity prices to their full level until 2011, and it remains to be seen whether such price increases will actually take place. Naturally, the increases will be unpopular and will have to be managed carefully to avoid causing the business and residential users too much pain. The main opponents of the reform are highly-placed members of the presidential administration who would like to keep the electricity monopoly intact. Thus, the fate of the reform will depend on the jockeying for power among the various clans that surround Putin.

The high profits from the oil and gas industry are not the direct cause for authoritarianism in Russia. However, they have provided resources for elite policies of expanding the state's coercive capacity, suppressing the formation of autonomous groups, and providing subsidies to the population to ensure the regime's continuing popularity. In this sense, the energy rents have facilitated the evolution of a non-democratic system.

Instability in a system based on political payoffs

Outside of the political sphere, Russia's leaders have adopted several useful policies, such as establishing a Stabilization Fund at the beginning of 2004 to absorb a considerable part of the oil profits, to prevent damaging inflation rates as oil prices remain high, and to set aside money now that will be available if the price of oil drops in the future. However, while the Russian government has used its energy resources to build up the powers of the state, repress society's involvement in political processes, and continue subsidies, it has not managed to create a stable political system.[39] Russian politics has now concentrated power in the hands of a small elite whose hold on power depends on its ability to continue spending Russia's energy wealth in a costly effort to maintain political control.[40] As this section shows, under the political system existing at the end of Putin's second term, top members of the political elite held key positions in the energy industry. Unfortunately, the resulting combination of political and economic power has promoted corruption throughout the economy and society.

Merger of political and energy industry leadership

In addition to maintaining high energy subsidies for the population, Putin's government bought off the political elite with powerful management positions in the state energy sector. During Putin's tenure, numerous high-level political leaders acquired powerful positions on the boards of Russian energy corporations, as shown in Table 3.1.[41] These interlocking positions essentially allowed a state takeover of the energy sector. This merger of state and energy industry posts shows the interconnected nature and mutual influence of energy and politics in Russia.

Under Putin, the state's coercive capacities increased at a faster rate than administrative competence. State officials typically lack the technical skills to run large corporations in the energy sphere or other sectors of the economy. Likewise, the personalization of control and the state's limited ability to manage corruption meant that its administrative levers were limited. In this regard, Putin did nothing to strengthen the weak institutions for oversight that he inherited from the Yeltsin era.[42] Accordingly, Russia's state companies in the oil and gas sectors have not performed as well as their private counterparts.

The state takeover and the on-going battle for control have not served the interests of the oil companies that have moved from private to public control. The performance of the assets once controlled by Yukos since the 2003 expropriation has not been as robust as it had been under private ownership. Russian oil production grew by only 2.4 percent in 2005, after expanding by an average

Table 3.1 Political leaders with powerful corporate positions at the end of Putin's second presidential term

Name	Executive branch position	Corporate position
Vladislav Surkov	Presidential advisor	Transnefteprodukt board chairman
Igor Sechin	Presidential administration deputy head	Rosneft board chairman
Sergei Naryshkin	Deputy prime minister	Rosneft board deputy chairman
Aleksey Kudrin	Finance minister	ALROSA supervisory board
Dmitry Medvedev	First deputy prime minister	Gazprom board chairman
Viktor Khristenko	Minister of Industry and Energy	Transneft board chairman; Gazprom board
Yevgeny Shkolov	Presidential aide	Transneft board of directors
Sergei Sobianin	Presidential Chief of Staff	TVEL chairman
German Gref	Minister of Economic Development and Trade (to 2007)	Gazprom board

Source: The Brookings Institution, *The Russian Federation*, The Brookings Foreign Policy Studies Energy Security Series (Washington, DC: The Brookings Institution, October 2006), 2; Marshall Goldman, "Putin, Petroleum, Power, and Patronage: The Dog Barks but the Caravan Moves On," presentation at the Jamestown Foundation, 7 December 2006; Mark Franchetti, "A Clean Sweep for Putin Cronies," *Sunday Times*, 11 November 2007.

of 8 percent in the previous seven years.[43] Similarly, the manner in which the company is run is not nearly as transparent as had previously been the case. Such problems were entirely predictable and already visible in the state-managed gas monopoly. Gazprom essentially functions as a rent-redistribution mechanism benefiting numerous inside players. In recent years, its production has declined, while all new production in Russia has come from independent, privately-owned companies working in the gas field. Reform is extremely unlikely in the near future, since it would trample so many well-entrenched interests.[44]

The enormous cost of maintaining this system highlights its instability.[45] Rather than transferring energy sector profits to the benefit of society, this system works to channel much of the control over this income to the key political elites. By combining political and economic power in Russia, elites are loathe to leave office, because their departure from the height of the political system means that they will likely also lose their access to economic power as well. Thus, Russia's resource wealth is not only deforming the political sector, but there is a reverse feedback in which state intervention in the energy sector decreases the ability of the latter to work effectively and produce profits efficiently. The Russian elites benefit from the fortuitous rise in oil prices, which is a function of the fluctuations in international markets rather than of their own skill in managing the economy. By the same token, however, they are vulnerable to possible downturns on notoriously unstable commodities markets.

Even though the state and energy sector have merged to a large extent, the elite running them is not monolithic, as the unsuccessful attempt to unite

Gazprom and state-controlled oil company Rosneft in 2004–5 showed.[46] The main conflict among the individuals at the apex of Russian power is for control over the rents generated by the energy sector and other lucrative parts of the economy. The Yukos case, in which valuable assets were transferred from a privately-held company to Rosneft, whose chairman is deputy head of the presidential administration Igor Sechin, was the crucial element in developing this system because it made possible state efforts to reassert control over a much broader array of Russian energy assets. Such efforts continued with Gazprom's acquisition of Sibneft, described above, and the August 2007 state takeover of Russneft, once Russia's seventh largest oil company. The head of Russneft, Mikhail Gutseriev, apparently annoyed the authorities by seeking to purchase Yukos assets that had been designated for state-owned companies.[47]

Nevertheless, despite these disputes among the elites, by the nature of the system, the Russian state had extensive control over the energy sector. The constitution and federal law give ownership of Russia's resources to the state. The state-owned monopoly Gazprom controls the production of the vast majority of Russia's natural gas and the distribution of all Russian gas. Since oil can only be extracted under license, bureaucrats decide which companies have this right.[48] The state also has monopoly control over Russia's pipeline network for distributing oil and gas.

The Russian state is in a position of strength vis-à-vis big business that is unusual for a middle-income country – or indeed for any country.[49] Russia differs from post-war Japan and Italy because most businesses in Russia began with shady deals and because big businesses are associated with the oil and gas sector, which means that they must rely on state licenses. As a result, the Russian state holds considerable leverage over its companies because it can threaten them at any time with legal action, drawing on illegal activities from the past, or the removal of their licenses.[50] Russia also lacks an independent judiciary that can expose corruption.

Extensive corruption

High levels of corruption have coincided with the concentration of Russia's political and economic power. In Transparency International's 2007 Corruption Perceptions Index, Russia was ranked 143 out of 180 countries with an absolute score of 2.3 on the 1–10 scale, where 10 is the best possible.[51]

The pervasive corruption that influences almost every aspect of the Russian state makes it necessary to draw a clear distinction between the public interest of the state as a whole and the private interests of the individuals who control the powers of the state. Because a relatively small number of individuals can control the Russian energy industry, the key individuals around the Russian president can set energy policies. But this does not mean that they have final control over the rents produced by the energy industry. Clifford G. Gaddy and Barry W. Ickes have shown that these rents are siphoned off in a variety of informal ways.[52] For example, Russia's energy producers can gain control of some of the rents by inflating the costs associated with actually producing the energy. Additionally, there are numerous informal taxes, such as bribes or contributions to projects supported by regional officials that the energy companies must pay in order to continue doing business.[53] Likewise, as noted earlier, outside investors in the natural gas monopoly Gazprom demonstrated that considerable amounts of money in that company are wasted. Even the seemingly great power of the Russian state in the energy sector is severely circumscribed by the inability of the top leadership to control where all of the rents go. In this sense, the Russian state has very weak administrative capacity.

Corruption exists in Russia not because of the presence of extensive oil resources, as some argue, but because the authorities are not sufficiently accountable to society at large.[54] If the Russian government were more transparent and less repressive, social groups would be able to track the flow of these funds with greater precision. The emphasis here on state–society relations, particularly on the development of independent watchdog groups, focuses analytical attention on this interaction as the cause of corruption rather than the presence of the resources per se. Continuing to rely on a system of corporate payoffs to the political elite severely undermines the ability of Russian society to evolve in a socially useful direction.

Conclusion

Russia is not using its resources in an intelligent way. So far, the increased income from the energy sector has helped to bolster an authoritarian government. Only wise policies will be able to take advantage of the windfall gains Russia has received in the first decade of the twenty-first century to diversify the economy away from its current reliance on raw materials production.

Russia has built a state with extensive coercive capacity, but the political system that Putin has created is not stable. A small group of people who managed the key political, security, and energy institutions led Russia at the end of Putin's second term. The concentration of power in the hands of a few individuals means that the state lacks the ability to develop policies that best address the needs of Russian society overall. The suppression of a free media and a viable opposition makes it hard for new ideas to emerge, which, in turn, stymies necessary structural changes. Rather than stressing the inclusion of the broadest possible participation in the Russian system, Putin's government represses all viable opposition to the incumbent authorities. Although it has raised energy prices somewhat during the 2000s, the government has also used its extensive energy resources to provide subsidies to residents and business to insure its continuing popularity and the quiescence of the population. While Russian energy consumers now face higher prices than they paid in the past, the increases have not kept pace with the rapidly rising world prices. The result is a powerful political elite that can protect its position for the short to medium term, but most likely will lose this ability over the long term. While there was no sign of political change in Russia at the end of Putin's second term, the long-term prospects for a system built on the forceful suppression of the opposition are not good.

Russian leaders can only buy stability through costly measures that are not sustainable. The key elites now have extensive control over the country's resources. In order to facilitate his hold on power, Putin and his allies need to use the rents that they obtain from energy sales to ensure that all other political actors in the system remain loyal to them. Effectively, Putin has to use Russia's public resources to pay off other groups to prevent them from grabbing political power for themselves. The leadership also must buy the political acquiescence of the population through measures such as providing energy subsidies for residents who rely on extensive supplies of natural gas to heat homes in Russia's cold climate. While it will be difficult for the population to make the transition to market prices, and any move in this direction must be managed responsibly to prevent undue economic dislocation, ultimately such a step will be necessary. Making such progress will be extremely difficult. Under the current system, Russia's leaders are dependent on high oil prices. In the absence of these resources, they would have to rely on extensive repression, greatly strengthening the measures already in place.

Without the feedback of a free media, an articulate political opposition, and social oversight by informed citizens, the policies of the political elite will eventually start to diverge from those required by the population for the most stable forms of political and economic development. While clever leaders can manipulate the system enough so that they may be able to stay in power for decades, ultimately their policies do not promote the broader institutional strength of the state, namely one that has the administrative capacity to respond to social needs, and secure the overall well-being of society.

With its tendencies to concentrate power and gain control of productive assets, the incumbent regime has little interest in implementing key reforms to increase the efficiency and effectiveness of Russia's energy companies and the larger business community. In this sense, Russia's strength in the energy sector is likely to stunt the long-term development of the country, both in the energy sector itself and in other parts of the economy. In particular, Putin and his colleagues have talked extensively about trying to diversify the Russian economy away from its heavy reliance on natural resource exports, but they have yet to make much progress in this direction. In fact, the continuing concentration of power in the hands of a small elite makes it less and less likely that Russia will be able to diversify effectively. Given the on-going crackdown on civil society, there is likewise little chance that energy revenues will be directed toward a democratic evolution of the political system. As long as Russia's energy revenue remains strong, such political change is highly unlikely and the authoritarian regime will only further entrench itself. Only a drop in energy prices might force the Russian leadership to create the political space that would make it possible to search for more innovative ways to diversify the economy.

Notes

1 Peter Reddaway and Dmitri Glinski, *The Tragedy of Russia's Reforms: Market Bolshevism Against Democracy* (Washington, DC: United States Institute of Peace Press, 2001), 2.
2 Thomas Carothers, "The End of the Transition Paradigm," *Journal of Democracy* 13, no. 1 (2002): 5–21.
3 Samuel Huntington, *Political Order in Changing Societies* (New Haven: Yale University Press, 1968).
4 See the discussion in Thane Gustafson, *Capitalism Russian-Style* (New York: Cambridge University Press, 1999), 29f.
5 Eugene Huskey, *Presidential Power in Russia* (Armonk: M.E. Sharpe, 1999), 29.
6 See, for example, the account of Berezovsky's acquisition of Sibneft and the loans-for-shares auctions in Pavel Klebnikov, *Godfather of the Kremlin: Boris Berezovsky and the Looting of Russia* (New York: Harcourt, 2000), 188–211. For a more positive view of the privatization process written at the time, see Joseph R. Blasi, Maya Kroumova, and Douglas Kruse, *Kremlin Capitalism: Privatizing the Russian Economy* (Ithaca: Cornell University Press, 1997).
7 Anders Aslund, "Putin's Economic Legacy," *Russian Analytical Digest*, no. 36 (March 2008): 5–8, www.res.ethz.ch/analysis/rad/ (accessed 27 August 2008).
8 See Peter Reddaway and Robert Orttung, eds., *The Dynamics of Russian Politics: Putin's Reform of Federal-Regional Relations*, 2 vols. (Lanham: Rowman & Littlefield, 2003 and 2005).
9 For a clear overall description, cf. Andrew Jack, *Inside Putin's Russia: Can There Be Reform Without Democracy?* (New York: Oxford University Press, 2004).
10 Konstantin Simonov, *Russkaia neft': poslednii peredel* (Moscow: Algoritm, 2005), 5.
11 For a useful summary of energy policy under Putin, see Miriam Elder, "How the State Got a Grip on Energy," *Moscow Times*, 14 March 2008.
12 Michael L. Ross, "Does Oil Hinder Democracy?," *World Politics* 53, no. 3 (2001): 325–61, at 356. See also Kevin K. Tsui, "More Oil, Less Democracy? Theory and Evidence from Crude Oil Discoveries," paper, 11 November 2005, http://home.uchicago.edu/~ktsui/OilDemocracy.pdf (accessed 27 August 2008).
13 See also the discussion in section two of Harley Balzer, "Knowledge Economy or Nigeria? Russia's Hydrocarbons in Comparative Perspective," paper prepared for the Annual Meeting of the American Association for the Advancement of Slavic Studies, New Orleans, LA, 15–18 November 2007.
14 William Tompson, "A Frozen Venezuela? The 'Resource Curse' and Russian Politics," in *Russia's Oil: Bonanza or Curse?*, ed. Michael Ellman (London: Anthem, 2006), 194ff.
15 Along these lines, see Boris Nemtsov and Vladimir Milov, *Putin. Itogi* (Moscow: Novaia gazeta, 2008), 5, www.nemtsov.ru/docs/putin-itogi.pdf (accessed 31 August 2008) and Tompson, "A Frozen Venezuela?."
16 See particularly the discussion in Ross, "Does Oil Hinder Democracy?." See also: Larry Diamond, *The Spirit of Democracy: The Struggle to Build Free Societies throughout the World* (New York: Times Books, 2008), 74–9; Terry Lynn Karl, *The Paradox of Plenty: Oil Booms and Petro-States* (Berkeley: University of California Press, 1997); Nathan Jensen and Leonard Wantchekon, "Resource Wealth and Political Regimes in Africa," *Comparative Political Studies* 37, no. 7 (2004): 816–41; Benjamin Smith, "Oil Wealth and Regime Survival in the Developing World, 1960–1999," *American Journal of Political Science* 48, no. 2 (2004): 232–46; Erika Weinthal and Pauline Jones Luong, "Combating the Resource Curse: An Alternative Solution to Managing Mineral Wealth," *Perspectives on Politics* 4, no. 1 (2006), 35–53.
17 Kryshtanovskaya as cited by "Russia Under Putin: The Making of a Neo-KGB State," *The Economist*, 24–31 August 2007.

18 Francesca Mereu, "Putin Made Good on Promise to FSB," *Moscow Times*, 8 February 2008.
19 Syuzanna Farizova, "Gosduma naznachala FSB otvetstvennoi za terrorizm," *Kommersant*, 26 February 2006.
20 See Daniel Treisman, "Putin's Silovarchs," *Orbis* 51, no. 1 (2007): 141–53.
21 Viktor Yasmann, "Siloviki Take the Reins in Post-Oligarchy Russia," *Radio Free Europe/Radio Liberty*, 18 September 2007.
22 Masha Lipman, "Russia's Apolitical Middle," *Washington Post*, 4 June 2007, A15.
23 See the Office of the Chief Economist presentation of the European Bank for Reconstruction and Development (EBRD) Transition Report 2007, slide 18, www.ebrd.com/pubs/econo/tr07p.pdf (accessed 27 August 2008).
24 Larry Diamond, *The Spirit of Democracy: The Struggle to Build Free Societies throughout the World* (New York: Times Books, 2008), 75.
25 Sergey Guriev and Georgy Egorov, "The Resource Curse and Media Freedom," *Beyond Transition* 17, no. 2 (2006), 8.
26 Human Rights Watch, *Choking on Bureaucracy: State Curbs on Independent Civil Society Activism* (New York: HRW, February 2008), http://hrw.org/reports/2008/russia0208/ (accessed 27 August 2008).
27 Yevgenia Zubchenko, "The Adventures of Foreigners in Russia," *Novye Izvestia*, 17 October 2006.
28 Philip Hanson and Elizabeth Teague, "Big Business and the State in Russia," *Europe–Asia Studies* 57, no. 5 (2005): 657–80.
29 Henry Hale, *Why Not Parties in Russia: Democracy, Federalism, and the State* (New York: Cambridge University Press, 2006).
30 www.eitransparency.org (accessed 27 August 2008).
31 Andrei Makarychev and Olga Paleeva, eds., *Neftianoi sector rossiiskoi ekonomiki: diagnostika problemnykh zon i tekhnologiia sotsial'nogo deistviia* (Nizhnii Novgorod: Rus-Expert Transit, TraCCC, OSI, 2006), 57f.
32 Clifford J. Levy, "An Investment Gets Trapped in Kremlin's Vice," *New York Times*, 24 July 2008.
33 Alexander Dyck, Natalia Volchkova and Luigi Zingales, "The Media's Effect on Corporate Governance in Russia," *Beyond Transition* 17, no. 2 (2006): 19f.
34 Tompson, "A Frozen Venezuela?," 199.
35 Natalya Grib, "Plus Gasification of Entire Europe," *Kommersant*, 26 June 2007.
36 See Daniel Simmons and Isabel Murray, "Russian Gas: Will There Be Enough Investment?," *Russian Analytical Digest*, no. 27 (September 2007): 2–5, at 2, www.res.ethz.ch/analysis/rad/ (accessed 31 August 2008).
37 Vladimir Milov, "Anatomy of an Error," *Kommersant*, 6 September 2006. The authors cite a figure of 85 percent in Vladimir Milov, Leonard L. Coburn, and Igor Danchenko, "Russian Energy Policy, 1992–2005," *Eurasian Geography and Economics* 47, no. 3 (2006), 286. Matthew J. Sagers accepts this figure, but suggests looking at primary energy consumption, where the figure for subsidies is closer to 50 percent, see "Russia's Energy Policy: A Divergent View," *Eurasian Geography and Economics* 47, no. 3 (2006), 316.
38 See Susanne Wengle, "Power Politics: Electricity Sector Reform in Post-Soviet Russia," *Russian Analytical Digest*, no. 27 (September 2007): 6–9, www.res.ethz.ch/analysis/rad/ (accessed 31 August 2008).
39 For a very cautious analysis along these lines, see Yegor Gaidar, *Collapse of an Empire: Lessons for Modern Russia* (Washington, DC: Brookings Institution Press, 2007), 253.
40 See Diamond, *The Spirit of Democracy*, 77.
41 See also: Anders Aslund, *Russia's Capitalist Revolution: Why Market Reform Succeeded and Democracy Failed* (Washington, DC: Peterson Institute for International Economics, October 2007), 251f.

42 Rajan Menon and Alexander J. Motyl, "The Myth of Russian Resurgence," *The American Interest* II, no. 4 (2007): 96–101.
43 These figures and comparison are taken from Leon Aron, *Russia's Oil: Natural Abundance and Political Shortages* (Washington, DC: American Enterprise Institute for Public Policy Research, Spring 2006). See also Anders Aslund, "Russian Resources: Curse or Rents?" *Eurasian Geography and Economics*, 46, no. 8 (2005): 613f. David Woodruff argues that the earlier growth resulted "was largely a one-off, short-term opportunity to use new technology to improve yields from mature fields discovered in the Soviet era," so the production drops cannot all be attributed to the new state ownership. See David M. Woodruff, "The Expansion of State Ownership in Russia: Cause for Concern?," *Development and Transition*, no. 7 (July 2007): 11ff.
44 Rudiger Ahrend and William Tompson, "Unnatural Monopoly: The Endless Wait for Gas Sector Reform in Russia," *Europe–Asia Studies* 57, no. 6 (2005): 801–21.
45 See Dmitry Furman's expression of this hypothesis in: Dmitry Furman, "Medvedev's Dilemma, or the Price of 'Stability'," *Russia Beyond the Headlines*, 27 February 2008, www.rbth.rg.ru/articles/price_of_stability.html (accessed 31 August 2008).
46 Pavel K. Baev, "Russian Super-Giant in its Lair: Gazprom's Role in Domestic Affairs," in *Europe's Energy Security: Gazprom's Dominance and Caspian Supply Alternatives*, ed. Svante Cornell and Niklas Nordling (Washington, DC: Institute for Security and Development Policy, 2007), 61f., www.isdp.eu/files/publications/books/0802energysecurity-4-Baev.pdf (accessed 31 August 2008).
47 Fred Weir, "Kremlin Extends Grip on Oil," *Christian Science Monitor*, 10 September 2007, www.csmonitor.com/2007/0910/p01s04-woeu.html (accessed 31 August 2008).
48 Leslie Dienes, "Observations on the Problematic Potential of Russian Oil and the Complexities of Siberia," *Eurasian Geography and Economics* 45, no. 5 (2004): 319–45, at 330.
49 Hanson and Teague, "Big Business and the State in Russia," 657.
50 See Robert Orttung, "The Role of Business in Russian Foreign and Security Relations," in *Russian Business Power: The Role of Business in Russian Foreign and Security Relations*, ed. Andreas Wenger, Jeronim Perovic, and Robert W. Orttung (London: Routledge, 2006), 28f.
51 www.transparency.org/news_room/latest_news/press_releases/2007/2007_09_26_cpi_2007_en (accessed 31 August 2008).
52 Clifford G. Gaddy and Barry W. Ickes, "Resource Rents and the Russian Economy," *Eurasian Geography and Economics* 46, no. 8 (2005): 559–83.
53 The Brookings Institution, *The Russian Federation*, The Brookings Foreign Policy Studies Energy Security Series (Washington, DC: The Brookings Institution, October 2006), 8.
54 M. Steven Fish argues that the natural resource endowment, economic policy, and the power of the legislature are the key determinants shaping how open the political system is. "Too much oil, too little economic liberalization, and too weak a national legislature" explain the country's failure to democratize, according to his logic. See: M. Steven Fish, *Democracy Derailed in Russia: The Failure of Open Politics* (New York: Cambridge University Press, 2005), 247. According to Robert Klitgaard's famous formula, the level of corruption = monopoly + discretion − accountability. See Robert Klitgaard, *Controlling Corruption* (Berkeley: University of California Press, 1987).

4 Developing Russia's oil and gas industry
What role for the state?

Heiko Pleines

Should the energy sector be in private hands or run by state-owned companies? Most of the world's major energy-producing countries have decided that their energy sectors should be state-controlled. After the global wave of privatization during the 1980s and 1990s, there has been a marked trend toward re-nationalization of the oil and gas sectors. As a result, as of 2008, state-owned companies accounted for over 85 percent of worldwide production and over 95 percent of global reserves. Only four of the world's 20 largest oil and gas companies, measured by oil equivalent reserves, are in private hands. And the world's largest private oil company, Russia's Lukoil, ranks only fifteenth, closely followed by ExxonMobil, BP, and Chevron.[1]

There are multiple reasons for the dominance of the state in the energy sector. As fossil fuel is vital to the functioning of modern economies, countries tend to consider oil and gas a matter of national security, and thus, often restrict foreign ownership in this sector. For the major energy-producing countries, oil and gas is a key source of income for the state budget.[2] Accordingly, the governments in these countries tend to favor national companies in order to secure these vital financial flows. The dominance of state-owned companies can be further explained by the fact that the market is extremely capital-intensive and only very few companies are able to compete in it successfully – naturally, a powerful national company with state support is in a good position to compete for large projects. Through bilateral agreements or multilateral organizations such as OPEC, national oil companies also effectively coordinate their activities at the international level and are thus in a good position to compete with international private oil companies.

Similar considerations have prompted Russia, which privatized much of its oil industry during the 1990s, to gradually increase the role of the state in the energy sector (the gas sector was never privatized to the same extent). In fact, the share of state-owned companies in oil production increased from a mere 13 percent in 2004 to about 40 percent in 2007. The Russian government also adopted a more active role in developing the industry.

Yet the crucial question is whether state-owned companies are more effective managers of the energy sectors than private companies. Empirical evidence does not completely support the neo-liberal view that private companies are more effective than state-owned companies, as the case of Norway's state-owned oil company demonstrates. Joseph Stiglitz writes: "By most accounts, Norway's state oil company was both efficient and incorruptible. [...] Norway's story is important because it destroys the shibboleth that efficiency and welfare maximization can be obtained only through privatization."[3]

Russia is another case in point. Contrary to the expectations of neo-liberal theory, Russia's private companies performed very poorly during the 1990s. In fact, some privatized companies, including the major oil company Sidanko, were brought to bankruptcy through systematic asset-stripping by their new owners.[4] However, the key to understanding the Russian developments of the 1990s is that the market environment was unstable and property rights insecure. As oil companies were privatized in manipulated auctions, owners were not sure whether they would be able to hold on to the assets that they had acquired and were therefore unwilling to develop long-term investment plans.[5]

State ownership as such seems not to be the key determinant explaining the performance of a company. What is more important is the market environment in which a company is operating. If there is a functioning market with clear rules and secure property rights, companies are likely to operate efficiently. If not, they tend to engage in asset-stripping rather than long-term development. The role of the state is thus crucial: the state can work to improve the efficiency of private and state-owned companies by subjecting them to market pressures through the establishment of clear rules of the game and secure property rights, or it can become a factor of instability itself.

State regulation of the oil and gas industry poses very specific challenges, with the main issues being the treatment of foreign investors, the role of state ownership, and the regulation of related markets. This chapter will examine how the Russian state under President Vladimir Putin has dealt with these challenges. It argues that the market environment created by Putin's state does not encourage effective management and good governance in Russia's energy sector. The chapter starts by looking at how foreign investors have been treated in Russia. The second section analyzes the privatization/re-nationalization trends from the early 1990s through Putin's second term as president, with a focus on the Yukos affair. Sections three to five consider the role of the state in a regulated market environment, including the state's activities in the downstream sector and the reform of gas prices. The final section draws some conclusions assessing the effectiveness of Russia's energy sector.

Restricting foreign investment

As the oil and gas industry is one of Russia's most important and most profitable businesses, it has attracted considerable foreign investment. As a result, Russia's oil and gas production accounts for about a third of total foreign investment in the country. In addition, oil refining contributes another 7 percent.[6] The biggest foreign direct investors in the oil and gas industry so far are the participants in the major Sakhalin production sharing agreement (PSA) projects (Sakhalin-1 and Sakhalin-2), concluded in 1996; BP, which merged its Russian activities

Developing Russia's oil and gas industry 73

with the Tyumen Oil Company in 2003; and Germany's BASF, which entered gas production in Russia through joint ventures with Gazprom. Additionally, ConocoPhillips (USA) and E.ON Ruhrgas (Germany) bought into the Russian oil and gas industry through portfolio investments. ConocoPhillips now holds 20 percent of Lukoil, and E.ON Ruhrgas owns a stake of 6 percent in Gazprom.[7]

However, fears of a sell-out to foreigners have always been a part of Russian political debates and often strike a chord with Russian voters. The population strongly opposes any foreign involvement in strategic sectors of the economy and in the energy sector, in particular. Experts from the state sector, such as high-ranking bureaucrats from the relevant ministries and members of the respective parliamentary commissions, are more open to foreign investment in general, but half of them speak out against foreign investment in the oil and gas industry (see Figure 4.1).

Ambivalence characterizes the attitude of the Russian state toward foreign direct investment in the Russian oil and gas industry. Policymakers must balance a need for investment to modernize one of the most important sectors of Russian industry against the fear of surrendering control over this important sector to foreign interests. Prevailing political and economic conditions influence which policy dominates at any given time. In the early 1990s, when enthusiasm for market reforms was growing, lawmakers laid the legal foundations for joint ventures. When public sentiment against capitalism and any sign of kowtowing to

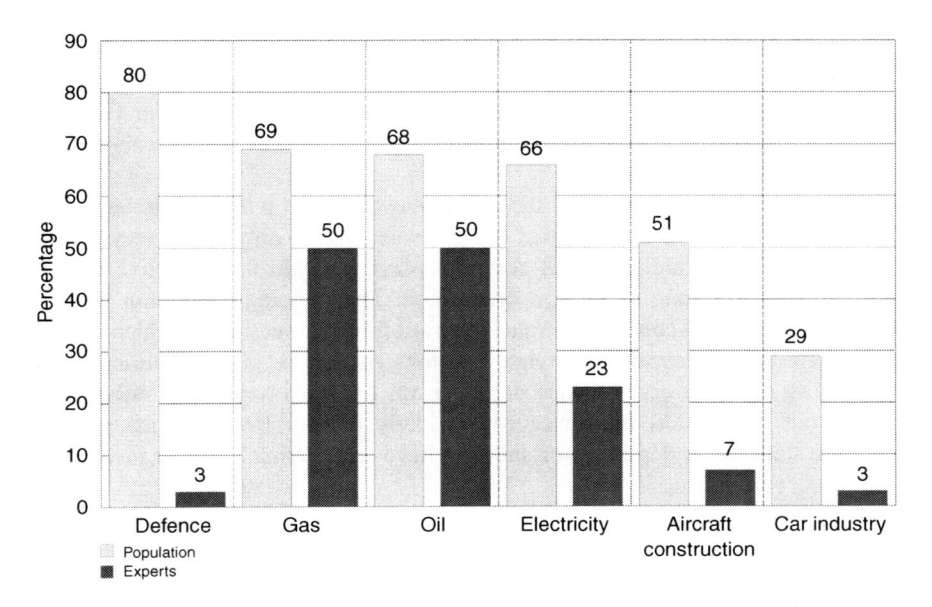

Figure 4.1 There should be no foreign investment in this sector of the economy! (Representative poll of the Russian population and expert poll of state actors, 2005 and 2006).

foreign investors was rising, regulators tightened restrictions for foreign investment. When the financial crisis of 1998 made foreigners the only possible source of cash, the parliament quickly enacted a more attractive PSA law. A few years later, increased earnings, resulting from the rise in world market oil prices, cooled interest in foreign direct investment.[8]

As a result, during Putin's second term as president and during the initial stage of Dmitry Medvedev's time in the Kremlin, foreign investors in the Russian oil and gas industry faced increasing pressure from the state. The Sakhalin-2 project, with projected investments of $10 billion, became the most prominent case. The project, operated by Shell together with Japanese companies, was the only major foreign investment in the oil and gas industry without a Russian partner. When Shell and its partners started to realize the project's potential in 2006, the Russian state forced the foreign companies to include Gazprom, threatening otherwise to shut down activities because of environmental concerns. As a result, the foreign partners were forced to sell part of their share to the state company.[9]

In reaction to concerns about legal security for foreign investments, President Putin in autumn 2005 promised clear regulation. However, it took the government until spring 2007 to prepare a draft law on foreign investment in strategic branches of the Russian economy. The bill was then passed by the lower chamber of parliament in a first reading in September 2007 and in a second and third reading in spring 2008, and was signed by President Putin on 30 April, just before his term ended.[10]

According to the law, any foreign purchase of a controlling stake in a state-owned or private company in strategic sectors or a purchase of more than 10 percent in larger oil and gas deposits[11] are subject to approval by a government commission, made up of representatives of economy-related ministries and security structures including the Federal Security Service (FSB).[12] Vladimir Putin, in his post-presidential role as prime minister, became head of the commission set up in July 2008.

The most important aspect of the law, however, is that it took the government so long to produce it. The fact that the law was enacted only at the very end of Putin's presidency indicates that powerful players within the executive branch are debating the issue of foreign investment. The ongoing discussion implies that the state has no consistent strategy toward foreign investment, which in turn leads to lasting insecurity for foreign investors. As the law gives a political body the ability to make case-by-case decisions on foreign investments rather than laying out clear rules, this insecurity is likely to last. However, attempts to increase state ownership in the oil industry have created much greater insecurity.

Increasing state ownership

Whereas the gas industry on Russian territory was transferred to a single state-controlled company, Gazprom, when the Soviet Union fell apart, the Russian oil industry had by the mid-1990s been reorganized into 13 major vertically-integrated companies. Of these 13, eight were privatized by 1998, while three remained under the control of the federal government and two under the control of regional governments. As a result, in 1999, the share of state-owned companies in gas and oil production stood at 92 percent and at less than 25 percent, respectively, as Figure 4.2 shows.

Following a first wave of consolidation, the number of major vertically-integrated oil companies dropped to eight by 2004. Of these, the federal state owned only Rosneft, while regional governments continued to control two oil companies. At this time, the combined share of state-owned companies in oil production fell to less than 15 percent. State-controlled Gazprom, on the other hand, still accounted for 87 percent of Russia's gas production, although it was facing increasing competition from newly founded independent gas producers.

Since the late 1990s, the Russian government had considered plans to create a national oil company around Rosneft in order to increase the role of the state in the oil industry. However, these plans did not materialize. The situation changed in the wake of the Yukos affair. When it became clear in 2004 that the Yukos oil company would be taken over by the state, a conflict emerged between Rosneft and Gazprom. The Rosneft management assumed that the liquidation of Yukos would lead to the long-delayed creation of a national oil company. The Gazprom management, however, developed ambitions to enter the oil business through a purchase of major Yukos assets. As both sides had good connections to key decision-makers in the government and as the liquidation of Yukos included a number of judicial pitfalls, limiting the scope for maneuver, the power struggle continued for nearly a year. In the end, Rosneft took over Yukos, while Gazprom acquired another private oil company, Sibneft, which was then renamed Gazprom Neft.

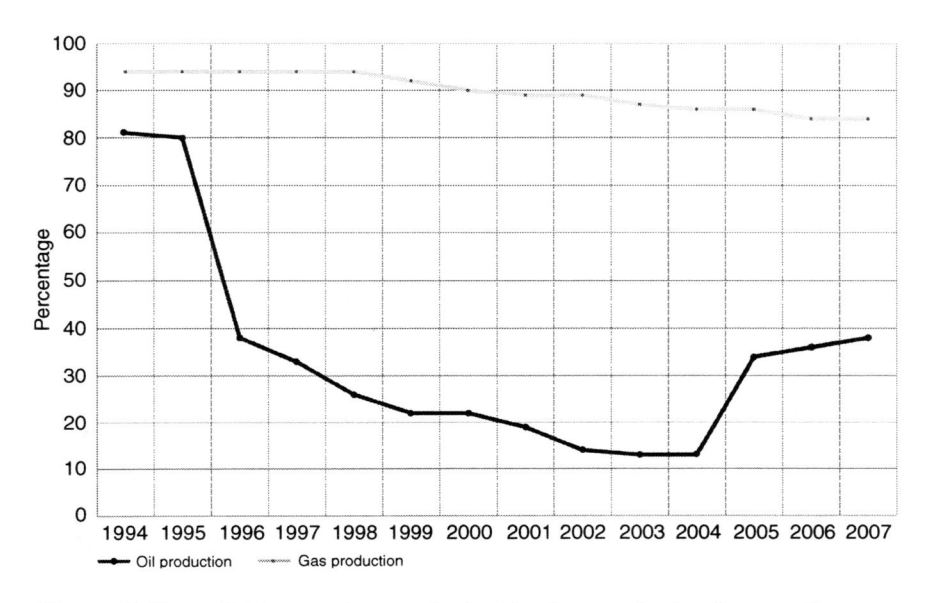

Figure 4.2 Share of state-owned companies in oil and gas production (in percent).

At the end of this second wave of consolidation, the share of state-owned companies in oil production had risen to nearly 40 percent. In mid-2008, the Russian oil and gas industry was dominated by five major companies (see Figure 4.3), of which Gazprom (with Gazprom Neft) and Rosneft are majority state-owned while Lukoil, Surgutneftegaz, and Tyumen Oil Company-British Petroleum (TNK-BP) remain private. In addition, there are a number of smaller private as well as state-owned companies active in the oil and gas industry.

An important feature in the process of increasing state ownership in the oil industry was the state's reliance on heavy pressure and legally dubious measures. The Yukos affair has become the prime example of this.[13] The oil company Yukos had been acquired by financial magnate Mikhail Khodorkovsky's Menatep group in two manipulated (though not illegal) privatization auctions in December 1995.[14] In the second half of the 1990s, the company became notorious for bad corporate governance, especially asset-stripping and further manipulations against the interest of minority owners. However, after the financial crisis of 1998, when Khodorkovsky took over company management, corporate governance as well as economic performance improved considerably, and Yukos was set to become Russia's biggest oil company.[15]

The Yukos affair started in June 2003 with the arrest of Yukos security chief Alexei Pichugin, on charges of ordering a contract killing. In the following month, a major owner of Yukos, Platon Lebedev, was arrested for alleged privatization fraud (not related to Yukos). In October 2003, the authorities incarcerated Khodorkovsky, accusing him of tax evasion. In the following months, the general procurator started investigations against all major owners of Yukos and most of the company's senior managers. Three owners escaped to Israel, and the

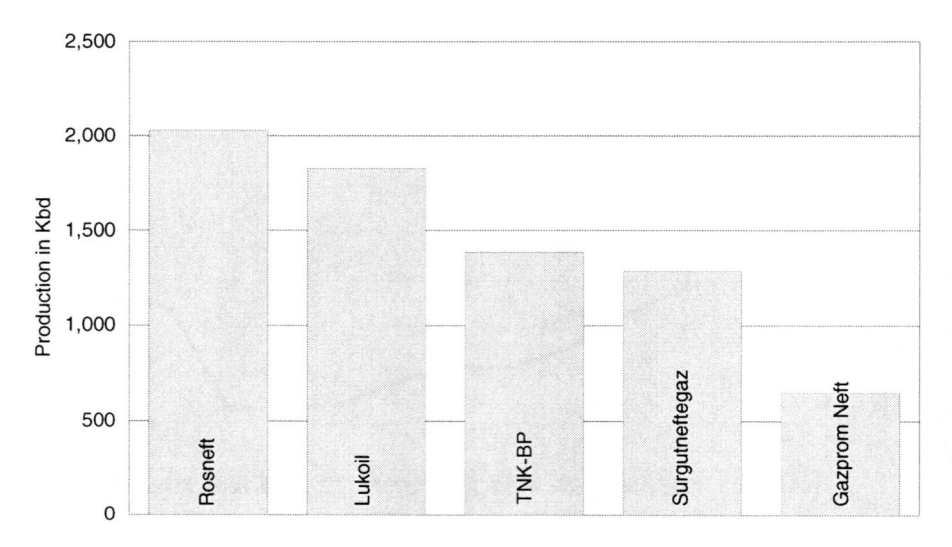

Figure 4.3 Russia's five biggest oil companies (2007 production in kbd).

company management moved to London in November 2004. Courts sentenced Lebedev and Khodorkovsky to long prison terms in May 2005.

The main instrument to gain control over Yukos was back tax claims. By the end of 2004, tax claims against Yukos, made in the wake of investigations into alleged tax evasion, added up to $28 billion. For two years, tax claims were higher than company turnover. As a result, the company's tax debts could only be settled through sales of company assets. The company was finally liquidated in summer 2007 as a result of bankruptcy proceedings. The state's strategy to gain control over Yukos consisted of three main elements:

First, the selective enforcement of rules, which has been conceptualized as suspended punishment by Alena Ledeneva,[16] is a clear feature of the Yukos affair. The tax authorities had previously approved the relevant tax reports by Yukos, with then prime minister Mikhail Kasyanov describing the tax evasion by Yukos as unethical, but legal. The State Audit Chamber named Sibneft as the biggest sinner, but Yukos became the only company to be confronted with big back claims and trials. Other companies that exploited the same loopholes as Yukos did were not charged or got away with minor fines. In addition, charges and tax claims made against Yukos subsidiaries were often dropped as soon as the subsidiary had been taken over by a state company.

Second, state actors repeatedly violated the rules of due process in the lawsuits against Lebedev/Khodorkovsky as well as in the tax and bankruptcy proceedings concerning Yukos. For example, instead of non-core assets, the company's major production subsidiary, Yuganskneftegaz, was confiscated first in order to settle tax debts. A sham firm then won the auction for this facility and sold the asset to state-owned Rosneft within a month.

Third, state agencies exerted heavy pressure on persons close to Yukos. They collectively charged Yukos management with forming an organized crime group and threatened to withdraw the licenses of company lawyers. A foreign lawyer saw his visa annulled during an unannounced night visit by the state authorities to his hotel room. The bank accounts of organizations funded by Yukos were frozen on charges of money-laundering.

Though the state applied its greatest pressure in the Yukos affair, it used similar measures on other occasions as well. In the case of the Kovykta gas deposit license, for example, the State Subsoil Agency in 2007 threatened RUSIA Petroleum, the private license holder that was majority owned by TNK-BP, with the immediate loss of the license due to the non-fulfillment of a clause on production volumes. As soon as TNK-BP had sold RUSIA to state-owned Gazprom, the clause was removed from the license agreement. However, Gazprom paid a fair price of close to $1 billion for the deal.[17]

In sum, the Russian state has used various methods to take over private companies and increase state ownership in the oil industry. While negotiated takeovers prevail across the economy as a whole, state enforced takeovers have received much greater publicity, particularly because of their application in the energy industry. In most cases, the state does not directly acquire ownership, but rather acts through state-owned companies, such as Gazprom or Rosneft. In a negotiated takeover, state companies buy additional stakes at market prices, as happened in the case of the Sibneft takeover by Gazprom. Enforced takeovers are based on manipulated or selective allegations of legal wrongdoing (especially concerning taxes as well as safety and environmental regulations), typically followed by pressure in the form of bad publicity, office searches and the confiscation of company documents, frozen bank accounts, threats of license withdrawals, hefty fines, and the arrest of senior managers.

Since the state decided to play a larger role in the oil industry, state-owned companies tripled their share in oil production within a year. Yet another major outcome of increased state involvement is the heightened insecurity that private oil companies face regarding their property rights. When state agencies make claims against oil companies, the media as well as investors do not weigh the merits of the claim as such, but start speculating about the political interests behind the claim. When the state makes large claims against a company, rumors begin to circulate that the respective company may be the next to face an unfriendly takeover by a state company. The result is that efforts to increase state ownership in the oil industry have also strongly increased the insecurity of property rights and considerably weakened the rule of law. At the same time, they leave the state to address the corporate governance challenges of the companies it controls.

Managing state-owned enterprises

Gazprom offers a prime example of the challenges the state faces in managing huge enterprises. As successor to the Soviet gas ministry, Gazprom holds a monopoly in gas production, transport, and export and is the world's largest producer and exporter of natural gas. As a result of the privatization process, the state reduced its stake in Gazprom to around 40 percent in the mid-1990s. However, as most of the other shares were held by small investors and company employees, the state's share was big enough to dominate the company board.

Nevertheless, in the 1990s, the Gazprom management under Rem Vyakhirev was able to act independently of the state, as it held the state's stake in trust. The management used the lack of outside oversight to engage in large-scale asset-stripping. Profitable subsidiaries were transferred to the children of top managers or to politicians close to the company.[18] An account of the major cases of asset-stripping from 1997 to 2001 estimates the foregone value for Gazprom at more than $5 billion.[19] Under President Putin, the Russian government started to regain control over Gazprom. In 2001, Vyakhirev was sacked; under his successor, Alexei Miller, the company recovered many of the stripped assets through court proceedings and informal pressure from the state. However, in a report published in 2004, Hermitage Capital Management claimed that Gazprom had lost more than $2 billion in the preceding year due to misuse of funds by company managers. The key problems were overpayment for services rendered and non-transparent financial flows to the intermediary company responsible for gas exports to Ukraine.[20] Obscure intermediaries, partly controlled by Gazprom management, remained responsible for gas exports to Ukraine through 2008.[21]

Whereas financial losses related to asset-stripping have been reduced drastically under the new Gazprom management, the giant gas company still operates inefficiently. Compared to independent gas producers, which face numerous restrictions imposed by Gazprom's monopoly position in gas transport and by state bureaucrats close to Gazprom, Gazprom is clearly underperforming and, as a result, accounts for a continuously declining share in Russian gas production.[22] An analysis of Gazprom's expenditures in 2004, conducted by Vadim Kleiner, shows that the company overpaid for many projects. Construction of 1 km of the Russian part of the Blue Stream pipeline, for example, was twice as expensive as the Turkish part. Costs are seen as very high in comparison with other Russian companies as well as in comparison with the international gas business, mainly due to excessive profits for intermediaries and inefficient organization. Kleiner also criticizes Gazprom for heavily investing outside its core business, whereas investment in exploration and development of new fields is relatively low.[23]

Similar inefficiencies can be observed in Russia's state-owned oil companies. As an empirical analysis of the corporate governance performance of Russian oil companies shows, since the financial crisis of 1998, private companies have been much more likely to react to increased market pressures with improvements in performance.[24]

Promoting domestic downstream activities

The Russian state is not only focused on increasing ownership, but also on expanding economic development in the energy sector. In order to add value to the country's oil and gas production, the government wants to encourage domestic downstream business. The top priority is the oil industry, where profit margins for high-quality refined products (mainly fuels) and petrochemical products (plastics, fibers, and synthetic rubbers) are much higher than for crude oil. For the gas industry, on the other hand, the main way to add value is to get closer to foreign end consumers, i.e. to invest in retail distribution businesses abroad.

Russian domestic demand for refined petroleum products is rising rapidly due to increased consumer spending, especially on cars. Since 1998, retail gasoline prices have risen much more rapidly than average consumer price inflation, thus increasing the profits derived from such sales. The industry's limited capacity for the production of high-octane gasoline for cars has led to a pricing premium in the domestic market for gasoline. At the same time, refining margins have been rising worldwide, driven by a global move toward cleaner fuels. As utilization rates have risen, the long-distance trade in refined products has become an important aspect of the business, increasing the international demand for Russian exports of oil products.

In order to promote downstream activities in the domestic oil industry, the Russian government has adjusted taxes and export tariffs to favor domestic oil refining. Since export tariffs were changed in 2005 to make exports of refined products more attractive than crude exports, exports of oil products have soared, rising above 100 mmt in 2006 and generating revenues of $44 billion. In addition, tax levels are no longer rising in line with refining depths. Accordingly, profit margins for high-quality products have increased, thus encouraging investment in new production technology.

While demand is rising, Russia's refining capacity has been in decline since the end of the Soviet Union. As a result, the average capacity utilization at Russian refineries has risen from about 65 percent in 2000 to about 80 percent in 2005, not too far below the average worldwide rate of 86 percent.[25] In reaction to these developments, Russian oil companies have announced ambitious investment plans for their refineries. The total planned costs of these projects add up to more than $20 billion. Although it can be expected that not all of the projects will be realized, Russia's refining industry faces a period of rapid modernization.[26]

The Russian government also wants to develop the petrochemical industry in its move to add value to oil production. In 2006, the Ministry for Industry and Energy completed a development strategy for the chemical and petrochemical industry of Russia until 2015. For this period, the base case of the strategy expects investments of about $50 billion in the chemical industry, which have to be fully financed by private investors.[27] As the Russian government does not consider the branch to be of strategic relevance and as the branch needs foreign money and know-how to reach international standards, foreign direct investment is explicitly mentioned as a major source of modernization. The government also expects the major national oil and gas companies that have entered the petrochemical industry to invest heavily in the modernization of the branch. As the largest Russian petrochemical company, SIBUR, is controlled by Gazprom, the state is in a position to promote investments directly. SIBUR plans to invest about $3 billion in the modernization and expansion of petrochemical production by 2010.[28] While the plans seem to be overambitious and some Russian oil companies are likely paying lip service to state demands for increased investments, foreign investment in the petrochemical industry has been rising sharply since 2006, and domestic production is set to replace an increasing part of Russia's petrochemical imports.

In summary, the combination of a supportive world market and an incentive-based development strategy by the state have promoted considerable investment into Russian downstream activities and revitalized a branch of industry that was close to collapse in the 1990s. It is interesting to note that the Russian state has not created similar incentives in the oil industry itself, where, for example, preferential tax treatment for enhanced oil recovery could improve productivity by up to 60 percent, according to a McKinsey study.[29]

Liberalizing product markets

In 2005, about 50 percent of primary energy consumption and about 85 percent of final energy use in Russia were still sold at government-regulated rather than market-based prices.[30] However, while the state is increasing control over production, it continues to liberalize product markets.

Russia liberalized domestic prices for oil and oil products in 1992, and legislation blocks any attempt to reassert price regulation. Therefore, the state has

Developing Russia's oil and gas industry 81

only indirect influence on prices, which it exercises mainly through taxes. However, as the number of oil companies is small, oil product markets are nearly by definition oligopolistic. In addition, the privatization of the oil industry in the first half of the 1990s was based on regionally-concentrated, vertically-integrated oil companies. As a result, there are wholesale monopolists in many regions, which in turn determine retail prices, although independent retail traders have emerged in most regions. According to an estimate by the Russian Anti-Monopoly Commission, in about two-thirds of Russian regions, the market for oil products is either monopolistic or oligopolistic.[31]

Nevertheless, an analysis by Cambridge Energy Research Associates comes to the conclusion that "domestic wholesale prices for refined products are not excessive" and that "there is no evidence of monopoly rents in retail prices even in highly monopolized regions."[32] This finding suggests that limited competition in oil product markets does not lead to excessive price distortions, at least not when compared to the (also oligopolistic) world market. In summary, the Russian oil product market is largely free from direct state intervention and is on average as efficient (or inefficient) as the world market.

Whereas prices for oil and oil products have been liberalized, the price for gas supplied by Gazprom is regulated by the state, acting through the Federal Tariff Service. In mid-2008, prices were differentiated on the basis of 13 pricing zones, defined by their distance from the wellhead. Moreover, prices for private households are on average about 25 percent lower than those for industrial consumers. Whereas industrial customers pay for gas actually consumed, the gas consumption of more than 80 percent of households is not metered, and their gas bill is, therefore, based on living space or registered persons.

In line with rising export prices, average domestic gas prices have increased considerably. From 2000 to 2006, they rose nearly threefold. However, prices for domestic industrial customers are still far below export prices and also far below prices paid at free domestic auctions organized since the end of 2006 as a test for full market liberalization. Independent gas producers are not subject to price regulation. However, their access to consumers is restricted by Gazprom's monopoly on transport pipelines. As a result, the biggest independent gas producer, Novatek, had to sell its gas at a discount rate of between 10 and 20 percent in recent years. In addition, independent gas producers have been excluded from gas exports since 2006. This means that, in contrast to the oil products market, the domestic gas market displays clear distortions in prices due to restricted competition and state regulation.[33]

Gazprom has for years been lobbying for an end to the state regulation of gas prices, since doing so would lead to an immense increase in company earnings. As a result, the Russian government has decided to liberalize the gas market for industrial customers by 2011 on the basis of full netback parity between domestic and international markets, while gas deliveries to private households will remain subject to price regulation by the state. However, the major question is whether this liberalization will grant independent gas producers unrestricted access to consumers and thus increase competition. If this is not the case, the liberalization will simply cause higher domestic gas prices, but will not change the market structure. Accordingly, the real test for a competitive gas market is not the liberalization of prices, but equal treatment for independent gas producers, including foremost fair pipeline access to domestic and foreign customers.

Conclusion

From the very beginning of his presidency, Vladimir Putin made clear that it was his main aim to re-establish Russia as a world power and that he saw economic strength as the main attribute of a modern world power. Accordingly, ambitious targets for Russia's macroeconomic growth were central to his political agenda. During his presidency, the strategies employed to promote economic growth became increasingly statist.[34]

As Medvedev took over the presidency, Russia's state policy was to increase state control in strategic sectors of the economy mainly through ownership of big enterprises in these sectors, which are then united into a state holding company. In the gas industry, Gazprom has performed this function. In the oil industry, Rosneft and Gazprom compete for it. In machine building, a transformed Rosoboronexport is to become a dominant state holding. Additional state-owned strategic companies have been created in shipbuilding, aviation, nuclear power, and nanotechnology. Through these state holding companies, the state can then influence the development of the respective economic branch directly. State representatives to company boards are state employees either from the responsible ministry or, in the case of chairpersons, sometimes with a secret service background.[35]

It seems that the state wanted to increase its share in the oil industry considerably and rapidly, and, therefore, used heavy pressure to increase state ownership, whereas in other branches of the economy deemed strategically important, the state has primarily used negotiated buyouts to create "national champions."

However, even in the oil industry, the state's share in production still stands below 50 percent, and in the gas industry, where it is much higher, a downward trend is continuing. At the same time, shares of the state-owned Rosneft company have been issued through an IPO, and Gazprom is only 51 percent state-owned. This situation seems to indicate that, on the one hand, the state wants majority ownership in the major oil and gas companies, but, on the other hand, loyal (majority Russian-owned) companies can continue to operate without the state as a shareholder and foreign investors can be active as (friendly) minority owners.

In addition, contrary to restrictions in sectors deemed to be of strategic relevance, foreign investment is promoted in the rest of the economy. As Julian Cooper summarizes in his account of Russian competitiveness in global markets:

> In sectors viewed as not as sensitive from a national security point of view, foreign investment is being encouraged, but in these cases it appears that there is also a desire to foster a number of Russian national champions to work alongside the foreign-owned companies and joint ventures. The policy option of developing higher value-added processing activities in established

materials producing sectors will probably require substantial foreign direct investment.[36]

A prime example of this is the Russian petrochemical industry, where the state expects the Gazprom subsidiary SIBUR and foreign investors to support the modernization of production technologies together.

However, as the history of the new law on foreign investment in strategic enterprises clearly indicates, this differentiation between sectors of the economy is subject to controversial debates within the state executive. The definition of a branch as strategically relevant may change easily and, according to the new law, treatment of foreign investors in strategic enterprises will depend on the mood of a governmental commission.

In summary, foreign as well as domestic companies in the Russian oil and gas industry are facing high insecurity concerning their property rights and the legal regulation of their business activities. This insecurity is highlighted by selective law enforcement and consistent rumors of a further unfriendly expansion of state ownership in the sector. Such a situation promotes inefficiency in private as well as state-owned companies.

An efficiently functioning private industry requires secure property rights, competition, clear rules for the market players, and respected regulatory agencies. For state-owned enterprises to work efficiently, there must be competent management separated from politics and a functioning market environment based on competition. After the end of socialism, Russia in the 1990s had none of these, and there has so far been no consistent attempt at improvement. As a result, the political mood of the leadership will continue to determine the role of the Russian state in the oil and gas industry. The bottom line, though, is that if the state does not create the conditions for a competitive market environment, neither state-owned nor private companies will perform to the full extent of their potential.

Notes

1 Based on the list of biggest oil and gas companies (data for 2006) compiled by the *Oil and Gas Journal* of 17 September 2007 (special issue).
2 In most of the major oil-exporting countries, revenues from the oil and gas industry account for more than 50 percent of state budget revenues. Among the ten biggest exporters, only Russia (40 percent), Mexico (32 percent), and Norway (24 percent) have a lower share. International Monetary Fund (IMF), *Draft Guide on Revenue Transparency* (Washington, DC: IMF, 2004).
3 Joseph E. Stiglitz, "What is the Role of the State?," in *Escaping the Resource Curse*, ed. Macartan Humphreys, Jeffrey D. Sachs, and Joseph E. Stiglitz (New York: Columbia University Press, 2007), 23–52, at 30.
4 Valerii A. Kriukov, "Ownership Rights, Bargaining and Globalization in the Oil Sector," in *Explaining Post-Soviet Patchworks*, vol. 2, *Pathways from the Past to the Global*, ed. Klaus Segbers (Aldershot: Ashgate 2001), 170–92, at 182; and Valery Kryukov, "Adjustment to Change: The Case of the Oil and Gas Industry," in *Shaping the Economic Space in Russia*, ed. Stefanie Harter and Gerald Easter (Aldershot: Ashgate 2000), 102–26, at 120.

5 On the Russian auctions, see: Heiko Pleines, "Large-Scale Corruption and Rent-Seeking in the Russian Banking Sector," in *Economic Crime in Russia*, ed. Alena Ledeneva and Marina Kurkchiyan (The Hague: Kluwer, 2000), 191–207. On the resulting property rights problems, see: Stiglitz, "What is the Role of the State?," 34–8.
6 Figures are from the Russian Federal Service for Statistics as of the end of 2005, www.gks.ru.
7 For a list of major foreign investments in Russia's oil and gas industry, see *Russian Analytical Digest*, no. 27 (October 2007): 15, www.res.ethz.ch/analysis/rad (accessed 31 August 2008).
8 Andreas Heinrich, Julia Kusznir, and Heiko Pleines, "Foreign Investment and National Interests in the Russian Oil and Gas Industry," *Post-Communist Economies*, 14, no. 4 (2002): 495–507.
9 Michael Bradshaw, "Sakhalin-II in the Firing Line: State Control, Environmental Impacts and the Future of Foreign Investment in Russia's Oil and Gas Industry," *Russian Analytical Digest*, no. 8 (October 2006): 6–11, www.res.ethz.ch/analysis/rad (accessed 31 August 2008).
10 For a more detailed discussion, see: Peeter Vahtra, Kari Liuhto, and Harri Lorentz, "Privatisation or Re-Nationalisation in Russia? Strengthening Strategic Government Policies Within the Economy," *Journal of East European Management Studies* 12, no. 4 (2007): 273–96, esp. 287–93.
11 For state-owned foreign companies, the thresholds are 25 percent and 5 percent, respectively.
12 Law "On the Procedure of the Realization of Foreign Investment in Companies of Strategic Relevance for the Defense and National Security of the State," Moscow, 7 May 2008.
13 Fuller accounts of the Yukos affair are given by: Wojciech Kononczuk, *The "Yukos Affair," its Motives and Implications*, CES Studies, no. 25 (Warsaw: Centre for Eastern Studies, 2006), http://osw.waw.pl/files/PRACE_25.pdf (accessed 9 August 2008); William Tompson, "Putting Yukos in Perspective," *Post-Soviet Affairs* 21, no. 2 (2005): 159–81; Philip Hanson, "Observations on the Costs of the Yukos Affair to Russia," *Eurasian Geography and Economics* 46, no. 7 (2005): 481–94; Julia Kusznir, "Russland: Die Jukos-Affäre und ihre machtpolitischen Hintergründe," *Ost-West-Gegeninformationen* 18, no. 2 (2006): 8–11; Heiko Pleines and Hans-Henning Schröder, eds., "Die Jukos-Affäre, Russlands Energiewirtschaft und die Politik," *Working Papers of the Research Centre for East European Studies*, no. 64, 2nd edition (Bremen: Research Centre for East European Studies, 2005). An overview of shortcomings of legal proceedings in the Yukos affair is given in resolution 1418 (2004) of the Council of Europe. The fullest accounts of manipulations by state actors are provided in: Otto Luchterhandt, "Rechtsnihilismus in Aktion: Der Jukos-Chodorkovskij-Prozeß in Moskau," *Osteuropa* 55, no. 7 (2005): 7–37; Angelika Nußberger and Dmitrij Marenkov, "Quo vadis iustitia? Der Fall Chodorkovskij im Licht der Rechtsprechung zur Europäischen Menschenrechtskonvention," *Osteuropa* 55, no. 7 (2005): 38–51; Pleines and Schröder, *Die Jukos-Affäre, Russlands Energiewirtschaft und die Politik*.
14 Heiko Pleines, "Large-Scale Corruption and Rent-Seeking in the Russian Banking Sector," *Economic Crime in Russia*, ed. Alena Ledeneva and Marina Kurkchiyan (The Hague: Kluwer, 2000), 191–207. In 2007, a Russian court ruled that the Yukos auction had been legal.
15 Andreas Heinrich, Aleksandra Lis, and Heiko Pleines, *Corporate Governance in the Oil and Gas Industry. Cases from Poland, Hungary, Russia and Ukraine in a Comparative Perspective*, KICES Working Papers, no. 3 (Koszalin: Koszalin Institute of Comparative European Studies, 2005), 18–20. See also: Yuko Adachi, "The Ambiguous Effects of Russian Corporate Governance Abuses of the 1990s," *Post-Soviet Affairs* 22, no. 1 (2006): 65–89.

16 Alena Ledeneva, *How Russia Really Works* (Ithaca, NY: Cornell University Press, 2006), 12f.
17 Deutsche Bank Research, *Russia Morning Comment*, 1 February 2008, 6. For a chronology of events, see the regular reports in the *FSU Oil and Gas Monitor* (www.newsbase.com) and in the Russian newspaper *Kommersant* (www.kommersant.com).
18 The results of an investigative report (supported by a company insider) have been published in: Florian Hassel, "Alles bleibt in der Familie: Wie die Gasprom-Manager Russlands reichstes Unternehmen ausplündern," *Frankfurter Rundschau*, 21 May 2001, 7. See also: United Financial Group, *Russia Morning Comment*, 13 June 2001, 7; Heiko Pleines, "Scrutinizing the Gazprom–Itera Relationship," *FSU Oil and Gas Monitor* (NewsBase), 6 February 2001.
19 V. Kleiner, "Korporativnoe upravlenie i effektivnost' deiatel'nosti kompanii (na primere OAO 'Gazprom')," *Voprosy ekonomiki*, no. 3 (2006): 86–103.
20 *Moscow Times*, 8 June 2004.
21 Simon Pirani, *Ukraine's Gas Sector* (Oxford: Oxford Institute for Energy Studies, 2007), 29–42.
22 The fullest account is given by: Andreas Heinrich and Julia Kusznir, "Independent Gas Producers in Russia," KICES Working Papers, no. 2 (Koszalin: Koszalin Institute of Comparative European Studies, 2005).
23 Kleiner, "Korporativnoe upravlenie i effektivnost' deyatel'nosti kompanii (na primere OAO 'Gazprom')." The official reply of Gazprom to these accusations is given by the press secretary of the head of management: C. Kupriianov, "Otvet 'Gazproma': Kritika effektivna, kogda ona obosnovana," *Voprosy ekonomiki*, no. 3 (2006): 104–10.
24 Heinrich, Lis and Pleines, *Corporate Governance in the Oil and Gas Industry*.
25 A concise overview of these developments is offered by Julia Kusznir and Heiko Pleines, "Russia's Refining Assets," *Hydrocarbon Engineering* 12, no. 9 (2007): 12–18.
26 For a list of planned investments see ibid., 18.
27 Ministry of Industry and Energy (Minpromenergo), *Strategiia razvitiia khimicheskoi i neftekhimicheskoi promyshlennosti Rossii na period do 2015 goda* (Moscow: Minpromenergo, 2006).
28 "Russian SIBUR to Invest $3 Billion to Increase Output," *Bloomberg*, 3 July 2007, www.sibur.ru/eng/640/1567/218/index.shtml?id=2623 (accessed 9 August 2008).
29 D. Ramazanov, "Organizatsionno-ekonomicheskie problemy povysheniia nefteotdachi na mestorozhdeniiakh Rossii," *Voprosy Ekonomiki*, no. 7 (2008): 123–33, at 133.
30 Matthew J. Sagers, "Russia's Energy Policy: A Divergent View," *Eurasian Geography and Economics* 47, no. 3 (2006): 314–20, at 316.
31 Vladimir Milov, Leonard Coburn, and Igor Danchenko, "Russia's Energy Policy 1992–2005," *Eurasian Geography and Economics* 47, no. 3 (2006): 285–313, at 308–11.
32 Cambridge Energy Research Associates (CERA), "Russian Domestic Oil Price Outlook," workshop held at CERA, Washington, DC, April 2006.
33 Yuli Grigoryev, "Today or Not Today: Deregulating the Russian Gas Sector," *Energy Policy* 35, no. 5 (2007): 3036–45; Rudiger Ahrend and William Tompson, *Russia's Gas Sector. The Endless Wait for Reform?*, OECD Economics Department Working Papers, no. 402 (Paris: OECD, 2004).
34 For a more profound analysis, see: Jakob Fruchtmann, "Putins Konzeption von Wirtschaftspolitik," in *Nur ein Ölboom? Bestimmungsfaktoren und Perspektiven der russischen Wirtschaftsentwicklung*, ed. Hans-Hermann Höhmann, Heiko Pleines, and Hans-Henning Schröder (Münster: LIT, 2005), 151–68.
35 For more detailed analyses of the development of state holdings, see: William Tompson, "Back to the Future? Thoughts on the Political Economy of Expanding State Ownership in Russia," in *Changes in Economic Power and Strategic Government Policies in Russia*, ed. Peeter Vahtra and Kari Liuhto (London: Routledge, forthcoming); Kari Liuhto, "Genesis of Economic Nationalism in Russia," *Electronic Publications of the*

Pan-European Institute, no. 3 (2008), www.tse.fi/pei (accessed 20 August 2008); Vahtra, Liuhto, and Lorentz, "Privatisation or Re-Nationalisation in Russia?"; Philip Hanson, "The Turn to Statism in Russian Economic Policy," *International Spectator* 42, no. 1 (2007): 29–42; A. Radygin and G. Malginov, "Rynok korporativnogo kontrolia i gosudarstvo," *Voprosy ekonomiki*, no. 3 (2006): 62–85.

36 Julian Cooper, "Can Russia Compete in the Global Economy?," *Eurasian Geography and Economics* 47, no. 4 (2006): 407–25.

Part II
Russia's role in international energy markets

5 Russia's key customer
Europe

Stacy Closson

Media reporting and Western security discourse tend to portray Russia as the aggressor in its energy relations, increasingly able to convert its hydrocarbon supply to Europe into economic and political capital. Likewise, many Western scholarly works and analytical reports suggest that Europe is dangerously dependent on Russia.[1] Some NATO members have even urged the creation of an "energy NATO" or suggested that the alliance define a shutoff of energy by Russia as an attack justifying the invocation of Article V on collective defense.[2] Part of this perception has to do with the way Russia is pursuing business interests in Europe, a policy once described by Russian President Vladimir Putin as "energy supremacy."[3] Russia's tactics regarding the pricing of gas to its Commonwealth of Independent State (CIS) customers and related shutoffs of gas and oil transiting Belarus and Ukraine to Europe, as well as its subsequent championing of transit options that bolster its near monopoly of gas supplies to Europe, concern many end-users. Moreover, Russia's continued recalcitrance toward ratifying the Energy Charter Treaty (ECT) and its recent effort to limit foreign investment in upstream ventures, such as Kovykta and Sakhalin, are viewed by some as unwarranted, given its demands for access to markets in Europe.[4] However, as alarming as these recent developments have been for Europe and the US, the warnings emphasizing an encroaching Russian energy giant do not consider the strong interdependency between Russia and Europe that benefit both parties. This interdependency will remain well into the future, creating conditions that favor cooperation over confrontation.

While it is recognized that in the near-term, Russia will remain Europe's single most important source of hydrocarbons, particularly for natural gas, Russia's share of the European market will decline over time, increasing Russia's dependency on Europe. Already, the quality of the relationship makes Europe indispensable to Russia in terms of overall trade volumes. The European Union (EU) in 2005 accounted for some 56 percent of Russia's exports and around 45 percent of its imports, with Russia's exports to the EU generally being confined to oil and natural gas. Around two-thirds of Russian gas and oil exports currently go to EU member states, the rest to other European countries and the CIS states. These exports have been critical to Russia's welfare, as one-third of all Russian GDP growth over the recent period has come from the natural resources sector, with taxation of oil and gas providing almost 50 percent of federal government fiscal revenue.[5] Moreover, Russia's dependence on hydrocarbon exports is likely to grow, as Russia has failed to invest its energy profits in sectors that would ensure long-term, sustainable economic development. This lack of investment could especially hurt the development of Russia's hydrocarbon sector, as the International Energy Agency (IEA) forecasts require energy investment at around €800 billion by 2030. In order to meet this requirement, Russia would have to supplement domestic funds by encouraging more foreign investment through a revised legal framework that provides secure property rights for the assets of foreign companies operating in Russia.[6]

Meanwhile, as European states are making moves to diversify their hydrocarbon resources, Russia appears to be less active in securing alternative markets beyond the West. Europe is strengthening relations with African producers, developing liquefied natural gas (LNG) markets, and moving toward greater use of renewable resources. Russia, on the other hand, continues to make business arrangements to construct more pipelines linking its oil and gas fields westwards, obtain rights for the use of gas storage sites in Europe, and sign long-term purchase guarantees with European customers. These plans are taking priority over the construction of pipelines to Asia, investment in upstream gas sector projects, and construction of the infrastructure required for exporting LNG globally. Given these developments, Russia will remain a major player in the European market in the foreseeable future, accounting for roughly a quarter of EU hydrocarbon consumption or 40 percent of imports. Nevertheless, even with the Russian energy sector concentrated on the European market, it will not be able to meet European demand for gas, which is forecast to grow 70 percent by 2030.[7]

The disjuncture between, on the one hand, the actual interdependency between Russia and Europe and, on the other hand, the portrayal of Russia as the aggressor and Europe as the dependent actor, may be more the result of semantics than of facts. Since the early 2000s, the Russian government has tended to understand the context of its energy business in Europe better than Europeans understand Russia. Russia has done a good job of playing a weak hand by engaging with individual European states and their mostly nationally-owned companies to create a series of business arrangements that suit the interests of both sides. Today, Russian and European energy companies are creating joint stock companies, constructing oil and gas pipelines within the EU, investing in hubs and storage facilities, refineries, and terminals, and swapping Russian sales to customers on Europe's market for European exploration and technology in upstream projects in the Russian Far East. This has created a visible map of Russian state-owned assets dotted across Europe and North Africa.[8] It is this visual that concerns many in Europe and America and contributes to calls for less dependency on Russia.

However, the increasingly politicized debate around the issue of Russia's activities in the European energy market has impeded a more even-handed approach to examining their interdependent relationship. Missing from the discussion is an analysis of the relationship over time and of the implications for present and future developments. To this end, this chapter will first provide an overview of energy relations between Russia and Europe, beginning with the Soviet Union. It will then examine more closely the statistical evidence of the interdependency between Russia and Europe in the hydrocarbon sector. Next, various intersecting influences on Russia's energy strategy in Europe will be discussed in order to expand the analysis of how Russia might perceive its role in Europe. The final section will review the range of possibilities for Europe's and Russia's interdependency, based on past and present trends.

Overview of Russian–European energy relations

In order to place the current debate on Russian–European energy relations in perspective, a review of this relationship dating back to the post-Stalin Soviet Union is useful. After all, the discussions taking place today over whether Europe should cooperate with Russian companies and whether Europe's increasing supply dependency on Russia could strengthen an increasingly confrontational Russia are merely repetitions of earlier debates relating to the Soviet Union. This section will begin with an overview of the early European–Soviet oil and gas pipeline projects, followed by the collapse of the Soviet Union and the creation of new legal frameworks for cooperation, including the ECT and the energy dialog as part of the EU–Russian Partnership and Cooperation Agreement (PCA). This will provide the basis for an analysis of the growing interdependency since the late 1990s.

Hydrocarbon relations between Europe and the Soviet Union date back to the late 1950s, when oil and gas pipelines to the Eastern European member states of the Council for Mutual Economic Assistance (CMEA) were constructed. Recipient states of Soviet hydrocarbons included Poland, East Germany, Czechoslovakia, Hungary, Romania, and Bulgaria. Energy exports to Western Europe began to flow in the late 1960s as European states sought to diversify away from oil into other forms of energy, notably natural gas. Negotiations were held between the Soviet Union and Austria, France, Italy, Finland, Japan, West Germany, and Sweden. Starting in 1968, Austria was the first non-Communist state to receive Soviet gas via Czechoslovakia based on a 20-year contract.[9] Multi-decade contracts were signed beginning in 1970 between the USSR and the Ruhrgas corporation for the delivery of gas to the Federal Republic of Germany and on to France.[10] Rising world energy prices (particularly the oil spike in 1973–4) and growing volumes meant that energy exports as a share of total Soviet energy produced grew steadily, interrupted only by the difficulties with oil production after 1977.[11] This trade provided the Soviet Union with over 60 percent of its hard currency earnings.

Beginning with the fall of the Pahlavi monarchy in Iran in 1979, Soviet leaders suggested to Western Europeans that they should consider importing greater volumes of alternative sources of energy supply. In 1980, the Soviet Union began negotiations with Western European banks, gas companies, and equipment manufacturers for an East–West pipeline to increase deliveries of natural gas to Western Europe. In a high-profile break with the Reagan administration, Western Europeans in 1982 delivered equipment for the construction of the East–West pipeline despite US protests. While Europeans viewed the project as a source of domestic employment and diversification from oil, the US government was concerned that greater volumes of trade would help to finance the Soviet military arsenal.[12] Moreover, the USA worried that French or German dependency on Soviet gas could provide the Soviet Union with a stronger bargaining position against the West.[13] Nevertheless, the pipeline project went ahead, and the Soviets lost any potential diplomatic leverage that the project might have offered when they threatened to enact penalties against Western European firms should they side with the USA.[14] These threats backfired, and eventually the Europeans and the USA agreed to limit Soviet gas imports to 30 percent of the total, while simultaneously developing Norway's Troll field in the North Sea.[15]

Despite these diplomatic disagreements, overall European imports of Soviet oil and gas continued to rise through the end of the Cold War. Soviet oil exports to Western Europe grew in the 1980s, from 30.7 mt pa in 1980 to 44.8 in 1983 and 44.0 mt in 1984, declining by 1985 to 33.3, but rising once again to 37.6 mt in 1986.[16] By 1982, West Germany, France, and Italy were importing between 15 to 30 percent of their gas supplies from the Soviet Union. These figures rose to between 30 and 36 percent by 1990 and more than doubled in the case of France (see Table 5.1).

The next phase in European–Russian energy relations began after the collapse of the Soviet Union in 1991. Russian oil and gas production levels dipped due to the chaos caused by the transition to a market system and did not reach 1990 levels again until 2005. Additionally, Russia experienced a major economic crisis in 1998, resulting in its default on state loans and precipitating the collapse of most of its private banks. This financial meltdown, coupled with record low market prices for hydrocarbons, meant that Russia's foreign currency reserves all but disappeared. However, despite these setbacks, Russia was still able to meet hydrocarbon supply commitments to European states. Russia maintained gas supplies to its 14 European customers, increasing export volumes to nine of these, and added Greece as a client in 1996. Crude oil exports to 11 European countries increased as well, including new customers in the Czech Republic, Finland, Germany, Hungary, Italy, and Lithuania.[17] Expanding exports was possible partly due to a significant decline in domestic consumption of hydrocarbons as a result of the

Table 5.1 Natural gas supplies in 1982 and 1990

Country	Total gas consumption (billion cubic meters)		Soviet gas share of total gas consumption	
	1982	1990	1982	1990
Federal Republic of Germany	38.4	52.9	20.6	29.7
France	21.2	26.3	14.6	35.7
Italy	22.0	32.9	31.8	35.9

Source: John Van Oudenaren, *The Urengoi Pipeline: Prospects for Soviet Leverage* (Santa Monica, CA: Rand, 1984), 21.

collapse of the industrial complex throughout the former Soviet space and Central Europe. The growth was also the result of some Western investment in Russia and Central Asia in up-stream development and pipeline construction for export.

There were, however, incidences of temporary stoppages of Russian supplies to some Central and Eastern European customers. Western experts argue that the stoppages to the Baltic States during the early 1990s marked the beginning of Russia's use of its hydrocarbon supply as a political tool.[18] Between 1998 and 2000, Russia's state-owned oil transit monopoly company Transneft stopped the flow of oil to Lithuania nine times despite Lukoil's contractual obligation to supply this oil.[19] Lithuania then was negotiating the sale of 33 percent of its Mažeikių Nafta refinery to US-based energy company Williams, as well as planning the construction of new port facilities and pipelines in order to diversify its oil imports away from Russia.[20] In defiance of previous agreements, Russia terminated oil deliveries by pipeline to Latvia's Ventspils terminal in 2003. Subsequently, in 2007, as the Estonian government removed a Red Army monument from the center of Tallinn, the state-owned Russian Railways suddenly halted oil deliveries to Estonian ports.

During this period, Russia engaged in disputes with Belarus and Ukraine, the two countries that transit most of its exports to Europe, over hydrocarbon prices and nonpayments. These disputes sometimes resulted in temporary shutoffs of oil and gas from Russia. After the dissolution of the Soviet Union, Belarus and Ukraine faced rising energy prices for Russian hydrocarbons, which they could not pay, compounding their debt to Russia annually. These countries had grown accustomed to low prices and a barter system employed during the Soviet era, and factories were built with little consideration for energy efficiency and conservation. Neither the Siberian gas fields, where the gas originated, nor homes throughout the Soviet Union were metered. The newly independent governments experienced difficulties in convincing their citizenry to pay for the energy they consumed. Barter deals and debt-for-equity swaps of state assets with Russia were sufficient to pay off their debt.[21] In response to nonpayment, Russian stoppages of gas to Ukraine began in 1992–3, but did not receive international attention until the pricing dispute in winter 2005–6. In response to Russian pressure, Belarus agreed to privatize Beltransgaz, including the pipeline infrastructure, to Gazprom, while Ukraine avoided such concessions.[22]

Starting in the mid-1990s, Europe and Russia began to formalize their energy relations through international treaties and regular consultations. In 1994, the EU and Russia signed a Partnership and Cooperation Agreement (PCA), which came into force in 1997. Article 65 of the PCA addressed a range of prescriptions for enhancing EU–Russian energy cooperation, offering a set of liberal economic prescriptions, including the provision of institutional, legal, technical, and financial assistance for the purposes of increased energy trade based on market principles.[23] In 2000, the EU and Russia launched an energy dialog within the framework of the PCA. Additionally, both the EU and Russia published energy strategy documents, respectively projecting 20 and 30 years into the future, in which they recognized their mutual dependency and complementary interests in strengthening energy cooperation.[24] Senior officials were designated to steer the dialog, and working groups were established to address investments, infrastructures, and energy efficiency issues. The long-term shared objective, as stated in the 2001 Joint Statement by the EU and Russia, was not only to establish an energy partnership, but also for Russia to participate in the development of the EU's internally integrated market as part of a larger common economic area.[25]

To nurture this dialog the EU opened a Technological Centre for Information and Technology Exchange in 2002, followed by a Permanent Council for Mutual Cooperation in 2005. After the establishment of these bodies, the EU–Russia dialog on infrastructure and conservation improved. Positive developments were realized in the integration of Europe's and Russia's energy markets, including the interconnection of electricity grids, agreement on regulator principles for internal markets and long-term supply contracts, and cooperation in nuclear energy and advanced energy technologies. However, the EU–Russia energy consultations, particularly those concerning hydrocarbons, were often considered difficult and seen as falling short of their stated objectives. The reasons for these problems are rooted in the two sides' different objectives for an energy dialog. For Russia, the priorities are long-term contracts for natural gas, attracting investments and technology, participation of the European Investment Bank, and removing limits on imports of energy products into the EU. The EU, on the other hand, wants to advance supply security by opening up Russian energy markets and promoting a more favorable climate for investments in Russia. This divide is made even more difficult by the fact that different EU member states have diverging priorities depending on their energy imports from Russia.[26] Granted, it was never the objective of the EU–Russia dialog to replace private companies in contracting energy supplies, nor was it meant to provide a master plan for future gas and oil pipelines.[27]

Moreover, Russia never felt it necessary to ratify the Energy Charter Treaty (ECT) that it had signed in 1994, despite continued urging by the EU. The ECT includes provisions for free transit across the territory of all signatory states, as well as for international mediation to settle disputes. Russian critics of the ECT suggest that it will be used by the EU to impose too many obligations on the Russian side and that Russian energy companies will gain few advantages in return. Russian politicians object to the right of first access to their pipelines, transit tariffs, and the role of regional economic organizations.[28] At the Sochi EU–Russia Summit in 2006, Russian President Vladimir Putin said the ECT meant free access for European companies to production and transportation infrastructure in Russia, but added: "The question is, what will we get in return? We ask where your deposits and pipelines are. If [Europe] does not have any, then we have to look for other areas of cooperation."[29] Recognizing that the ECT would not be ratified by Russia in its current form, in October 2006, the EU proposed to extract those relevant provisions and incorporate them into a new legal framework called the Strategy Partnership Agreement.[30] In fact, despite not ratifying the ECT, Russia is legally bound and has accepted provisional application of the treaty where it is consistent with its laws in order to promote cooperation.

The debate over the ECT represents a larger reality for Russia – that it will likely be the dependent actor in its energy relationship with Europe in the future. As was mentioned in the introduction, the EU is Russia's main economic partner both in terms of imports and exports. Oil and gas volumes flowing from Russia to Europe constitute a larger share of Russia's exports than of Europe's imports of these fuels. Two-thirds of Russia's oil exports are directed to the EU. Approximately 15 percent of EU oil consumption is of Russian origin, and 30 percent of EU oil imports come from Russia.[31] According to the 2003 Russian Energy Strategy to 2020, oil exports will increase from 145 mt to 300 mt in 2020 (30 million of this to Europe, increasing from 127.5 to 160 mt or 1.1 percent pa). However, this will only meet 30 percent of Europe's demand growth. Thus, a hypothetical stop of Russian oil deliveries would hurt Europe, which imports the bulk of its energy with tankers and where shortfalls could theoretically be balanced out with imports from other places. While in the short term, Europe's opportunities for supply diversification are limited, the picture will improve in the long term. By 2030, most new oil imports to Europe will come from OPEC, and not from Russia or Central Asia.

In the gas sector, Russia's ability to meet commitments in Europe will either require it to increase imports from Central Asia or to reform its domestic patterns of demand. Gazprom, through its subsidiary Gazexport, has shifted much of its gas exports to serve the rising demand of European countries and Turkey. The gas imports of the EU-30 (the current EU members plus Switzerland, Turkey, and Norway) are expected to grow by 40 percent, equaling 200–250 bcm pa, far exceeding Russia's potential. Russia estimates that it will only cover about 23 percent of total demand.[32] Unlike in the case of oil, gas transport and storage facilities are limited, at least until LNG gains a larger share of the market. Therefore, a hypothetical stoppage of gas supplies would hurt Europe. Additionally, the pipelines coming to Europe from other directions are at full capacity in peak winter months, limiting alternatives for imports to Europe.[33] This gas bottleneck, coupled with the fact that gas is a strategic resource for industry and residential use in Europe, as well as the preferred alternative to other hydrocarbons because it helps curb carbon emissions, makes Europe as dependent on Russia's delivery of gas as Russia is on receiving the money in return for its deliveries.

It should be underscored, however, that there are different "Europes." Depending on the compilation of states, whether it is the EU-30, the 27 current EU members, or the 15 states that made up the EU before the enlargement round of 1 May 2004, the level of dependency on Russia varies. For example, 70 percent of the EU-30's imported gas comes from Russia. However, Russia's share in Europe's overall gas consumption is only 25 percent. Russia's most valued customers are high-paying Western European states, such as Germany and Italy, whose dependency is growing, and who are willing to fund joint projects and invest in Russia's up-stream activities. There is another group of European states whose dependency on Russia is even higher than that of Germany and Italy, such as the Baltic States, Finland, and Central Europe. In a third category are states that are less dependent on Russia, but whose gas reserves are waning, including

Norway, the Netherlands, and the United Kingdom. Thus, how Russia views its role in Europe likely depends on which "Europe" is under consideration.

Challenges for Russia in Europe

Russia faces at least three major challenges operating in the European energy sector. First, as has been noted, Europe is Russia's most important energy partner. However, as Europe will remain its only major partner in the near term, Russia faces a potential problem of insecurity of demand. Russia is therefore searching for new buyers to diversify its customer base, particularly in Asia. Second, Russia has major problems with Eastern European transit countries, which reflect negatively on relations with wider Europe. Thus, it strives to redirect oil and gas through new pipelines bypassing these states in order to stabilize relations with its key European customers. Third, a major issue in Russian–European relations is reciprocity. Russia and the EU have different understandings of this concept. While Russia strives for EU approval of its investments downstream in the European market, Europe measures reciprocity by the degree of investment its companies are allowed to make upstream in Russia.

First, regarding Russia's demand security, despite the previously mentioned October 2007 warning from Russia that it would diversify deliveries of hydrocarbons to Asia should Europe impose limitations on Russia's investments in Europe, its transit infrastructure going east remains underdeveloped. There are plans to build the East Siberia Pacific Ocean (ESPO) pipeline to Japan with an eventual branch to China, but it is not expected to come on line until 2015 at the earliest (see Nina Poussenkova's chapter in this volume). Moreover, the participation of China and South Korea in Russia's Kovykta gas project, bringing gas to Northeast Asia through a new Angarsk–Daqing pipeline, was halted in June 2007, in part due to pricing disagreements between Gazprom and Chinese officials.[34] In the interim, Kazakhstan has already built the first oil pipeline to reach the Chinese market from a former Soviet state. Furthermore, Russia must compete with a gas pipeline under construction from Turkmenistan to China through Uzbekistan and Kazakhstan.

To meet Europe's demand, Russia currently imports 60 bcm of gas from Central Asia annually. These imports are projected to increase from 80 to 100 bcm in the coming years, after the May 2007 agreement between the presidents of Russia, Turkmenistan, Uzbekistan, and Kazakhstan to build another pipeline skirting the eastern Caspian seashore to Russia.[35] Russia opposes alternative Caspian–Europe extensions, including Trans-Caspian pipelines, which it argues are impossible to construct given that the legal status of the Caspian Sea remains unresolved. Russia has also warned against the idea of a pipeline from Georgia through Ukraine to the EU, called White Stream, citing potential complications for its Blue Stream pipeline to Turkey under the Black Sea.[36]

However, Russia must also be careful to avoid a confrontation with Europe over pipeline construction, such as its offer of alternatives to Europe's favored pipeline projects. Russia and some European states, such as Bulgaria and Serbia, prefer the South Stream project.[37] Should South Stream materialize, those countries committed to the Nabucco project with Bulgaria, including Ukraine, and European consumers may be forced to drop their plans.[38] Moreover, as Gazprom's South Stream concept would carry Russian and Central Asian gas to Europe across Bulgaria, the pipeline would bypass Turkey, thus shelving Gazprom's earlier plan, Blue Stream Two, designed to pass through Turkey. It would also divert some gas volumes away from Ukraine's transit system into South Stream via Bulgaria. Another project, the construction of Nord Stream with Germany through the Baltic Sea, would likely mean that the Yamal–Europe pipeline through Poland would not be built, as they both have capacities of 27 bcm a year. The Netherlands and the United Kingdom have signed on to building trunk pipelines from Nord Stream. However, issues involving rising costs (50 percent increase in the three years since agreements were reached with Germany in October 2005), disagreements about the pipeline path in the Baltic Sea, and Poland's continued protests against the rerouting of hydrocarbons from Russia could significantly delay its completion.

The second challenge facing Russia concerns difficult relations with transit states, particularly Ukraine and Belarus. Ukraine is the primary transit country of Russian and Central Asian gas to Europe (over 80 percent), as well as the largest consumer of Russian gas. Russia is striving to repair its image in Europe after the Ukraine gas crisis in 2006, during which, as a result of a pricing dispute between Russia and Ukraine, there was a temporary shutoff of gas to Ukraine and EU member states. Russia is conscious that it must be seen to be a reliable and long-term supplier of gas to Europe. Russia's failure to consult paying European customers prior to the shutoff made them question the reliability of Russia and search for alternative supplies. It has also led some Europeans to assume that the shutoffs were part of an effort to destabilize Ukraine as the victors of the "Orange Revolution," aiming to integrate their country with Europe, were consolidating power.[39] While Russia claims that it increased prices to Ukraine simply as a matter of ending long-term subsidies, most analyses of this event portray Russia as pursuing political goals.[40]

Russian supply interruptions can be interpreted in two ways. On the one hand, former Soviet states should not expect perpetual subsidies. The new prices imposed have been related to sales prices in the West, and the transition from subsidies to market prices may simply represent a passing phase as countries adjust their relationships and adapt to market realities. Moreover, Russia's imposition of government influence on energy exports is not much different from that in other major energy-exporting states. On the other hand, in the energy industry, contract renegotiations normally do not involve cutting off supplies. The shutoffs were widely seen as having political as well as commercial motivations, particularly when Russia has used similar techniques earlier in the cases of the Baltic States, as well as Georgia and Azerbaijan. The interruptions were also interpreted in the context of the Russian government's efforts to limit the activities of independent Russian and international energy companies, such as Yukos and Shell, from operating in Russia.[41]

At the same time, Russia has perceived several moves by European states to block its companies' procurement of Western energy assets as retribution for its actions. These include Lithuania's Mažeikių Nafta oil refinery, previously owned by Yukos and sold to Poland's PKN Orlen rather than to Gazprom. This disappointment was followed in early 2006 by the British government's decision to block the sale of Centrica, owner of British Gas, to Gazprom. This incident resulted in Gazprom CEO Alexei Miller issuing a warning to ambassadors of the EU member countries in Moscow that Gazprom would gradually reorient its market toward China and the US. Finally, in October 2006, Lukoil's attempt to procure Kuwait Petroleum International's Europort refinery in Rotterdam, The Netherlands, was overturned.

Despite these perceived moves to keep Russian companies out, however, Russia's oil transit monopoly company, Transneft, is expanding into Europe as set out in a variety of agreements with European states and companies to construct pipelines. There is the forthcoming Burgas–Alexandropolis oil pipeline, in which Russia's stake is 51 percent (33.34 percent is owned by Transneft and 33.3 percent each by Rosneft and Gazpromneft). This would be the first Russian-controlled pipeline to be built entirely within the EU. The second project is the Baltic Pipeline System (BPS) to send crude from the Russian Timan-Pechora region, Western Siberia, the Urals, and Volga to the Primorsk port near St. Petersburg for transshipment to Europe. The pipeline could ship as much as 150 mt of oil annually. There are also plans to construct a parallel gas pipeline along the Baltic seabed for LNG. The third is the Druzhba–Adria integration project, which would enable Russian oil to flow directly to the Adriatic, by reversing the flow in the existing pipeline.

Moreover, Russia is expanding its role as a supply bridge between Europe and the rest of the world by means of maximizing the range of its investments in global upstream projects, as well as expanding the number of export routes to Europe under full or partial Russian control. Russian companies are investing in upstream projects in potential supplier states for Europe's gas market. These include Northern Africa and the Middle East (Algeria's Salah field, Libya's Green Stream pipeline, and Egyptian supply via Jordan and Turkey), Nigeria, Trinidad, Venezuela, and the Caspian region. Russia also wishes to keep Turkey as a major gateway to Europe for Russian oil and gas. Gas now comprises three-quarters of Russia's exports to Turkey through the previously mentioned Blue Stream pipeline across the Black Sea. Plans are underway between Gazprom and Turkey's Botas to construct underground gas storage facilities in Turkey and to expand Turkey's gas pipeline infrastructure to Israel and Greece.[42] Finally, Russia continues to invest in the rich Iranian hydrocarbon market; Russia owns the gas pipeline connecting Armenia to Iran, and has invested in a new oil pipeline from Iran to Armenia with plans to construct a refinery on the Armenian side of the border.

The third challenge for Russia in Europe is the notion of reciprocity. Russia does not want to be unilaterally dependent on Europe; it strives for interdependency and mutual benefit through symmetrical interaction between Russian and European companies.[43] For Russia, energy security has tended to mean security of demand by foreign customers at fair and preferably high prices. This approach runs counter to Europe's concept of energy security as the diversification of supply. The EU Commission talks about creating a "level playing field" by bringing about "predictability and reciprocity" in terms of domestic and foreign investment, opening markets, and fair access to transport networks in Russia. This is ideally achieved through the convergence of energy policies, legislation, and regulations, while complying with the "high standards of EU regulations concerning safety, security, and the environment."[44] Since the Russian 2006 G-8 presidency and the Sochi EU–Russia Summit in 2006, interdependency has come to represent a bridge linking security of supply and security of demand. Russia stated at this summit that it wanted to convert its economy from oil and gas to an innovation-based society by selling hydrocarbons in exchange for access to technology.[45] Thus far in practice, however, Russia has used the concept of "interdependency" to push ideas of long-term supply contracts with customers, as well as to facilitate Russian expansion into downstream markets in Europe.[46]

As a result, Russia has increasingly come under pressure from US and European companies to balance investments in Europe with European plans to invest in Russian projects. The latest move by the EU Commission to pass legislation limiting investments in its domestic market to only those companies that separate production, transport, and sales in the European market would effectively block Gazprom's plans to be engaged in all three.[47] The Commission's stated intention, however, was not so much directed at foreign companies, but an effort to encourage the unbundling of domestic European energy giants, particularly E.ON Ruhrgas and Gaz de France. Likewise, Russia will have to consider whether it will continue to place restrictions on European participation in pipeline transit, most upstream projects, and generation in its internal market. In the interim, Russia's medium- to long-term concerns are that it will be denied access to downstream markets in Europe, that it will waste investment in unneeded production capacity should Europe diversify sooner, and that Europe will try to gain greater access to its natural resources.[48]

The three challenges facing Russia in the European market – ensuring sustained demand from Europe, addressing troubles with transit states while avoiding confrontation with European customers, and addressing European companies' demand for greater access to the Russian market – are intertwined. If Russia redirects resources to Asia, it will jeopardize relations with Europe. However, if it relies too much on European demand and the market falls, then Russia will suffer. In the interim, attempts to find alternatives to the traditional former Soviet transit states are undermining transatlantic plans for alternative supply routes across the Caspian and into southern Europe, bypassing Russia. The question of how or whether these challenges are resolved will shape the next several decades of Russia's relations in the European energy market.

Russia's future in the European energy market

There are a range of possible outcomes for Russia's future in the European energy market, from cooperation to conflict, or a combination of the two. The possibilities depend on many intersecting factors, some of which are more or less controllable by one or the other party. For Russia, these include a rise or drop in Russian production, a rise or fall in Russian domestic demand, and the future role for domestic and foreign companies in Russia's domestic market. For Europe, relations with Russia may be affected by an increase or decrease in Europe's demand as a result of changes in efficiency levels, the amount of gas provided by new suppliers (e.g. Central Asia, Iran, North Africa, and the LNG market), and the role of alternative sources other than gas. For both Russia and Europe, the extent to which the EU is able to liberalize its domestic market will directly affect Russian companies' investments in Europe, setting a marker for how much foreign investment Russia will tolerate in its domestic market. Finally, the role of Russian and European companies, and whether they work together in extracting and transporting hydrocarbons from new or expanding markets in the Middle East, Africa, or South America will also alter the dynamics in their relations.

First, Russia's future in the European energy market could be as a reliable and transparent partner that meets its commitments for supply. A balance regarding the pipelines would have to be realized between Europe and Russia, as well as agreement reached on foreign investments in the European market in relation to Europe's investments in Russia. This new understanding could be indicated in an agreement reached between the EU and Russia in a "post-Partnership and Cooperation Agreement" outlining the objectives and principles of energy cooperation in a balanced and mutually binding manner.[49] This legal and regulatory framework could then serve as a basis for agreeing to joint projects in areas of upstream and downstream projects in Russia, Eurasia, and Europe. As the multi-party pipeline and storage projects in Europe progress, Russian and European companies could continue to extend their cooperation to other parts of the world, as is already the case in North Africa.

Proponents of partnership argue that Russian investments in the European market will require Russian businesses to act in a more transparent, accountable, and responsible manner. As Russian companies integrate their up-, mid-, and downstream business, they are more likely to be responsible suppliers to European customers, given that disruptions would directly hurt their interests. Among those espousing partnership are European bureaucrats working on the EU Russia Energy Dialogue and European energy company directors cooperating with Russia in joint projects, such as E.ON Ruhrgas, ENI, Total, and Statoil.[50] Other advocates of this approach are Russian energy analysts who document the objectives of Russian state-owned energy companies investing in Europe, such as Gazprom.[51] It is a fact that as Russian companies invest in European assets, they are increasingly bound by European law and regulations. Furthermore, the European Commission's Directorate-General for Energy and Transport has announced that projects such as Nord Stream will be subject to review. These measures, it is argued, should ensure that Russia's investments in the EU's common economic space advance Europe's energy security objectives, while also strengthening the interdependent relationship based on a mutually acceptable legal framework.

The second possibility for Russia's future in the European energy market is the prospect of confrontation. Russia could operate in a non-transparent and sometimes challenging manner, deterring investments in its internal markets, monopolizing investments in the CIS, and using various points of leverage to assert itself more forcefully in Europe's energy sector. Those who believe that this trend will dominate future relations warn that Russia will gain a firm foothold in domestic EU politics as a result of many of the European states' dependency on Russian gas supplies.[52] Some believe that Russia is planning to take over internal generation facilities and distribution networks in Europe, linking them to the larger supply networks, thus dominating a chain that would eventually put Russia in a politically advantageous position. There is much speculation as to the potential for Russia to, for example, gain an unofficial, yet significant veto on issues by threatening to halt oil and gas supplies to European states.[53] Contentious issues at the moment include the installation of a missile defense system in Central Europe (Poland and the Czech Republic), the support of many European states for the independence of Kosovo, and NATO expansion into the former Soviet space (Georgia and Ukraine).

On the other hand, confrontation could result from a weakened Russia. Should the EU remain Russia's primary market, it could be in a stronger position in the future to apply more effective sanctions against Russia in the case of a major disagreement.[54] Conversely, some analysts predict that Russia's energy sector will be unable to sustain current levels of development, state enterprises will stagnate, and new fields will not be brought on-stream in time to meet both growing domestic and European demand.[55] The growth rate of added value in the extractive industries sector for hydrocarbons slowed from 7.9 percent in 2004 to 1.9 percent in 2005.[56] In 2005, Gazprom registered only a 0.5 percent increase in the volume of extracted gas as compared to the previous year, despite its absorption of minor independent gas producers.[57] The same trends held steady through 2007. Should Gazprom be unable to meet supply commitments to Europe, then European gas companies could eliminate the take-or-pay conditions in their contracts with Russia, meaning that they would no longer agree to pay for a fixed amount of gas even when a lesser amount is actually used. This, in turn, would threaten Gazprom's ability to borrow for future development projects.[58]

The same could happen to the oil industry, as the Russian government attempts to consolidate the industry into several large state-owned companies, such as Rosneft and Gazpromneft. Such consolidation would restrict the amount invested by several smaller companies. The effects of this state policy are already apparent when comparing the respective oil extraction rates for 2004 and 2005, which slid from 10 percent to 2 percent. State owned companies gave the poorest performance, including Yuganskneftegaz (acquired from Yukos by Rosneft) and Sibneft (acquired by Gazprom).[59] Additionally, if world energy prices should experience a downturn, accumulated debt combined with high taxation of oil production and export could have a negative impact on the incentive for oil companies to increase production.[60]

A third possibility is that Russian–European energy relations could continue as they are, sometimes in cooperation and other times in conflict. Russia could continue to cooperate with Western European states, enhancing aspects of its "circles of influence" through a network of commercial relationships and quid pro quos with governments and companies. Such practices are likely to continue as long as the EU does not have a fully coordinated and executed energy policy. The development of Austrian–Russian relations to the exclusion of Hungary regarding asset ownership is one example. Gazprom intends to use Austria as a transit corridor to capture other EU markets, developing a Central European Gas Hub and Gas Transit management Center at Baumgarten. In July 2007, Austria's OMV announced its intent to take over MOL, a private Hungarian energy company. Likewise, Russia's July 2006 closure of an oil pipeline to Lithuania appears to be part of an effort to phase out oil deliveries through the Druzhba pipeline transiting Belarus and Central Europe, in favor of the aforementioned Baltic Pipeline System and a tanker line operating out of the Russian ports of Primorsk and Ust-Luga directly to Western Europe. Finally, the German–Russian business cooperation in the Nord Stream project has alienated the Baltic states and Poland, who had hoped to be transit states for Russian gas and fear future stoppages of supply.[61]

However, this game of "circles of influence" could also harm Russia. Recent history shows that if Russia raises the price of gas too high, or attempts to monopolize the direction of Central Asia gas too much, it can lose markets. As a result of raising gas prices for Azerbaijan and Georgia, Russia lost 100 percent of Azerbaijan's market, and 50 percent of Georgia's, in part due to Shah Deniz coming online and the inauguration of the Baku–Tbilisi–Erzurum pipeline. Further, the support for alternative pipeline routes to Russia is growing, with firmer commitments for supply coming from Azerbaijan, Kazakhstan, and maybe even Turkmenistan to Europe through the planned Trans-Caspian pipelines. Finally, Russia's decade-long game of "circles of influence" with Asian customers in China and Japan has not made either potential recipient secure with the as-yet unrealized supply.

Nevertheless, the EU remains vulnerable as a result of its inability to consolidate a common policy toward Russia. The EU, as it currently stands, is ill-equipped and lacks a policy mandate for speaking with a single voice on security issues. Rather, the general trend is that individual countries are attempting to recapture key competencies from the EU.[62] Some argue that there has been no actual energy crisis yet in Europe, but only the manufactured perception of such a crisis, and that the "Russia is unreliable" theme only appeared after Britain, experiencing a particularly difficult time in relations with Russia, became a net gas importer.[63] Even if a common policy toward Russia were to be agreed, its practical implementation would meet with various agendas among European countries according to where they are located on the resource–transit–recipient route.[64] Thus, Europe has, for the most part, been reacting rather than taking an active role in reshaping its domestic capabilities and developing a coherent strategy that would link the domestic and external strands. As a result, some European and Russian companies are moving forward in designing new projects, but with heavy interference from political actors, which makes it impossible to assess the risks and costs of various options responsibly.[65]

It is unclear at the moment whether the relationship will move more toward partnership or conflict. Instead, it is likely to be characterized by a combination of the two. Obviously, cooperation is most desirable, but unlikely in the near term, as Europe is beginning to promote policies that foster diversification from Russian gas and move to alternative sources, as well as to limit monopolies, such as Gazprom, from freely investing in its internal market. Nevertheless, real partnership is taking place among European and Russian energy companies in Europe and in Northern Africa. Therefore, cooperation in the private sector will continue, even as the public sector adopts a more confrontational rhetoric. This difference arises because energy relations will remain embroiled in broader political issues between Europe and Russia, such as military security arrangements in the region. Moreover, the relationship could oscillate between cooperation and conflict depending on how several unknowns unfold. These factors include the matter of whether Russia will allow independents in the gas industry to compete with Gazprom and whether such competition enhances production levels, how and when Russia will develop the Yamal Peninsula for gas supply, and how domestic demand in Russia will develop and how this will affect supply to Europe.[66] Thus, cooperation and conflict are likely to coexist in parallel for the foreseeable future.

Conclusion

Historically, the 30-year Soviet movement downstream into the Central European market (from the 1960s to the 1990s) is being repeated in Russia's expansion downstream into the Western European market over the last decade. As during the Soviet era, Russia has remained a reliable supplier to Western Europe. However, since 1990, Russia has begun to exercise its threat of supply stoppages to gain leverage in business and political processes in the Central and Eastern European markets. Likewise, as during the Soviet era, the tactics employed by Russia to divide different states in their energy relations with it has actually had the opposite effect. Then, threats to Europe over the East–West pipeline brought the US and Europe closer together in expanding exploration in the North Sea. Now, Russia's tactics in dealing with the transit states of Central and Eastern Europe have united the US and Europe in advancing their efforts to seek alternative resources and could eventually unite Europe in a fully integrated system that secures all states' supplies.

Up to this point, Russia has realized its actual dependency on Europe, and has shaped its policies and practices to address this fact. Russia has capitalized on Europe's internal inaction, creating the appearance that Europe, in fact, is dependent on Russia. It is true that no single European country, or even a bloc of several of the more powerful countries, will likely be able to compete with Russian state-owned companies in the near-term. Moreover, Europe's gas demand will continue to increase, along with its dependency on Russian supply. In the long term, however, Russia is confronted with several difficult choices that will affect its future role in Europe's energy sector. These include establishing a policy of compromise in several correlated developments: re-nationalization versus the productivity of its energy sector; market pricing of gas versus variegated pricing; increasing global demand versus limited exploration investments; and encouraging the construction of more pipelines to Europe, while limiting alternative projects beyond Russian control. As these issues unfold, it appears that Russia's role in Europe is likely to be characterized both by cooperation and by conflict.

Notes

1 See Janusz Bugajski, "Energy Policies and Strategies: Russia's Threat to Europe's Energy Security," *Insight Turkey* 8, no. 1 (2006): 141–8; Svante Cornell and Niklas Nilsson, eds., *Europe's Energy Security: Gazprom's Dominance and Caspian Supply Alternatives* (Washington, DC and Stockholm: Central Asia Caucasus Institute & Silk Road Studies, 2008), www.isdp.eu/files/publications/scornell/sc08europesenergy.pdf (accessed 3 August 2008); Marshall L. Goldman, "The Dog Barks but the Caravan Moves On," *The Journal of Post-Soviet Democratization* 15, issue 4 (2007): 360–70; Frank Umbach, "Europe's Next Cold War. The European Union Needs a Plan to Secure Its Energy Security," *Internationale Politik* (Transatlantic Edition), 20 July 2006, 64–71, www.dgap.org/publikationen/view/49c634c0180611dba3d6c352aa4ae fb0efb0.html (accessed 3 August 2008).
2 These suggestions have been made by the Polish and US governments in 2006 and 2007, respectively.
3 President Putin's Candidate of Sciences dissertation at the St. Petersburg Mining Institute, completed in 1997, emphasizes the role of gas in projecting Russian influence, as a means of re-entering the ranks of great powers.
4 At Kovykta, British Petroleum (BP) was forced to sell its 62.9 percent majority stake to Gazprom in 2007; at Sakhalin-2, Royal Dutch Shell had to start paying dividends of about US$1 billion a year due to delayed production.
5 European Commission (EC), *Russian Federation: Country Strategy Paper 2007–2013* (Brussels: EC, 2007), 33, http://ec.europa.eu/external_relations/russia/docs/ 2007–2013_en.pdf (accessed 3 August 2008).
6 Ibid., 36.
7 EC, *Green Paper: A European Strategy for Sustainable, Competitive and Secure Energy* (Brussels: EC, 8 March 2006), 317, http://ec.europa.eu/energy/green-paper-energy/doc/2006_03_08_gp_document_en.pdf (accessed 3 August 2007).
8 Agata Loskot-Strachota and Katarzyna Pelczynska-Nalecz, *Gazprom's Expansion in the EU – Co-operation or Domination?* (Warsaw: Centre for Eastern Studies, April 2008), www.osw.waw.pl/files/GP_EU_en.pdf (accessed 3 August 2008).
9 Robert E. Ebel, *Communist Trade in Oil and Gas: An Evaluation of the Future Export Capability of the Soviet Bloc* (New York: Praeger Publications, 1970).
10 For a history of the USSR's gas exports to Europe, see www.gazpromexport.ru/ history/?pkey1=00004 (accessed 2 September 2008).
11 Thane Gustafson, *Crisis Amid Plenty: The Politics of Soviet Energy Under Brezhnev and Gorbachev* (Princeton: Princeton University Press, 1989), 263f.
12 Daniel Yergin, *The Prize: The Epic Quest for Oil, Money and Power* (London: Simon & Schuster, 1991), 742f.
13 Thane Gustafson, "Energy and the Soviet Bloc," *International Security* 6, no. 3 (1981–2): 65–89.
14 Gustafson, *Crisis Amid Plenty*.
15 Yergin, *The Prize*.
16 Yegor Gaidar, *Collapse of an Empire* (Washington, DC: Brookings, 2007), 107.
17 International Energy Agency 2007 database. Requested from: www.iea.org/Textbase/ stats/index.asp (sent by e-mail, 12 March 2008). The following states were Russia's

gas customers from 1990–2000: Austria, Czech Republic, Finland, France, Germany, Greece, Hungary, Italy, Poland, Slovak Republic, Switzerland, Turkey, Bulgaria, Romania, Croatia, Latvia, and Lithuania. The following were Russia's oil customers 1990–2000: Austria, Czech Republic, Finland, France, Germany, Greece, Hungary, Italy Poland, Turkey, Bulgaria, and Lithuania.

18 Keith C. Smith, *Security Implications of Russian Energy Policies*, CEPS Policy Brief, no. 90 (Brussels, Centre for European Policy Studies, January 2006), http://shop.ceps.eu/downfree.php?item_id=1293 (accessed 11 March 2008).
19 Goldman, "The Dog Barks but the Caravan Moves On," p. 362.
20 *City Paper: The Baltic States*, weekly archives, www.balticsww.com/wkcrier/0201_0215_99.htm (accessed 11 March 2008).
21 Ustina Markus, "Energy: Ukraine and Belarus Seek Help Abroad," *Transitions Online*, 3 May 1996, www.tol.cz/look/Transition/article.tpl?IdLanguage=1&IdPublication=8&NrIssue=33&NrSection=1&NrArticle=2533 (accessed 3 August 2008).
22 Marcin Kaczmarski, "The Influence of Russian Federation on Energy Security in Europe", in *The Future of European Energy Security*, ed. Leszek Jesien (Krakow: Tischner European University, 2006), 155–64.
23 *The Partnership and Cooperation Agreement* (PCA, 1997) and the *Protocol to the PCA* of 27 April 2004 are available at: www.delrus.ec.europa.eu/en/p_243.htm (accessed 23 February 2008).
24 EC, *Green Paper Towards a European Strategy for the Security of Energy Supply*, COM(2000) 769 final (Brussels: EC, November 2000); EC, *European Energy and Transport Trends to 2030* (Brussels: EC, January 2003); Ministry of Industry and Energy (Minpromenergo), *Energeticheskaia strategiia Rossii na period do 2020 goda*, approved as decree no. 1234-r by the Russian government on 28 August 2003, www.minprom.gov.ru/docs/strateg/1/ (accessed 13 December 2007).
25 Joint Statement by the EU and Russia, 3 October 2001, http://ec.europa.eu/external_relations/russia/summit_10_01/dc_en.htm (accessed 1 March 2008).
26 Susan Handke and Jacques J. de Jong, *Energy as a Bond: Relations with Russia in the European and Dutch Context* (The Hague: Clingendael International Energy Programme, Netherlands Institute of International Relations, September 2007), 45.
27 Sunam S. Haghighi, *Energy Security: The External Legal Relations of the European Union with Major Oil- and Gas-Supplying Countries* (Oxford: Hart Publishing, 2007), 345.
28 Tatyana Romanova, "Energy Partnership – A Dialog in Different Language," *Russia in Global Affairs*, no. 1 (January–March 2007), http://eng.globalaffairs.ru/numbers/10/1085.htm (accessed 26 January 2008); Valery Yazev, "I am Against the Ratification of the Energy Treaty," *Kommersant*, 15 November 2006, www.kommersant.ru/application.html?DocID=720405&IssueId=36111 (accessed 2 December 2007).
29 "Energy Sector Openness Must be a Reciprocal Arrangement," *RIA Novosti*, 25 May 2006, http://en.rian.ru/russia/20060525/48621904.html (accessed 27 January 2008).
30 Romanova, "Energy Partnership – A Dialog in Different Language."
31 Energy Information Administration (EIA), *Russia Country Analysis Brief: Oil Exports* (Washington, DC: Department of Energy, Energy Information Administration, May 2008), www.eia.doe.gov/emeu/cabs/Russia/Oil_exports.html (accessed 2 September 2008).
32 The Institute for Energy Strategy in Moscow has released a Conception of Russian Energy Strategy to 2030, supposedly requested by factions within the government. However, its status of official approval is unknown (on the draft concept until 2030, see also Philip Hanson's chapter in this book).
33 John Gault, "Energy Security: What Role for the EU?," presentation at the 22nd International Training Course in Security Policy, Geneva Centre for Security Policy, Geneva, 23 January 2008.

34 The project also became embroiled in a conflict between the Russian government and TNK-BP, a joint British–Russian company. The Russian government threatened to revoke the license for the Kovykta consortium's (RUSIA-Petroleum) alleged failure to fulfill production quotas by the deadlines. Eventually, TNK-BP sold its share in RUSIA-Petroleum to Gazprom in June 2007.
35 Total Central Asian gas deposits are estimated to be as much as 22 tcm, comprising 12 percent of world reserves. Turkmen and Uzbek gas combined allow Russia to supply its domestic market with gas at $100/kcm, selling Western Siberian gas to Europe at $230–$250.
36 Initially named GUEU (Georgia–Ukraine–European Union), White Stream envisages a seabed pipeline from Georgia to Crimea, with options to continue toward EU territory either through Ukraine's gas transit system or, alternatively, from Crimea to Romania's Black Sea coast, entering EU territory there. At present, however, GUEU White Stream project developers are also envisaging a direct route from Georgia to Romania on the seabed.
37 The South Stream pipeline would run from Russia's Black Sea coast on the seabed to Bulgaria and from there to Italy. Two options are under consideration for the Bulgaria–Italy route: through Greece and the Adriatic seabed to southern Italy and/or through Romania, Hungary, and Slovenia to northern Italy. In either case, Bulgaria would become the linchpin country for this project, with a planned volume of 30 bcm annually.
38 The Nabucco pipeline is planned to originate in eastern Turkey and run for 3,300 km via Bulgaria, Romania, and Hungary to Austria, with a projected annual capacity of 30–35 bcm of gas. The consortium includes Turkey's pipeline company Botas, Bulgaria's pipeline operator Bulgargaz, Romania's Romgaz, Hungary's MOL, and Austria's OMV as project leader.
39 For a more thorough discussion, see Jeronim Perovic and Robert Orttung, "Russia's Energy Policy: Should Europe Worry?," *Russian Analytical Digest*, no. 18 (April 2007): 2–7, www.res.ethz.ch/analysis/rad/details.cfm?lng=en&id=29825 (accessed 15 October 2007).
40 See, for example, Vladimir Socor, "Kremlin Stops Gas Deliveries To Ukraine," *Eurasia Daily Monitor*, 3 January 2006 and Keith C. Smith, "Russian Energy Policy and Its Challenge to Western Policy Makers," Statement before the House Government Reform Subcommittee on Energy and Resources and the Subcommittee on National Security, Emerging Threats, and International Relations, Washington, DC, 25 June 2007, www.csis.org/media/csis/congress/ts070625smith.pdf (accessed 3 August 2008). Tensions over Ukraine grew once again in late 2007 over the alleged $1.3 billion owed to Gazprom (or RosUkrEnergo, the intermediary company) for non-payment of nine months' worth of deliveries. This announcement was made in the same month when the Orange Coalition re-established itself as a ruling coalition, controlling both the presidency and the position of prime minister. Partly to allay fears of European customers, Russia offered to establish an early-warning mechanism with the EU, so as to notify customers before a gas shutoff occurs.
41 Gault, "Energy Security: What Role for the EU?"
42 The Brookings Institution, *The Russian Federation*, The Brookings Foreign Policy Studies Energy Security Series (Washington, DC: The Brookings Institution, October 2006), www.3.brookings.edu/fp/research/energy/2006russia.pdf (accessed 23 October 2007).
43 Interview with Tatiana Mitrova, Russian Academy of Sciences, Zurich, October 2007.
44 EC, *Communication from the Commission to the European Council: External Energy Relations from Principle to Action*, COM(2006) 590 final (Brussels: EC, 12 October 2006), http://ec.europa.eu/external_relations/energy/docs/com06_590_en.pdf (accessed 28 January 2008).

45 Government of Russia, "Energy Security at the G8," http://en.g8russia.ru/press/facts/global_energy/ (accessed 24 October 2007).
46 See: The Brookings Institution, *The Russian Federation*.
47 The energy reform suggested by Europe and the reform United Energy Systems of Russia (UES) would close the door on Gazprom buying energy networks in the EU until Russia and the EU sign a cooperation agreement and Gazprom is divided into production and transportation components.
48 Gault, "Energy Security: What Role for the EU?"
49 See: EC, *Communication from the Commission to the European Council*.
50 These perceptions are gleaned from reading European Commission documents on the EU–Russia Energy Dialogue and various companies' annual reports.
51 Tatiana Mitrova, "Gazprom's Perspective on International Markets", *Russian Analytical Digest*, no. 41, (May 2008): 2–6, www.res.ethz.ch/analysis/rad/ (accessed 5 June 2008).
52 See Robert L. Larsson, *Russia's Energy Policy: Security Dimensions and Russia's Reliability as an Energy Supplier* (Stockholm: Swedish Defense Research Agency FOI, 2006); Smith, *Security Implications of Russian Energy Policies*; Ariel Cohen, *Europe's Strategic Dependence on Russian Energy*, Backgrounder, no. 2083 (Washington, DC: Heritage Foundation, 2007), www.heritage.org/Research/Europe/bg2083.cfm (accessed 10 March 2008).
53 See compilation of articles by Vladimir Socor, Jamestown Foundation Eurasia Daily Monitor, available at: www.jamestown.org/authors_details.php?author_id=105; Centre for Eastern Studies, *Gazprom in Europe: Faster Expansion in 2006* (Warsaw: Centre for Eastern Studies, February 2007), http://pdc.ceu.hu/archive/00003360/ (accessed 12 January 2008).
54 Andrew Monaghan, "Russia–EU Relations: An Emerging Energy Security Dilemma," *Pro et Contra* 10, issue 2–3 (2006), in English at www.carnegieendowment.org/publications/ index.cfm?fa=view&id=18494&prog=zru (accessed 3 March 2008).
55 See German Institute for Economic Research, "Threat of Gas and Oil Supply Shortage from Russia," summary available at: www.wieninternational.at/en/node/6594 (accessed 19 January 2008); Andreas Goldthau, "Rhetoric Versus Reality: Russian Threats to European Energy Supply," *Energy Policy* 36, no. 2 (2008): 686–92; Robert F. Price, "Energy Reform in Russia and the Implications for European Energy Security," *The Journal of Post-Soviet Democratization* 15, issue 4 (2007): 390–407.
56 World Bank, *Russian Economic Report*, no. 12 (Washington, DC: The World Bank, April 2006), http://web.worldbank.org/WBSITE/EXTERNAL/COUNTRIES/ECAEXT/RUSSIANFEDERATIONEXTN/0,,contentMDK:20888536~menuPK:2445695~pagePK:1497618~piPK:217854~theSitePK:305600,00.html (accessed 20 October 2007).
57 Iwona Wisniewska, *The Invisible Hand ... of the Kremlin Capitalism "a la Russe"* (Warsaw: Center for Eastern Studies, 2007), 54, http://pdc.ceu.hu/archive/00003066/01/the_invisible_hand.pdf (accessed 20 October 2007).
58 Vladimir Milov, "How Sustainable is Russia's Future as an Energy Superpower?," speech delivered to the Carnegie Endowment for International Peace, Washington, DC, 16 March 2006, www.carnegieendownment.org/events (accessed 19 October 2007).
59 Wisniewska, *The Invisible Hand ... of the Kremlin Capitalism "a la Russe"*, 55.
60 Simon-Erik Ollus, "Natural Resources – a Blessing or a Curse?," in *New Conditions for Growth in Russia*, BOFIT Online, no. 7, ed. Seija Lainela, Simon-Erik Ollus, Jauko Rautava, Heli Simola, Pekka Sutela and Merja Tekoniemi (Helsinki: Bank of Finland, 2007), 4–11.
61 For background, see Kirsten Westphal, "Germany and the EU–Russia Energy Dialogue," in *The EU–Russian Energy Dialogue: Europe's Future Energy Security*, ed. Pami Aalto (Aldershot: Ashgate, 2008), 93–118.
62 For background, see: Janne Halland Matlary, *Energy Policy in the European Union*

(London: Palgrave Macmillan, 1997); Aad Correlje and Coby van der Linde, "Energy Supply Security and Geopolitics: A European Perspective," *Energy Policy* 34, no. 5 (2006): 532–43; Sanam Salem Haghighi, *Energy Security: The External Legal Relations of the European Union with Major Oil and Gas Supplying Countries* (Oxford: Hart Publishing, 2007).
63 Jerome Guillet, "Don't Blame Gazprom for Europe's Energy Crunch," *Foreign Policy*, January–February 2007, www.foreignpolicy.com/story/cms.php?story_id=3696 (accessed 1 March 2008).
64 Andrew Monaghan, *Russia and the Security of Europe's Energy Supplies: Security in Diversity?*, Special Series 07/01 (Swindon: Conflict Studies Research Centre, 2007), http://se2.isn.ch/serviceengine/FileContent?serviceID=10&fileid=E01719FD-5CEE-6B5D-EF48-181E39EDFC83&lng=en (accessed 20 November 2007).
65 Roland Götz, *Russian Gas and European Energy Security*, SWP-Study RP 10 (Berlin: SWP, November 2007), www.swp-berlin.org/en/common/get_document.php?asset_id=4470 (accessed 15 October 2007).
66 "Securing the Future: A Conversation with Daniel Yergin and Thane Gustafson," CERA audiotape, 22 March 2007, www.cera.com/aspx/cda/public1/news/video/interviewList.aspx (accessed 19 January 2008).

6 Russia's role in the Eurasian energy market
Seeking control in the face of growing challenges

Julia Nanay

The Caspian is important for Russia's broader energy considerations for a number of reasons. This region contains significant oil and gas resources. Controlling the direction and volumes of exports from the states of this region is essential for Russia in order to reduce competition for its own energy exports on the international markets. Russia is particularly concerned with maintaining control over its relations with Europe: The greater Russia's control of energy flows from the Caspian, the more dependent Europe will be on it. In the oil market, Russia ideally could use the Caspian as a "swing producer." If it is able to control oil flows from the Caspian, it can calibrate the timing of all exports from the region so that if the market should need the extra oil production, the Caspian would be there to supply it, and if there were a glut in one market, Russia could switch supplies to another or reduce volumes from the south. If Russia also built the East Siberia Pacific Ocean (ESPO) pipeline, it could switch supplies among routes and markets. In the future, as Russia's own West Siberian production declines further, Caspian oil could provide the output for Transneft's pipelines.

Caspian gas is also important for Russia's domestic energy balance as well as its international energy sales. Until now, as long as the Caspian countries did not have other significant export outlets than through Russian pipelines, Russia has been in a position to buy this energy at a lower price than that at which it could be sold on world markets. However, because Turkmenistan has concluded an agreement for gas sales to China and a new pipeline is being constructed for these shipments to the east, the dynamics of the regional gas trade are undergoing an important change: Russia has agreed to work out a system in 2009 whereby the Caspian countries can receive world prices for their sales to Gazprom.[1] A complicating factor, however, is the empowerment of the Caspian countries now vis-à-vis Russia, since they are allegedly reluctant to conclude long-term contracts and will argue for European prices with contracts to be negotiated on an annual basis, defeating Gazprom's purpose in granting market pricing terms.[2] Gazprom wants to tie up this gas under long-term contracts.

Russia is the single most important buyer of gas from the region that it currently uses to supply Ukraine's domestic demand. These supplies, in turn, free up an equal volume of Russian gas for export to Europe. Russia sees Caspian gas as an important factor in its relations with Europe. As long as

Russia controls large volumes of Caspian energy flows, Europe continues to be dependent on it.

Russia is still in a very strong position vis-à-vis the individual states of the Caspian because most of the region's oil and gas pipelines pass through Russian territory. But Russia's position has been seriously challenged in recent years. In the oil sector, the most significant development is the opening of the Baku–Tbilisi–Ceyhan (BTC) pipeline in 2006. This pipeline, which was constructed with the strong backing of the US government, is the first major oil pipeline circumventing Russia. Other major developments in the oil sphere since 1991 include the opening of a relatively small-capacity oil pipeline from Kazakhstan to China, which began to be used for shipments in early 2006. Otherwise, Caspian oil flows mainly north through Russia – not only via the old Soviet transportation system, but also through a new pipeline built after 1991. The Caspian Pipeline Consortium (CPC) pipeline, which opened in 2001, is designed to transport Kazakh oil through Russian territory westwards.

The gas market is even less diversified than the oil market, with all the major Eurasian pipelines still running through Russia. Russia has also built some new transportation routes, including the Blue Stream pipeline, which was the first project to bypass Ukraine by transporting Russian gas to the Turkish market. Blue Stream connects Russia to Turkey by a pipeline under the Black Sea. So far, the only major gas pipeline circumventing Russia is the South Caucasus Pipeline (SCP), which follows the BTC oil pipeline route into Turkey and started to ship gas at the end of 2006. This pipeline is running below capacity, however, because it only transports gas from the first phase of the Shah Deniz field in Azerbaijan. Azerbaijan, Georgia, and Turkey consume the gas that is shipped through the SCP. There is also a small-capacity gas pipeline running from Turkmenistan to Iran.

Against the background of high oil prices and increased competition from Western energy companies, the Russian government and Russian energy companies have made efforts to advance Russian influence in the region, especially following President Vladimir Putin's election in 2000. These efforts include the intensification of diplomatic ties and contacts, as well as agreements to upgrade and expand gas pipelines from the Caspian and to purchase gas at much higher prices than previously.

However, the challenges to Russia's position remain significant. The West is lobbying for the construction of a gas pipeline under the Caspian Sea that would allow direct access to Turkmen and eventually also Kazakh gas. China has also emerged as a serious additional outside competitor for Caspian energy. Beijing has an agreement with Turkmenistan on the construction of a gas pipeline and has signed a production sharing agreement (PSA) for the rights to exploit a gas field in eastern Turkmenistan. There is already an oil pipeline running from Kazakhstan to China, and the Chinese are already building a gas pipeline from Turkmenistan through Uzbekistan and across southern Kazakhstan into China.

This chapter provides an overview of Russian energy policies toward the post-Soviet Caspian region, in particular by looking at Russia's approach to the three main Caspian energy-producing and exporting countries of Azerbaijan, Kazakhstan, and Turkmenistan. After a short historical overview of Russian policy changes from the early 1990s until Vladimir Putin, the chapter looks at the main challenges Russian policy is facing with regard to each of the three Caspian states. A further section then analyzes current trends of the pipeline game in the Caspian, and the final section assesses trends for the future.

Russian Caspian policies from Yeltsin to Putin

Prior to 1991, the Caspian region, with its significant oil and gas resources, was submerged in a centralized political and economic structure, with all key decisions being made in Moscow. Well before the break-up of the Soviet Union and before most observers in Europe and the US took notice, Moscow had orchestrated some of the region's most important oil and gas discoveries: Azerbaijan's Azeri-Chirag-deepwater Guneshli (ACG) oil fields and Shah Deniz gas and condensate field;[3] Kazakhstan's Tengiz oil field and Karachaganak gas and condensate field; and Turkmenistan's Dauletabad gas field. While they were either not developed at all or not fully developed, these crown jewels of the Caspian energy industry date to Soviet times.

It should come as no surprise that after the break-up of the Soviet Union, Moscow would eventually come to view with dissatisfaction the loss of these lucrative gems of its former empire. Nevertheless, during the whole of the 1990s, Russian companies, other than privately-held Lukoil, preferred to concentrate on shoring up their Russian assets. Lukoil, whose CEO Vagit Alekperov was born in Baku, was the only company that staked out important upstream positions in Azerbaijan and Kazakhstan.[4] Due to the problems Russia itself was having in regaining its own political and economic footing, it took nearly a decade for Moscow to pay more serious attention to the Caspian.[5]

Western companies, on the other hand, rushed to the Caspian in the early 1990s. While Turkmenistan remained largely sealed off from outside influence, the US and Europe became intensively engaged in Azerbaijan and Kazakhstan. The energy resources of these two countries were seen as offering a possible repeat of the success of the North Sea, where oil production has been declining. For the US, which kept a watchful eye on both Russia and Iran in the 1980s, the opening of this energy-rich area in the 1990s was a golden opportunity to win political influence and economic gain. The US goal in the Caspian has been to maintain Iran's isolation and reduce Russia's influence and role, while US and European companies increased their involvement in the Caspian's largest oil and gas fields and embarked on building private export pipelines in order to break the Russian monopoly on exports. Europe's goal in the Caspian has never been as clear-cut as that of the US because its energy ties to Russia are more pronounced. Europe was not, at the time, a strong advocate of pipelines that bypass or weaken Russia, yet it benefited from the US policy of creating multiple export routes.

During Russia's absence from the region in the 1990s, Western companies were successful in signing PSAs and joint ventures in Azerbaijan and Kazakhstan.

Between 1994 and 1998, 26 companies from 13 countries signed 15 PSAs for offshore resources in Azerbaijan, including for the ACG and Shah Deniz fields, which to this day are the only two big producing assets in that country. In contrast, Kazakhstan's oil industry was concentrated onshore, where major international oil companies signed for Tengiz and Karachaganak, which now form the backbone of Kazakhstan's oil industry. In both Azerbaijan and Kazakhstan, it was European and US companies that negotiated PSAs for the most important fields in the early 1990s.

November 1997 marked the start of a year characterized by enormous upheavals and changes in the oil industry when Saudi Arabia engineered a 10 percent increase in the production ceiling of the Organization of Petroleum Exporting Countries (OPEC). The output increase could not have been timed worse in terms of creating a glut of oil on world markets. This oversupply coincided with a financial crisis in Asia, which hit Russia in 1998 and resulted in financial and political chaos. These outside shocks had a knock-on effect on the oil industry in the Caspian, where low oil prices made it less attractive economically to develop expensive fields.[6] But the uncertainty that marked the end of the 1990s turned in Russia's favor after 2000.

President Vladimir Putin came into office in 2000 after Russia had suffered through a debt default in 1998 and at a time when the price for Russian Urals blend crude hovered around $27 per barrel. He began his presidency by trying to shore up Russia's regional relations, and in May 2000, Putin traveled to Turkmenistan accompanied by then-Gazprom head Rem Vyakhirev.[7] At the end of the 1990s, Putin had watched as the US tried to get former Turkmen President Saparmurat Niyazov to commit gas to a pipeline under the Caspian Sea and across Azerbaijan into Georgia and Turkey. He was determined to court Niyazov and to get him to keep his gas firmly committed to a northern route to Russia.

In 2001, Putin did not prevent the first private oil export pipeline, the CPC project, from opening in Russia. It linked Kazakhstan to the Black Sea port of Novorossiisk and broke Transneft's export monopoly. BP was able to complete a 50/50 joint venture with the Russian company TNK in 2003, which received Putin's blessing. The US was actively engaged in promoting a second private oil export pipeline across Russia to the northern port of Murmansk. Yet, in November 2002, Lukoil, which had refused to join the BTC pipeline consortium, seemed already to be taking its cue from Putin by selling its 10 percent stake in the BTC-linked ACG fields, saying that it would concentrate more on its Russian projects.[8]

In October 2003, Putin dramatically changed the outlook for foreign involvement in the region. He arrested Mikhail Khodorkovsky, founder of the Russian company Yukos, and halted the planned merger of Yukos with a US oil company. Talk of a private oil pipeline to Murmansk stopped, and negotiations for doubling the size of the CPC pipeline became bogged down in what has turned into years of Russian intransigence. After the US invaded Iraq in March 2003, the price of oil began rising. The price of Russian Urals oil inched upwards past $34 per barrel in 2004.

In 2004, as higher oil prices gave Russia more financial confidence, Putin began asserting greater state control over the entire Russian oil and gas industry. He also took a more hands-on approach to the Caspian countries and to oil and gas exports from this region. Russia had been unable to stop construction of the BTC oil pipeline, the private pipeline linking Azerbaijan's ACG fields with Georgia and Turkey, or of the SCP gas pipeline from Azerbaijan's offshore Shah Deniz gas and condensate field through Georgia to Erzurum (Turkey) (see Maps 6.1 and 6.2).

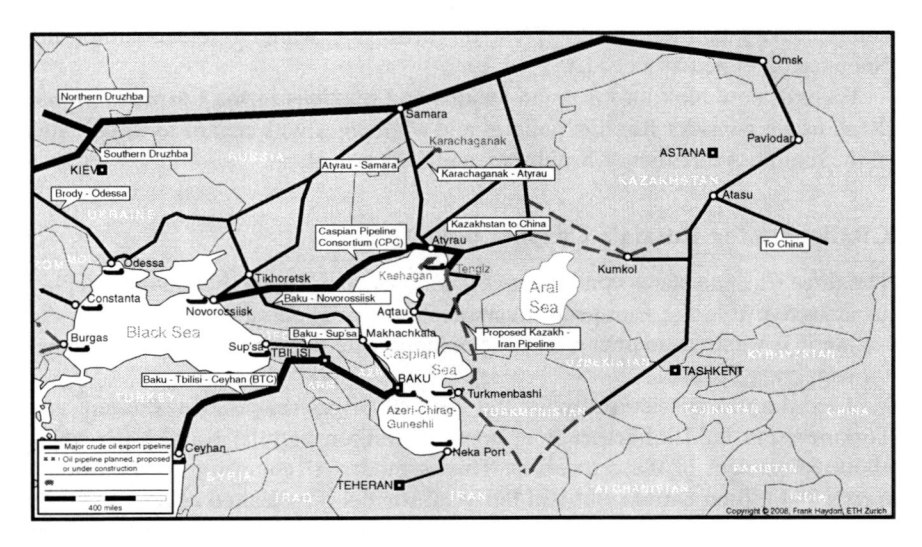

Map 6.1 Caspian oil pipelines.

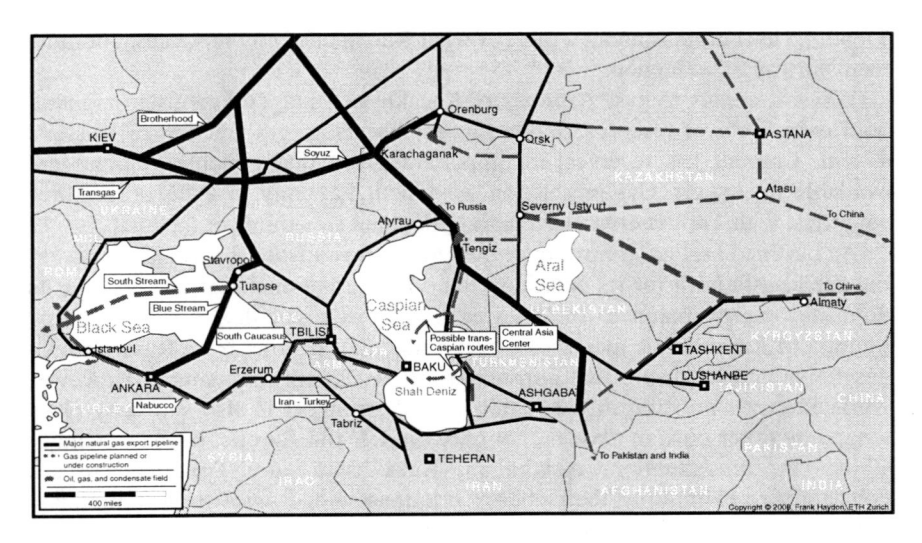

Map 6.2 Caspian gas pipelines.

It is the SCP project that has galvanized Russia into action because it threatens to take Caspian gas into Gazprom's lucrative European market. The last months of Putin's presidency in 2007 and 2008 were marked by aggressive efforts to prevent the construction of the Nabucco gas pipeline, which would bring Caspian gas from the SCP into Europe. Putin's successor, Dmitry Medvedev, who previously served as the chairman of Gazprom's Board, will continue the effort of derailing Nabucco. He is likely to pay greater attention to wooing Azerbaijan along with Turkmenistan. Both of these countries are also being heavily courted by the West for their gas, which is essential for the Nabucco pipeline to succeed.

We will now look into Russian actions and relations in the Caspian in more detail as we consider Russian policies and challenges with regard to three states in the region: Azerbaijan, Kazakhstan, and Turkmenistan.

Challenges for Russia's Caspian policy

The three Caspian states contain less oil and gas than Russia, but enough to play an attractive role for European diversification plans. Russia cannot ignore the region if it wants to maintain its near-monopolistic position as the key channel for supplying Europe.

According to BP estimates for the year 2006, Azerbaijan, Kazakhstan, and Turkmenistan hold oil reserves of some 47 billion barrels; Kazakhstan holds about 85 percent of these reserves. This is modest if compared to the Middle East's 743 billion barrels, but still fairly substantial if measured against Russia's 79 billion barrels.[9] According to PFC Energy estimates, oil production from Azerbaijan, Kazakhstan, and Turkmenistan reached 2.3 mbd in 2007, with over half of this extracted in Kazakhstan. Oil production by 2010 will be about 3 mbd.[10] This output is about a third of what Russia currently produces, but more than Norway's production.

When it comes to gas, Azerbaijan, Kazakhstan, and Turkmenistan together hold over 7 tcm of reserves. While this represents only a fraction of Russia's 47 tcm, Caspian gas reserves are important given that sizeable volumes are available for export. Gas production was about 92 bcm/y in 2006 in the three countries, with Turkmenistan accounting for about two-thirds of the total.[11]

As outlined earlier, control over the energy flows from this region is essential for Russia both for its position vis-à-vis international markets and for its domestic energy balance. In the area of gas in particular, Caspian energy imports to Russia are a means to offset a potential decline from Russia's own gas fields and to ensure that current export levels are maintained. However, while Russia's position in the region is still strong, it is also seriously challenged by other outside players, not only the US and Europe, but increasingly China. In this situation, Azerbaijan, Kazakhstan, and Turkmenistan are constantly re-calibrating their energy relations with Russia to accommodate their neighbor to the north while achieving maximum independence for themselves.

Azerbaijan

Initially, all of the Caspian leaders and the elite groups tied to these leaders were part of the Soviet generation with decades of links to Moscow. After independence, the leaders of the oil- and gas-producing countries began reordering these links, trying to shift away from Moscow. They got a taste of power and realized that control over their resources was essential for staying in power.

Of the three Caspian states under consideration, Azerbaijan was the most adept at using oil and gas to create a protective shield as it became the darling of the West. More than any other regional resource-holder, Azerbaijan understood the benefits of diversifying investors and reaching out to key Western powers that could ensure the country's political and economic survival and guarantee its independence from Russia.

During the 1990s, Russia's engagement in the South Caucasus was rather heavy-handed. Unable to provide economic incentives to attract the former Soviet republics into its orbit, Moscow used a divide-and-rule approach when it decided to back Armenia during the bloody conflict over Nagorno-Karabakh, which lasted from 1988 to 1994. Russia's assistance, which included extensive military support to Armenia and the Armenian-dominated Nagorno-Karabakh region, weakened Azerbaijan, which lost the territory of Nagorno-Karabakh and experienced an influx of hundreds of thousands of Azeri refugees fleeing the conflict zone. In addition to the Armenia–Azerbaijan lever, Russia tried to influence Georgian politics and sought to prevent the construction of pipelines from Azerbaijan across the latter's territory.

Russian interference in the southern Caucasus, however, had the unintended consequence of driving Azerbaijan and Georgia closer to the US and Europe. Certain personalities played a critical role at the time. Baku would have been less able to conduct business in the mid-1990s had it not been for the determined leadership of then-President Heidar Aliev and his skilled oil contract negotiators. During the time of Russian military assistance to Armenia, Aliev was able to attract Western companies, which were essential in helping Azerbaijan to develop its oil and gas resources and to build pipelines that bypassed Russia.

Azerbaijan's oil and gas prospects lie largely offshore in the Caspian Sea, with some of these in waters also claimed by Turkmenistan and Iran.[12] The inability to resolve water boundary disputes with these neighbors has made Azerbaijan vulnerable to the contested issues surrounding the Caspian Sea's legal status and stopped the development of potential prospects in joint waters.

Of the 15 offshore PSAs signed in the mid- to late-1990s in Azerbaijan, only two projects met with success: the BP-led oil project with the Azerbaijan International Operating Company (AIOC) and the Shah Deniz gas project. Ten PSAs were abandoned, one remains subject to Iranian claims, and two are still being worked on, but there is no production. Russia is represented through private oil company Lukoil in the Shah Deniz gas condensate field PSA and in the Yalama (D-222) PSA.

AIOC, which has oil reserves of 5.4 billion barrels, began producing oil in 1997, just three years after the September 1994 signing of its PSA for the offshore ACG fields. AIOC groups ten companies: BP (34.13 percent), Chevron (10.28 percent), State Oil Company of the Azerbaijan Republic – Socar (10 percent), Japan's Inpex (10 percent), Statoil (8.56 percent), ExxonMobil (8 percent), TPAO (6.75 percent), Devon (5.62 percent), Itochu (3.92 percent), and Amerada Hess (2.7 percent). AIOC became the second significant foreign-led consortium in the Caspian to produce oil, after TengizChevroil (known as TCO) in Kazakhstan, which started up in 1994. With AIOC producing close to 700,000 b/d by the end of 2007, Azerbaijan's total oil production topped 900,000 b/d. AIOC's output will reach 1 mbd in 2008, and the country's output level in 2009 will be close to the volumes realized in Kazakhstan.

The Shah Deniz offshore condensate and gas field PSA was signed in June 1996. Participants in the project include BP (25.5 percent), Statoil (25.5 percent), Socar (10 percent), Lukoil (10 percent), Naftiran Intertrade Company – NICO (10 percent), Total (10 percent), and Turkish Petroleum Corporation – TPAO (9 percent). Shah Deniz has 1.2 tcm of gas reserves, comparable to Karachaganak, and 1.75 billion barrels of condensates. Shah Deniz began production in 2007, with 2.7 bcm/y of gas and 15,000 b/d of condensate output. Production in 2008 should reach 8 bcm/y of gas and 30,000 b/d of condensate. During peak production under Stage-1, the field will produce annual volumes of 8.6 bcm of gas and 2 mt of condensate. Statoil is the commercial operator of the Shah Deniz field and heads the Azerbaijan Gas Supply company during Stage-1 of the field's operation. Gas from Stage-1 of the field will be sold to Turkey (6.3 bcm/y), Azerbaijan (1.5 bcm), and Georgia (up to 800 mcm). While Stage-1 gas has been fully committed, state company Socar says that no volumes have been sold yet for Stage-2.[13] Socar has said that it wants to be in charge of future sales, with Statoil's role only assured for Stage-1. One possibility that Socar has mentioned is selling gas to Gazprom for the market in neighboring Dagestan, freeing up these volumes for Gazprom sales elsewhere, including for the South Stream pipeline.

Azerbaijan's gas production could grow in the future from the development of deep gas under the ACG fields, which would be subject to a separate agreement. The existing AIOC partners would like to develop the ACG deep gas, while the Shah Deniz partners could look to future developments of deep gas layers under Shah Deniz.

Western companies – backed by their governments – are keen to get energy to market through private pipelines bypassing Russia. In fact, the construction of two major oil and gas pipelines that stretch across Azerbaijan, Georgia, and into Turkey, has enhanced Azerbaijan's role as a hub for collecting oil and gas exports from the entire Caspian region. Oil from Azerbaijan's own fields or oil that is transported by tankers across the Caspian Sea from Kazakhstan and Turkmenistan is exported from Baku via Georgia to several outlets, including the Turkish Ceyhan port (BTC pipeline) and the Georgian ports of Supsa and Batumi, while gas is currently shipped via the SCP pipeline to Erzurum for consumption along the way in Georgia and then in Turkey. The goal is eventually to export Azeri and Turkmen gas on to Europe through the Nabucco pipeline.

The construction of the BTC oil pipeline was a politically complicated and technically complex project and was achieved with enormous US government political backing and with limited US company participation. Over the five years that it took to form the consortium and finance and build the pipeline, the BTC partners – BP (30.1 percent), Socar (25 percent), Chevron (8.9 percent), Statoil (8.71 percent), TPAO (6.53 percent), Itochu (3.4 percent), Amerada Hess (2.36 percent), Eni (5 percent), Total (5 percent), ConocoPhillips (2.5 percent), and Inpex (2.5 percent) – faced numerous delays, cost overruns, and technical difficulties. The BTC became operational in July 2006. It is the only private oil pipeline in this region that bypasses both Russia and Iran. According to the US government's vision, it has also anchored at least the southern Caspian's oil exports in Turkey, moving routes away from Iran. Because it empties into a deepwater port in Ceyhan, Turkey and bypasses the Bosporus Straits, it is a highly attractive export route for Caspian oil. In 2026, ownership of the BTC will revert to Azerbaijan.

The BTC's current capacity of 1 mbd is adequate to accommodate Azerbaijan's own oil exports. AIOC will ramp up its production to 1.2 mbd by 2010 and can extend this peak output beyond 2017. Expanding BTC in increments to 1.2 mbd and 1.6 mbd is not difficult. Beyond that, expansion to 1.8 mbd and eventually to 2.2 mbd is possible, but this would be costly and might not be necessary, since AIOC's production will start to decline over the next decade. Two smaller pipelines – a 140,000 b/d route from Baku to Supsa on the Georgian coast and a 100,000 b/d pipeline from Baku to Novorossiisk, Russia – are also available, giving Azerbaijan's oil access to multiple pipeline routes.

The SCP partners are the same companies as those in the Shah Deniz consortium and include Russian company Lukoil and Iran's NICO. The SCP has a current capacity of 9 bcm/y but could be expanded to 20 bcm/y by constructing five additional pumping stations in 2012–14, when Stage-2 Shah Deniz with another 12.5 bcm/y and significant volumes of condensate is due to come onstream. In Stage-2, the SCP would be extended to Europe and could connect with the planned 3,300-km Nabucco gas pipeline (to be constructed by Austria's OMV, Hungary's MOL, Romania's Transgaz, Bulgaria's Bulgargaz, and Turkey's Botas) and would link these additional gas customers to gas from Azerbaijan and other potential sources, such as Turkmenistan.[14]

In sum, Azerbaijan's relatively independent posture vis-à-vis Russia was achieved by the construction of the BTC oil pipeline and solidified with the SCP gas pipeline. These pipelines will continue to provide Azerbaijan with enormous political and commercial leverage. Azerbaijan will end up being a smaller oil and gas producer than Kazakhstan, but will play a critical role in the region as a pipeline corridor contributing resources for the energy security of the West.

Kazakhstan

Of the 15 former Soviet republics, Kazakhstan is the second largest country after Russia. As large as Western Europe, it is likely to hold the most commercial prospects in the Caspian for the oil and gas industry. Russia's oil presence in

Kazakhstan was weak during the 1990s, although Lukoil did begin to establish a presence there as in Azerbaijan. Given the country's importance as the largest Caspian holder of oil reserves, Russia under Putin has been keeping its eyes on Kazakhstan's resources and has been mindful of Kazakhstan's oil and gas potential.

Putin visited Kazakhstan 15 times during his presidency, the most foreign visits he has made to any country except Ukraine.[15] Russian companies are involved in the coal and mining industries, with Lukoil continuing to be the dominant Russian company in oil. At the same time, Putin has directed Lukoil to pay greater attention to the Russian section of the North Caspian and indicated that he is monitoring Lukoil's activities there.[16]

Kazakhstan has proven gas reserves of 3 tcm, which is in excess of Norway's 2.89 tcm. However, this potential is far from being exploited to the fullest. Annual gas production of about 24 bcm/y is a fraction of Norway's 87 bcm/y. With 2007 production of oil and condensates of 1.3–1.4 mbd, Kazakhstan's liquids output is just about half of Norway's 2.7 mbd. It exports over 1 mbd of crude and condensates, with the majority of its exports going out through Russia.[17]

Kazakhstan's oil and condensates reserves could eventually grow in size and match Russia's 79 billion barrels. Kazakhstan could potentially also be the richest country among the post-Soviet states after Russia because, like Russia, it is blessed not only with a vast array of fossil fuel resources (oil, gas, and coal), but has also significant deposits of chrome, copper, lead, zinc, gold, bauxite, magnesium, and the list goes on. All this wealth is used to satisfy a small population base of just 15 million people.

Kazakhstan's onshore and offshore oil and gas reserve base is large, but to date, all of its production is onshore. Unlike Azerbaijan, Kazakhstan has not been seriously impacted by Caspian legal status issues. It has settled its offshore water boundary disputes with Russia, and the two countries have agreed on terms for developing joint fields, which are still in the exploration phase.

Kazakhstan's oil industry today is underpinned by just two very large onshore fields: the Tengiz field contains 6–9 billion barrels of oil reserves and upwards of 280 bcm of gas, and Karachaganak holds 2.3–6 billion barrels of condensate reserves and 1.3 tcm of gas. Offshore, the potential could be much greater, with the north Caspian's Kashagan field alone holding at least 13 billion barrels of recoverable oil reserves and large volumes of gas.

These three large fields (Tengiz, Karachaganak, and Kashagan) are all being developed with significant participation from Western energy companies, while Russia is underrepresented. Lukoil has a small share through a BP joint venture, LukArco (5 percent), in the Tengiz field. The other companies in the TengizChevroil joint venture, which was signed in September 1993, are Chevron (50 percent), ExxonMobil (25 percent), and Kazakhstan's state company KazMunaiGaz (KMG, 20 percent). Lukoil holds a 15 percent share in the Karachaganak project. The other major partners in the Karachaganak PSA, which was signed in November 1997, are BG (32.5 percent), Eni (32.5 percent), and Chevron (20 percent). There is no Russian participation in the Kashagan field.[18] Companies other than Lukoil are not represented in any significant way in Azerbaijan, Kazakhstan, or Turkmenistan.

Russia feels that it should have a greater stake in the Tengiz and Karachaganak fields, which were discovered in Soviet times. In the early to mid-1990s, there was even talk of splitting Kazakhstan up, with the Russian-populated north joining Russia. This split could possibly even have included the Tengiz and Karachaganak fields. In order to make sure that such a split would never happen, in June 1997, Kazakh President Nursultan Nazarbaev inaugurated a new capital in the north central part of the country – in a predominantly Russian city called Akmola (which means White Tomb). Nazarbaev renamed the city Astana (which means capital). This brought Kazakhstan's seat of power closer to Russia from its previous location in the southeastern city of Almaty, which is closer to China.

Russia's frustration with losing control over Kazakhstan's resources may explain its reluctance to help the country with its exports. In the 1990s, when the contracts with Western companies were signed, Russian energy companies – with the exception of Lukoil – were largely focused on production in Russia, while also lacking the financial means and technical know-how to successfully compete with Western companies in the Caspian. The only role for Russia to play was that of a spoiler. Kazakhstan's two large operating onshore fields are located in the north of Kazakhstan close to Russia's borders, and the energy produced from these fields is shipped north through Russia's pipeline system. In addition, the bulk of Kazakh gas is processed in the Orenburg plant located on Russian territory. All this meant that Russia was in a strong position to exert pressure on Kazakhstan by dictating the terms and conditions of Kazakh exports through its territory.

In fact, there have been problems through the years with oil and gas extraction in both the Tengiz and the Karachaganak fields. Lukoil's inclusion in both the Tengiz and Karachaganak projects and in the CPC pipeline was seen as a potential way to gain positive influence with the Russian government in order to obtain its cooperation for exporting Kazakh oil and gas.[19] The CPC is to date the only private oil pipeline through Russian territory. Both Tengiz crude and liquids from Karachaganak feed into CPC. Lukoil's presence, however, has not helped greatly in getting Russia to smooth the way for doubling CPC capacity to 1.34 mbd, and in fact, Lukoil has now sided with Transneft in blocking CPC expansion.[20] CPC is currently delivering over 700,000 b/d to Russia's Black Sea port of Novorossiisk, of which more than 300,000 b/d is from the Chevron-operated TCO joint venture. TCO production is set to rise to 540,000 b/d by 2009 and eventually reach 700,000 b/d or more. Kazakhstan counts on a larger CPC to accommodate an expected increase in production. Without an expanded CPC, however, other export avenues will need to be found.

Other Kazakh oil is shipped through a pipeline that dates from the Soviet era from Atyrau, Kazakhstan, to Samara in Russia and can carry about 300,000 b/d of Kazakh oil, which feeds into the Russian Druzhba pipeline system and is exported as Russian Urals Blend to Central and Eastern Europe. Russia would like to see Atyrau–Samara expanded to 500,000–600,000 b/d, and discussions over this issue may bear fruit before any decision on CPC expansion is taken. Oil can also move by rail to Ukraine and to China. It can be sent by tanker to Baku and by railway to Batumi on Georgia's Black Sea coast.

While transportation options to the west other than through Russia are still not available, some of Kazakhstan's oil is now flowing east through a pipeline to China. Oil from China's National Petroleum Cooperation (CNPC)-led onshore PetroKazakhstan Kumkol fields in the south-central part of the country has been flowing through the Chinese-backed 962-km Atasu–Alashankou pipeline since 2006. Atasu–Alashankou can accommodate up to 200,000 b/d into northwest China. Once this pipeline is extended by 2010 to feed oil from western Kazakhstan to Atasu and China, its capacity will be doubled and accommodate 400,000 b/d.

The pipeline, owned by state companies in Kazakhstan and China, is a strategic project initiated by the two countries for political and commercial goals. It is not a private pipeline like the CPC. The Atasu–Alashankou pipeline has allowed Kazakhstan to break Russia's grip on its oil exports and was meant to serve as a negotiating chip with its neighbor to the north. But due to its small size, the pipeline has not provided Kazakhstan with the leverage that would convince Moscow to move CPC expansion forward. Instead, this pipeline has marked the beginning of a more expanded commercial relationship with China that has also allowed a thaw in the political mistrust that marks the Kazakh–Chinese relationship.

In terms of gas, all pipelines still point to Russia. Kazakhstan has two different gas pipeline links to Russia: One ties Karachaganak to Orenburg, and the other, the Central Asia-Center (CAC) pipeline, carries mostly Turkmen and some Uzbek gas to Russia. Because of the CAC, Kazakhstan has a central role in getting gas from the southern part of the Caspian to Russia. Russia has an interest in making sure gas continues to flow north through the CAC. Karachaganak's gas reserves are as large as those of a number of major gas fields in West Siberia, and Putin worked assiduously to capture Karachaganak gas flows for Russia's Orenburg gas processing plant.

Thus, after long and difficult negotiations, in January 2008, most of the outstanding commercial issues between Kazakhstan's Ministry of Energy and Mineral Resources (MEMR) and Gazprom were finally settled.[21] The sour gas from Karachaganak will be shipped across the border to Orenburg, Russia, for processing under a 15-year contract. The agreement calls for increasing Karachaganak gas shipments from the current 7 bcm/y to 16 bcm/y. Expansion and upgrade of the 40-year-old CAC system will be completed by 2009. The CAC is scheduled for expansion from 45 to 80 bcm/y.

Despite a gas agreement for shipping Karachaganak gas to Orenburg for processing, Kazakhstan is planning to build a new gas processing facility on its side of the border. This new plant would allow future supplies from Karachaganak, exceeding volumes for Russia, to feed both the domestic market and eventually connect to a yet-to-be-built gas pipeline to China.

While Kazakhstan's small population does not require vastly increased supplies of oil and gas for the domestic market, greater efficiency could be achieved by connecting the oil and gas production in the west of the country by pipelines to the major population centers in the east. The current structure of the oil and gas pipeline networks, which were designed to heighten dependency on Russian,

Turkmen, and Uzbek resources in eastern Kazakhstan, prevents these efficiencies from being realized. The Soviet leadership never liked to make things simple and created highly inefficient mutual interdependencies among the former republics for oil and gas supplies and pipelines. The Kazakh government will now emphasize finding a way to get gas supplies to the new capital Astana in the north central part of the country and to southern Kazakhstan, where there are large population centers.

With increased volumes of oil and gas coming online in Kazakhstan between now and 2012, when production at the Kashagan offshore field is expected to begin, pipeline constraints for exports in the next few years could become a serious brake on growth. Despite progress in creating new export channels, Russia continues to exert unparalleled influence on the country's ability to break out of its isolated landlocked position.

Turkmenistan

Prior to the break-up of the Soviet Union, Turkmenistan's role was that of a major cotton producer. It was also a supplier of natural gas within the Soviet Union and a small oil producer. Between 1991 and 1993 cotton ceased to be the primary revenue earner and was replaced by gas. The revenues from gas created a false sense of independence and resulted in former President Saparmurat Niyazov believing that Turkmenistan was on the way to becoming an economic success story. The natural resource wealth fed into his creation of a cult of personality, which is slowly being dismantled by the country's new president, Gurbanguly Berdymukhammedov.

Turkmenistan's economic development remains largely dependent on gas even today. Through the years, Niyazov learned that gas is a difficult business, particularly for a landlocked country sitting between two of the world's largest holders of gas reserves (Russia and Iran) and next to two other potential gas powerhouses – Azerbaijan and Kazakhstan. From production of 82 bcm/y during the Soviet era, Turkmenistan's production collapsed to 32 bcm/y in 1996 and just 17 bcm/y in 1997. In March 1997, access to the Russian pipeline system – which was the only export outlet for the country's gas – was cut because of a dispute with Gazprom. The country became virtually bankrupt.

In reaction to the difficulties Niyazov encountered in his dealings with Gazprom, in February 1998, Turkmenistan became the first country among the post-Soviet republics to establish a non-Russian export route for its gas, when it began exporting gas through a new pipeline to northeast Iran. The pipeline to Iran was constructed in 1997 and was able to carry up to 14 bcm/y from Turkmenistan's western Korpedzhe oil and gas field to northeast Iran.

Russia, who believed that Iran would remain isolated due to US pressure, was taken by surprise at Turkmenistan's feat. Because of the US isolation of Iran, Russia thought that the countries of the Caspian region would have to continue their reliance on Russian-controlled export routes. Turkmenistan's Iran gas pipeline was the first to challenge this premise, with Azerbaijan's Supsa and

BTC pipelines being the second and third. After Turkmenistan's achievement, the US in 1998 was keen to divert gas exports from Iran and began promoting a pipeline under the Caspian Sea, the so called Trans-Caspian Pipeline (TCP) project, to move Turkmen (but potentially also Kazakh) gas across the Caspian to Azerbaijan and on to Georgia and Turkey.

The TCP pipeline did not materialize then, because Niyazov was not prepared to settle his offshore boundary disputes with Azerbaijan, nor to drop his own demands for financial reward in return for agreeing to this politically sensitive pipeline, which was heavily opposed by Russia. In addition, the acceleration of the development of the Shah Deniz gas field in Azerbaijan after 2000 made the need for Turkmen gas in a pipeline that would cross Azerbaijan less urgent.

Nevertheless, Turkmenistan's unexpected decision to build a pipeline to Iran as well as the interest of Western companies and governments in building a pipeline under the Caspian Sea prompted Russia to engage in a more hands-on policy toward this country. In April 2003, Russia signed a deal with Turkmenistan for long-term gas imports, under which Turkmenistan agreed to ship gas to Russia for the next 25 years.[22] During the first three years of the contract period, the payments for natural gas supplies were made by way of cash and equipment deliveries in equal portions. The method of payment in subsequent years was to be agreed upon later.[23]

While Russia thought it was in a strong bargaining position, since Turkmenistan's major export outlet was still to the north, this changed in 2004 when prices for oil (and gas) started to rise rapidly on world markets. Turkmenistan felt confident enough to start demanding higher prices for its gas deliveries to Russia and Ukraine. Turkmenistan was especially angered by Gazprom's practice of using Turkmen gas for deliveries to Ukraine while freeing Russian gas for export to Western markets, where it fetched prices that were approximately three times those paid to Turkmenistan.[24]

Gazprom agreed in April 2005 to pay Turkmenistan entirely in cash at a price of $44/kcm; a year earlier, Gazprom had paid as little as $18–22/kcm.[25] The price has risen further since. As of 1 January 2007, Gazprom raised the price for Turkmen gas from $65/kcm at the Turkmen border to $100/kcm. The new price represented a 54-percent increase, which made it bigger in both dollar and percentage terms than any price hike that Gazprom had paid any source before and further illustrated the importance of Turkmen gas to Gazprom.[26]

Also in January 2007, Gazprom agreed to quadruple its imports of Turkmen gas from the 12 bcm it purchased in 2006 to 50 bcm,[27] directing these volumes to Ukraine through the RosUkrEnergo (RUE) Russian–Ukrainian joint venture. By supplying Ukraine, Gazprom ensured that Europe would be supplied with Russian gas through Ukraine's transit pipelines. Turkmen gas today is an important supply source for Gazprom, largely because of the need to meet Ukraine's gas import requirements. Ukraine's gas transit pipelines to Europe, in turn, are essential for meeting Europe's requirements. If Ukraine is not supplied, there is a danger that Europe's supplies will see shortfalls, as was already experienced in January 2006. This dependency on Turkmen gas for Gazprom, Ukraine, and

Europe creates a dilemma for the EU as it seeks to route Turkmen gas through a southern pipeline corridor, with talk of the revival of the TCP back on the table.

Gazprom thus contracted to get 50 bcm/y at this higher price. The price hike was so large that Turkmenistan would realize significant revenue increases and would presumably be forced to appreciate its Russian relationship. Then former president Niyazov died in December 2006 and a new president, Gurbanguly Berdymukhammedov, was elected in February 2007. Berdymukhammedov decided that $100/kcm was not enough for Turkmenistan's gas. He spent months haggling with Moscow. In return for his agreement to a new gas pipeline project, the Pri-Caspian gas pipeline, in December 2007, Moscow gave in to his demands to raise the gas price yet again. In 2008, the price reached $130/kcm for the first half of the year and $150/kcm for the second half.[28] The gas price for Ukraine increased to $179.50/kcm starting 1 January 2008. A long-term gas price/supply deal between Gazprom and Turkmenistan for the period 2009–28 was to be negotiated. Any such long-term agreement, however, was preempted by the surprise Gazprom announcement in March 2008 that it would accept paying European prices for Central Asian gas in 2009. Subsequently, Kazakhstan, Turkmenistan, and Uzbekistan said they would no longer negotiate long-term agreements, instead favoring annual contracts for their gas sales.[29]

The US and EU would like to see greater volumes of Turkmen gas moving west, especially since Berdymukhammedov has also concluded a gas supply agreement with China, which could see 30 bcm/y from fields in eastern Turkmenistan flowing to China in the next decade. China's CNPC signed the one and only foreign onshore PSA for gas in July 2007 to develop a gas field on the right bank of the Amu Darya River near the border with Uzbekistan. The gas is planned for shipment through a new 30 bcm/y pipeline that CNPC is constructing through Uzbekistan and Kazakhstan to China.[30] CNPC envisages production of 13 bcm/y, with Turkmenistan agreeing to supply an additional 17 bcm/y from other fields for the new pipeline.[31] A gas price of $145/kcm has reportedly been agreed to by CNPC for gas purchases from Turkmenistan, about the same as the price being paid by Russia.[32]

Overall, Turkmenistan still lags behind Azerbaijan and Kazakhstan in terms of attracting investment. Four foreign consortia operate onshore and offshore in western Turkmenistan, and produce close to 80,000 b/d. Major international oil companies are starting to look more seriously at investing in Turkmenistan, encouraged by the new president. Turkmenistan produces about 200,000 b/d of oil, only a fraction of which is attributed to foreign companies. Its major gas field, the Dauletabad field along the border with Iran, belongs to the government and is the source of gas exports to Russia.

Other than the Chinese, foreign investors have not been active in gas, although the associated gas from existing producers is now under discussion for monetization. While gas from offshore could satisfy supply plans for a US- and EU-backed TCP, which would then feed into the Nabucco pipeline, it is also being sought by Russia for the new Pri-Caspian pipeline that Putin has signed up for the north. It is planned to be constructed by 2010, with Russian, Kazakh, and

Turkmen participation.[33] As a result of US and EU meddling in Turkmenistan's gas business, Russia and Iran may see their interests converge in this region. Their interests could collide with those of Turkey, the US, and the EU. This collision of interests could create further obstacles for the TCP.

Pipeline politics

In the landlocked Caspian region, it is the geography and capacity of pipelines that determine energy politics and relations among countries. Until a few years ago, Russia was able to call all the shots, since all the major pipelines pointed north through Russian territory. However, 2006 and 2007 saw major changes, especially since the construction of the pipelines from Baku through Georgia to Turkey. Energy geopolitics in this region remains tense, and Russia is now trying to challenge alternative pipeline projects to prevent a further erosion of its influence in the region.

Looking back, it has been more difficult for both Kazakhstan and Turkmenistan to balance their relations with Russia because of their location on the eastern side of the Caspian, farther away from the European market, and less difficult for Azerbaijan on the western side with the possibility to link up with Turkey through Georgia. However, Azerbaijan's success in reducing its Russian dependency is also owed to the vision of its former leader Heidar Aliev, who opened up the oil and gas sector to foreign investment prior to the election of Vladimir Putin in Russia in 2000. Azerbaijan moved forward with a series of Western-backed upstream and pipeline projects before Russia began consolidating its oil and gas sector and reverting it to state ownership in 2004. By then, Azerbaijan had tied itself to the West.

Kazakhstan's Nursultan Nazarbaev proceeded with much greater caution in the years prior to 2004, when he, too, could have solidified his Western ties more completely. This careful approach is due not least to the fact that there is a sizeable Russian population in the north of Kazakhstan and many of Kazakhstan's Moscow-educated elites are closely tied to Russian interests. Rather than bringing in foreign companies to develop the Caspian offshore at the same speed as Azerbaijan had done in the 1990s, Nazarbaev was satisfied to allow existing large onshore consortia (Tengiz and Karachaganak) to dominate the scene and, in the offshore sector, largely depended on Kashagan with a few other deals signed more recently. There has been no flurry of offshore activity as in Azerbaijan. This caution has meant that Kazakhstan's ties to the West are more tenuous, and the country's location has created a greater pull toward China than the West. In the future, a pull toward Iran, in addition to orientation toward Russia and China, is also possible.

Turkmenistan has been even more cautious in diversifying its energy relations. Under the heavy hand of the now deceased Niyazov, Turkmenistan began to nurture its close relationship with Gazprom, which proved personally lucrative for the former president. At the same time, in the 1990s, the region's first non-Russian gas export pipeline was built from an oil and gas field in western Turkmenistan to

Iran. Under its new president Berdymukhammedov, Turkmenistan is now making some tentative efforts to reach out to other foreign partners. Nevertheless, in order not to upset Russia, rather than overtly seeking to strengthen ties with the West, Turkmenistan has so far decided to strengthen its ties to China.

Looking at current developments, one cannot but note that the Caspian energy game remains extremely fluid, and Russia is active on various fronts in order to make sure it maintains control. As mentioned before, a key pipeline project that Russia seeks to prevent is the TCP. This project touches a raw nerve not only with Russia, but with Iran as well, with both Russia and Iran insisting that a settlement of the Caspian Sea legal status is required before any such pipeline projects are considered. To block progress on any undersea pipelines, Russia and Iran will also raise opposition on environmental grounds. A gas pipeline from Turkmenistan across northern Iran to Turkey has been considered as an option in the past.

Still, Russia knows that time is not on its side and has proposed alternative options that it hopes will lessen the need to construct the TCP. One such option is the expansion of the existing pipeline capacities from Central Asia (the CAC gas pipeline, running from Turkmenistan through Uzbekistan and Kazakhstan to Russia). The other is to construct a new pipeline along the Caspian Sea coast that would connect to the CAC pipeline system. In January 2008, Russia, Turkmenistan, and Kazakhstan signed an intergovernmental agreement (IGA) to build the Pri-Caspian pipeline, but many details still need to be worked out. Should Turkmenistan stick to this agreement, the West will see its hopes for additional gas from Turkmenistan dashed in the near future. All the gas Turkmenistan produces now or plans to produce in the next few years would then be committed to Russia and China. About 13 bcm/y of gas for China will come from a field China is developing in eastern Turkmenistan, but an additional 17 bcm/y will be required from other fields to make up the 30 bcm/y that Turkmenistan has promised to deliver to the Chinese. It is not clear whether the 17 bcm/y of additional supplies to China could eventually compete with supply sources for Russia.

Despite good commercial relations with both Russia and China, Turkmenistan has indicated that it wants to leave its options open. One indication of its desire to establish closer relations with the West is Berdymukhammedov's lack of complete commitment to the Pri-Caspian gas pipeline. Until agreement is reached on the final details of this pipeline, Turkmenistan has room to maneuver. In addition, on 1 January 2008, Turkmenistan unexpectedly shut off of its gas exports to Iran over a price dispute from a field in western Turkmenistan that is connected to Iran by a pipeline that eventually could carry 14 bcm/y, up from about 8 bcm/y now. After receiving $150/kcm from Russia for its gas and $145/kcm from China,[34] Turkmenistan wants Iran to agree to a higher price than the $85/kcm it has been paying. Turkmenistan has said it will not resume shipments until a new price is agreed. If Iran refuses to pay a higher price, Turkmenistan may try to sell this gas elsewhere, and the TCP then still remains an option.

Another question is how Russia plans to accommodate growing oil and gas production from Kazakhstan. Russia would like to prevent larger volumes of

Kazakh oil from flowing through the BTC. The only way for Russia to circumvent this would be to expand its own pipeline capacity for Kazakh oil. The Atyrau–Samara pipeline from Kazakhstan that feeds into the Transneft system currently carries about 300,000 b/d, and there has been consideration of a doubling of its capacity. Russia could also agree to an expansion of the CPC pipeline, but it continues to block all activity on this. Russia may try to delay Kazakhstan's ability to move oil to export markets, but now that Kazakhstan has a China option, it could decide to move more exports in an eastern direction in the future. If Russia continues to block CPC expansion, Kazakhstan will look for alternative routes to export its oil. The CPC pipeline is not in Russia's interest because it is not part of the Transneft system and thus undermines Russia's ability to control oil flows from the region. As of now, Russia's actions in the Caspian indicate that it is more interested in first securing the necessary export routes through its own territory in order to accommodate its own available oil supplies, and then securing control of all other oil regional transport routes.

From Kazakhstan's point of view, it will be very challenging to calibrate the timing of all of the elements for increasing its oil exports in the western direction – beginning with production volumes in Kazakhstan, pipeline capacity of the CPC and other Russia-oriented pipelines, new pipeline infrastructure in Kazakhstan, new port infrastructure in Kazakhstan and Azerbaijan, new-build tanker availability for cross-Caspian trade, and Azerbaijan's pipeline capacity availability. Not only are there many variables in this equation, but the costs of realizing the various parts will be high. While Kazakhstan's government talks about production rising to 3 mbd by 2020, this can only happen if export solutions are in place.

As far as gas is concerned, Kazakhstan's major gas producer is the Karachaganak field, with traditional links to the Orenburg gas processing plant in Russia, where the majority of its gas production is committed to flow over the next years. If Karachaganak succeeds in significantly increasing its gas output beyond what is committed to Orenburg, however, China – and not the West – is likely to be the potential market, with some volumes also sold domestically, particularly as Kazakhstan seeks to launch into petrochemicals. For the near future, however, the Karachaganak field's most important outlet will remain with Russia.

The one country in the Caspian that has largely escaped Russian control is Azerbaijan. But it remains part of the larger geopolitical energy game in the region. The decision to expand the BTC, for example, remains dependent on whether or not Kazakhstan decides to send increasing volumes of oil westwards and in what timeframe. In the gas sector, Azerbaijan is important as an alternative supplier to Europe, but Azeri gas will not be enough to fill the planned Nabucco pipeline. Nabucco will cost upwards of €5 billion and have a capacity of 31 bcm/y. This implies that more than just Azerbaijan's available 10–12 bcm/y will be required. Other gas supply options for Nabucco that are under consideration include gas from Turkmenistan and Iran. While Europe cannot count on Iranian gas as long as the situation around Iran remains tense, Turkmen gas will not be available either as long as there is no means of transporting it via a pipeline under the Caspian Sea.

At the same time, Russia and Gazprom have been actively undermining Europe's attempts to construct the Nabucco pipeline, proposing an alternative project – the South Stream gas pipeline that will link Russia under the Black Sea to Bulgaria. South Stream, which is planned for construction by Gazprom and Italy's Eni, will cost more than €10 billion, and will have a similar capacity to Nabucco and target many of the same markets.[35] Bulgaria, Hungary, and Serbia have agreed to join the South Stream project, further undermining Nabucco. In order to make Nabucco even less viable, Russia has been actively trying to convince Azerbaijan to sell Shah Deniz gas to Gazprom instead of Nabucco, with no success so far. However, newly elected Russian President Dmitry Medvedev may put more emphasis on relations with Azerbaijan and may try to find ways to make it worthwhile for the Azeris to sell their gas to Gazprom.

Russia is also promoting an oil pipeline to bypass the Bosporus. Russia has moved quickly to finalize the necessary agreements for the construction of a 700,000 b/d, 280-km oil pipeline from Bulgaria's Black Sea port of Burgas to the Greek Aegean Sea port of Alexandroupolis. Russia, Greece, and Bulgaria signed an IGA in April 2007 for Russia to hold 51 percent of the project that will involve state companies Transneft, Rosneft, and Gazpromneft, with Greece getting 24.5 percent (23.5 percent of this through a joint venture between Hellenic Petroleum and Thraki, and 1 percent for the Greek government), and Bulgaria's Bulgargaz and Technoexportstroy taking the remaining 24.5 percent stake.[36] In December 2007, an international project company was created, to be headquartered in Amsterdam. This step was formalized through a signing ceremony in Sofia, Bulgaria, attended by both current Transneft head Nikolai Tokarev and Rosneft President Sergei Bogdanchikov.[37] In January 2008, Putin visited Sofia, along with Medvedev, to seal the deal and finalize the formation of the international project company, which is now undertaking a business plan.[38]

These two new pipeline projects, in addition to the already existing Blue Stream gas pipeline across the Black Sea, which was completed in 2002 and opened in 2003, represent key elements of Russia's Caspian energy politics and are evidence of a coordinated attempt to remain a key player in this region and the hub for transporting energy to Europe. If the new projects are realized, they will seriously jeopardize EU efforts to diversify energy imports and establish direct links to the Central Asian energy producers. Such Russian successes will also put an end to Turkey's ambitions to become the key hub for transporting Caspian energy westwards.

Conclusions

The years 2008–12 will determine what access to Caspian resources the West can expect and what volumes might be available to move in a western direction. By 2011–12, Kazakhstan's Kashagan oil field will start production, and the third-phase expansion of the Karachaganak gas condensate field will be completed. Each of these projects will start to yield larger quantities of oil and gas searching for markets. How much of this new production will move north, east, or west remains to be determined. By 2011–12, important decisions will have been implemented for numerous pipeline routes. The key decisions affect CPC expansion and possible BTC expansion. These two oil pipelines are considered pivotal today for Western-dominated consortia to be able to access Western markets. But by then, an extension of the Kazakhstan–China pipeline to run from western Kazakhstan to the east will also have been built, and a new gas pipeline from Turkmenistan across Kazakhstan will be in place. In addition, there will be clarification as to the possibility of linking the SCP to the US- and EU-supported Nabucco gas pipeline to Europe. How much progress is achieved in many of these projects depends on Russia.

Russia is now calling the shots on the CPC, the original framework agreement which expired in September 2008. Transneft's influence in the day-to-day functioning of this project is already growing. The SCP pipeline aims to gain access to gas from Turkmenistan for Europe, but Russia is seeking to capture additional Turkmen gas in a new pipeline project to the north, raising questions as to how much will be available to go west. The BTC's expansion will be complicated by difficult negotiations with Azerbaijan, Georgia, and Turkey – but most important will be the ability of producers in Kazakhstan to get significant volumes of their oil across the Caspian to the BTC. This ability could be impeded by Kazakhstan's cautious approach toward allowing any project to be realized that could potentially upset Russia. Turkmenistan may be in the same boat when it comes to shipping gas under the Caspian to Azerbaijan – it may decide to exercise caution because of Russia's reaction; or, if Gazprom keeps increasing its purchase price, Turkmenistan may just decide to keep shipping its gas to the north.

Both Kazakhstan and Turkmenistan may see the creation of export routes to China as an alternative that is less politically threatening for Russia than options to the West. This may be more the case for gas than oil, since Gazprom depends so heavily on European markets for its sales and revenues. For gas, anything that threatens Gazprom's European lifeline might be considered too politically risky for Kazakhstan and Turkmenistan. For oil, Kazakhstan could eventually find that due to its geographic location, its natural markets are in Russia, China, and Iran. Some oil will also get across the Caspian, but the uncertainty is over just how much. By 2011–12, there will be greater clarity concerning Kazakhstan's intentions for creating the necessary infrastructure for Kazakh oil to reach the BTC.

Notes

1 "Russia Makes Financial Gamble to Retain Control of Central Asian Energy Exports," *Eurasianet*, 14 March 2008.
2 "Kazakhstan, Uzbekistan, and Turkmenistan Do Not Wish to Have Long-Term Contracts With Gazprom," *Vremia Novostei*, 19 March 2008.
3 Shah Deniz was a known field in 1992 when BP/Statoil started negotiations. In Soviet times, the field's high pressure prevented its development. What made it attractive to BP/Statoil was the prospect of oil, associated with the gas. In 1999, Shah Deniz was confirmed to be a large gas and condensate field.

4 Lukoil is involved in several key projects in Kazakhstan, including the Tengiz oil field, the Karachaganak condensate and gas field, and the CPC pipeline. In Azerbaijan, it is engaged in the Shah Deniz gas and condensate field. Russia is counting on production from Lukoil's offshore fields in the Russian section of the North Caspian to provide gas for the new South Stream pipeline. Just prior to traveling to Bulgaria in January 2008 to sign an intergovernmental agreement between Russia and Bulgaria for the South Stream gas pipeline, Putin met with Alekperov to discuss progress at the Korchagin and the Filanovskoye offshore fields. Alekperov told Putin that 12 bcm/y could be produced from these two Russian offshore Caspian fields. "South Stream Starts to Take Shape," *FSU Argus*, 25 January 2008.

5 "The Future of the Caspian Basin," talk by Julia Nanay at Harvard University's Kennedy School, 12 January 2001, before general officers of the US and Russian militaries:

> Now that Russian oil and gas companies feel secure in their home base, more of them are spreading their activities to Central Asia: Gazprom/Itera, Tyumen/Access Industries, Yukos, and Rosneft. Additionally, over the last year, Russian President Putin has zealously courted the leadership of the oil and gas producing countries in this region to win back their allegiance to Moscow. President Putin's diplomacy in the Caspian Basin has been heavily marked by a form of 'energy diplomacy'. In courting the Central Asian and Caucasian heads of state, he generally includes the chief executives of one or more of Russia's oil and gas enterprises, urging these governments to conclude deals with them.

6 While lower oil prices benefit oil-importing nations like the US, they hurt oil-producing nations. Oil prices at levels of $10–$11 per barrel in 1998 made many developments uneconomic, such as deepwater West Africa, deepwater US Gulf of Mexico, and exploration projects in the Caspian. Had oil companies foreseen oil prices at these levels, many would not have ventured into the Caspian. In August 1998, BP announced a merger with Amoco. Suddenly, there was a focus on streamlining and cost-cutting in the oil industry. This union submerged Amoco, the major US player in Azerbaijan, into BP, creating a British realm of interest in what the US had very much considered its own sphere. In December 1998, with oil prices hovering at 25-year lows, Exxon and Mobil announced that they would merge to create what became the world's largest oil and gas company.

7 "Putin Visits Turkmenistan," *RFE/RL*, 22 May 2000.

8 "Lukoil Sells Azeri Assets to Shift Focus to Russia," *Nefte Compass*, 21 November 2002.

9 British Petroleum (BP), *Statistical Review of World Energy 2007* (London: BP, 2007).

10 PFC Energy.

11 BP, *Statistical Review of World Energy*.

12 In 1997, Turkmenistan laid claim to the AIOC's Azeri field and part of the Chirag field in a dispute with Azerbaijan that has been left unresolved, but which could resurface as talks begin on joint development of the Serdar/Kyapaz field (referred to as Serdar by Turkmenistan and Kyapaz by Azerbaijan). Also, as attempts continue to connect Turkmen offshore gas to Azerbaijan's pipeline networks, water boundary disputes between the two countries need to be solved. Iran is another player that has outstanding claims. BP's efforts to develop the Alov–Sharg–Araz field, called Alborz by Iran, were halted by an Iranian warship in July 2001, and although this is one of the more attractive offshore structures in the South Caspian, work has not been able to resume since.

13 "Russia Not Excluded from Buying Azeri Gas, but Gazprom Will Have to Join Queue," *International Oil Daily*, 18 January 2008.

14 "Nabucco: 2008 Will be an Important and Decisive Year," *FSU Argus*, 26 January 2008; "Gazprom Eyes Shah Deniz Gas," *FSU Argus*, 18 January 2008.
15 "Globe Trotting Putin Landed in 64 Countries," *Moscow Times*, 22 January 2008.
16 "Lukoil Head Briefs Putin on Caspian Offshore Project," *Interfax*, 24 January 2008.
17 BP, *Statistical Review of World Energy*.
18 The Kashagan PSA was signed in November 1997, and its partnership was revised in January 2008 to accommodate an equal share for KMG alongside the largest IOCs. The new shareholding structure is Agip (16.81 percent), ExxonMobil (16.81 percent), Shell (16.81 percent), Total (16.81 percent), KMG (16.81 percent), ConocoPhillips (8.40 percent), and Inpex (7.55 percent).
19 The US-backed 1,580-km Caspian Pipeline Consortium (CPC) system includes Chevron (15 percent), Russia (24 percent), Kazakhstan (19 percent), Oman (7 percent), LukArco (12.5 percent), Rosneft/Shell JV (7.5 percent), ExxonMobil (7.5 percent), Agip (2 percent), BG (2 percent), Kazakhstan Pipeline Ventures (KMG-BP JV, 1.75 percent), and Oryx Caspian Pipeline (now Shell, 1.75 percent).
20 "Transneft Blocks CPC Expansion," *International Oil Daily*, 10 March 2008.
21 "Kazakhstan and Russia Agree on Karachaganak Gas Supply to Orenburg," *Interfax*, 15 January 2008.
22 Igor Torbakov, "Russian–Turkmen Pacts Mark Strategic Shift for Moscow in Central Asia," *Eurasia Insight*, 15 April 2003, www.eurasianet.org/departments/insight/articles/eav041503.shtml (accessed 8 July 2008).
23 Jeronim Perovic, "Russian Energy Companies in the Caspian and Central Eurasian Region: Expanding Southward," in *Russian Business Power: The Role of Russian Business in Foreign and Security Relations*, ed. Andreas Wenger, Jeronim Perovic, and Robert Orttung (New York: Routledge, 2006), 88–113, at 101.
24 John Roberts, "What Role Can Eurasian Gas Play in Europe?" *Energy Economist* (London), issue 266 (December 2003): 7.
25 *Neue Zürcher Zeitung*, 18 April 2005.
26 Julia Nanay, "Turkmenistan Gas Talk," Heritage Foundation, Washington DC, 16 January 2007.
27 Fifty bcm/y is the volume that the Central Asia Center gas pipeline system is able to accommodate from the Turkmen border via Uzbekistan and Kazakhstan to Russia.
28 "Deals Tighten Russian Grip on Central Asia," *International Oil Daily*, 21 December 2007.
29 "Turkmenistan, Uzbekistan, Kazakhstan to Raise Gas Prices to European Level in 2009," *Interfax*, 18 March 2008.
30 "Turkmenistan Allows China to Develop Gas Field Near Uzbekistan," *Eurasianet Partner Post from BBC Monitoring*, 19 July 2007. The gas-rich territory of Bagtyyarlyk in Eastern Turkmenistan, near the Uzbek border, is where the Chinese signed a contract. It has gas reserves of 1.7 tcm and includes the Samandepe and the Altyn Asyr gas fields. "Petrochina, China National Oil and Gas Exploration and Development Corp. (CNODC) to Invest $2.2 billion in Building Gas Pipeline from Turkmenistan," *Interfax*, December 2007. PetroChina and CNODC will each hold a 50 percent stake in CNPC Exploration and Development Company Ltd, (CNPC E&D – a joint venture with its parent China National Petroleum Corporation), which will cooperate with Kazakh and Uzbek state companies in the development of the pipeline.
31 "CNPC Targets 13 bcm/y Turkmen Output," *Platts*, 24 August 2007.
32 "China's Turkmen Pipe," *WGI*, March 2008.
33 "Pri-Caspian Gas Pipeline," *Kazakhstan Energy Monthly*, January 2008. A formal agreement on the pipeline was signed in Moscow on 20 December 2007 between Russia, Kazakhstan, and Turkmenistan. It is to be built from the Belek compressor station near Turkmenbashi on the existing CAC-3 pipeline to the Aleksandrov Gai measuring station in Saratov Province, Russia. CAC-3 runs from Okarem, Turkmenistan up the coast as far as Novi Uzen, Kazakhstan, from where it runs northeast to the CAC

pipeline at Beineu. This pipeline is planned for reconstruction with the new pipeline running parallel to it. Turkmenistan will build a new 10 bcm/y pipeline to the Karabogaz gas measuring station on the Turkmen–Kazakh border. Turkmenistan will guarantee 10 bcm/y of gas for this pipeline, the capacity of which will be expanded to 20 bcm/y in Kazakhstan, so that an additional 10 bcm/y of Kazakh gas will move in this direction. The pipeline will be operational in 2010, and with additional compressor stations can be expanded in the future.

34 "China's Turkmen Pipe," *WGI*, March 2008; CNPC pays Turkmenistan $145/kcm plus $50/kcm in pipeline fees to Uzbekistan and Kazakhstan for a border price in China of $195/kcm.
35 "South Stream Starts to Take Shape," *FSU Argus*, 25 January 2008. "From Bulgaria, a line may run through Serbia to Hungary and Austria, while another spur will run from Bulgaria to Italy, crossing Greece."
36 "Burgas–Alexandroupolis Operating Company Set Up," *Platts*, 19 December 2007.
37 "Burgas–Alexandroupolis Agreement Signed On Project Company," *Interfax*, 18 December 2007.
38 "Russia and Bulgaria Signed an Agreement on Construction of South Stream Gas Pipeline and the Burgas–Alexandroupolis Oil Pipeline," *WPS*, 23 January 2008.

7 Russia's future customers
Asia and beyond

Nina Poussenkova

Until recently, Russia's primary orientation was toward the West. Historically, Europe, linked to its eastern neighbor by oil and gas pipelines, was Russia's main energy partner. During the 1990s and early 2000s, Russian oil and gas companies made sporadic efforts to diversify beyond Europe, but these efforts were one-off attempts that did not win the full support of the state, whose energy strategy was mainly focused on the European Union (EU).

Now, however, Russia's energy security is one of the top priorities for the Russian government, which is interested in developing the eastern vector of its energy policy. Since the long-productive oil and gas fields in West Siberia are beginning to decline, Russia needs to create a new petroleum province in order to remain an important energy player, and East Siberia and the Far East are obvious candidates.

Russia intends to diversify its oil and gas exports, which are now predominantly focused on Europe, by establishing a foothold in the rapidly growing Asian market and by accessing US consumers. The urgent need to strengthen Russia's national security through the revitalization of East Siberia and the Far East, including the development of their huge untapped hydrocarbon potential, is driving the imperative to "turn east." Geopolitically, Russia also needs to develop a new type of relationship with China, since there is now serious concern that Russia's east may turn into a "resource hinterland" for its rapidly growing neighbor.

Therefore, Russia's evolving eastern energy strategy will have to cope with a tangled web of commercial, economic, social, political, and geopolitical issues. There are numerous obstacles for Russia to overcome in developing these resources, so it is unlikely that its efforts will succeed in the short-term future. In fact, Russia will most likely need to work with foreign partners, since its own financial and human resources will not be sufficient to address the challenges ahead.

This chapter examines opportunities for developing Russia's east. The first section analyzes East Siberia's and the Far East's hydrocarbon potential and describes the main economic and social problems there. It then studies Moscow's new attitude toward the eastern regions and provides insight into the most important new energy actors working in East Siberia and the Far East. The second section analyzes the main economic, financial, social, political,

Map 7.1 East Siberia and the Russian Far East.

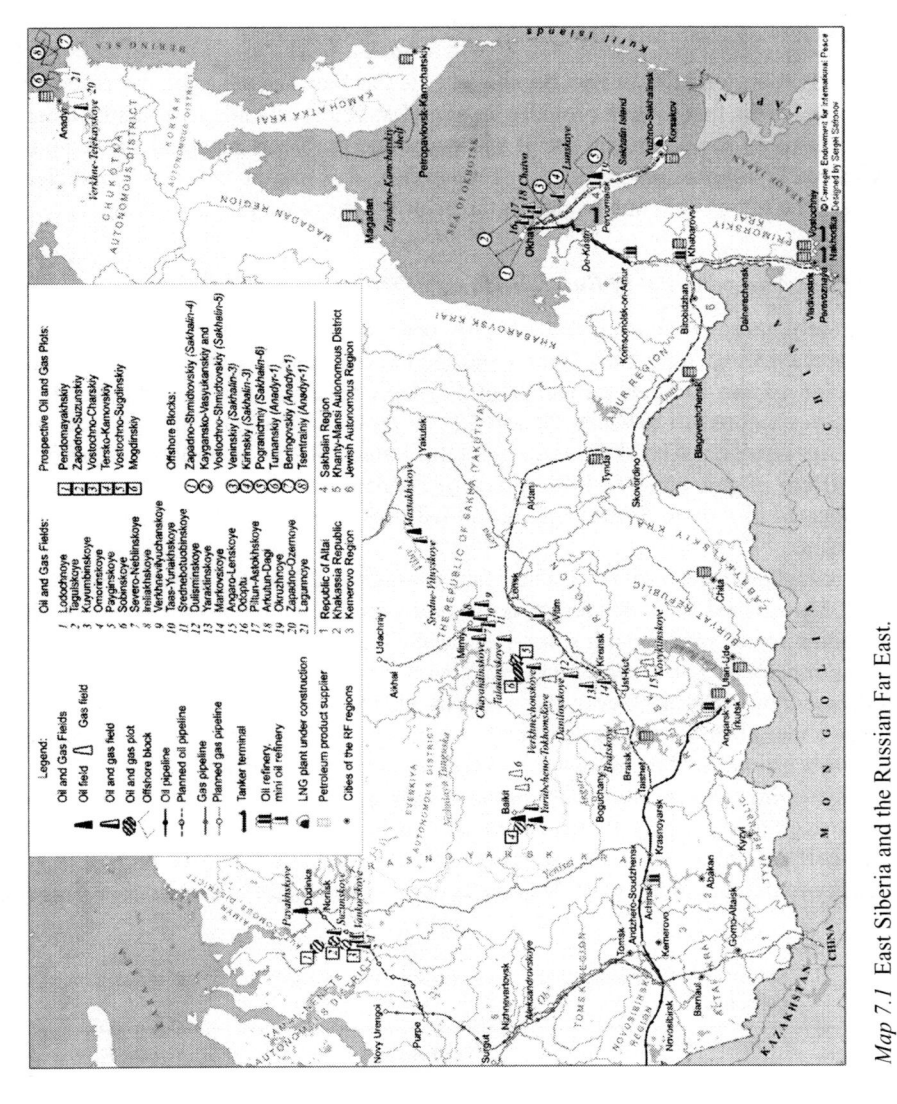

environmental, and geopolitical challenges that the country will face in developing these regions. The third section investigates the domestic and foreign implications of the new eastern vector of Russia's energy policy. Finally, the conclusion examines the prospects for Russia to implement its eastern policies.

Overview of Russia's East

Russia's energy wealth in East Siberia and the Far East has yet to be measured or exploited. This first section provides an overview of the oil and gas potential there and examines the enormous social and economic problems plaguing the region. After outlining the possibilities and obstacles, it looks at Moscow's policies toward the region and, finally, details the nature of the new players working there.

Hydrocarbon potential of East Siberia and the Far East

Currently, there are four oil and gas provinces in Russia (as listed in Table 7.1). Resource estimates for East Siberia and the Far East range widely. The Siberian Division of the Russian Academy of Sciences believes that their recoverable resources amount to between 20 and 22 billion tons of oil and 58 to 61 tcm of gas. Academician Alexei Kontorovich cites values of 15–20 billion tons of oil, 35–40 tcm of gas, and 3–4 billion tons of condensate.[1] Most of these resources are located in remote Arctic regions and will not be in demand for another 20 to 30 years.

Production level estimates also vary enormously. Russia's Energy Strategy to 2020, adopted in 2003, forecasts that oil production in the east could reach 3 million tons a year under a worst-case scenario and 80 million tons a year under an optimistic scenario, while gas production could increase to between 55 and 110 bcm/y by 2020.[2] However, these figures represent educated guesses rather than precise measures. Gazprom and the Academy of Sciences also provide radically different estimates of the maximum eastern oil and gas production (see Table 7.2).

The estimates vary so widely because only a small part of Russia's east has been explored (roughly 9 percent of the onshore territories and 6 percent of the shelf), while some Arctic seas are practically uncharted. The average drilling density in the region is 2 m of deep wells per 1 sq km, while in Russia on average

Table 7.1 Estimated distributions of total initial oil and gas reserves by region (in percent)

Region	Oil reserves	Gas reserves
West Siberia	53.5	41
East Siberia and the Far East	13.5	19
Continental shelf	12.4	32
European part of Russia	20.6	8

Source: "Waiting for the Eastern Program," *Oil and Gas Vertical*, no. 17 (2005), 35.

Table 7.2 Maximum oil and gas production levels in Eastern Siberia and the Far East

	Gas production, bcm		Oil production, million tons	
	Gazprom	Academy	Gazprom	Academy
Sakhalin	72.2	30.0	23.1	35.0
Yakutia	53.0	47.1	8.8	10.8
Irkutsk Region	46.3	53.0	9.1	13.4
Krasnoyarsk Krai	35.3	19.9	7.1	35.8
Total East Siberia and the Far East	206.8	150.0	48.1	95.0

Source: "Eastern Program: Expert Conclusion of the Siberian Division of Russian Academy of Sciences," *Oil and Gas Vertical*, no. 17 (2005), 43.

it is 23 m per 1 sq km.[3]

Since all previous hydrocarbon discoveries were made during the Soviet era before 1991, modern prospecting and exploration technologies will likely identify significantly more reserves. In particular, the discovery in 2007 of the major Angaro–Lensk gas field in Irkutsk Oblast by the Petromir company seemed to confirm these hopes.

The purely geological question of the size of the eastern resource potential has important political implications, since competing governmental agencies offer different assessments depending on their particular interests. The Ministry of Natural Resources (MNR), for example, is quite optimistic, anticipating extraction figures of 30 million tons of oil and 50 bcm of gas in the immediate future, since the available oil and gas reserves of the biggest fields can ensure these annual output levels.[4] By contrast, railroad representatives are more skeptical: they doubt that oil production in East Siberia will increase from the current 0.5 million tons to 30 million tons by 2011. This skepticism reflects a desire to continue the ministry's lucrative practice of delivering oil to China by railway rather than building a pipeline.[5]

There are currently four hydrocarbon production centers in Russia's East: Irkutsk, Krasnoyarsk (including the Taimyr and Evenk districts), Yakutsk, and Sakhalin. They all boast substantial hydrocarbon reserves and have achieved some progress in the development of their oil and gas fields. However, with the exception of the Sakhalin Island projects, where commercial petroleum production for export is under way, all other centers mainly extract hydrocarbons for local needs.

Russia must develop this region for reasons that go beyond its huge hydrocarbon potential. The problems that the region faces are a major threat to Russia's economic and political security, and they stem both from the Socialist legacy and the turbulent transition period that followed the collapse of the USSR.[6]

Problems of East Siberia and the Far East

Despite their natural resource sectors and export-oriented industries, these regions have sunk into a profound depression. The crisis of the 1990s was deeper and longer-lasting in the Far East than in the rest of Russia. Today, Russia's average national GDP is growing faster than that of the regions, and this gap is widening. Since the late 1960s, mining industries have been developing more rapidly in both East Siberia and the Far East than manufacturing sectors, and both regions have now turned into "resource colonies" for the rest of the country.

Demographic problems in the East threaten Russia's national security. In the period from 1989 to 2002, the population of the Far East declined by 16 percent, from eight million to 6.7 million people, through natural attrition and emigration, compared to a 4 percent decline for Russia as a whole. The average population density is 2.1 persons/sq km in East Siberia and 1.1 in the Far East.[7] There is an acute shortage of manpower, particularly of highly skilled workers, combined with a heavy flow of illegal immigration from neighboring countries.

Despite salaries that are higher than the national average, the living standards of the local population are lower than elsewhere because goods and services are more expensive. The huge disparity in economic development and social indicators in the various parts of the east may result in serious discontent.

Due to the growing centralization of power in Moscow, the regions in East Siberia and the Far East have been deprived of many prerogatives and much autonomy, breeding dissatisfaction with the federal government. The ability of the eastern regions to resolve their problems largely depends on the lobbying capacity of their gubernatorial administrations and their financial and industrial groups to influence Moscow. Unfortunately, Moscow's policy toward the regions is often to the detriment of the local economies, sometimes aggravating disparities among various areas.

All the regions' inherent problems worsened following 1991, as economic ties to European Russia were disrupted. The current status of East Siberia and the Far East is the main domestic threat now facing Russia, according to Dmitry Trenin of the Carnegie Moscow Center. After the disintegration of the USSR, these two regions suffered from depopulation, deindustrialization, and general degradation. Therefore, it is vital for Russia to achieve the "dual integration" of its eastern provinces by keeping them a part of Russian territory while also incorporating them into dynamically-growing Asian markets.[8] Gennady Chufrin of IMEMO fears that Russia may lose its sovereignty over these regions, and not because of international intrigues or external conflicts.[9] Therefore, the "eastern problem" is one of the most serious domestic challenges that the RF leadership has to resolve.

Moscow's eastern policy

During the 1990s, Moscow largely forgot about East Siberia and the Far East. However, the arrival of a new president caused a shift in Moscow's attitude toward its "Eastern stepchild." Vladimir Putin frequently traveled to Siberia and the Far East, trying to understand their problems, and often visited key Asian countries to gain insight into this region. During this period, Russia began to cooperate more closely with China, India, and other Asian countries, and Moscow's approach to its eastern regions changed accordingly. Putin formulated the goal of developing East Siberia and the Far East as one of the priorities for his second term in office, from 2004 to 2008. With the income generated by high oil prices, Russia now had the financial resources to achieve this goal.

In late 2006, Putin assessed the situation in the Far East as "a threat to national security" and stressed the need "to invest money in the Far East."[10] Consequently, the Ministry of Economic Development and Trade is now preparing a targeted federal program on "The Development of the Far East and Zabaikal Region up to 2013."

During Putin's second term, the Kremlin implemented several practical measures to transform these underdeveloped territories. First, the federal government merged several eastern regions into larger units: Thus, the Taimyr and Evenk autonomous okrugs were merged with Krasnoyarsk Krai, and the Ust-Orda Buriat Autonomous Okrug was included into the administrative structure of Irkutsk Oblast in 2007. Presumably, Moscow is combining the regions in order to strengthen its control over them.

Second, a major personnel reshuffle is underway, in line with the president's new prerogative of appointing governors, implemented since 2004. The new appointees either have St. Petersburg backgrounds or demonstrate unquestionable loyalty to the Kremlin. They replace men who frequently had strong local power bases and did not necessarily rely on Moscow for their authority.

Third, the Far Eastern governors, together with the relevant federal ministries, are engaging big business in revitalizing the Far East on the basis of the now fashionable public–private partnerships. This trend was likely inspired by a successful experiment in Chukotka, where magnate Roman Abramovich, after becoming governor in 2000, managed to improve the living standards of the local population radically, largely through donations from his vast personal wealth. As a result, in 2007, President Putin did not allow him to resign, viewing Abramovich as a guarantor of social stability in the region.[11]

Simultaneously, the government is trying to promote oil and gas development in Russia's east through a variety of measures. In terms of fiscal policy, the lack of appropriate tax incentives has been a serious obstacle for Russian companies that wished to work in the area. Lawmakers are considering changes to the tax code that envisage tax reductions for production from depleted fields and hard-to-recover reserves, and tax breaks for work in new fields in previously undeveloped territories, including in East Siberia and the Far East. Preferential treatment for domestic companies developing new fields off-shore, mainly in the Arctic Ocean and the Far East, are also under discussion. Majority state-owned Gazprom and Rosneft, which have divided the continental shelf among themselves, will benefit most from this fiscal innovation.[12]

The government is also making amendments to the Law on Subsurface Resources. Efforts to modernize the 1992 text have been underway since 2004.

Here, the Ministry of Natural Resources has a conflict of interest with the Federal Security Service (FSB). The ministry proposed designating oil and gas fields with booked reserves of more than 70 mt and more than 50 bcm, respectively, as "strategic," while the FSB considers this criterion to be "too mild" and wants to declare more fields as strategic, limiting foreigners' access to them.[13] Since many fields in Russia's east are strategic, the ultimate text of the law will have a large impact on the region.

The delay in approving amendments to the subsurface resource law creates significant uncertainty for foreign companies operating in Russia. However, it is now clear that the involvement of foreign majors in the development of Russian strategic deposits will be limited: They will have to be content with the role of junior partners to Russian companies. By denying international oil companies access to future auctions, Russian companies such as Gazprom and Rosneft will likely be able to pay a lower price.

Finally, the government has adopted a new pipeline strategy. Moscow has made the decision to build the East Siberia–Pacific Ocean (ESPO) pipeline to diversify Russian exports by bringing them to Asian customers. Of course, the government hopes that this plan will improve the economic situation and living standards in Russia's east (see below).

New eastern players: Gazprom and Rosneft

The desire of the Kremlin to control strategic sectors of the economy, particularly oil and gas, and to strengthen its positions in the crucial eastern region will affect the speed of progress in developing the hydrocarbon potential of East Siberia and the Far East. The government is only willing to entrust the monumental task of developing Russia's east and forging energy ties with Asia to select companies. To this end, Moscow is creating conditions to displace private actors from this territory in favor of state-owned organizations and to limit the role of foreign companies to allow greater room for domestic entities (see Figure 7.1).

Until recently, state-owned companies were poorly represented in this region, where private corporations dominated the landscape. Gazprom had almost no presence in the region, while Rosneft, though having eastern holdings, was too weak to be considered a serious player. Now Gazprom has significantly strengthened its eastern positions, and Rosneft has become the leading oil company in Russia. These two heavyweights grabbed the most important assets in the region; their success in implementing key projects and their conflicts of interests will largely determine the east's progress, relations between Russia and the Asian countries, and the future direction of the region's hydrocarbon exports.

During the 1990s, Gazprom was not interested in East Siberia and the Far East; at that time, the gas monopolist was tied up with problems elsewhere. However, Gazprom's approach changed after 2000, when the company began to promote its own vision of regional development and quickly founded its eastern empire. It has moved forward by making a number of prominent acquisitions. In 2005, it purchased Sibneft, an important oil company with several licenses in the area.

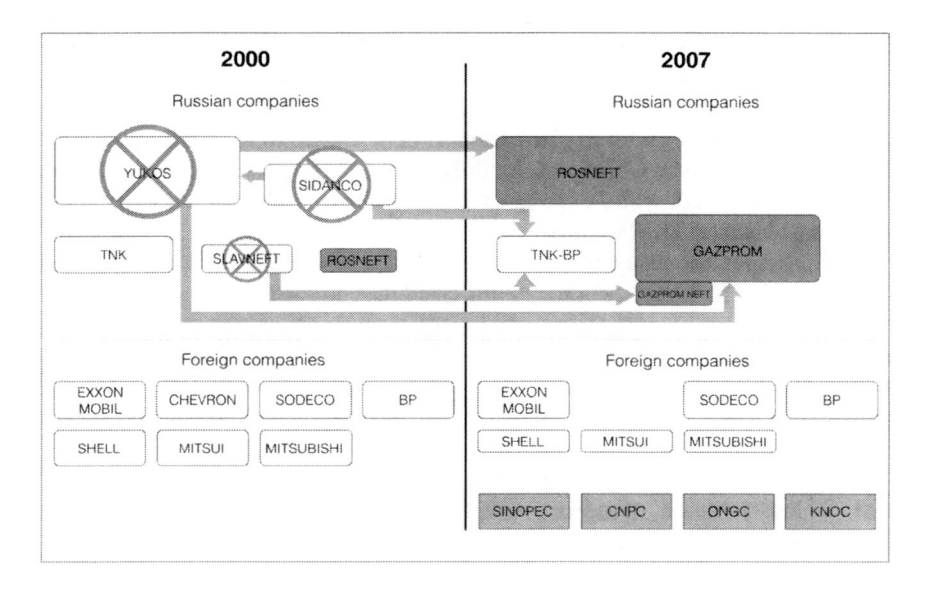

Figure 7.1 Key players in Russia's east, 2000–7.

In 2006, Gazprom made a significant step forward by joining Sakhalin-2 as the majority shareholder, and thus entering the LNG market that it had coveted for a long time. This project has total reserves of 155 mt of oil and condensate and 490 bcm of gas, and has enormous export potential. Until Gazprom joined the project, Sakhalin-2 had been the only Russian energy project developed exclusively by foreign companies.

In 2007, Gazprom gained control of the giant Kovykta gas field in Irkutsk Oblast, which boasts 2.13 tcm of gas and 108 mt of condensate. TNK-BP had hoped to develop the field on its own, but could not proceed without Gazprom's approval.

Gazprom has further ambitions to strengthen its eastern positions. It has officially declared its intention to acquire the Chayandinsk field in Yakutia with 1.24 tcm of gas reserves and blocs of Sakhalin-3 uncontested, for which changes in legislation will be required. It argued that bypassing competitive bidding would best serve state interests.[14]

Gazprom's dominance in the region has been further enhanced because in 2002, the Russian government appointed it as coordinator for implementing the state's eastern gas policy and instructed Gazprom and the Ministry of Energy to develop a program to create a unified system of gas production, transportation, and supply, taking into account the possibility of exporting gas to China and other Asian countries (dubbed the Eastern Gas Program). This work was completed only in 2007 after numerous revisions. Even the latest version of the program contained 15 different scenarios for the development of eastern hydrocarbon fields through 2030.[15] Total investments in the Eastern Gas Program to 2030 would be some $100 billion. The program envisages gas production at 27 bcm/y by 2010, and at 162 bcm/y by 2030. It is expected that domestic gas consumption in Russia's east (excluding gas chemical enterprises and technological needs) will grow from 13 bcm/y in 2010 to 32 bcm/y in 2030. Pipeline gas exports to China and South Korea might increase to between 25 and 50 bcm/y after 2020, while exports of LNG to Asian countries are expected to rise from 14 bcm in 2010 to 28 bcm in 2030.[16]

The program, the result of a five-year effort, leaves much to be desired; even the Ministry of Industry and Energy criticized it. A ministry spokesman said that "the program does not contain anything destructive or anything that does not allow for an alternative solution," and admitted that the versions of the program were selected "under conditions of equal economic inefficiency."[17] It would probably be too optimistic to expect that this document will help achieve a real breakthrough in the development of the gas industry in Russia's east.

Gazprom has further entrenched itself in the region by developing relations with China. In 2006, Gazprom and China National Petroleum Cooperation (CNPC) signed a protocol on deliveries of some 68 bcm of gas to begin in 2011, and Gazprom is now working on the Altai gas pipeline project to pump West Siberian gas to China.

Thus, through aggressive asset-grabbing, Gazprom has turned itself from a virtual player with great authority but no actual assets into a formidable force in the region. However, a key question remains: Can Gazprom provide enough gas to meet its commitments to Europe, satisfy the growing domestic demand, and supply China?

With the acquisition of most of Yukos' oil assets, Rosneft grew from a relatively minor player to become the undisputed leader of the domestic oil industry. It now aspires to equality with ExxonMobil and BP by 2010. Russia's leadership wants to have a national oil company that can match the global supermajors, and Rosneft is increasingly being positioned as such an entity.[18]

East Siberia and the Far East are the zone of Rosneft's strategic interests. It has a strong presence in the Far East: Its subsidiary Sakhalinmorneftegas is involved in the Sakhalin-1, -3, -4, and -5 projects. Sergei Bogdanchikov, Rosneft's CEO, originally headed Sakhalinmorneftegas, and this region is psychologically important to him.

In addition to Sakhalin, Rosneft established a foothold in East Siberia by acquiring the Vankor field with 250 mt of oil and 76.8 bcm of gas.[19] In 2005, Rosneft further strengthened its eastern positions by buying 25.9 percent of Verkhnechonskneftegas, the license holder for Verkhnechonsk field, from Interros. The Verkhnechonsk field is located in Irkutsk Oblast and has C1+C2 reserves of 201.6 mt of high-quality oil, 3.4 mt of condensate, and 95.5 bcm of gas.[20] In 2007, Rosneft acquired Yukos' holdings in the Yurubcheno–Tokhomsk Zone,[21] which the company needs to fill the ESPO pipeline.

Rosneft's downstream positions in the east are also strong and expanding. Initially, it owned the Komsomolsk refinery, two petroleum product distributors, and three export terminals. Then, Rosneft acquired all of Yukos' refineries in 2007, including the East Siberian Angarsk and Achinsk refineries and its fuel stations, including those located in East Siberia. Subsequently, the company fully inherited Yukos' eastern positions; yet it remains to be seen whether Rosneft will be able to utilize them as efficiently as its predecessor did. Also, Rosneft intends to build a refinery with a capacity of 20 mt/y at the final point of ESPO by 2012 – in line with Russia's declared intentions of shifting from exports of crude to products with higher added value. The refinery is expected to produce gasoline and diesel fuel under Euro-4 and Euro-5 standards, with 95 percent of output exported and 5 percent consumed in the Primorsky Krai.[22]

Rosneft now plays an important role in Russia's relations with China, South Korea, and India through the projects it is undertaking in the east. Rosneft seems to have a special relationship with China, as the Chinese banks provided $6 billion for Rosneft's Yuganskneftegas acquisition, to be repaid by crude deliveries. Chinese companies have aspired to player status in the Russian oil industry for many years, but their achievements were practically nil before the Yugansk deal, which seems to have changed their fortunes.

In 2005, Rosneft invited Sinopec to conduct and co-finance exploration of the Veninsky bloc within Sakhalin-3, allowing it to purchase a 25.5 percent stake. Then, in mid-2006, the Vostok Energy joint venture was established between Rosneft (51 percent) and CNPC (49 percent) to deal with hydrocarbon production and exploration in Russia; the joint venture has already won a license for two small fields in Irkutsk Oblast close to the ESPO route.[23] The Chinese successes may be attributed to the Socialist legacy of both countries, which makes it easier for the Chinese to understand the specifics of doing business in Russia. Another key to Chinese companies' successes in Russia is the fact that they not only try to access the Russian upstream business, but also admit Rosneft into their downstream market. A Rosneft–CNPC joint venture will be established in China to deal with refining and marketing; a 10-mt refinery will be built in Tientsin port[24] along with a network of 300 to 400 fuel stations.

Rosneft is also cooperating with other Asian countries. Rosneft is working with South Korea by allowing Korea National Oil Corporation (KNOC) to participate with a 40 percent stake in the West Kamchatka shelf exploration. India, through its Oil and Natural Gas Corporation (ONGC), is another important partner of Rosneft. Their cooperation started in 2001 on Sakhalin-1. Then, in 2007, Rosneft and ONGC signed a memorandum under which the Indians would access Russian offshore fields, in return paying for their development and admitting Rosneft to the Indian downstream business.

Through these various moves, Gazprom and Rosneft radically strengthened their positions in the Russian east, where they are aggressively implementing the state's policy of "etatisation" and "russification."

Challenges

Tapping the east's enormous hydrocarbon potential requires overcoming significant domestic and global challenges. Among the issues that need to be addressed are: a lack of strategic vision among Russia's leaders about how to proceed with developing the region; enormous financial requirements; organizational issues; environmental concerns; infrastructure challenges; ownership conflicts among state-owned and private companies; the role of foreign companies; and the establishment of new markets in Asia.

Lack of strategic vision

Developing the energy resources of East Siberia and the Far East will be more difficult for Russian leaders than developing the fields of West Siberia, with greater national, economic, political, and demographic implications. In the face of this enormously complex challenge, the government has yet to put together a comprehensive plan for the revitalization of Russia's east that would not only include the development of the oil and gas industry, but embrace all major resources and aspects of life in the region. However, as of today, the government has not yet decided on whether it is more feasible to focus on the oil and gas industries or the manufacturing sectors.

It will be particularly important not to repeat the strategic mistakes made in West Siberia. There, Soviet leaders emphasized a short-term focus on producing as much oil and gas as quickly as possible. Their programs went forward with little concern for the long-term development of the region and were extremely wasteful.

Even if it had a clear idea of what it wanted to do, the Russian government would have difficulty implementing its plans. Contemporary Russia will hardly be able to repeat the breakthrough of the 1960s and 1970s, when the USSR launched the West Siberian petroleum province in virgin territory. Today's Russian leaders do not have the Socialist command-and-control mechanisms that their Soviet counterparts had at their disposal. Moreover, Russia's current leadership, which is focused on using windfall oil revenues to meet its short-term goals, is either unwilling or unable to apply market mechanisms efficiently, either by providing appropriate incentives to domestic companies ready to work in the east or by involving foreign majors in the efforts.

Moreover, it appears that the Russian government does not have a clear idea regarding practical methods for developing the East. For example, debates continue over whether it is appropriate to use "fly-in crews," a method widely applied in West Siberia, to develop the remote fields in Russia's east. The use of these crews is probably more efficient than establishing permanent settlements in remote locations with extremely harsh climatic conditions, but the practice of bringing in rotating groups of personnel will not help resolve the crucial problem of increasing the population in the Russian east.

Financial requirements

Oil and gas exploration and production in East Siberia and the Far East will be more expensive than in other parts of the country, largely because of the harsh climatic and geological conditions in these areas. Most of the territory is covered by permafrost, which increases construction costs. In the Far East, the temperatures vary between well below freezing (as low as −70° in Oimiakon) to extremely hot conditions, making for one of the most dramatic climatic variations in the world. Additionally, the region presents drillers with complicated geological conditions. For example, the Yurubchen deposit has a complex structure with an extensive gas cap, even though its oil is light, sweet, and quickly flowing. Other fields contain oil, gas, and condensate, which means that all components must be produced simultaneously, requiring the construction of oil, gas, and condensate pipelines. The major gas fields of Krasnoyarsk Krai, Irkutsk Oblast, and Yakutia are rich in ethane, propane, butane, and helium, which are valuable to the chemical industry. So, in addition to the construction of the fields, it is necessary to establish chemical enterprises and maintain storage facilities for helium.

Due to the difficult conditions, exploration costs in the east will be much higher than in other parts of Russia. According to Academician Kontorovich, future oil exploration will cost between $2.40 and $2.60 per ton in West Siberia, while gas exploration will cost $1/kcm. However, in East Siberia and the Far East, onshore oil exploration will cost between $3.70 and $4.50 per ton, and gas extraction will cost up to $1.50/kcm. On the Far Eastern shelf, oil exploration will cost $5.60 per ton, and gas will cost around $2/kcm.[25]

Production costs will also be much higher than they are elsewhere. TNK-BP predicts that gas lifting costs will be from $28 to $35/kcm in the east, though in West Siberia, Gazprom reports costs of $3 to $4, and independent gas producers incur costs of some $2/kcm.[26]

Basic infrastructure and investment to support these operations will also be costly. Kontorovich estimates that $87bn is needed to create major oil production centers in Russia's east. To ensure crude production levels of 80 mt before 2030 in East Siberia and Yakutia, some $14.5 billion will have to be invested in exploration, and $2.8 to $3 billion on the Sakhalin shelf.[27] When expenditures for establishing the appropriate social infrastructure and general-purpose industrial facilities are factored in, the sums become truly awe-inspiring. Despite the windfall oil revenues that Russia enjoys today, domestic sources of funding will hardly be sufficient to develop this area.

The government plan is for companies to bear the financial burden of developing the eastern oil and gas industry. According to MNR, $13 to $16 billion will be needed to ensure the necessary increment of reserves by 2020. Currently, the federal budget outlays for the development of East Siberia are about $40 million/y, and by 2020 the government will have invested approximately $800 million in total. Accordingly, the companies will have to put up most of the investments.[28]

Organizational, environmental, and infrastructure challenges

Organization, environmental, and infrastructure problems present particularly thorny issues for the companies seeking to develop the East. The shortage of highly trained and educated workers presents a major organizational challenge to energy companies working in the area. Russia's east has one of the lowest population densities in the world, and people continue to leave the region. The situation with respect to specialists prepared to work in the region is particularly alarming: During the 15 years following the collapse of the Soviet Union, numerous geological and geophysical organizations and drilling teams that had worked in East Siberia and Yakutia have ceased to exist. The shortage of qualified workers became evident during the construction of ESPO's first phase, when in 2007 Transneft decided to hire about 1,500 Chinese for the project, since the contractor, Krasnodarstroitransgas, did not have enough qualified Russians available.[29]

Environmental problems are especially serious in these regions. Because of the prevailing low temperatures, fragile ecosystems have a weaker recuperative capacity. Also, under Socialism, many highly polluting industries were established there, while no attention was paid to protecting the environment. To complicate the situation further, it is nearly impossible to close down a polluting factory that provides employment for the majority of the population in a town because of the ensuing social problems. The wasteful consumption of valuable natural resources (timber, fish, fur animals), which had always characterized the Soviet approach to this "colonial" part of the country, became practically extreme in the years that followed the Soviet collapse.

These organizational and environmental issues only make it more difficult to set up the appropriate infrastructure. Poorly developed transportation links[30] and the shortage of trunk pipelines are the key obstacles to developing this region. This situation evolved into a vicious circle: Oil was not produced due to the lack of an export pipeline,[31] which failed to be constructed because oil was not produced.

ESPO is supposed to resolve this conundrum; however, this ambitious project also faces serious problems. ESPO is often compared to the Baikal–Amur Mainline (BAM) railroad, a massive construction project from the Soviet era that now mostly stands idle because there is not enough cargo to transport on it. Whether ESPO will suffer the same fate remains unclear. Already, construction has been delayed because Putin changed the route of the pipeline to move it farther away from Lake Baikal.

The most serious risk the project faces is uncertainty about the resource base. West Siberia will provide the pipeline with 30 mt/y of oil in the foreseeable future. Some 7 to 10 mt of East Siberian oil will be supplied to ESPO in 2009. Afterwards, volumes of East Siberian oil should reach 20 mt in 2010 and 40 to 45 mt by 2015. However, East Siberia's proven reserves are still relatively small, and no one knows whether they will be sufficient to supply the pipeline.

Another uncertainty is connected with ESPO's competition with the Russian Railways (RZD), a company that has always played an important role in transporting crude and petroleum products in Russia's east. It plans to increase shipping capacity on the China-bound route to 30mt/y. RZD is a formidable competitor because the railway lobby is quite powerful in Russia; besides, the Russian government wishes to revitalize BAM, which can be used to transport some of the oil.

The question of pipeline tariffs also remains open. Initially, the tariff for pumping oil through ESPO was to be $38.80/ton for the Taishet–Skovorodino section. This tariff meant that transportation costs to deliver oil from East Siberia to the Pacific Ocean were more than double the cost of using existing routes. Higher costs were to be partly offset by premium prices paid for the high-quality East Siberian oil in the Asian markets as compared to Europe, which mainly receives the lower-quality Urals blend. However, the additional 400 km added to the pipeline as the result of the rerouting will result in even higher tariffs. To make exports through ESPO profitable, the highest pumping tariff should not exceed $50/ton, in which case the payback period for the first stage of the pipeline will be ten years.[32]

Given the extended pipeline route, the project costs rose quite sharply. Originally, the entire pipeline was expected to cost $11.5 billion, with the first stage estimated at $6.65 billion. Now, the first stage alone will likely cost $11 billion. Moreover, it is difficult to forecast the cost of the second stage because of the rapidly growing price for pipes, according to Semen Vainshtok, former chief of Transneft.[33] If the decision to build ESPO were made today, the officials would have second thoughts, according to Valery Nesterov of the Troika Dialog investment bank.[34] Nevertheless, the decision was a political one and probably would have ignored considerations of commercial feasibility in any case.

Problems connected to Russia's companies

Russia's evolving business climate has a powerful influence on developments in the region, particularly with the destruction of the private Yukos company, the behavior of the state-owned natural gas monopolist Gazprom, and its battles with state-owned oil company Rosneft. Corporate ownership changes in the region caused considerable difficulties because they delayed project implementation. Thus, in 2001, Yukos planned to achieve peak production of 13 mt/y from the Yurubchen field by 2008. Investment requirements in the Yurubcheno–Tokhomsk Zone were estimated at $17 billion. Some $3 billion was to be spent on building a pipeline and a road. However, the Kremlin's decision to destroy the private company brought progress to a halt. In 2005, when the state seized Yukos' shares, oil production essentially stopped, and, as a result, financing was suspended. Construction of the oil pipeline was also shelved. Rosneft acquired the field in 2007, but was not able to start activities quickly because its numerous acquisitions had run up a debt of $26 billion (as of spring 2007),[35] spreading the company too thin to undertake major projects.

Another challenge is the attitude of Gazprom, which has its own corporate agenda that differs in some respects from national objectives. The company sometimes seems more interested in acquiring non-core assets, building export pipelines, and joining projects that are already underway than in commissioning new fields. Therefore, it is hindering the development of certain areas in the Russian East.

Thus, when Gazprom was designing the Eastern Gas Program and studying different options for developing the region, it chose the cheapest alternative with minimum export risks. However, this scenario envisaged conservation of the Chaiandinsk field in Sakha until at least 2030. Evidently, Gazprom was not eager to invest $4 billion and create the necessary infrastructure; instead, the monopolist found it easier to buy gas from Central Asia. This choice caused serious concern on the part of Sakha's leadership, which had hoped that Gazprom's program would speed up the development of the republic. Therefore, in 2005, the State Assembly of Yakutia (Il Tumen) sent an appeal to Putin and to then Prime Minister Mikhail Fradkov warning them about serious social and economic implications that could result from Gazprom's decision. The Sakha legislators asked the Russian leadership not to allow "corporate interests and motivations to prevail over the strategic interests of Russia" and to take action to develop the Chayandinsk oil, gas, and condensate field.[36] Presumably, Gazprom will ultimately gain control of the Chayandinsk field; however, it is unclear whether the company will commission it quickly and efficiently, or will just "sit on the reserves" since it wishes to have all of the country's important gas assets in its portfolio.

Rivalry between the two dominant players in Russia's East, Gazprom and Rosneft, represents another important challenge to the development of the region. In the past, Rosneft was too weak to think about competing with the almighty Gazprom. Recently, however, it has emerged as Gazprom's rival on a variety of fronts – and it is winning in many instances. After fending off plans for a merger with the gas giant, Rosneft purchased the bulk of Yukos' former assets, beating back tough competition from the gas monopolist. It also bought Udmurtneft, a TNK-BP subsidiary, with financial support from China's Sinopec, though Gazprom was also a contender.

The rivalry between Rosneft and Gazprom reflects power struggles among various Kremlin clans. Dmitry Medvedev, the former chairman of the Gazprom board, is a "civilian" with no experience in the Russian security services, while Igor Sechin, chairman of the Rosneft board, was a leader of the "siloviki," politicians with backgrounds in these agencies. In March 2008, Medvedev was elected Russian president, but the rivalry between the two companies is expected to continue. However, the positions of Rosneft might become less stable now because Medvedev, who used to be an ardent advocate of Gazprom's interests, has become truly all-powerful, and it is unclear to what extent Igor Sechin will be able to oppose him in supporting Rosneft.

In the future, the companies are expected to clash over exports of Sakhalin-1 gas. Gazprom views Sakhalin-1 gas as a resource that could make it a major player in the east and seeks to maintain its monopoly over Russia's gas exports. ExxonMobil and Rosneft, which currently control the exports from Sakhalin-1, are considering various directions for gas exports from Sakhalin-1, including China, Japan, and South Korea. Although ExxonMobil and Rosneft have the right to export Sakhalin-1 gas independently of Gazprom because the project is implemented under the terms of a production-sharing agreement (PSA), they may eventually have to work with the gas giant. Gazprom is particularly interested in eliminating the competition from ExxonMobil, since an agreement with the Sakhalin-1 shareholders permits the Chinese to lower prices in negotiations with the concern.

This competition between Gazprom and Rosneft aggravates the instability in the domestic oil and gas industry and does not contribute to the efficient development of Russia's east. However, it is better to have two dominant companies in the domestic energy sector than one; they ensure a system of checks and balances, whereas a single player would encounter no barriers in its expansion drive.

The role of the foreign majors

The policy of limiting foreign involvement in the development of Russia's strategic resources is particularly visible in the east. As noted above, Gazprom joined the Sakhalin-2 and Kovykta projects, limiting the foreign companies who had been leading these projects to a minority role. Likewise, Rosneft let BP participate in the Sakhalin-4 and Sakhalin-5 projects by financing part of the expenditures, but limiting it to a 49 percent stake.

The willingness of Russian companies to invite international oil companies (IOCs) to participate in projects depends on the volume of reserves in a given field, world oil prices, the technological complexity of the field, and the financial requirements of the project. Thus, Rosneft's view concerning potential foreign involvement in the development of the Vankor field evolved as its estimates of the field's reserves increased. In 2003, Rosneft head Sergei Bogdanchikov said that his company would need a foreign partner for Vankor (either French company Total or the Indian ONGC). A year later, however, he stated that the company would not think about engaging a partner until it had a full picture of reserves. By 2006, when the size of Vankor's reserves was clear, Bogdanchikov gave an unambiguous answer to the question about inviting a foreign partner: "We'll never make such a gift to anybody. It is one of the most promising assets in the world, and we'll develop Vankor by ourselves."[37]

However, the policy of going it alone has a serious downside. Sakhalin-1 and Sakhalin-2, the only eastern projects led by IOCs, were also the only efforts that showed serious progress. Limiting the involvement of international companies might further slow the development of the region. Today, the international majors remain the main providers of essential funding, technology, know-how, and managerial experience.

New markets

Another difficulty is related to the fact that Russia is now trying to enter a completely new energy market, the Asia-Pacific region, where the rules of the game differ from what Russia is used to in Europe. Also, Russia will have to learn to skillfully maneuver between the conflicting interests of China and Japan, two leading countries in Asia, both of whom are competing for Russian hydrocarbons.

Russia will face tough competition in Asia from other suppliers, particularly those from the Middle East. Thus, over the last decade, Saudi Aramco has embraced a strategic oil policy of "looking east." For the Saudis, the US and Europe have taken a back seat to the East. China, Japan, South Korea, and India now receive about 60 percent of Saudi crude exports, as well as the bulk of its refined petroleum products exports.[38] Additionally, several former Soviet republics are establishing a foothold in Asian oil and gas markets. Some analysts expect that by 2010, China will receive some 20 mt of oil and 30 bcm of gas per year from Kazakhstan and Turkmenistan.[39]

China is becoming an increasingly important trading partner for Russia, included in the energy sphere, and it considers Russia to be an energy supplier that could help it mitigate its dependence on Middle Eastern oil. Following a pragmatic line, China seeks oil and gas at the lowest possible price from diversified sources. If the two sides can reach an agreement, Russian crude deliveries to China could grow from 46,000 b/d in 2003 to 442,000 b/d in 2020.[40]

Russia has always had complicated relations with its southern neighbor, and the Russian public's attitudes toward China are mixed: On the one hand, people fear "the Chinese threat," particularly Chinese penetration into the Russian Far East; on the other hand, popular attitudes toward the Chinese are evolving. The Levada Center's polls show that respondents in 2006 included China in the list of Russia's top five friends – placing it in the third position – while just a year earlier, China had only ranked among the top ten.[41]

Doing business with the Chinese will require significant flexibility and skills on the part of Russian oil and gas companies. As Gazprom's negotiations indicate, the Chinese have taken a very tough position on gas pricing issues, since they assert that gas must compete with the cheap and abundant local coal[42] that accounts for some 70 percent of Chinese energy consumption.[43] The Chinese believe that Russian energy supplies are overpriced, and they are not ready to pay prices comparable to what European consumers pay for Russian gas.[44]

Also, the Chinese are put off by Russia's hesitation and delay in building pipelines to China and increasing energy exports. Russia, however, is worried that if it builds a pipeline to China, it will be at China's mercy because China will be the only possible buyer of the energy. When Russia built the Blue Stream gas pipeline to Turkey, that country was able to demand lower prices after the pipeline had been built. However, the danger for Russia is that it may delay too long and overplay its hand by overestimating its position.[45]

Japan, also eager for new energy supplies, is a long-standing rival of China in the scramble for Russian oil and gas. It made some attractive proposals when Russia was debating the relative merits of building a pipeline from East Siberia to the Pacific coast (Angarsk–Nakhodka) or directly to China (Angarsk–Daquing). Japan offered to put up $5 billion for pipeline construction and $2 billion for oil field development, while indicating that a pipeline to the Sea of Japan could handle oil exports to America, as well as Japan.[46] In Russia's thinly populated Far

East, oil cooperation with the Japanese was seen as a counterbalance to China, a partner Russians view with some misgivings.

However, the energy dialog with Japan is fraught with serious difficulties, largely stemming from the poor political relations between the two countries. Japan and Russia never signed a peace treaty at the end of World War II, and the territorial dispute over the Kurile Islands still continues.

Given the host of problems, including the lack of a strategic vision, enormous financial requirements, corporate problems, difficulties for foreign companies, and the need to open up new markets, there are major obstacles standing in the way of Russian efforts to develop East Siberia and the Far East. The enormity of the challenge naturally raises questions about the likelihood of Russian development efforts succeeding. The next section considers the potential respective implications of Russia's ability or non-ability to foster such development efforts.

Domestic and foreign implications

The ultimate fate of East Siberia and the Far East holds enormous implications for Russia and its neighbors. The problems listed in the previous section pose a significant challenge for development there. This section examines what kind of results will come about if the development does not happen and the likely implications if it does. The consequences of failure and success are starkly different.

The scale of the obstacles to be surmounted suggests that Russia will have great difficulty in developing East Siberia and the Far East. The implications resulting from failure would be extensive. Most importantly, there would be negative consequences for Russia's internal stability, because continuing economic stagnation in the east would aggravate the already serious social and demographic problems in these vast regions. Jobs would become harder to obtain, and many more residents would leave in search of better opportunities elsewhere. Without expansion into Asian markets, Russia would remain dependent on Europe as its most significant consumer and not be able to diversify its energy sales.

There would also be numerous negative consequences for Russia's neighbors. China would have to continue its search for new sources of energy. To some extent, this search would entail continuing reliance on the country's extensive coal supplies, with predictable negative environmental consequences. China would also undertake a variety of efforts to find new energy supplies in other areas, such as Africa and Latin America, perhaps putting strains on these markets. There would be even greater competition in Central Asia as Russia and China both battle for energy resources from these countries. The Central Asian countries would benefit from this situation and would be able to command higher prices for their exports.

If Russia achieves even a partial success in creating an eastern petroleum province and entering the Asian markets, it will seriously affect the global energy sector. Presumably, the era of practically exclusive energy relations between Russia and Europe would come to an end, since the construction of eastbound oil and gas pipelines and an LNG plant on the Pacific Ocean would allow Russia to target Asia and the US as new customers. This diversification of customers would also permit the Russian government and corporations to adopt a tougher negotiating position with their European counterparts. For example, Moscow would probably make stronger demands to remove barriers blocking the expansion of its companies in the West, especially the obstacles to Gazprom's entry into gas distribution and retail sales in Europe.

Serious complications for Europe could arise if the oil and gas provinces of West and East Siberia were joined together. Such a link could be made possible with the construction of ESPO, which could carry hydrocarbons from West Siberia that had been mainly exported to Europe or consumed domestically in the east. Additionally, rail transportation of oil and petroleum products to China might expand in the future. Another problem for Europe is emerging in the gas sector: Though Russia has enormous gas reserves, with stagnating domestic production, there might be insufficient production of the blue fuel to meet long-term export commitments to Europe while simultaneously satisfying growing domestic demand and servicing new consumers in Asia. Meanwhile, Europe is also trying to diversify away from Russia, partly increasing its reliance on other energy sources that do not seem to be very stable politically. Such moves add to long-term uncertainty in the energy markets.

New trends would emerge in relations between Russian and Middle Eastern oil producers competing for the same Asian markets. Iran might turn out to be a "wild card," since it might view Russia as a rival for the Chinese market, where Teheran is an important energy supplier. Thus, Iran could use China as a counterbalance not only to the US, but to Russia as well.

Japan, China, and South Korea, all seeking to diversify away from their current dependence on the Middle East, are vitally interested in Russian oil and gas because of the geographical proximity of this hydrocarbon source and the relatively greater political stability in Russia. Russia's intensified efforts in the east will probably aggravate the already bitter rivalry between China and Japan for Russian hydrocarbons. The bilateral ties that Russia favors with each of them will inevitably affect their relations with each other.

Politically, Russia's energy cooperation with China could trigger unexpected complications in the relationship between Russia, China, and the US. This rapprochement between Russia and China in the energy sphere might seem undesirable for the US, which perceives China as its main competitor for the mid-term perspective and does not want it to become stronger through energy ties with Russia.

The opening of the 9.6 mmt/y LNG plant within the Sakhalin-2 project (and plans to double LNG production capacities in the future) will have important consequences for the global LNG market. This additional major LNG source could affect existing LNG flows and contracts because Gazprom could use its power as the majority shareholder in Sakhalin-2 to influence decisions regarding potential future customers.

In the longer-term perspective, Russia plans to enter the US oil and LNG markets. In addition to expanding the diversity of Russia's customers, such a move might cause friction with long-standing hydrocarbon suppliers to the US, such as Mexico and Canada.

There are a variety of other global implications as well. Russian state companies working in the east are joining forces with national oil companies (NOCs) from China and India within the framework of the new Moscow–Delhi–Beijing axis. This process of creating NOC alliances is currently taking place around the world, and a key purpose is to counterbalance the influence of IOCs. This combination of Russian companies, with their considerable hydrocarbon reserves, and Indian and Chinese companies, with their money and hunger for energy resources, might become a formidable force, which could aggravate the already uneasy global relationship between NOCs and IOCs. Today NOCs control extensive resources, while the IOCs remain the most active market players. Probably, the only way to achieve some compromise among these opponents is to promote a constructive dialog among them and foster mutually beneficial exchanges of technology and know-how for reserves.

Another complication may arise in Russia's relations with the Central Asian states that are now entering the Asian market, where they find themselves in competition with Russia. Russia is still the main gatekeeper for supply from Central Asia, as most of this landlocked region's oil and gas pipeline infrastructure connects into the Russian system. Naturally, Moscow wants to maintain its influence over Central Asian supply patterns and benefit from them. Accordingly, oil and gas transit issues will remain at the top of the political agenda for a long time.

Along these lines, Russia's plans to divert part of its gas flows from Europe to Asia increase the significance of Turkmenistan as another "wild card" in the game. Russia intends to use Turkmenistan's gas to cover part of the potential shortage of domestic gas supplies and to meet the demands of European customers while increasing its own gas supplies to China. However, since Ashgabat has also promised gas to China, it is unclear whether Turkmen supplies are sufficient for both directions, increasing the level of uncertainty in the global gas markets.

Therefore, Russia is now searching for the most economically and politically attractive consumer for its hydrocarbons, since Russia's oil and gas will not be enough for everybody. The geopolitical choice it makes in the energy sphere will have profound implications for the global energy scene.

Conclusion

The most important overall conclusion from this analysis is that Russia is facing a number of incredibly difficult challenges in its efforts to develop East Siberia and the Far East. Taking into account all the challenges inherent in the eastern energy policy, a major breakthrough in the development of a new hydrocarbon province appears unlikely in the immediate future. It is more probable that sporadic progress will be achieved in areas that are easier to access and with projects that are easier to implement, where national objectives coincide with the corporate interests of Gazprom and Rosneft.

Nevertheless, Russia has a very strong national interest in developing the energy resources of East Siberia and the Far East. Russian leaders argue that without developing the region, existing economic, social, and demographic problems, such as high levels of unemployment and the exodus of the most skilled workers, will continue, representing a threat to Russia's national security and territorial integrity. Worries among Russian leaders help to explain the strong desire of the national leadership to use Russian oil companies to sew together Russia's broad territory into a coherent whole. It also explains why the Russian authorities have sought to reduce the role of foreign companies operating in the region to one of junior partners. Thus, given these important domestic concerns, analysts should not underestimate the degree to which Russia's plans to develop the East are driven by domestic factors.

It is also clear from this analysis that Russia's eastern regions will have to develop much stronger economic ties with Asia. To survive economically, East Siberia and the Far East will have to play a much larger role on Asian energy markets. Without this economic boost, the regions will continue to deteriorate. Such a policy is naturally risky, because the Russian regions could easily be pulled into the rapidly growing Chinese economic machine. But, most likely, as the economy of Russia's east becomes more integrated with Russia's Asian neighbors, the region will maintain its strong political and cultural ties with the rest of Russia.

In working on the Asian market, Russia will need to balance among the various powers of China, Japan, South Korea, and even the US. The interests of these countries are often conflicting, and Russia can maneuver among them in the same way that it is able to play off the various countries within Europe. In this sense, Russia is not really balancing Asia against Europe, but working within Asia and, to some extent, North America. Russia's relationship with Europe is still its anchor and priority. Thus, there is a possibility for an optimistic scenario in which Russia can develop both in the east and Europe. What happens in Asia does not necessarily have to have an impact on Russia's European ties.

In fact, Russia's interest in developing its east is so vital to its efforts to preserve the territorial integrity of the country that it will have an interest in working with foreign partners to overcome the enormous obstacles to development in the region. East Siberia and the Far East offer enormous potential for global cooperation between Europe, Asia, and the US on the state level, and between Russian companies, global majors, and NOCs at the corporate level. Clearly, the development of this huge and complex region will be impossible on the basis of Russia's resources alone. Foreign involvement is essential for the success of projects that are extremely capital-intensive and technologically and managerially challenging. However, the current state of affairs in the Russian oil and gas sectors, and trends in relations between Russia and other energy suppliers and consumers indicate that the development of these regions, particularly their export programs, unless properly managed, can provoke conflicts between key interested parties and general instability in global energy markets.

Notes

1 Recommendations from the Parliamentary Hearings "Legislative Basis for Creating Pipeline Systems in East Siberia and the Far East," RF State Duma, Moscow, 25 April 2006.
2 Ministry of Industry and Energy (Minpromenergo), *Energeticheskaia strategiia Rossii na period do 2020 goda*, approved as decree no. 1234-r by the Russian government on 28 August 2003, www.minprom.gov.ru/docs/strateg/1/ (accessed 13 December 2007).
3 *Promyshlennye Vedomosti*, 20 May 2005.
4 Report of Deputy Minister of Natural Resources A. Temkin "On the Program of Geological Prospecting and Exploration of Oil and Gas Fields in East Siberia and the Far East of Russia," Parliamentary Hearings, RF State Duma, Moscow, 17 February 2005.
5 See, for example, *Energy Vector of Russia's Eastern Geopolitics* (Moscow: Ekonomika, 2006), where one of the authors is V. Yakunin, head of Russian Railroads.
6 See, for example, *Strategy of Siberia's Economic Development*, approved as decree no. 765-r by the Russian government on 7 July 2002.
7 For a geographical overview on the demographic situation in Russian regions, see: www.perepis2002.ru/ct/grf_map.htm (accessed 15 September 2007).
8 Dmitry Trenin, "National Security: Big Eastern Strategy," *Vedomosti*, 14 February 2005.
9 Gennady Chufrin, "Russia in APR," *Russian Expert Review*, no. 5 (2003).
10 "Who will Help the Far East," *Vedomosti*, 10 April 2007; "The East will Get $16.7 Billion. That is, Even More than Sochi," *Vedomosti*, 2 August 2007.
11 "Man of the Week: Putin's Victory," *Vedomosti*, 12 February 2007.
12 "Holidays on the Shelf," *Vedomosti*, 4 May 2007.
13 "Subsurface under Supervision," *Vedomosti*, 21 February 2008.
14 *Regional Economic Digest*, 22 June 2007.
15 "When Will They Drill Kovykta," *Vedomosti*, 23 March 2007.
16 Minpromenergo, *Programma sozdaniia v vostochnoi Sibiri i na Dal'nem Vostoke edinoi sistemy dobychi, transportirovki gaza i gazosnabzheniia s uchetom vozmozhnogo eksporta gaza na rynki Kitaia i drugikh stran Aziatsko-Tikhookeanskogo regiona*, approved as order no. 340 by Minpromenergo on 3 September 2007, www.minprom.gov.ru/activity/energy/strateg/3 (accessed 15 January 2008).
17 *Regional Economic Digest*, 22 June 2007.
18 Nina Poussenkova, "Lord of the Rigs: Rosneft as a Mirror of Russia's Evolution," paper written for "The Changing Role of National Oil Companies in International Energy Markets," a project jointly sponsored by the Japan Petroleum Energy Center and the James A. Baker III Institute for Public Policy, Rice University, Houston, March 2007, www.rice.edu/energy/publications/docs/NOCs/Papers/Rosneft_Nina.pdf (accessed 3 September 2008).
19 Nodari Simonia, "Russian Energy Policy in East Siberia and the Far East," paper written for "The Energy Dimension in Russian Global Strategy," a project jointly sponsored by the Japan Petroleum Energy Center and the James A. Baker III Institute for Public Policy, Rice University, Houston, 2004, www.rice.edu/energy/publications/docs/PEC_SimoniaFinal_10_2004.pdf (accessed 3 September 2008).
20 "Peace Treaty Signed by Shareholders of Verkhnechonskneftegas," *Oil and Capital*, no. 9 (2006): 9–12.

21 The Yurubcheno–Tokhomsk Zone in the Evenk District has total geological resources of between 2.5 and 3.5 billion tons of oil and 0.5–1.2 tcm of gas.
22 "Where to Find a Refinery: Rosneft is Considering Refining its Crude," *Vedomosti*, 15 September 2006.
23 "A Profitable Partnership: The Rosneft-CNPC Joint Venture Gets Irkutsk Fields," *Vedomosti*, 1 August 2007.
24 *Prime-TASS*, 26 November 2007.
25 "Eastern Program: Expert Conclusion of the Siberian Division of Russian Academy of Sciences," *Oil and Gas Vertical*, no. 17 (2005): 35.
26 "There is No Money to Develop the East," *Oil and Gas Vertical*, no. 14 (2005): 60f.
27 "Replacement of Reserves is the Key Challenge," *Oil and Gas Vertical*, no. 10 (2005): 12–15.
28 See the report by Temkin "On the Program of Geological Prospecting and Exploration of Oil and Gas Fields in East Siberia and the Far East of Russia."
29 "Chinese Section of the Pipeline: There are not Enough Russian Workers for ESPO," *Vedomosti*, 19 July 2007.
30 In East Siberia, the density of railroads is 21 km per 10,000 sq km versus 50 km in Russia on average, and the density of car roads is 15 km per 10,000 sq km versus 31 km in Russia on average. Therefore, winter roads (*zimniks*) and rivers are widely used for transportation purposes.
31 Thus, Verkhnechonskneftegas produced only 2,500 tons of oil in 2006 in the absence of transportation infrastructure, and crude was sold to the local boiler houses.
32 "Gref Will Take Care of the Oilmen: He Proposed to Limit Oil Transportation Tariff in the Far East to $50," *Vemodosti*, 20 July 2007.
33 *RIA Novosti*, 12 July 2007.
34 "A Virtual Pipeline: Transneft Won't Be Able to Commission ESPO in 2008," *Vedomosti*, 25 December 2007.
35 A very high level, given its capitalization of $88.5 billion. "Rosneft is Betting on the Ruble," *Vedomosti*, 3 September 2007.
36 "Will the Chayandinsk Field Remain an Orphan?," *Oil and Gas Vertical*, no. 3 (2006): 41.
37 "President of the State Company," *Oil and Capital* (special supplement), no. 7 (2007): 5.
38 Amy Myers Jaffe and Jareer Elass, "Saudi Aramco: National Flagship with Global Responsibilities," paper written for "The Changing Role of National Oil Companies in International Energy Markets," a project jointly sponsored by the Japan Petroleum Energy Center and the James A. Baker III Institute for Public Policy, Rice University, Houston, March 2007, 27, www.rice.edu/energy/publications/docs/NOCs/Papers/NOC_SaudiAramco_Jaffe-Elass-revised.pdf (accessed 3 September 2008).
39 "From Rhine and Danube to Yangtze and Ganges," *Oil of Russia*, no. 1 (January 2008): 88–93, www.oilru.com/nr/177/4103/ (accessed 3 September 2008).
40 *Supply and Demand Analysis on Petroleum Products and Crude Oils for Asia and the World* (Tokyo: The Institute of Energy Economics, April 2006), 55.
41 www.levada.ru/interrelations.html (accessed 25 August 2006).
42 China has a coal R/P ratio of 48 years, according to British Petroleum (BP), *Statistical Review of World Energy 2007* (London: BP, 2007), 32.
43 "Russia Looks Both East and West," *The Straits Times*, 20 July 2006.
44 www.energystate.ru/news/363.html (accessed 15 September 2007).
45 www.iags.org/n0119063.htm – 4 (accessed 15 September 2007).
46 "Japan and China Battle for Russia's Oil and Gas," *New York Times*, 3 January 2004.

Part III
International policies toward Russia

8 European perspectives for managing dependence

Pami Aalto

This chapter focuses on the nature of the European Union's (EU) energy dependence on Russia. It analyzes the main challenges resulting from this dependence for the formulation of a common EU energy policy and for the relations that the EU and its individual member states have with Russia. While "energy dependence" in general suggests an asymmetric type of relationship, the term itself remains highly contested. Given the currently politicized nature of the debate on Europe's energy relations with Russia, we need to arrive at an exact understanding of the nature of this dependence. The dependence is reciprocal, with Europe dependent on Russia and Russia dependent on Europe. However, the situation is not so simple, since it is not Europe as a whole that is dependent on Russian energy, but only several of its states. The specific nature of an individual European country's dependency on Russia impacts the way that this dependency is socially framed and used within the EU and in domestic political debates.

This chapter argues that Europe's dependencies on Russian fossil fuel imports are best managed if the high level of existing interdependencies and the different interests within Europe and between individual European states and Russia are acknowledged. An important condition for putting the relationship between Europe and Russia on a firm footing is to address some of the tensions between the EU and individual European states, which due to different historical trajectories have developed different types of relations with Russia, resulting in different views on how best to manage these relations. In contrast to some European countries whose energy relations with the Soviet Union/Russia date as far back as the 1960s and 1970s, the EU as a political entity only began in the early 1990s to apply some of its energy principles to its foreign energy relations. Thus, the EU has been promoting policies based on three principles: open, free, and competitive markets; reliability and security of energy supply; and sustainability in the exploration and exploitation of energy resources. It has also consequently sought to make its relations with Russia and other key energy-producing and transit states dependent on adherence to these values.

Individual EU member states, however, have implemented these three principles selectively. These diverging policies are in part due to the fact that many of them developed their energy relations with Russia well before the EU started to institutionalize its energy principles and apply these to its foreign relations. EU efforts to speak with a single voice toward Russia are bound to conflict with the different interests of individual EU countries should the EU seek more convergence in its approach toward Russia. While the future is likely to see some intra-EU tensions, a radical shake-up in European–Russian energy relations is unlikely in the short to medium term. Even in the long term, the EU–Russia energy trade is likely to maintain its current high volumes, while gradually becoming more regionalized when different sub-regions of the EU conclude different deals with Russian actors. Beyond the fossil fuel trade, sustainability issues and the electricity sector are set to become important integration platforms.

This chapter starts with an overview of European–Russian relations. The overview includes an analysis of Europe's energy situation and the development of a common EU energy policy, the role of Russia in the EU energy market, and an analysis of current debates on Russia within the EU. The second part looks more closely into the diverging approaches of EU and EU member policies vis-à-vis Russia and discusses in particular the cases of Germany, Poland, and the UK as a way of illustrating the difficulties of forging a common EU-wide strategy toward Russia. The third part considers potential trends shaping the future of European–Russian relations and the formulation of a common EU approach.

Overview

In this first section, we look into the nature of Europe's dependence on Russia and seek to arrive at a deepened and more balanced understanding of what this term actually means. First, we demonstrate that increasing energy poverty within the EU has prompted nearly all of the main actors to look to Russia, and this has brought the differences between the "short story" of EU relations with Russia and the "long story" of individual member states' relations with Russia to the fore. We then argue that in this situation, the tensions between two possible models of development for European energy policy illustrate the policy options and obstacles facing the EU and its member states in their energy relations with Russia. These models are best defined as focusing on either a cooperative energy security society or a converging energy security society. We examine the applicability of these models by analyzing the role of Russian energy in the European market and the related debates at the EU, member state, company, and citizenry levels.

Europe's energy situation

Assuming that current consumption patterns do not change, Europe will need to import an increasing amount of its energy, in particular oil and gas, from abroad. EU oil production is set to decline sharply in the medium to long term. Natural gas production from the fields in the North Sea may at best rise slightly, but will not be enough to meet Europe's quickly increasing demand for gas. The EU currently imports half of all the energy resources it uses; by around 2030, this share will rise to 70 percent. The EU's increasing energy poverty has meant that Russia, which is rich in hydrocarbons and close to Europe, emerged as Europe's single most important energy supplier. Today Russia accounts for approximately a quarter of EU consumption of oil and gas, and around 40 per cent of the EU's imports of these two types of hydrocarbons that together make up 61 percent of the EU's energy consumption.[1]

Russia's importance is further highlighted by several accompanying factors: although Europe has announced plans to develop renewable energy sources and increase efficiency, implementing these proposals will take a long time, and they will not replace oil and gas in the near term. At the same time, Europe's indigenous potential to exploit other sources of energy like coal, nuclear power, or hydropower are constrained, given either the limits in the availability of these sources or environmental concerns. Moreover, there are limits as to the degree to which Europe will want to diversify away from Russia, given the potential problems with the reliability of supplies from other major energy-exporting regions like the Middle East, or West Africa, where deposits of energy resources are simply insufficient to satisfy Europe's huge needs. Simultaneously, Europe will face increasing competition for Russia's resources from other major consumers, in particular China, Japan, and other countries of the Asia-Pacific region.[2]

Against this larger background of Russia's importance to Europe, we will now analyze the two stories of Europe's energy relations with Russia: the long European bilateral state story and the much shorter EU story.

History of European–Russian energy relations

The long story of European energy relations with Russia starts with the Austrian and West German pipeline projects of the late 1960s and early 1970s. These deals, which the US government unsuccessfully sought to prevent, introduced Soviet gas into the West German and Austrian energy mixes in order to reduce the share of imports from the Middle East, which was increasingly perceived as an unstable supplier of energy – especially after OPEC stopped shipping oil to the US and its allies in response to the Yom Kippur War of 1973. For West Germany and Austria, these deals, motivated by *Ostpolitik* and détente, created a new dependence on the Soviet Union. West Germany sought to manage this new dependence by building new storage facilities while simultaneously working to ensure that alternative supplies were available.

For the Soviet Union, the deals stimulated economic growth by means of export pipelines paid for with credits secured against gas supplies.[3] The long story, thereafter, charts the gradual extension of dependence on Russian gas and oil to many other EU member states, in increasing volumes and with the help of expanding pipeline networks. The peak of crude oil output from Britain and The Netherlands led to reduced indigenous European production and pushed a growing number of member states toward Russia. Furthermore, the central and east European (CEE) enlargements of the EU in 2004 and 2007 included ten new member states that had developed strong energy ties with the Soviet Union. As a legacy of the past, most of these countries are today heavily dependent on Russian oil and gas imports.

For the Soviet Union, and later, Russia, the long story charts the growing dependence on European continental markets through pipelines, which creates a "physical" connection between producer and consumer that cannot be broken easily. The main ports through which the Soviets shipped their oil, and the majority of export ports that the Russians built since the 1990s, rely on the Baltic Sea and the Black Sea waterways, which limit annual tanker shipments to some 150,000 deadweight tons. Such limitations make long-distance oil deliveries to the US and Asia too expensive to be commercially viable, and tie Russia closely to the European oil market.[4] Such infrastructure ties are strengthened by Russia's oil pipelines to Europe, which account for about a quarter of Russia's oil deliveries to the EU.

In the gas sector, all of the export pipelines inherited by Russia from the Soviet Union and also those built in the post-Soviet era are oriented westwards and connect with former Soviet states, Turkey, or Europe. The EU is by far the most lucrative market for Russian energy exports and has long yielded the highest prices for Russian gas export monopolist Gazprom. Russia will be locked firmly into gas pipeline supplies to the EU area at least for the next 10–15 years.

The possible reorientation of energy exports toward Asia, as well as the shifting of Russia's oil exports toward its Arctic ports, will be gradual and partial. Production of liquefied natural gas (LNG), which can be shipped to Asia, will only come online on Sakhalin Island in Russia's Far East around 2008–9, initially in small quantities. LNG will not be shipped from European Russia before 2015–20.[5] Hence, when the long story of energy relations between individual European countries and Russia is examined from both the EU and Russian sides, what emerges is a picture of mutual dependence, or historically developed and durable *interdependence*, between the majority of EU member states and Russia.

The short story of Europe's energy relations with Russia, by contrast, starts with the emergence of the first elements of the then European Economic Community's (EEC) own energy policy in 1988. This policy consisted mainly of intra-EEC measures intended to create an internal energy market based on competition as a follow-up to the single European act of 1987.[6] In 1994, the European Energy Charter Treaty (ECT) was signed by a large number of EU member states as well as energy-producing and transit countries in the EU's neighborhood, including Russia. In the treaty, the centerpiece of the EU's energy policy continued to be the *market rules and competition* principle, but alongside that appeared important references to the *security of supplies* and *sustainability* concerns. By proceeding from these three principles, the ECT marked the first effort of the EU and its member states to persuade Russia to take into consideration European energy priorities, as Russia had by that time become a major supplier to the EU area, and as the EU typically attempts to extend its own models to its partners.

However, Russia refused to ratify the ECT because it objected to the treaty's transit protocol that would have obliged Russia to give up its near-monopolistic control over energy transit within the former Soviet territory, where Central

Asian energy producers relied on Russian-controlled pipelines. The Russian objections meant that the treaty had no practical impact, because its most important signatory refused to accept it. The failure of the all-encompassing multilateral route, together with the poor energy production outlook in Western Europe, helped the European Commission (EC) in October 2000 persuade member states to give it a mandate on proposing an "energy dialog" with Russia.[7] This dialog is mostly conducted between the EC, which functions as the EU's integration motor and main bureaucratic body, and the Russian government. It aims to offer a politico-institutional framework for the intense EU–Russia energy trade, and as a desirable side-effect, to promote intra-EU convergence around the EU's energy policy principles. For Russia, it also offers the possibility of additional technology transfers and the modernization of its infrastructure and economy by means of European investments and mutual interaction.[8]

The differences between the long and the short stories are significant because they help to highlight the changing dynamics of European–Russian energy relations due to the entrance of a new actor (the EU) and the implementation of new principles put forward by this actor. During the past two decades, the EU has gradually acquired some competences in energy policy-related questions in order to push through its energy policy principles. These competencies mostly pertain to the EU's role in regulating the internal market, competition, the environment, and technology, with EU-designed transport corridors and logistics chains also entering the picture.[9] In addition, the EC has the integrative task of convincing member states to agree multilaterally on new targets and benchmarks for energy policy. The EU thus attempts to institutionalize its energy policy principles among its member states, while simultaneously trying to extend them to energy providers like Russia as well as transit states.[10] Although the EU has in this manner become the most important agenda-setter in European energy policy, it constantly runs into conflict with the historically-evolved energy relations between individual European countries and Russia.

Toward an EU-centered energy security society

In order to analyze the tensions between the recently developed EU approach toward Russia and the approaches to energy relations of individual EU member states with Russia as they have historically developed, we consider the type of *energy security society* that the EU and its member states may form, and how such a society may help them to engage in a coherent and fruitful approach toward Russia.

The idea of an energy security society draws on the so-called English school of International Relations (IR) theory and focuses on interstate ties, with the aim of applying this framework to an analysis of European energy policy. This means conceptualizing the EU-led effort of promoting the three principles of energy policy – markets and competition, security of supplies, and sustainability – as a project of developing an energy security society. Ideally, this society includes not only the EU member states but Russia as well, together with transit countries and other important energy producers exporting to Europe. Borrowing from the classic English school literature, we use the term "energy security society" to refer to a *group of states that have established common rules and institutions for the conduct of their mutual energy relations with a firm interest in maintaining these arrangements.*[11]

Analytically, various degrees of integration can be discerned binding such an interstate society together. In other words, depending on the degree of integration, we can distinguish between different actually existing and possible societies. Currently, in practice, the situation among EU member states is best characterized as a *cooperative energy security society*. Within this arrangement, important elements of the three EU energy policy principles are shared by many member states, but not to the extent of having convergent domestic energy sectors and giving the EC a leading role in external energy policy questions. There is a practice and expectation of co-operation, but a simultaneous lack of deeply-internalized mutual solidarity and consistent implementation of joint EU positions.[12]

A *converging energy security society* is a more ambitious, yet realistic, aim for the EC. It would mean identical energy-policy governance structures at the domestic level. In external energy relations, the EU would have essentially unconditional support for managing ties with energy suppliers. This society would ultimately achieve domestic and foreign energy policy convergence.

A *confederative energy security society* would mean the application of an identical set of energy-policy principles at the domestic level. In external energy relations, intergovernmental coordination would gradually lead to an unequivocal transfer of loyalties to the EU level so that the EC, together with the EU's high representative for foreign affairs or a possible double-hatted energy representative, sitting both in the supranational EC and the intergovernmental European Council, would obtain a full mandate for managing energy relationships with major providers. This set-up would be close to a new political entity that on a more general level was envisioned by the federalist movement and, in part, by neofunctionalist integration theorists. However, for the foreseeable future, this model remains a possibility in name only. Nevertheless, it deserves mention as a yardstick that is often implicitly used in critical analyses of EU energy policy performance.

The range of options for integration in the area of energy policy presented here makes us more sensitive to the role of such social factors as common rules, institutions, and interests in interstate arrangements in Europe. However, while interstate arrangements indeed play a large role in the present cooperative society within the EU, the individual *states* and their governments remain mainly responsible for energy security issues on their territories, as it is part of their jurisdiction to decide on the energy type, energy mix, and origins of the energy they use.

Companies and transnational financial actors are in charge of concrete energy projects from field development and finance to energy transport and consumer sales. They often prefer convergence-type arrangements. However, the nature and strength of their preferences depends on the extent of state control over the companies, and thus on whether they emphasize state sovereignty or a lack of borders in their business plans.

The *citizenry* represent an emerging popular component in energy policy integration due to the heightened role of energy in policy and media debates and the increased likelihood of energy policy issues entering election campaigns. Unlike companies, the political orientation of the broader publics with regard to energy can be said to have remained predominantly national in Europe, even though an EC-coordinated poll published in 2006 revealed that 47 percent of EU citizens wanted more European-level activities regarding energy policy.[13] The nature and extent of the relationship of these three components – states, transnational actors, and the broader publics – determines the level of integration of any energy security society within the EU and its persistence over time.

Role of Russian energy in the European market

Russia is an important outside force impacting what kind of EU energy security society is likely to emerge. Russia's influence is due to the fact that the country plays a very important role as an energy supplier to Europe. The actual application of the three principles formulated by the EU (markets and competition, security of supplies, and sustainability) will thus be impacted by the nature of Europe's relations with Russia.

The member states have over time developed very different energy relationships with Russia.[14] The high degree of dependency on Russia is best seen in the gas sector, where seven EU members depend 100 percent on Russian pipeline supplies, and six others rely on Russia for more than 50 percent of their gas supply. However, the maximum figures for the share of Russian gas in overall primary energy consumption do not rise higher than the 30 percent mark in any individual case, due to the fact that the energy mix also contains other energy sources (see Table 8.1).

Although Russia's weight in the overall European energy supply appears to be modest, the real issue for those states close to Russia is that there is no alternative provider of natural gas in the absence of LNG terminals or linkages to pipelines other than Russia's transportation system. Norway is the second most important gas supplier to the EU after Russia, supplying 25 percent of EU imports, but the bulk of its supplies at present go to Germany, France, and the UK. Southern European member states are the best placed to establish linkages to northern African resources. In total, 19 percent of the EU's gas imports come from Algeria.[15] In the oil sector, the degree of dependence on Russia can be highly significant as well, despite the more globalized nature of the oil market. The problem is well manifested in the difficulties encountered by Latvia's Ventspils oil port and Lithuania's Mažeikių oil refinery when Russia turned off pipeline supplies in 2003 and 2006, respectively, necessitating their replacement with less economical railroad and maritime supplies.

The EU's overall natural gas dependence on Russia is unlikely to grow much higher in absolute terms because of the slow development of new gas fields in

Table 8.1 The role of gas imports from Russia among EU member states

EU member state	Share of total gas imports in % (2004)	Share of gas imports from Russia in total primary energy consumption in % (2006)
Bulgaria	100	12
Estonia	100	–
Latvia	100	–
Lithuania	100	–
Finland	100	16
Romania	100	13
Slovakia	100	35
Greece	82	7
Austria	82	18
Hungary	81	32
Czech Republic	74	15
Poland	63	7
Slovenia	60	–
Germany	45	9
Italy	37	11
France	21	3

Source: European Commission (EC), *EU Energy Policy Data*, SEC(2007)12 (Brussels: European Commission, 2007); Vladimir Milov, "Nabucco, European Energy Supply Diversification, and Russia," presentation at the FT "Gas for Europe" conference, Budapest, 14 September 2007.

Russia. Jonathan Stern of the Oxford Institute for Energy Studies, for example, argues that Russia is unlikely to ship much more than the 185 bcm of gas it shipped in 2006 in the next few decades.[16] Most likely, the total will remain under 200 bcm. Europe's overall consumption of gas is, however, bound to grow considerably faster.[17] The gas gap may be closed by increasing imports from Algeria, Norway, Nigeria, Libya, Egypt, and Qatar, and negotiations are under way with suppliers from Azerbaijan and Turkmenistan.[18] Gas deliveries from Iran and Qatar, both of whom have bigger reserves than the above-mentioned suppliers, could also help to meet Europe's growing gas needs. Most of these prospects will mean building new pipelines; in some cases, such as Qatar's, deliveries are likely to be in LNG, which requires building gasification plants in Europe. Thus, if LNG imports are set to double by 2010,[19] effective utilization would presuppose developing LNG ports in the UK from which the gas would then feed into the continental system through the Interconnector pipeline.[20] Other similar measures include LNG terminal projects in Germany's Wilhelmshaven, the island of Krk in Croatia, Poland's Gdansk, and the Hellenic-Bulgarian ports on the Aegean coast.

However, due to the fact that Russia controls close to a third of the globally known gas reserves and is geographically proximate to the EU, it is clear that other individual suppliers can not, in the long run, completely replace Russian gas, but can only at best complement Russia and reduce its relative weight.[21] On top of gas supplies, Russia will also remain important for Europe as a supplier of oil (although Russia's oil reserves are much smaller than its gas reserves) and, to a lesser extent, it will supply electricity, coal, and uranium.

Debate at the EU level on Russian energy

The debate within the EU on the role of Russia as an energy supplier to Europe became almost hysterical after Gazprom shut down its gas deliveries to Ukraine in January 2006, which ultimately led to a temporary drop in gas supplies to a number of European countries. In the European media, Russia was portrayed as the cause of the shortage in Europe when in fact it was Ukraine that had tapped into the shipments destined for Europe in order to balance out its loss from Gazprom deliveries.[22] The framing of "Russia as the villain" stands in sharp contrast to the situation in 2000, when, in the EC's security of supplies document, efforts to decrease dependence or increase self-sufficiency were not as prominent as was the aim of trying to manage the risks related to dependence.[23] The plan of the then president of the EC, Romano Prodi, was in fact to increase gas supplies from Russia to some 240 bcm a year by 2020.[24] Such has been the recent rush to diversify the sources of supplies away from Russia that Andrew Monaghan has described the situation between Europe and Russia as an "energy security dilemma" whereby the EU's suddenly desperate diversification drive in the face of largely unfounded concerns forces Russia in response to these concerns to diversify away from the EU, which appears to have become less dependable as a consumer.[25]

Another strand of the newly alarmist debate, albeit one based on more concise efforts for a balanced analysis, is the thesis of the coming Russian "gas shortage." While the official Russian position (as expressed, for example, in the Energy Strategy up to 2020) does not subscribe to the gas shortage thesis, numerous Western as well as a few Russian analysts warn of Russia's inability to meet its European supply commitments in the face of declining production in the gigantic fields of Western Siberia, insufficient investment in the upstream sector, aging transportation infrastructure, and uncertainty as to the possibility that Central Asian gas might offset declining production in Russia's own fields.[26]

Recent documents produced by EU High Representative on Foreign Policy Javier Solana and the European Parliament accentuate the importance of achieving more transparency, as well as *reciprocal*, i.e. non-discriminatory, equal market access conditions in both the EU and Russia. The liberalizing European market is characterized by efforts to unbundle production, distribution, and consumer sales. Unless equal access is granted to the Russian market, where a few companies maintain monopolistic positions (e.g. Gazprom in the gas sector and Transneft in the oil transportation sector), representatives of the EU have indicated their willingness to consider imposing restrictions on the activities of the fully integrated gas export monopolist Gazprom in the EU market. Along these lines, the EU still adheres to the principles of reciprocity as they are laid out in the ECT, and in particular to its Transit Protocol.[27] An energy clause in the new EU–Russia partnership treaty might be a way of renegotiating the deadlocked issue of ECT ratification.

Debate at the member state, company, and citizenry level

There is a high degree of variation as to the extent to which individual European countries are dependent on Russian energy imports. In particular, the states in the western and southwestern parts of Europe (for example, Spain, Portugal, Belgium, The Netherlands, Ireland, and the UK) do not import any pipeline oil or gas from Russia, which, for the time being, makes them relative outsiders in EU–Russia energy relations. Germany and Italy represent the most Russia-confident end of the European spectrum. They are intent on maintaining or even expanding the present levels of energy supplies from Russia. Some countries in the southeastern part of Europe (Bulgaria, Greece, Romania, and Hungary) are planning the construction of new pipelines from Russia. In northern Europe, Sweden, which to date does not import any pipelined oil or gas from Russia, has since the turn of the millennium increased its oil imports from Russia dramatically (despite the fact that some analysts have expressed worries about this development).[28]

Poland is typical of the more suspicious end of the spectrum, where the conflict between Gazprom and Ukraine at the beginning of 2006 was seen as a manifestation of the potential risks involved in relying on Russia. The Polish threat perception prevails regardless of the fact that 27 bcm of gas continues to arrive to the EU via the Yamal–Europe pipeline crossing Poland. In an energy conference of ten eastern European countries in Vilnius in October 2007, Poland's President Lech Kaczynski took up the contentious issue of the planned Russian–German Nord Stream gas pipeline project in the Baltic Sea, which bypasses Poland and makes the once planned second trunk line to the Yamal pipeline redundant. According to Kaczynski, Russia uses energy as a political weapon, while personal gains also play a role in the sector. Czech Deputy Prime Minister Alexandr Vondra complained that:

> Unjust manipulation or interruption of energy supplies is as much a security threat as is military action (...) Post-Soviet countries have been experiencing that on a daily basis, as Russia's appetite for using energy as a political weapon is growing.[29]

However, it must be borne in mind that out of the EU-27, only the Baltic states have experienced direct energy blockades. The first such events occurred during their independence struggles with the Soviet Union in the early 1990s.[30] After regaining independence and establishing themselves as independent actors, they went on to enjoy enormous benefits by collecting proceeds from Russia's energy transit that continued to flow through their territories as a legacy of the Soviet era, before Putin's Russia was able to open new ports that were rapidly built around St. Petersburg. Events such as the loss of the bulk of their transit income, the problems witnessed at the Ventspils port and Mažeikių refinery, as well as the experience of being bypassed by the Nord Stream pipeline, have prompted the Baltic states to seek diversification away from their former patron in an alarmist fashion together with Poland, and partly, the Czechs.

EU–Russian energy relations are extremely complex. Some EU member states view the EU–Russia energy dialog as the EC's business. Germany has its own energy dialog with Russia. Norway, which is a member of the internal energy market through its membership in the European Economic Area (EEA), has a separate energy dialog with Russia. Moreover, the EC has its own energy dialog with Norway. Most member states continue to strike bilateral deals with Russia. Nevertheless, as a rule, smaller EU member states with no large energy companies and high energy-import dependency have a latent interest in multilateralizing their energy relationship with Russia. However, to date, only a few member states have indicated willingness to assign more competence to the EC in this sphere, even though that might be the best means of securing their interests.

At the company level, the picture is more uniform. Most market actors want to continue and/or expand business with Russia even when lucrative PSAs are no longer offered or cancelled, and when their roles are becoming reduced to the provision of technical expertise with minority shareholdings at best. The UK-based company BP seeks to continue its involvement in Russia even after its subsidiary TNK-BP was forced to sell its 62.9 percent majority stake in the Kovykta gas field in eastern Siberia to Gazprom in the summer of 2007, with a buy-back option of 25 percent. Royal Dutch Shell is continuing the development of Sakhalin-2 oil field regardless of having to agree to pay dividends of some $1 billion a year to the Russian government after protracted Russian pressure because of delayed production. Even disillusioned actors, such as the Ventspils port in Latvia and the Mažeikių refinery in Lithuania, would probably welcome the re-opening of the now dry oil pipelines. The Finnish Fortum/Neste company has, however, left the Russian oil production sector altogether after selling its stakes in the Shapkino oil fields in the Timan-Pechora area to Lukoil.

On the more positive side from the European point of view, offers of 25- and 24-percent stakes, respectively, in the company developing the Shtokman gas fields in the Barents Sea have been made to the French Total corporation and Norwegian Statoil/Norsk Hydro, with the final decisions on their participation to be taken when the technical and financial details of the deal are agreed by 2009.[31] However, German companies tend to get the best deals for their Russian operations, due to having given Gazprom access to their own downstream operations in the course of several asset swaps, as will be explained below. Italy's Eni, for its part, is included in the building of the South Stream pipeline from Russia through the bed of the Black Sea and then through Bulgaria to Slovenia, Austria, and Italy. A key reason for the eagerness of these and many other European companies to continue their involvement in the Russian energy sector and develop joint projects is that the resources they control, mainly in the North Sea, are dwindling. Any stake in Russian energy helps to maintain their sales volume, in a situation where an increasing share of their sales is from "foreign" sources.

In most countries, the broader public is mostly a bystander in these developments, despite many trade unions having a keen interest in continued employment in the energy sector, sometimes by means of states supporting national energy champions in the same way as Gazprom and Rosneft receive state backing in Russia. However, Finland's partly state-owned electricity and heating power company Fortum illustrates how the typical European pattern of state ownership in an otherwise marketized environment may become increasingly problematic. There was widespread public criticism in 2006 of the huge option deals cashed in by the company's directors as a result of an executive incentive program that had been established when energy prices were low. On balance, however, the consumer voice is only emerging in energy policy and in debates on prices and the use of energy proceeds. Only in some EU member states do households actively make use of the opportunity to change their energy suppliers that is afforded by the internal EU market. In none of these instances is there any evidence of such moves being motivated by a perception that Russian energy is problematic.

On the whole, there is partial, but progressing, integration and coordination at the interstate level within the European energy security society, which remains mostly a co-operative model. In the transnational domain where energy companies operate, there is pressure for maintaining integral ties and even increasing interdependencies with Russia. Companies generally benefit from converging European markets, but may simultaneously face tightening competition in their home markets as a result of EU-induced liberalization. In foreign operations, both in the EU area and in Russia, they may encounter protectionist measures. Overall, in the business sector, there is a notable drive for developing the European energy security society. The broader publics are only emerging as actors in energy policy debates, but they may prove more important in the future when energy policy becomes a frequent topic in the media, even though the complexity of energy issues will always limit their active engagement.

Challenges

The second part of this chapter develops the idea of an energy security society further in order to assess the challenges ahead, both with regard to internal integration within the EU and energy relations with Russia. The cases of Germany, Poland, and the UK are highlighted as useful shortcuts in examining the extreme ends among these policy options and obstacles in terms of political, economic, and other considerations.

From challenges to options

The EU-led project of developing a European energy security society capable of coordinating energy relations with Russia faces pressure from several directions. Individual EU member states differ in the way they formulate and implement their energy policies. They have very different energy sectors, and each of the states has its own particular mix of primary energy sources. Furthermore, the states have diverging views on European integration in general, and they are integrated within general European market structures in different ways. Therefore, they represent, on the whole, *varying levels of socially framed integration capacity vis-à-vis EU energy policy*. Europe is also heterogeneous in terms of its energy relations with

Russia, as some members are very dependent on Russian energy imports, while others are not. Accordingly, these relationships are very differently framed in domestic debates, ranging from high levels of confidence about Russia to calls to diversify away from Russia. These differences mean that EU member states have *varying levels of socially framed integration capacity vis-à-vis energy relations with Russia*. Furthermore, the EU area's intensive energy trade with Russia faces pressures to exercise a more principled and value-based Common Foreign and Security Policy (CFSP) toward Russia. Many of these pressures emanate from the CEE member states and the debates in the European Parliament.

Combining these factors, the existing co-operative energy security society among EU member states reflects moderate integration capacity vis-à-vis the application of EU energy policy principles. The declared EU goal of "speaking with one voice" to Russia remains difficult to attain in this situation. As indicated in the table below, there are at least four possible outcome options: If moderate internal integration capacity goes hand in hand with a low integration capacity vis-à-vis energy relations with Russia, security of supplies might remain unstable in the short to medium term due to a dearth of good alternatives, particularly in the case of gas (option A in Table 8.2). High integration capacity in relation to Russia in conditions of moderate internal integration, for its part, is likely to lead to exclusive bilateral deals between member states and Russia (option B). High integration capacity vis-à-vis EU energy policy among member states, as suggested by the convergent energy security society model, would by virtue of the EU's energy poverty be largely ineffectual for securing supplies if integration capacity vis-à-vis Russia remains low (option C). Finally, high internal convergence coupled with high EU–Russian energy sector integration would represent an ideal combination for finding one voice and securing supplies (option D).

The challenges and options for developing a European energy security society, conditioned by the factors of integration capacity vis-à-vis EU energy policy and

Table 8.2 Challenges and options for European energy security society

Socially framed integration capacity vis-à-vis energy relations with Russia

		Low	High
Socially framed integration capacity vis-à-vis EU energy policy	Moderate	A. Co-operative intra-EU society with unstable security of supplies in the short to medium term	B. Co-operative EU society with member states making exclusive deals with Russia to secure supplies
	High	C. Convergent intra-EU society with unstable security of supplies in the short to medium term	D. Convergent European society extending towards Russia with a high degree of supply security

energy relations with Russia, are best illustrated by concrete examples. We focus on Germany, Poland, and the UK because they are all major EU member states and large energy consumers with varying levels of indigenous production, particularly coal. They either have influenced significantly or have the potential to influence the conduct of EU energy policy and energy relations with Russia. They also manifest very different combinations of the EU and Russian integration capacity factors.

Germany

Germany liberalized its energy market in 1997–8, but the oligopolistic structure of its energy sector and its reluctance to change the situation hinders further energy policy integration within the EU. For example, politicians pushed through the merger of E.ON and Ruhrgas in 2003 against the wishes of the federal anti-cartel agency partly in order to create a company weighty enough to deal with Gazprom's increasing strength. German–Russian relations are built on decades of positive experience of *Ostpolitik* and Cold War era détente, the Kohl–Gorbachev deal over the re-unification of Germany, and most recently, the Schröder–Putin alliance that culminated in the decision to build the Nord Stream gas pipeline. This project marked a watershed in European energy debates and European–Russian energy relations. Schröder became the company's honorary chairman after his term as German chancellor ended in late 2005. In this venture, the 51-percent majority shareholder Gazprom works with E.ON Ruhrgas, BASF Wintershall, and the Dutch Gasunie, which have minority stakes of 20, 20, and 9 percent, respectively.[32]

The Nord Stream gas pipeline perhaps best illustrates the crucial and highly geopolitical nature of the German–Russian relationship. It would have been far cheaper to upgrade the operating capacity of the Bratstvo gas pipeline that runs through Ukraine to Germany. At present, the Bratstvo pipeline transports only 115 bcm instead of its theoretical maximum of 175 bcm. However, German–Russian–Ukrainian talks to expand this pipeline failed in 2002. The Russo-Ukrainian gas dispute in 2006 made this option even less attractive. Given the conflict-ridden Russo-Baltic and Russo-Polish relations, as well as energy conflicts between Russia and Belarus in 2004 and 2007, building a second trunk along the Yamal–Europe line running through Poland and Belarus, with or without a Baltic "Amber line," also became a dead option.[33] From Germany's point of view, Nord Stream provides the first direct connection to Russian gas without potentially (or actually) unreliable transit states that could disrupt the energy flow. It is, however, a far costlier option. In fact, it is exceeding its estimated €10 billion cost and it is falling behind the original schedule that called for the first trunk line to become operational by 2010. Nevertheless, it cements the energy alliance between Germany and Russia as both parties aim at cutting off transit states.

In the medium term, Germany has no other option than purchasing large amounts of gas from Gazprom. The Nord Stream project makes the most economic sense in bolstering ties between German and Russian energy companies. It provides Germany with the gas it needs, and gives German energy companies something to sell at a time when Germany's own production is dwindling. Gazprom gains access to a downstream market with the help of asset swaps. The Nord Stream project was mentioned in the memorandums of understanding that E.ON Ruhrgas signed with Gazprom in 2004 and 2005, promising the German company a 24.5 percent stake in the Yuzhno Russkoye gas field in Western Siberia. Gazprom has, in return, received assets in three Hungarian companies controlled by Ruhrgas. BASF's subsidiary Wintershall has another 24.5 percent of Yuzhno Russkoye in addition to its Achimgaz joint venture to develop the Novy Urengoi field. The two companies also explore fields together in Libya and are partners in WINGAS, which operates long-distance pipelines in Germany.[34] The strong German–Russian energy ties can be viewed as being well in line with the EU's need for establishing channels to influence and deal with Russia. Those more critical of Russia, however, consider these ties to be a threat, since they potentially make Germany hostage to Russia and Russian energy.[35]

It is, for the time being, hard to see any serious challenges to the German–Russian energy relationship, apart from the criticism advanced against it from some of the CEE states, which are reduced to bystanders as their former role as pivotal energy transit countries diminishes. Not only is the Russian–German relationship strong, it may even expand in the future, especially in more unconventional energy areas: Germany holds a global leadership position in renewable energy technology, despite the fact that renewable energy provides a mere 6 percent of energy and 10 percent of electricity consumption in the country.[36] Germany produces half of the windmills and one-third of the solar cells worldwide, and has one-third of the hydropower installations market, in addition to producing bio-fuel plants.[37] Given Russia's future need to develop its massive potential in renewable energies, Germany's competence in this field may supplement the present hydrocarbons trade.

The currently strong and expanding German–Russian energy relationship may not, however, fully translate to the benefit of the whole EU unless Germany manages to re-establish its lead in EU-wide energy policy integration, where it is the weightiest actor. Germany lost that lead through its oligopolistic domestic market, which hinders EU-wide convergence, and because of its focus on establishing strong bilateral ties with Russia (moving from option D to B).

Poland

Poland joined the EU in 2004, but was poorly equipped for integrating with EU energy policy. Despite ongoing reforms, no properly functioning energy market has emerged in Poland to date. Poland's gas sector remains closed at least until 2010, despite EU directives to open it up; the Poles argue that the country first needs to diversify away from its high 63 percent dependence on Russia before any serious liberalization can be attempted. In the oil sector, Poland receives 95 percent of its supply from Russia.

Given that the Polish government considers its position vis-à-vis Russia to be precarious even after attaining EU and NATO memberships, Poland has, on the regional level, attempted to build various counter-coalitions that are, at least in part, directed against Russia. These measures include, for example, Poland's call on Europe to support Ukrainian presidential candidate Viktor Yushchenko in his struggle against the Russian-backed Viktor Yanukovich in 2004, or the rather strange Polish proposal in 2006 to create an "energy NATO" of mostly energy "have-nots," which would only include Norway as a major supplier, but exclude Russia. Between late 2006 and autumn of 2007, as a response to Russia's blockade of Polish meat exports on alleged hygiene grounds, Poland blocked all negotiation attempts to sign a new EU–Russia treaty, insisting that the ban on its meat be lifted first. During this time, Poland also called for a liberalization of Russia's energy sector. Prime Minister Donald Tusk's government, which replaced the very anti-Russian government of Jaroslaw Kaczynski in late 2007, promised to continue seeking alternatives to Russian supplies, but left the door open for modifying his predecessor's anti-Russian policy.[38]

The serious political difficulties between Poland and Russia instruct Poland to seek diversification away from Russian sources, even though piped Russian oil and gas continue to be the cheapest option alongside domestic coal in a purely economic sense. There are, however, also a number of economic motives explaining Poland's anti-Russian policies. With the construction of the Nord Stream gas pipeline, it is likely that the second trunk line of the Yamal–Europe pipeline through Poland will not be built as originally planned. Nord Stream's 27 bcm a year capacity in the first phase of the project is almost the same as the current 28 bcm capacity of Yamal–Europe. The expansion of Nord Stream to 55 bcm after the second phase is about the same volume as the Yamal–Europe would have provided if the second trunk had been built. Given that absolute volumes of supplies from Russia to the EU area are not likely to increase much, in some scenarios the present pipeline crossing Polish territory and supplying Poland along the way may even turn out to be obsolete. Such a scenario would leave Poland without any transit leverage in relation to Russia. Also, Poland would remain dependent on gas imports outside of its control, as it would eventually need to import Russian gas via other EU states.[39]

To reduce dependence on Russia, the Polish gas monopoly PGNiG and the German natural gas trading and energy service provider Verbundnetz Gas agreed on gas sales from Germany to Poland.[40] They also are working on a project to import natural gas from Norway via an extension to the planned Scanled gas pipeline running from southern Norway to Sweden, and potentially to Denmark. However, realization of this plan might require upgrading the capacity of the whole Scanled pipeline, incurring high costs. Together with the planned LNG port in Gdansk, the costs look prohibitive to many outside observers, especially given that the timeframe for both projects is set for 2010–11.[41]

In the oil sector, Poland hosts the northern Druzhba pipeline that runs from Russia through Belarus to Germany. In order to gain direct access to Caspian oil, bypassing Russian-controlled pipelines, the Poles want to extend the current Odessa–Brody oil pipeline in Ukraine northwards to Plock in Poland, and possibly even as far as to Gdansk and the Lithuanian port of Klaipeda on the Baltic

Sea shores. Finally, the Polish company PK Orlen's acquisition of a majority stake in Lithuania's Mažeikių refinery in 2006, defeating the efforts of Russian energy companies to acquire the same assets, will not help to increase Poland's integration capacity vis-à-vis energy relations with Russia.

In the face of increasing pressure to comply with EU market rules, Poland must devise an energy policy that enhances its own drilling in the Baltic Sea, implements clean coal technologies to utilize Poland's rich coal reserves, develops extensive renewable energy technologies, and promotes energy efficiency in what is currently a relatively energy-intensive economy. The sustainability challenges in particular are formidable: Only 5 percent of Poland's overall energy and 3 percent of electricity consumption in 2005 came from renewable energy sources.[42] In the mid-term, a more marketized and sustainable energy agenda would be pertinent for developing a convergent intra-EU energy security society. The drawback of this approach is that Poland's interaction capacity in relation to Russia is likely to stay low, a fact that has already influenced EU–Russia relations negatively in the past (option C). During the first five years of its EU membership, Poland, thus, only offered a model of poor integration capacity vis-à-vis EU energy policy, coupled with a weak integration capacity vis-à-vis Russia in conditions of on-going high dependency (option A).

United Kingdom

The UK is traditionally a laggard when it comes to European integration, with the exception of security and defense sector co-operation. Nevertheless, in energy policy, the UK is clearly at the forefront of implementing the markets and competition principle, and has acted as an influential advocate of energy market reforms throughout the EU. The UK's own reforms were started in the late 1980s and finalized in 1998. Today, the UK boasts a more advanced energy market than EU directives stipulate, and has also started to speak in favor of more energy sector integration within the EU.[43]

As far as its integration capacity with Russia is concerned, the UK has little to boast about. The British tradition of political relations with Russia is weak. In the post-Soviet era and in the new millennium, the UK has had several political disputes with Russia. Among these were its decision to give political asylum to Russian oligarch Boris Berezovsky and Chechen rebel leader Akhmed Zakaev, both of whom Russian prosecutors are seeking to have extradited. Neither the UK's pro-US position in the war in Iraq, nor the UK–Russian spying rows during 2006–7 have made relations any easier.

Economically, the UK can, at least to some extent, afford all these shortcomings. The significance of Russia is negligible in terms of UK trade, despite Britain being the number one EU investor in Russia. Moreover, the UK is currently not dependent on Russian energy, which by EU standards puts the country into a small and shrinking group; the UK will not need to rely on Russian energy supplies as long as its own supplies from the North Sea (which are rapidly declining) and Norwegian supplies continue to flow into the country.[44]

So far, the Russian gas that flows into continental Europe through the Bratstvo and Yamal–Europe pipelines has been too expensive for the UK market as a result of tariffs that each transit country adds to the price. Gas from the Nord Stream pipeline delivered in the future would be more viable economically, but Gazprom would like to own its own distributor in the UK. Toward this end, in early 2008 Gazprom continued earlier efforts to buy Centrica, the largest actor in the UK market. This attempt provoked domestic debate, but the UK government did not propose any countermeasures. Nevertheless, the deal has not gone through. While Russia seeks to work in the UK, BP has experienced many problems with its operations in Russia. For example, BP had to cede to Gazprom its majority stake in the Kovykta gas field. Despite the concession, however, BP announced that it was creating a strategic alliance with Gazprom for major joint investments and asset swaps. This announcement may have been a face-saving measure for BP, or the start of energy co-operation based on the German model.

Experts fault Britain's renewable energy policy for oscillating between partly incompatible global environmental goals, national export industry targets, and rural development efforts.[45] The share of renewable energy is a negligible 1 percent in overall energy consumption and only 4 percent in electricity consumption.[46] While the UK lacks large-scale hydropower or biomass sources, the country has a high capacity for energy integration with the EU and a pro-market orientation, while the UK–Russian energy relationship may deepen regardless of BP's severe problems in Russia. The UK can offer Russian actors a large and open downstream energy market, and the significant upstream investment capacity of its oil and gas majors.

On the whole, the UK case suggests significant support for a convergent EU energy security society, but regardless of the strong potential, it is questionable whether the UK's interaction capacity in relation to Russia may be enough for such a society to extend to Russia and to help stabilize supplies. (Thus option C is most likely; while option D is possible, but not likely in the short term).

Trends

The final part of this chapter first discusses the lessons learned from the three case studies regarding the prospects for further convergence vis-à-vis internal EU integration and energy relations with Russia, as well as regional stability. The second section of this part then outlines some elements for a sustained European–Russian energy partnership.

Toward more regionalized European–Russian energy relations

The cases of Germany, Poland, and the UK illustrate well the need for a balance between integration capacity vis-à-vis the EU, on the one hand, and Russia, on the other. The way in which various EU member states position themselves within these two "poles" to a large extent determines the kind of energy security society that may form in the EU and the wider European area.

The German case suggests a route toward a mostly unproblematic energy relationship built on a high degree of interdependence with Russia. However, it is not likely to be copied across the EU because it relies on a strong bilateral relationship with Russia and reflects some reluctance toward building a more developed intra-EU energy market. Together, these factors undermine intra-EU solidarity and reduce the prospects for putting the less well-placed EU member states on a more equal footing vis-à-vis Russian energy majors under the EU flag. The Polish case suggests the necessity of switching toward a higher degree of integration within the EU in order to improve supply security. Concomitantly, it reflects the pain involved, and the partial nature of such steps in arranging energy security when capacity for engaging Russia positively remains low. The UK case underlines the sufficiency of intra-EU energy market integration when adequate energy reserves are accessible through EU and EEA area suppliers. In a situation of declining EU and EEA production, however, the British case emphasizes the need to start engaging Russia seriously and anticipating any possible new tendencies and changes to the domestic energy scene that this shift may imply.

Taken together, these three case studies imply some capacity for intra-EU convergence, but due to its imperfect nature, the need for further integration is clear. At the EU level, regardless of the prevailing imperfect application of joint energy policy principles that are required for a more convergent energy security society, it is not unreasonable to expect closer intra-EU integration in the mid-term. This integration will necessarily take a long time and require long and painful negotiations over reform. The EC's gradually increasing coordinating role and competence in energy questions will be pivotal, but so will political will on the part of the individual member states and the application of pressure from the EU bodies to engage in a more coherent common energy policy. Eventually, EU states will understand that it is in their best interest to increasingly act in unison against tightening conditions on the world energy market.

But it is important to note that simply agreeing on the importance of market, security of supplies, and sustainability within the EU falls short of actually implementing these principles into day-to-day policies in an environment where the EU is becoming more and more dependent on its neighbors for energy, particularly Russia. In other words, building a well-working energy security society within the EU becomes a question of arranging energy relations with Russia. In this regard, the key obstacles lie not only in member states' remaining sovereignty within the sector, but also in the variation of integration capacity among individual EU member states in relation to Russia.

At the level of EU member states' energy relations with Russia, some states are attempting to lessen dependence gradually. Succeeding in this endeavor will be a mid- to long-term process. Finding alternative supplies and sources is not easy. Poland and the Baltic states, for example, are handicapped because they do not control the keys for diversification projects, such as the construction of the Nabucco gas pipeline from Central Asia. In the oil sector, the autumn 2007 deal to bring Azeri oil to Poland and possibly to Lithuania via a pipeline to be extended from the existing Odessa–Brody trunk to Plock without crossing

Russian territory may not be feasible without the involvement of Kazakhstan's energy resources (which are now, however, completely tied up by Russia). Overall, this situation highlights the interdependent nature of the wider European energy scene and the fact that the large EU member states and Russia are in the best positions. Additionally, it highlights the importance of developing renewable sources of energy for states wishing to lessen their hydrocarbon dependence on Russia.

Some EU members, like Germany, Italy, and many southeastern European states, seek to maintain their present energy ties with Russia and even increase them. However, to cement the relationship as an interdependent one, keeping in mind the domestic pressures in Russia to start investing in energy sales to Asia, these EU members will need to offer Russia a long-term lucrative business perspective together with a strong political component in order to prevent its reorientation toward the Asian energy market. After all, Asian buyers will soon agree to pay the same high prices as the Europeans for Russian energy. This possibility raises the question of whether those EU members that are dependent on Russian supplies, whose number will grow in the future, should try to increase their own weight in dealing with Russia through fostering greater energy co-operation amongst themselves and strengthening supranational elements within the EU.

Even countries like the UK may slowly be drawn into the same game with Russia, while only countries such as those in the western Mediterranean with extensive LNG facilities and pipelines from northern Africa may afford to maintain a low level of energy relations with Russia. The EU members in the eastern parts of the Mediterranean are already reconfirming their position within the Russian energy orbit. Turkey partially falls into this latter category, but additionally has ambitions to become a hub for non-Russian energy from the Caspian on its way to the EU.

On the whole, the regional differences in how interaction with Russia is developing may lead to a more regionalized nature of EU–Russia energy relations. For the EU area, this may be a much better option than the present combination of Russian unilateralism and European bilateralism. The winners will likely be in the northeastern and southeastern corners of the EU where major energy projects from Russia are planned. The still pivotal CEE transit route is set to gradually lose its importance and faces the challenge of ageing infrastructure. It is also beset by questions regarding who is to pay for its improvement and who, in the long term, will need it. Consequently, the hopes of many CEE states for improved security after attaining EU membership may turn out to be unfulfilled as far as energy security is concerned, since they are losing their transit leverage on Russia. In short, achieving considerably greater cohesion vis-à-vis Russia within the EU will be difficult in the context of growing regionalization.

Elements for a sustained European–Russian energy partnership

Efforts to promote sustainability are likely to be a big winner in all this. Finding alternative supplies and meeting climate change prevention targets in the EU area will benefit alternative and clean energy industries working on new and renewable energy sources and energy efficiency. These efforts will create new jobs and produce a huge economic stimulus due to the rising global demand for these technologies. There will also be a need to find a means of exporting and transferring these technologies and sustainability practices to Russia in order to ensure that Russia has adequate supplies of hydrocarbons to meet both domestic and export needs, an interest shared by both the EU and Russia. In this way, sustainability, rather than any desperate effort to revamp the EU-defined ECT, or the narrowly-based EU–Russia energy dialog, can act as a cornerstone of a wider European energy security society embracing energy consumers in the EU, transit states, and Eurasian energy producers, including Russia.

Another issue of joint EU–Russian interest is electricity supply. Both parties faced reliability and capacity problems in their grids during the first years of the new millennium. With the electricity sector's ongoing liberalization in the EU, and the start of the sector's privatization and some unbundling in Russia in 2007, there is at least a possibility of a relatively level playing field emerging, and decent hopes for the market principle becoming well established in this sphere of the EU–Russia energy relationship. Trade and co-operation in nuclear fuels and technology may become a smaller co-operation component, although competition between Russian actors and domestic nuclear sector actors in some member states colors relations in this field as well.

Conclusion

In this chapter, we have argued that in order to understand European energy dependence on Russia, we must first analyze the different energy relations that the majority of individual European states have historically developed with Russian actors. This analysis forms the basis for understanding the prospects for and limits of energy policy integration within the EU, including the EU's efforts to extend the principles of its energy policy – markets and competition, security of supplies, and sustainability – into the conduct of what today is a heavily interdependent EU–Russia energy trade.

Broadening the set of principles governing EU energy policy and, in particular, relaxing the market and competition principle somewhat may be a way ahead in order to deal more effectively, first, with the EU member states, and second, with Russia, outside the electricity sector where markets may well start to work as suggested above. This concession would also mean accepting Gazprom's gas export monopoly in Russia, which is an issue where the European negotiating position looks very weak. Such a move would justify domestically removing the obstacles preventing a further Gazprom expansion into the EU downstream market unless reciprocal access is clinched.

A way out of this anti-market impasse in the gas sector may open up if Russia allows the small independent gas producers, which account for an increasing share of Russia's gas output, to develop, which, in turn, might gradually pave the way for the creation of more liberal conditions on Russia's energy market.

But even if the pressure for a relative closure of the downstream market continues within the EU, and even if some measures blocking Russian access are in fact adopted, that should not necessarily be read to mean that the EU and Russia are drifting apart, but rather as the establishment of a more level playing field.

Another aspect of leveling the playing field would be for the EU, in its thinking and actions, to start from recognition of the sovereignty concerns of energy producers such as Russia who have non-renewable resources. Gearing the thinking on both sides toward a joint agreement on what the whole energy chain should look like and how it should be arranged is much preferable to one-dimensional expectations of automatic supplies and markets.

Throughout this chapter, we have argued that regardless of the alarmist trends in European energy debates vis-à-vis Russia, the underlying very strong interdependence, not a one-sided dependence on Russia, is what drives the relationship. EU–Russia relations enter into a "crisis" at almost regular intervals, but rarely do these events push the parties permanently apart. There is a strong economic logic behind the relationship that locks the two sides into a mutually beneficial partnership; as long as this logic works, neither Europe nor Russia are likely to consider seriously disengaging from this relationship.

Notes

1 Pami Aalto and Kirsten Westphal, "Introduction," in *The EU–Russian Energy Dialogue: Europe's Future Energy Security*, ed. Pami Aalto (Aldershot: Ashgate, 2007), 1–8; European Commission (EC), *Green Paper: A European Strategy for Sustainable, Competitive and Secure Energy*, SEC(2006)317, (Brussels: EC, March 2006); Gawdat Bahgat, "Europe's Energy Security: Challenges and Opportunities," *International Affairs* 82, no. 5 (2006): 961–4.
2 Aalto and Westphal, "Introduction," 1ff.; Bahgat, "Europe's Energy Security," 961.
3 Kirsten Westphal, "Germany and the EU–Russia Energy Dialogue," in Aalto, *The EU–Russian Energy Dialogue*, 94f.
4 Vladimir Milov, Leonard C. Coburn, and Igor Danchenko, "Russia's Energy Policy, 1992–2005," *Eurasian Geography and Economics* 47, no. 3 (2006): 285–313, at 295.
5 Ibid., 294–9.
6 Janne Haaland Matlary, "The Nordic Countries and EU Membership: The Energy Factor," in *The European Union and the Nordic Countries*, ed. Lee Miles (London: Routledge, 1996), 239ff. The 1970s discussions on a common energy policy for Western Europe never came to any concrete results. See: Sebastian Mayer, "Path Dependence and Commission Activism in the Evolution of the European Union's External Energy Policy," *Journal of International Relations and Development* 11, no. 3 (2008): 251–78, at 254.
7 Mayer, "Path Dependence," 267.
8 Aalto and Westphal, "Introduction," 8–14.
9 Ibid., 13f.
10 Richard Youngs, *Europe's External Energy Policy: Between Geopolitics and the Market*, CEPS Working Document, no. 278 (Brussels: Centre for European Policy Studies, November 2007).
11 My definition is adapted from the classical definition of interstate societies of Hedley Bull and Adam Watson, "Introduction," in *The Expansion of International Society*, ed. Hedley Bull and Adam Watson (Oxford: Clarendon Press, 1985), 1.

12 The classification into cooperative, converging, and confederative societies is borrowed from Barry Buzan's recent work on the English School, which is here adapted to the sphere of energy policy; see Barry Buzan, *From International to World Society? English School Theory and the Social Structure of Globalisation* (Cambridge: Cambridge University Press, 2004), 158ff.
13 For the tripartite division into states, transnational actors, and peoples, see: Ibid., 118–38; on the cited poll, see Mayer, "Path Dependence," 269.
14 Pami Aalto, "Building-Blocks for a North European Energy Policy," in *The New Northern Dimension: From Regional Cooperation to High Politics*, ed. Pami Aalto (Brussels: Centre for European Policy Studies, 2008).
15 Aalto and Westphal, "Introduction," 7.
16 Jonathan Stern, *The New Security Environment for European Gas: Worsening Geopolitics and Increasing Global Competition for LNG*, NG 15 (Oxford: Oxford Institute for Energy Studies, October 2006).
17 Andrew Monaghan, *Russia and the Security of Europe's Energy Supplies: Security in Diversity?*, Special Series 07/01 (Swindon: Conflict Studies Research Centre, 2007).
18 See also Bahgat, "Europe's Energy Security," 967.
19 Jan Kjärstad and F. Johnsson, "Prospects of the European Gas Market," *Energy Policy* 35, no. 2 (2007): 869–88.
20 Alan Riley, *The Coming of the Russian Gas Deficit: Consequences and Solutions*, CEPS Policy Brief, no. 116 (Brussels: Centre for European Policy Studies, October 2006).
21 Kjärstad and Johnsson, "Prospects of the European Gas Market."
22 Tatiana Romanova, "Energy Dialogue from the Strategic Partnership Level to the Regional Level of the Northern Dimension," in Aalto, *The EU–Russian Energy Dialogue*, 89.
23 Susanne Peters, "Courting Future Resource Conflict: The Shortcomings of Western Response Strategies to New Energy Vulnerabilities," *Energy Exploration and Exploitation* 23, no. 1 (2003): 36–41.
24 Romanova, "Energy Dialogue," 98.
25 Monaghan, *Russia and the Security of Europe's Energy Supplies*, 9.
26 Milov, Coburn, and Danchenko, "Russia's Energy Policy"; Riley, *The Coming of the Russian Gas Deficit*.
27 European Parliament, *Resolution of 26 September 2007 on Towards European Foreign Policy on Energy*, 20072000(N) (Brussels: European Parliament, 2007); High Representative on Foreign Policy, *An External Policy to Serve Europe's Energy Interests*, Commission/SG/HR for the European Council, S160/06 (Brussels, 15–16 June 2006).
28 Robert L. Larsson, *Sweden and the NEGP: A Pilot Study of the North European Gas Pipeline and Sweden's Dependence on Russian Energy* (Stockholm: Swedish Defence Research Agency FOI, 2006), 41f.; Keith C. Smith, *Security Implications of Russian Energy Policies*, CEPS Policy Briefs, no. 90 (Brussels: Centre for European Policy, January 2006).
29 Vondra quoted in: "East Europeans Slam Russia's Political Use of Energy," *RFE/RL Newsline*, 12 October 2007, www.rferl.org/content/Article/1143971.html (accessed 11 September 2008).
30 Smith, *Security Implications of Russian Energy Policies*, 1f.
31 Indra Øverland, "Natural Gas Projects in the Russian North: Implications for Northern European Co-operation," in *The New Northern Dimension of European Neighbourhood*, ed. Pami Aalto, Helge Blakkisrud, and Hanna Smith (Brussels: Centre for European Policy Studies, 2008).
32 Westphal, "Germany and the EU–Russia Energy Dialogue," 93–100.
33 Ibid., 107–11.
34 Ibid., 102–5.

35 Robert L. Larsson, *Russia's Energy Policy: Security Dimensions and Russia's Reliability as an Energy Supplier* (Stockholm: Swedish Defence Research Agency FOI, 2006), 192ff.
36 From the EC's website: "Overview: Energy for the Future: Renewable Sources of Energy," http://ec.europa.eu/energy/res/index_en.htm (accessed 22 January 2008).
37 "Report: German Companies World-Leaders in Renewable Energy," *Deutsche Welle*, 19 February 2007, www.dw-world.de/dw/article/0,2144,2355370,00.html (accessed 11 January 2007).
38 "Tusk to Continue Poland's Energy Diversification," *Reuters*, 23 November 2007, http://uk.reuters.com/article/oilRpt/idUKL2310384120071123 (accessed 4 January 2008).
39 Aleksanteri Institute Eurasia Energy Group, "The Energy Dynamic on the Borders of the EU: Belarusian Russian Relations," policy presentation, www.helsinki.fi/aleksanteri/energy/publications/presentations.htm (accessed 4 January 2008).
40 Judy Dempsey, "Poland Intends to Cut Reliance on Russian Gas," *International Herald Tribune*, 18 December 2005.
41 "Poland Unveils New Gas Policy 'To Improve Energy Security'," BBC translated text of report by Polish newspaper *Gazeta Wyborcza* of 22 March 2007, www.redorbit.com/news/business/879360/poland_unveils_new_gas_policy_to_improve_energy_security/index.html (accessed 4 January 2008).
42 "Overview: Energy for the Future: Renewable Sources of Energy."
43 EC, *Communication from the Commission to the Council and the European Parliament: Prospects for the Internal Gas and Electricity Market: Implementation Report*, COM(2006) 841 final (Brussels: EC, January 2007), 163–6, http://eur-lex.europa.eu/LexUriServ/site/en/com/2006/com2006_0841en01.pdf (accessed 2 September 2008); Mayer, "Path Dependence," 268.
44 Graham Timmins, "Bilateral Relations in the Russia–EU Partnership: The British View," in *The Two-Level Game: Russia's Relations with Great Britain, Finland and the European Union*, ed. Hanna Smith (Helsinki: Aleksanteri Series 2006), 49–66.
45 Dan van der Horst, "UK Biomass Energy since 1990: The Mismatch between Project Types and Policy Objectives," *Energy Policy*, 33, no. 5 (2005): 705–16.
46 "Overview: Energy for the Future: Renewable Sources of Energy."

9 US energy policy and the former Soviet Union
Parallel tracks

Peter Rutland

Energy security has been a central concern of US foreign policy at least since the oil crisis of 1973. However, despite the fact that Russia is the world's leading source of natural gas and second only to Saudi Arabia in oil production, the US has viewed Russian energy mainly through the prism of larger strategic considerations, such as competition for influence in the Caspian region, or a Russian threat to the independence of Ukraine. Plans to develop direct energy relations between the US and Russia have been slow to come to fruition, and only a handful of projects involving US companies inside Russia have got off the ground.

Over the past 20 years, US–Russian relations have see-sawed between giddy cooperation and thinly-disguised hostility. This constant change makes it hard to predict the future path that relations between the two countries might take in the near or long term. The mutual fear that shaped relations in the Cold War was replaced by a period of partnership and cooperation, roughly from 1988 to 1999. Hopes for partnership were revived after the 11 September 2001 attacks united the two countries in what the US government of George W. Bush has referred to as the "war on terror," but this interlude was followed by a relapse into suspicion and disdain after 2003. It would be a mistake to exaggerate the degree of strategic partnership in the 1990s – but it would be equally unwise to underestimate the scope for cooperation in areas of common interest in the future.

In all of these various phases in US–Russia relations, energy has only played a secondary role. This is rather surprising, given the increasingly important place of hydrocarbons in Russian economic development, and the equally prominent role of energy in the US economy and in US foreign policy. But military and diplomatic factors have always taken priority in the relations between Washington and Moscow. Energy has become more visible as a topic of mutual concern in recent years – though its role has been that of a promise unfulfilled, or even a security threat, rather than a concrete partnership. Correspondingly, Russia has barely impacted the general course of US energy policy over recent decades.

The first section of this chapter provides an overview of US–Russian relations, focusing on the place of Russia in US trade and energy in particular. The second part addresses some of the major challenges facing these relations. These relations notably suffer from a Cold War hangover, as they are still largely based on strategic thinking and zero-sum considerations rather than mutual economic interests. In fact, when it comes to energy, the two sides have clashed most notably in their struggle for influence in the Caspian region. The two sides also have very different views on the functioning of the energy market, with Russia showing increasing reluctance to allow access for US companies in upstream projects. The third part then offers some prospects for the future and argues, in the concluding section, that the scope for partnership is limited, since Russian and US perceptions of their respective national interests are pulling in different directions.

Overview

This section puts Russian energy in the context of overall US trade and broader US energy policy. After a short historical account of US–Russia relations, the section discusses the various aspects of Russian energy that became relevant to the US and US energy companies after 1991. It also provides an overview of overall trade relations in order to explain the relatively modest place occupied by Russia in the overall foreign economic policy of the US.

Dealing with a new partner

During the Cold War, US diplomacy toward the Soviet Union and US energy policy ran on parallel tracks, with relatively little overlap between the two. Washington's relationship with Moscow was focused on preventing nuclear war and containing the arms race, while also striving to limit Soviet expansionism in the Third World. These strategic concerns crowded out any substantial US interest in the USSR as an energy supplier. The Soviet Union had been exporting oil and gas to Europe since the late 1950s, forging ties with companies such as Italy's Eni that are still relevant today.[1] The US strongly disapproved of these relationships on strategic grounds, trying, for example, to block the construction of the Urengoi–Uzhgorod natural gas export pipeline in the early 1980s.[2]

The 1973 and 1979 oil price surges filled the coffers of the Soviet state, but unrest in East Europe and the foolhardy invasion of Afghanistan increased the burdens of empire to the breaking point. The global oil price fell sharply after 1985, triggered by a Saudi decision to preserve its market share by doubling production.[3] The price slump cost the Soviet budget about $7 billion a year in lost revenue, increasing the sense of urgency behind Mikhail Gorbachev's desperate attempts at reform – efforts that actually brought about the system's collapse.[4]

After the break-up of the Soviet Union, the US national security interest lay in addressing urgent security concerns: downsizing of the Soviet nuclear arsenal and ending regional conflicts, such as the wars in the former Yugoslavia. Russia and the US did have one important common interest in the post-Soviet states – forestalling the emergence of new nuclear powers, and preventing the spread of nuclear weapons and know-how. Hence, in 1993–4, they were able to cooperate very effectively in persuading Kazakhstan to give up its nuclear weapons, and spirited away the nuclear-weapon materials.

The US was initially optimistic that what President Bill Clinton called a "market democracy" would take root in Russia. If Russia became a "normal" country, then its energy resources could become fully integrated into the global market. However, in the meantime, the chaos of transition and the battle to privatize oil industry assets caused Russian oil output to fall by nearly half, from 11.4 mbd in 1987 to 6.1 mbd in 1997.[5] Strobe Talbott was President Clinton's point man for relations with Russia as deputy secretary of state from 1993 to 2000. It is striking that oil and gas are not directly mentioned at all in Talbott's 478-page memoir.[6] Talbott's focus was crisis management: shoring up Yeltsin's authority, arranging International Monetary Fund (IMF) bailouts, dealing with unsecured nuclear weapons in Ukraine, and handling the humanitarian crises in Bosnia and Kosovo. The main energy connection was nuclear power – with the US committed to an ambitious and costly plan to buy and process Russian plutonium. The Gore–Chernomyrdin commission was tasked with developing economic cooperation – including energy – though their focus seems to have been on strategic issues such as space launches and Russian arms sales to Iran.[7] More important for economic relations was the team of Larry Summers and David Lipton at the US Treasury. They concentrated on macroeconomic stabilization, managing Russia's foreign debt, and the conditionality of IMF loans. Energy rarely featured in their deliberations, apart from periodic fruitless efforts to persuade Moscow to liberalize domestic gas and electricity prices as part of the transition to a market economy (domestic oil prices were mostly freed by 1995, and moved up to near world levels).

Russia as an energy source

The 1990s produced few concrete results for US energy interests in Russia. The privatization program mostly excluded foreign buyers from the energy sector, and Russia took in only $3.7 billion foreign direct investment in the course of the decade. The first energy project involving a foreign partner to come on-stream, in 1994, was Conoco's Polar Lights joint venture in the northern Timan–Pechora field (that proved to be only marginally profitable because of the ever-changing tax regime).[8] By the end of the 1990s, joint ventures still only accounted for about 5 percent of Russian oil output.[9] US companies did acquire stock in some of the newly-privatized Russian firms, but such investments rarely led to more active cooperation. ARCO purchased 8 percent of Lukoil stock in the early 1990s, but this did not lead to the joint projects that ARCO had hoped for.[10]

The first big direct investment in Russian energy came when British Petroleum (BP) paid $484 million for a 10 percent stake in Sidanco in 1997. But within a year, the venture was bankrupt due to the loss of a key subsidiary to rival Tyumen Oil. After BP took over Amoco, it quietly dropped Amoco's Priobskoe joint project with Yukos in March 1999. A persistent BP returned to the Russian market in 2003, paying $7.7 billion to form a 50/50 joint venture with Tyumen Oil (now renamed TNK). In September 2004, ConocoPhillips bought the last remaining Russian government block of shares in Lukoil, paying $2 billion for 7.5 percent of Lukoil's stock.[11] ConocoPhillips subsequently increased its holdings to an agreed limit of 20 percent, gaining a seat on Lukoil's board. Conoco is working with Lukoil in the Timan–Pechora basin, helping to develop the Varandei oil terminal on the Barents Sea. The company also pledged to support Lukoil's efforts to regain access to Iraqi oil fields, such as the West Qurna field, the rights to which it lost after the US invasion.

Three production sharing agreements (PSAs) were signed in 1993–4: two projects on the island of Sakhalin, led by Royal Dutch Shell and ExxonMobil, and the Kharyaga project in the Arctic, led by France's Total. PSAs exempt foreign investors from most tax liabilities until they recoup their investment costs. They are often seen by politicians, in Russia and elsewhere, as unfair deals that favor international corporations at the expense of weak states. Their advocates argue that PSAs may be the only way to get companies to invest in marginal fields and in countries where the risk of expropriation is high. The State Duma passed a law regulating PSAs in December 1995, but parliamentary opposition prevented any new projects from actually being authorized under the law. In January 2004, the Commission on PSAs cancelled a 1993 tender for the Sakhalin-3 bloc of oil and gas fields granted to Exxon, Mobil, and Texaco. Disputes delayed completion of the three initial PSAs, which did come on-stream in the early 2000s. Still, the Russian side complained that although $18 billion had been invested in the three projects by 2006, they had generated only $407 million revenue for the federal budget.[12]

By the 2000s, Russia had emerged as the world's second largest oil exporter, accounting for nearly 10 percent of global exports. But more than half of the world's oil reserves are still located in countries adjacent to the Persian Gulf. Russia's proven and probable oil reserves are nearly all located in remote regions of Siberia or north of the Arctic Circle, and it will be very costly to bring them to market. Russia has no spare capacity in either production or transportation to market, so it cannot hope to play the role of a swing producer, affecting the global price, now or in the foreseeable future. That role will continue to be played by Saudi Arabia. On the other hand, global discovery and development costs tripled between 1999 and 2006, to nearly $15 a barrel, so if this trend is sustained in the future, it is more likely that Russia's expensive reserves will be brought into production.[13]

In the 1990s, Russia's newly-privatized oil companies started looking for investment opportunities in Western markets to capture more of the downstream profits from refining and retailing. The US market was also in their sights, since it accounts for one-quarter of the world's gasoline consumption. A breakthrough came in 2000, when Lukoil bought Getty Petroleum with its 1,300 gas stations in the US northeast.[14] It started re-branding some of them as Lukoil outlets in 2003. Led by Lukoil and Yukos, Russia started serious exports of oil to the US in 1999, averaging some 100,000 b/d (crude plus refined combined).[15] Deliveries increased to roughly 300,000 b/d in 2003 – though with strong fluctuations, peaking at 550,000 b/d in July 2003. In 2006, Russia exported an average of 100,000 b/d of crude and 223,000 b/d of refined oil to the US, rising to 120,000 and 420,000 in 2007. Still, that only accounted for 2 percent of US imports and less than

4 percent of refined imports, making Russia the fourteenth largest source of US crude imports and the seventh largest in terms of refined product imports.[16]

Russia is the world's leading natural gas producer.[17] Sooner or later, this should lead to closer economic cooperation with the US. To date, Gazprom has only exported through pipelines to Europe, and has not operated any facilities to produce liquefied natural gas (LNG) that can be shipped in tankers to global markets. LNG sales accounted for 24 percent of the global gas market in 2006 and are expected to double by 2020.[18] The US, starting from nearly zero, is projected to become the second largest importer of LNG in the world (after Japan) by 2010 and the biggest in 2015.[19] Gazprom is keen to break into these lucrative new markets, but massive investments are needed. It is building two LNG facilities on Sakhalin, each with a capacity of 4.8 mt/y, which are expected to come on-stream in 2008. However, in February 2008, Gazprom announced it was dropping plans to build a $3.5 billion LNG plant in the Baltic, given the priority of completing the Nord Stream undersea pipeline to Germany.[20] That decision may cause PetroCanada to cancel its plan to build a new $1 billion re-gasification plant at Gros Cacouna, Quebec, since that was expecting to be supplied with Russian LNG. Pending construction of its own LNG facilities, Gazprom Marketing began selling LNG it had purchased from other countries to the US. Gazprom made its first LNG delivery to the US in September 2005, in cooperation with British Gas, and in September 2006 delivered to Maryland another shipment of gas it had bought from BP's plant in Trinidad.[21]

US companies were disappointed to find themselves shut out of development plans for Gazprom's giant Shtokman Arctic off-shore field. The original shortlist of five possible foreign partners issued in 2006 included ConocoPhillips and Chevron. After repeated delays, Gazprom announced in July 2007 that it had selected France's Total as a partner, giving them a 25 percent stake, and in October 2007, another 24 percent stake was awarded to Norway's StatoilHydro.

US–Russian trade and investment

The gradual and limited evolution of US involvement in Russia's energy sector reflects the general pattern of US–Russian trade and investment. According to Russian figures, the post-2000 Russian economic boom was accompanied by a doubling of Russian exports to the US, from $4.6 billion in 2001 to $8.9 billion in 2006. But as a proportion of total Russian exports outside the CIS the US share fell from 4.9 percent to 3.0 percent (see Table 9.1). Russian imports from the US also doubled during that period, from $3.3 billion to $6.4 billion, while declining as a share of total imports from 10.6 percent to 4.6 percent. In 2006, the US ranked ninth as a destination for Russian exports and fourth as source of imports (again, not counting CIS trade, which would push the US rank even lower). The falling US share of Russia's total trade means that at a macro level, Europe remains the most important player in Russian trade policy.

According to the US International Trade Commission, Russia was the twenty-fifth largest trade partner for the US in 2006, taking 0.4 percent of US

Table 9.1 US trade with Russia, 1995–2006 (Russian data)

	1995	2000	2001	2002	2003	2004	2005	2006
Exports to US ($ mn)	4,315	4,644	4,198	3,989	4,216	6,624	6,323	8,922
% total*	6.8	5.2	4.9	4.4	3.7	4.4	3.0	3.0
Imports from US ($ mn)	2,648	2,694	3,253	2,980	2,692	3,200	4,563	6,397
% total*	8.0	12.1	10.6	8.3	6.1	5.5	5.7	4.6

Source: Federal State Statistics Service, Foreign Trade of the Russian Federation with Far Abroad Countries, www.gks.ru/free_doc/2007/b07_12/25–05.htm (accessed 27 August 2008).

Note
* Percent of all Russian trade outside CIS.

Table 9.2 US trade with Russia, 2005–07 (US data)

	2005	2006	2007 (11 months)
Exports	3,658	4,215	6,148
% of total US exports	0.4	0.4	0.6
Imports	15,325	19,642	17,675
% of total US imports	0.9	1.1	1.0

Source: United States International Trade Commission, http://dataweb.usitc.gov (accessed 27 August 2008); U.S. Census Bureau, Foreign Trade Statistics, www.census.gov/foreign-trade/statistics/highlights/index.html (accessed 27 August 2008).

exports and providing 1.1 percent of US imports (see Table 9.2). That means the Russia trade is even less significant at a macro level for the US than is US trade for Russia. But the absolute rise in trade is encouraging, and it suggests that increasing numbers of Russian and US companies are engaged in and profiting from the relationship. Fuel accounted for 48 percent of the US imports from Russia, followed by steel (11 percent) and aluminum (10 percent). US exports were led by nuclear machinery (29 percent), meat (15 percent), and vehicles (14 percent). Russia is the fifth largest export market for US-made oil and gas field equipment. In 2002, US exports of oil and gas field machinery to Russia totaled $328 million.[22]

Foreign direct investment (FDI) has loomed large in the economic revival of many transition economies, from oil-rich Azerbaijan to the manufacturing giant of China. But post-Soviet Russia generally kept foreign investors at arm's length, despite its need for new capital to rebuild its obsolete industrial base. Total accumulated FDI as of June 2007 was $179 billion – less than 10 percent of GDP, compared to more than 60 percent for Kazakhstan and 85 percent for Azerbaijan.[23] One peculiarity of FDI in Russia is that a very large proportion of the money appears to be Russian export earnings recycled through offshore bank accounts, since Cyprus accounts for $37 billion and Luxembourg accounts for $29 billion of the incoming FDI.[24] The US was in sixth place, the source of

$7.4 billion of investments in Russia – 3 percent of the total stock. The pace of foreign investment has accelerated in recent years, hitting $29 billion in 2004 and $27 billion in 2005. US firms invested $1.6 billion in the first nine months of 2004 and $1.2 billion in the same period of 2005.

The United Nations Conference on Trade and Development (UNCTAD) data has the US as the top investor in Russia in 2002 (the most recent year for UNCTAD data), accounting for 22 percent of FDI stock, followed by Cyprus (19 percent) and Holland (12 percent).[25] The sectoral breakdown was food ($3.1 billion), petroleum ($2.4 billion), telecommunications ($2.8 billion), and transport and retailing (each $1.6 billion). By 1999, two of the top ten foreign subsidiaries by sales were US companies: Nevamash, a joint venture of Caterpillar and Kirovskii Zavod in St. Petersburg, founded in 1994 (65 percent owned by Caterpillar), and the Svetogorsk paper mill, bought by International Paper in 1998. Conoco ranked twenty-second, just behind Coca Cola. GM and Ford opened car assembly plants in Russia in 2002.

The largest single US investment in Russia is Chevron's 1,500-km, $1-bn pipeline, built to carry crude oil from Kazakhstan to the Russian Black Sea port of Novorossiysk. In 1993, Texaco (now Chevron) entered Kazakhstan to develop the giant Tengiz field, in which it held a 50 percent stake, along with ExxonMobil (25 percent), Kazakhoil (20 percent), and Russia's LUKarco (5 percent). Chevron and Lukoil formed the Caspian Pipeline Consortium (CPC) to build a new export pipeline with an initial capacity of 600,000 barrels per day. Construction began in 1999, and the first oil was loaded in October 2001.

A bilateral investment treaty between the US and Russia was signed in 1992 and approved by the US Senate that same year, but has still not been ratified by Russia. In 2005, the Overseas Private Investment Corporation (OPIC) provided $119 million in guarantees and insurance for 29 projects, compared to $99 million for 22 projects in the fiscal year 2004. President Clinton's International Clean Energy Initiative included efforts to promote US involvement in upgrading district heating systems, working through the joint Russian–American Center for Energy Efficiency in Moscow, founded in 1992.[26]

Challenges

What are the major challenges facing US–Russian energy relations? The key question is whether US energy policy will continue to be heavily influenced by military-strategic considerations, under the general rubric of "energy security." This approach has prevented the US from engaging with Russia on a more constructive basis on concrete economic and business considerations. Instead of strengthening the energy relationship with Russia, the US has looked for ways to contain the country's influence, especially in the energy-rich Caspian region. There were brief periods of rapprochement in the early Yeltsin years and after the 2001 attacks in the US, but otherwise, negative perceptions based on stereotypes from the Cold War have prevailed and form a major obstacle for the US to foster the partnership with Russia. Russia also must shoulder its burden of the blame for the sorry state of the relationship, since domestic political considerations have repeatedly thwarted efforts to promote international business cooperation.

Shifting the trajectory of US energy policy

For the past century, oil has been a key element driving the US economy, shaping US society, and propelling the US to superpower status. Japan's search for oil and the US embargo on oil sales to Japan were crucial factors triggering the Pacific War, from which the US emerged as the dominant world power.[27] The US itself began to import oil in the late 1940s, and securing a steady supply of oil for the world market became a key goal of US foreign policy. US domestic oil production peaked in 1970, and the share of imports in US oil consumption climbed from 34 percent in 1973 to 60 percent in 2007. Oil was viewed not just as a commodity, but as a component of national security, with uninterrupted supply seen as vital to US national interests. Given that the US alone accounts for one-quarter of global demand, for the past half century, US strategy has aimed at maintaining the *global* supply of oil. In contrast, for Europeans, energy security is more narrowly focused on diversity of supply, given that they get 44 percent of their natural gas imports and 30 percent of their oil imports from Russia.[28]

US energy policy has been built around the principle of maximizing supply to ensure cheap gasoline, preferably from a diverse range of sources to minimize the possibility of disruptions. The global price shocks of 1973, 1979, and 1990 rattled, but did not topple, this laissez-faire approach. The economic boom of the 1990s drove up commodity prices, with oil rising from $17 to $70 a barrel between 1997 and 2007. US dependence on imported oil became increasingly costly – to the tune of $450 billion a year.[29] World demand for oil is projected to rise by 47 percent by 2030, driven by the opening of huge new markets in China and India, so there is no relief in sight in the future.[30] Adding to the US woes is the fact that since the 1970s, there has been a shift of control over reserves from international oil companies to sovereign states. By 2006, only 30 percent of OPEC production was in the hands of the oil majors, and 13 of the top 15 firms in the world league table of proven oil and gas reserves were state-owned, national oil companies.[31]

In February 1991, then-US President George H.W. Bush announced a new National Energy Strategy that tried to stimulate domestic energy production, but his initiatives were largely blocked by the Democratic-controlled Congress.[32] Likewise, President Clinton did not implement any new policies to reduce US dependence on foreign oil. Despite mounting evidence of global climate change, the US did not join the 1997 Kyoto Protocol.

How can the stubborn continuity of US energy policy in the face of mounting global challenges be explained? The critical school, exemplified by Michael Klare's book *Blood and Oil*, argues that since the 1930s, US policy has been predicated on military action to ensure the flow of cheap oil.[33] The 1980 Carter Doctrine pledged military commitment to ensure the continuity of oil supplies.[34] The fall of the Soviet Union made it easier for the US to use its military force –

hence the 1991 and 2003 Iraq wars, which were at least in part aimed at securing the vast deposits of oil in and around the Gulf.[35] Klare's approach is dismissed by the mainstream of US policymakers, but it is taken seriously in Moscow and elsewhere around the world. For example, in a January 2008 speech, retired General Makhmut Gareev, the president of the Academy of Military Sciences, said: "With the growth of the dependence of its economy on access to world markets and natural deposits, the military-force component of US policy will be systematically intensifying, including toward Russia."[36]

Since 2000, US energy strategy has continued to follow familiar principles: diversification of sources; moderate efforts to reduce consumption; and political interventions to build stability in the Middle East and Africa.[37] The mainstream US approach, which can be found in the authoritative collection on *Energy and Security* edited by Jan Kalicki and David Goldwyn, is to assume that business as usual can persist for the foreseeable future. For example Adam Sieminski's chapter on world energy futures, written in 2005, assumes that the price of oil will drift down to the level of $35 a barrel – which was the average price over the past 30 years.[38]

US strategy is driven in large part by the simple geo-economics of oil. More than half of the proven oil reserves are located in the Gulf. Those fields have low extraction costs, and Saudi Arabia alone has sufficient excess capacity to serve as a stabilizing force on the global market, if it chooses to play that role. However, Saudi spare capacity has halved over the past decade, from 3–4 mbd to 1–1.5 mbd, while the Middle East's share of global output has fallen from 40 percent in 1974 to less than 30 percent today.[39]

The inertia of US policy in the face of these global changes is somewhat puzzling. Why is it that no new auto emissions targets were introduced between 1986 and December 2007 and gas taxes are still one-quarter of European levels?[40] The monthly petroleum-related trade deficit went from $6 billion in January 2002 to $26 billion in June 2006, and in 2007, oil accounted for about one-third of the US $450 billion annual trade deficit. The market has not forced adjustments in the US economy to correct this imbalance: the volume of imports has not decreased as price increased. Energy demand is inelastic, at least in the short run. Half of US oil consumption is for transportation, where machinery has a 10–15-year lifespan.

One additional factor contributing to the inertia of US energy policy is the fact that the countries with trade surpluses – not just the Saudis, but also China and Russia – prefer to save rather than buy goods. The recycling of super-profits from the petroleum industry has led to a surge of cheap capital that has made it easy for the US to fund its external and budgetary deficits (and its wars) through borrowing. In the long run, if high oil prices persist, we can expect investment to shift to less energy-intensive machinery. But in the short term, profits from oil go to elites and corporations with a vested interest in postponing policies to develop sustainable alternatives.[41]

In 2001, President Bush set up a controversial task force led by Vice President Dick Cheney, allegedly packed with oil and coal lobbyists, and whose membership the VP refused to divulge.[42] Despite conspiracy theories that hinted at dark machinations, the Cheney group produced an anodyne public report that reiterated long-standing policy principles of maximizing production, diversification of sources, and moderate promotion of conservation and renewable energy (including subsidized ethanol, a favorite of the farm lobby).[43] Russia only merited five paragraphs in the 170-page document. It was four years before the new national strategy was passed into law, in the form of the 2005 Energy Policy Act. Once again, this new legislation did not make any major changes in US energy policy.

In sum, the particularities of US domestic policy toward energy, which have very deep roots in the US political economy, have not been conducive to the emergence of a more fruitful relationship with Russia despite its role as a major energy exporter and the corresponding potential for mutually beneficial economic cooperation.

Getting beyond the great game: US–Russian rivalry in the newly independent states

While US companies encountered obstacles and delays in seeking involvement in energy projects inside Russia, they were generally welcomed as partners for the exploitation of oil and gas fields in Azerbaijan and Kazakhstan. The US had a strong strategic interest in bolstering the viability and legitimacy of the newly-independent states in Central Asia and the Caucasus. Oil-driven economic development would strengthen those regimes and help them secure their independence in the face of a possible resurgence of Russian influence. At the same time, developing a new export route for oil and gas across the Caucasus that by-passed Russian territory would be a way to reduce Western, especially European, dependence on Russia as an energy source. In addition, US corporations believed that the new governments of Azerbaijan and Kazakhstan would be more malleable than that of Russia, and perhaps offered better prospects for stable long-term partnership.

In September 1994, BP signed "the contract of the century" with the State Oil Company of Azerbaijan, and became the lead investor in the Azerbaijan International Operating Company (AIOC) developing the Azeri–Chirag–Guneshli (ACG) offshore fields. Production started in 1997, though the oil reserves proved to be below expectations and may peak as early as 2012.[44] BP operations in Azerbaijan became closely entwined with the rule of President Heidar Aliev, who had returned to power through a coup in June 1993.[45] A complicating factor for the US government was that the strong Armenian–American lobby persuaded Congress to enact Section 907 of the Freedom Support Act, effective January 1993, which barred direct US aid to the Azeri government so long as it maintains a blockade and state of war against Armenia. In addition to Chevron's involvement in Kazakhstan's Tengiz field, in 1997 the company signed a joint venture with Lukoil to develop Kazakhstan's Karachaganak gas field.

The main challenge was building a pipeline to bring Caspian oil to Western markets without crossing Russia. The US government put considerable effort into promoting the project. After several years of negotiation, in 2002, work started on a pipeline to carry the oil from Baku via Tbilisi to Ceyhan, a port on Turkey's Mediterranean coast. The BTC line became operational in 2006, with a capacity of 1 mbd. The $3.9 billion project received loans from the World Bank and European Bank for Reconstruction and Development. The consortium that built the pipeline is led by BP (with a 30 percent stake) and includes the State Oil Company of Azerbaijan (25 percent), Chevron (8.9 percent), Statoil (8.7 percent), and half-a-dozen others. ExxonMobil declined to participate in BTC, considering it too risky and expensive.[46] The US government delayed approving OPIC insurance for the pipeline, insisting that the project must be commercially viable in order to receive government assistance.[47] In 2003, OPIC did provide $142 million of financial support, but later criticized BP for failing to report corrosion problems with the pipeline that were revealed by environmentalists to the London *Sunday Times* in 2004.[48]

US interest in developing Caspian basin hydrocarbons was driven primarily by strategic concerns – the desire to build local state capacity and forge new pro-Western allies in the region, and to isolate Iran and Russia – rather than by a wish to increase the flow of oil to world markets, though these strategic and energy benefits were seen as developing in tandem. Despite US protestations that its involvement in the region was not aimed against Russia, Moscow tended to see the rivalry for Caspian oil and gas as a zero-sum game in which US advances would come at Russian expense. So the completion of the BTC probably hardened Russian resolve to continue its support for Armenia and separatist regions in Georgia, in a bid to block US strategic projection into the region.

The stakes increased with the realization in the early 2000s that there was insufficient oil in the Azeri sector of the Caspian to fill BTC. This meant that oil and gas supplies would have to be brought from the rich fields of Kazakhstan and Turkmenistan. Russia vigorously opposed such proposals, citing the lack of agreement over the legal status of the Caspian Sea to challenge plans to build pipelines across the seabed. At the same time, Moscow wooed Turkmenistan by offering higher prices for long-term gas delivery contracts, closing the gap between the price offered to Ashgabat and the price being paid by the Europeans.[49] Beginning in 2009, Russia will pay Turkmenistan "European" prices for the gas it buys.

NATO's decision to enlarge into Central Europe in 1997 was accompanied by an eastward expansion of the activities of the Partnership for Peace organization, with the first joint exercises in Uzbekistan in 1998. The leaders of Georgia and Azerbaijan welcomed the prospect of NATO projecting influence into their region, and looked to Western help to regain control over breakaway regions that had established de facto independence with Russian military support. Meanwhile in Central Asia, guerrilla incursions into Uzbekistan and Kyrgyzstan in 1999–2001 threatened the stability of those regimes, and stimulated Russia to adopt a more proactive security role in the region. China has also become involved, through what became the Shanghai Cooperation Organisation (SCO), and through the construction of a pipeline to carry oil imports east across Kazakhstan.[50] China's active policy of involvement in Central Asia was not welcomed by the US, but neither was it resisted through any concrete actions or statements from Washington.

US policy has been contradictory. The US wants to limit Russian influence in the newly-independent states, while at the same time trying to maintain a working relationship with Moscow by insisting that US policy in the region is not directed against Russia. Russian policy has been more consistent, and over time, the Russians have persuaded Kazakhstan and Turkmenistan to continue shipping oil and gas across Russia, in part by using the legal ambiguity of the Caspian Sea to block plans for a trans-Caspian pipeline. It has invested in expensive new gas export pipelines across the Baltic Sea and Black Sea to reduce its own dependency on transit countries. Domestically, the Kremlin has effectively renationalized the oil sector and has been forcing foreign partners, one after another, to give up their majority control over joint ventures on Russian territory. The US has not been able to stop these developments, and has often been reduced to carping from the sidelines.

Hopes of a new partnership

With the departure of Presidents Clinton and Yeltsin in January 2001, there were hopes that the two new leaders, Vladimir Putin and George W. Bush, could forge a new relationship. Initial conditions were not promising. The August 1998 financial crisis had shattered any illusions that Russia had completed the transition to a stable "market democracy." The angry Russian reaction to NATO's use of force in Kosovo in 1999, followed later that year by Yeltsin's nomination of 17-year KGB veteran Vladimir Putin as his replacement, and the outbreak of the second Chechen War, made Russia an even less attractive partner for the US.

However, President Putin espoused his commitment to market institutions and integration with the West. In June 2001, at his first summit with Putin in Slovenia, President Bush famously "looked the man in his eye" and "was able to get a sense of his soul."

Then came a series of attacks on the US in September 2001, and Putin's prompt offer of support. Putin seized the opportunity to align his interests with those of the US and fold the invasion of Chechnya into the so-called "global war on terror." US–Russia relations were back on track, and it looked as if a strategic partnership based on the solid ground of mutual national security interests might still be a realistic goal. At the same time, the fact that 15 of the 19 hijackers involved in the 11 September 2001 plot were Saudis raised severe doubts about the reliability of Saudi Arabia, the lynchpin of US energy strategy. Perhaps Russia, the world's second largest oil exporter, could be used to break the OPEC stranglehold on the global oil market.[51]

US business interests were also bullish because finally, in 1999, the Russian economy started rapidly growing, spurred by a 75 percent depreciation of the ruble and a rebound in the world oil price. By 2000, 70 percent of Russian oil production was in the hands of private companies, whose owners were aggressively modernizing their operations: hiring Western managers, introducing international accounting standards, and seeking foreign share listings and asset acquisitions. Russian oil output started to climb, accounting for 48 percent of the increase in world oil supply between 1998 and 2004.[52] Several of the Russian oil majors were actively looking for partnerships with Western companies. The merger of TNK with BP went through in September 2003, and Mikhail Khodorkovsky's Yukos, the largest Russian oil company, seemed to be preparing for a similar sale. Yukos was moving to break the monopoly of state-owned Transneft and build privately-owned export pipelines to Daqing in China and (in cooperation with other companies) to Murmansk on the Arctic Ocean.[53] It was argued that the rise of oil oligarchs was creating a new, pro-Western elite who could take control once Putin, a transitional post-Yeltsin figure, had stepped down. Khodorkovsky himself actively promoted such a scenario, investing heavily in Duma deputies (and Washington think-tanks) and hinting that he might challenge Putin for the presidency in 2004.

In this new spirit of cooperation, a joint US–Russian Energy Working Group met in Washington in April 2002. The following month, Bush and Putin issued a statement in Moscow promising "to develop bilateral cooperation on a mutually beneficial basis in accordance with respective national energy strategies and reduce volatility and enhance predictability of global energy markets".[54] The first meeting of a new US–Russia dialog convened in Houston in October 2002, attended by the two sides' energy and commerce ministers and dozens of oil and gas company executives.[55] Russian producers hoped for access to the US market, where margins are higher and demand was more buoyant than in Europe, where oil consumption is flat due to high taxes and conservation policies. The US government also promised to support Russian entry into the World Trade Organization, and to lift the 1974 Jackson–Vanik amendment that tied Russia's trade status to its emigration procedures. In return, there was talk of the creation of a US–Russian Strategic Energy Reserve, whereby the US would pay for reservoirs of Russian oil at sites such as Singapore and Nova Scotia that could be released in the event of a global market squeeze. The US side did acknowledge there were some "challenges" still to be overcome – such as the need for Russia to establish a clear legal framework and expanded export infrastructure. The US was still pushing for the revival of PSA agreements, which the Russian participants thought were no longer needed. Khodorkovsky was an enthusiastic participant in the Houston gathering, arguing that "Russia is a quite stable place" while recognizing that "there is clear resistance within the Russian energy sector elite and parts of the Russian government to changing the status quo."[56] The next year saw Russia attending an OPEC meeting for the first time as an observer in June 2003, followed by a state visit by Crown Prince Abdullah to Moscow in September 2003.

Even at the time, many independent US observers were skeptical about the scope for closer US–Russian cooperation. Victor and Victor wrote:[57]

> Both governments do have a durable common interest in boosting Russia's oil exports: this benefits the United States through a more diverse world

supply and helps Russia by creating revenue and jobs. Intergovernmental relations, however, are not capable of exerting much influence over the business conditions that actually determine private investment in Russia's oil sector.

However, the tide of US–Russia relations turned decisively for the worse in the course of 2003. The arrest of several Yukos executives in July was followed by the detention of Khodorkovsky himself in October, on grounds of tax evasion. That dramatic step came just one year after the heady Houston summit, and just six months after Khodorkovsky had signed a pipeline agreement in the Kremlin in the presence of Putin and President Hu Jintao of China. Khodorkovsky's arrest was triggered by his political ambitions, and Putin's fear that Khodorkovsky could help non-government parties gain a strong foothold in the upcoming December 2003 State Duma elections. The main fear was that a Khodorkovsky-backed candidate could challenge Putin for the presidency in the March 2004 election.

In the wake of Khodorkovsky's arrest, the pro-Kremlin United Russia went on to a sweeping victory in the December 2003 State Duma elections, and Putin sailed to re-election in 2004. Later that year, Putin announced the abolition of direct elections for regional governors. Russia's return to a centralized, authoritarian system of power seemed complete. In the meantime, Khodorkovsky was sentenced to nine years in jail for tax fraud (reduced to eight on appeal), while Yukos assets were progressively seized for tax arrears and sold to the state-owned Rosneft.

The Khodorkovsky affair vividly illustrated the close connections between domestic and international politics. The deterioration in US–Russian relations was not simply caused by Putin's desire to consolidate his domestic power base. It also reflected a growing rift between Moscow and Washington due to international developments. The US-led invasion of Iraq in March 2003 was vocally opposed by Putin (and by the leaders of France and Germany). The US-backed "Rose Revolution" in Georgia in December 2003 set off alarm bells in the Kremlin, which saw a new US plot to encircle Russia's borders with pro-Western governments. A year later, the "Orange Revolution" in Ukraine replicated the victory of pro-Western forces in Georgia. That was followed by a "Tulip Revolution" in Kyrgyzstan in March 2005.

Russia's testy reaction to these developments included a temporary shut-down in Ukraine's gas supplies in January 2006, a step that stoked European anxieties about their dependency on Russian energy. The US saw an authoritarian revival in Russia on both the domestic and international fronts – a development fueled by the surge of revenue due to the rising price of oil. Speaking in Vilnius, Lithuania in May 2006, US Vice President Cheney accused Russia of using energy as "an instrument of intimidation and blackmail".[58] It became common to refer to Russia as an "energy superpower". For example, US National Intelligence Director John Negroponte described Russia as an "energy superpower" (albeit a "regional" one) in a January 2007 Congressional briefing on "Current and Future Threats to the United States" – a point that was not lost on Russian observers.[59] Moscow wants to protect itself against future threats by building up its military muscle and by using its energy exports as a political weapon. Hostile countries will be punished by denial of energy supplies, while friendly powers will be rewarded by investments boosting energy supplies, perhaps a share for their companies in developing Russian oil and gas fields, and maybe even a price discount.

Over the five years since the Yukos affair, Russia's oil sector has been effectively re-nationalized. Apart from Rosneft's absorption of Yukos, Sibneft was forcibly sold to Gazprom. The future of Russian development is now in the hands of state-owned oil and gas corporations, directly controlled by the Kremlin officials who sit on their boards of directors. There are grave concerns that these quasi-political entities will focus their efforts on rewarding insider cronies and maintaining populist price subsidies. They are less likely to prioritize efficiency and rational investment planning.

The exclusion of TNK-BP from the Kovykta gas field and of Shell from the Sakhalin-2 energy project in 2006–7 were other clear signals of the change in course. A new subsoil resources law will bar foreign companies from holding more than 50 percent ownership of any field deemed "strategic."

The Russian government is confident that Russian oil and gas companies have the managerial skills to be the lead investors on new projects, contracting with Western firms for technical services as necessary. In ten years' time, we will have some idea whether they are correct. But in the meantime, these developments mean that US companies can only hope for service contracts and other junior roles in Russia's burgeoning energy empire.

Signs of progress

While the overall prospects for the future of US–Russia energy relations look rather dim, there have been some positive developments in the last couple of years. Among these was the US acceptance of Russia's bid for entry to the World Trade Organization (WTO) in November 2006.[60] The US had been holding out for Russian concessions on food imports, liberalization of the market for financial services, and improved legislation on intellectual property rights. Russia had been negotiating for WTO entry for 13 years, and the US was the main hold-out in the round of bilateral negotiations with member countries. After the two sides failed to close a deal at the G8 summit in St. Petersburg in June 2006, Russia's patience was exhausted. Moscow slapped a ban on US chicken imports, citing sanitary concerns, and passed up a $3 billion option to buy 22 Boeing 787 airliners. The WTO entry issue has some symbolic significance for the US–Russian relationship, but more than two years have passed (during which Ukraine was accepted for WTO entry), and it is still unclear whether Russia will actually join the organization.

Global warming remains an area of some promise for US–Russia relations. Although the two countries stand on opposite sides of the energy fence as an energy importer and exporter, respectively, they are both huge consumers of energy – and are the world's largest and third largest greenhouse gas emitters, respectively (with China in second place). This means that they have a common interest in developing technologies and incentive systems to promote *mutual* action to reduce greenhouse gas emissions.[61] Russia's energy use per unit of GDP is three times that of Europe, so there is massive scope for cooperative cost-saving. Russia agreed to join the Kyoto Protocol in May 2004, after the EU gave up its insistence that Russia liberalize its internal gas market and agreed to support Russia's entry to the WTO. But the US has to forge a domestic political consensus for its *own* entry into the Kyoto process before it can start making deals with Russia. Interestingly, even the Pentagon is recognizing the problem. The Defense Department released a report on climate change in 2003, and in 2007 sponsored a CNA Corporation report "National Security and the Threat of Climate Change."

If the Democratic Party should gain control of the White House and Congress in 2008, we *might* see a major shift in US energy security policy, away from unilateralism and output maximization, toward multilateralism and conservation. But then again, we may not: the domestic policy process has been built up around the existing energy paradigm for half a century, and will be hard to transform.

In any event, Russia is unlikely to feature prominently in US policy. Policy papers advocating conservation in the US rarely mention Russia as a relevant actor.[62] A recent study by the Brookings Institution grudgingly concedes that "Russia will remain a major energy player on the global market for the foreseeable future."[63] But as a high-cost producer with no excess capacity, it will not be a market maker. The study also doubts whether Russian oil and gas recovery is sustainable, since "behind the scenes, Russia's entire political and economic system is extremely tenuous."

Either way, it seems that US policy will continue to move in the direction of isolating Russia. If Russian oil and gas stagnates, due to lack of competition and bureaucratic inertia, then the US will have to look elsewhere for increments to the global energy market. If, on the other hand, Russia's oil and gas output grows, it will be seen as a strategic threat, given its willingness to use those petro-rubles to project Russian political influence

Conclusion

The past 15 years have seen the rise and fall of hopes for a breakthrough to partnership in US–Russian relations. Despite the ups and downs of the relationship, US energy policy toward Russia has remained fairly consistent. Key elements of the enduring US official policy remain as follows:

- Russia will need Western capital and technology to develop its oil and gas reserves. This is best done through foreign direct investment in projects where foreign companies have majority control.
- More oil and gas fields need to be developed and brought on-stream as quickly as possible.
- New producers outside Russia should be encouraged. Alternative export routes to bring their oil to world markets without transiting Russia are a priority.

- Oil and gas transit should not be a state monopoly and should not be used as a political weapon.

On almost every point, Russian policy has become diametrically opposed to US interests. Under Putin, the state sector's control has risen from 30 to 70 percent, and not even Russian private companies are allowed to have a majority stake, let alone foreign companies. Flush with cash, the Russian government is in no hurry to boost oil and gas production in the short run. Russia has tried its best to block or delay the construction of alternative export pipelines across the Caucasus and has used the North Stream and South Stream natural gas pipeline projects to forge closer ties with Germany, Italy, and other partners while blocking European efforts to develop a common strategy to decrease their dependency on Russia.

Overall, US energy policy toward the former Soviet Union has been something of a disappointment. This failure is partly because of the lack of imagination within the policy itself, and partly due to Russia's success in implementing its own policy agenda, which runs contrary to many of the US goals. US policy toward the post-Soviet states was predicated on false optimism about the speed of the transition to "market democracy" and on reservations about Russia's reliability as a strategic partner. US policy toward energy security has rested on a myopic assumption that cheap oil supplies can be secured from the Gulf for the foreseeable future.

Notes

1 Thane Gustafson, *Crisis Amid Plenty: The Politics of Soviet Energy Under Brezhnev and Gorbachev* (Princeton, NJ: Princeton University Press, 1989). The Friendship oil pipeline was built in 1964, and following West Germany's agreement to buy Soviet natural gas in 1970, the Soyuz (1978), Urengoi (1983) and Yamal (1997) pipelines were built.
2 Matthew R. Simmons, *Twilight in the Desert* (Hoboken, NJ: John Wiley & Sons, 2005); Rachel Bronson, *Thicker than Oil: America's Uneasy Partnership with Saudi Arabia* (New York: Oxford University Press, 2006).
3 Edward Morse and Amy Myers Jaffe, "OPEC in Confrontation with Globalization," in *Energy and Security: Toward a New Foreign Policy Strategy*, ed. Jan H. Kalicki and David L. Goldwyn (Washington, DC: Johns Hopkins University Press, 2005), 77. The world price fell from $20 to $10 a barrel "nearly overnight."
4 Yegor Gaidar, *Collapse of an Empire: Lessons for Modern Russia* (Washington, DC: Brookings Institution, 2007), chapter 3. Gaidar calculates that the Soviet Union lost $7 billion in annual oil revenue during the years 1984–7 (131).
5 John D. Grace, *Russian Oil Supply* (Oxford University Press, 2005).
6 Strobe Talbott, *The Russia Hand* (New York: Random House, 2002).
7 Ibid., 264.
8 According to Conoco chairman Archie Dunham, speaking at the US–Russia Commercial Energy Summit in Houston on 1–2 October 2002: James Baker III Institute for Public Policy, *U.S.–Russia Commercial Energy Summit*, Baker Institute Study, no. 21 (Houston: James Baker III Institute for Public Policy, February 2003), 6.
9 Grace, *Russian Oil Supply*, 146.
10 Ibid., 119.
11 Erin Arvedlund, "Conoco Wins LUKoil Bid," *New York Times*, 30 September 2004.

12 Igor Tomberg, "Russia has Outgrown PSA," *RIA Novosti*, 20 September 2006.
13 Jad Mouawad, "Quest for New Energy Supplies is Becoming Tougher," *International Herald Tribune*, 8 October 2007.
14 "Russia's LUKoil Plans East Coast Expansion," *Alexander's Oil and Gas Connections* 9, no. 16 (2004), www.gasandoil.com/goc/company/cnn43370.htm (accessed 3 September 2008).
15 www.economagic.com/doeme.htm (accessed 31 August 2008).
16 Energy Information Administration (EIA), *US Imports of by Country of Origin*, http://tonto.eia.doe.gov/dnav/pet/pet_move_impcus_a2_nus_ep00_im0_mbbl_m.htm (accessed 3 September 2008).
17 Jonathan Stern, *The Future of Russian Gas and Gazprom* (New York: Oxford University Press, 2005).
18 *LNG Observer* 4, no. 3, 1 July 2007. LNG still only accounts for 7 percent of total gas consumption.
19 Helmut Weisser, "The Security of Gas Supply – a Critical Issue for Europe?," *Energy Policy* 35, no. 1 (2007): 1–5.
20 "Gazprom Drops Baltic LNG," *Reuters*, 2 February 2008.
21 "BP and Gazprom Announce LNG Supply Deal," BP press release, 13 September 2006, www.bp.com/genericarticle.do?categoryId=2012968&contentId=7022601 (accessed 31 August 2008); www.gazprom.ru/eng/articles/article21387.shtml (accessed 31 August 2008). Norway's Statoil is a partner in the Cove Point, Maryland regasification plant.
22 "Mission Statement, Secretarial Oil and Gas Business Development to Russia," 21–25 September 2003, http://trade.gov/doctm/russia_0903.html (accessed 31 August 2008).
23 United Nations Conference on Trade and Development (UNCTAD), *Country profiles*, www.unctad.org/Templates/Page.asp?intItemID=3198&lang=1 (accessed 31 August 2008).
24 Data from: Federal State Statistics Service, www.gks.ru (accessed 31 August 2008). Legally reported capital exports amount to some 5 percent of Russian GDP.
25 See at UNCTAD, *FDI in Brief*, www.unctad.org/Templates/Page.asp?intItemID =3198&lang=1 (accessed 31 August 2008).
26 Information obtained from: Municipal Network for Energy Efficiency, www.munee.org/; www.cenef.ru/ (accessed 31 August 2008).
27 Daniel Yergin, *The Prize. The Epic Quest for Oil, Money and Power* (New York: The Free Press, 1993).
28 *The European Union and Russia: Close Neighbours, Global Players, Strategic Partners* (Brussels: European Commission External Relations, October 2007), 13, http://ec.europa.eu/external_relations/library/publications/34_eu_russia.pdf (accessed 31 August 2008).
29 David Sandalow, *Freedom From Oil: How the Next President Can End the United States' Oil Addiction* (New York: McGraw Hill, 2007).
30 EIA, *International Energy Outlook 2006* (Washington, DC: Department of Energy, EIA, 2006).
31 Margaret Polski, "The New Institutional Economics of Energy Security," paper presented at the International Society for New Institutional Economics, Boulder, CO, 21–24 September 2006.
32 Yergin notes that the 1990s was a decade of "overconfidence." Daniel Yergin, "Energy Security and Markets," in Kalicki and Goldwyn, *Energy and Security*, 51–64, at 53.
33 Michael T. Klare, *Blood and Oil: The Dangers and Consequences of America's Growing Dependency on Imported Petroleum* (New York: Metropolitan Books, 2004). In addition, see Jim Holt, "It's the Oil," *London Review of Books*, 18 October 2007 and Godfrey Hodgson, "Oil and American Politics," *Open Democracy*, 2 October 2005, www.opendemocracy.net/democracy-americanpower/oil_2887.jsp (accessed 31 August 2008).

34 In October 1999, Centcom was broadened to include Central Asia (but not the Caucasus). Klare, *Blood and Oil*, 137.
35 In his autobiography, former Federal Reserve Chairman Alan Greenspan writes "I am saddened that it is politically inconvenient to acknowledge what everyone knows: the Iraq war is largely about oil." Cited in: Bob Woodward, "Greenspan is Critical of Bush in Memoir," *Washington Post*, 15 September 2007. See also David Strahan, *The Last Oil Shock: Survival Guide to the Imminent Extinction of Petroleum Man* (London: John Murray, 2007), chapter 1.
36 Cited in: *Itar-Tass*, 19 January 2008.
37 Jan H. Kalicki and David L. Goldwyn, "Introduction: The Need to Integrate Energy and Foreign Policy," in Kalicki and Goldwyn, *Energy and Security*, 1–16.
38 Adam E. Sieminski, "World Energy Futures," in Kalicki and Goldwyn, *Energy and Security*, 21–50, at 30.
39 Oystein Noreng, "Restructuring World Economic Power Relations Through High Oil Prices," Seminar discussion held at the New America Foundation, Washington, DC, 25 April 2007, www.newamerica.net/events/2007/restructuring_world_economic_power_relations_through_high_oil_prices (accessed 31 August 2008); "Oil's Dark Secret," *Economist*, 12 August 2006.
40 Lex, "US Energy Policy," *Financial Times*, 4 October 2007.
41 Michele Cavallo, *Oil Prices and the U.S. Trade Deficit*, FRBSF Economic Letter, no. 2006–24 (San Francisco: Economic Research Federal Reserve Bank of San Francisco, September 2006), www.frbsf.org/publications/economics/letter/2006/el2006-24.pdf (accessed 31 August 2008). See also: Alessandro Rebucci and Nikola Spatafora, "Oil Prices and Global Imbalances," in *IMF World Economic Outlook: Globalization and Inflation* (Washington, DC: International Monetary Fund, April 2006), 71–96, www.imf.org/external/pubs/ft/weo/2006/01/pdf/c2.pdf (accessed 31 August 2008); Bob Lloyd, "The Commons revisited," *Energy Policy*, 35, no. 1 (2007): 5806–18.
42 Jane Mayer, "Contract Sport: What did the Vice-President do for Halliburton?," *New Yorker*, 16–23 February 2004.
43 National Energy Policy Development Group, *Reliable, Affordable, and Environmentally Sound Energy for America's Future*, Report of the National Energy Policy Development Group (Washington, DC: The White House, May 2001), www.whitehouse.gov/energy/National-Energy-Policy.pdf (accessed 31 August 2008).
44 Maureen Crandall, "Realism on Caspian Energy: Over-Hyped and Under-Risked," in *International Association for Energy Economics Newsletter* (Cleveland, OH: Energy Economics Education Foundation, 2005), 5–10, www.iaee.org/documents/05spr.pdf (accessed 31 August 2008).
45 David Leppard, "BP Accused of Backing 'Arms for Oil' Coup," *Sunday Times*, 26 March 2000.
46 Jonathan Elkind, "Economic Implications," in *The Baku–Tbilisi–Ceyhan Pipeline: Oil Window to the West*, ed. S. Frederick Starr and Svante Cornell (Washington, DC: SAIS, Johns Hopkins University, 2005), 42.
47 "The NEPD Group recommends that the President direct the Secretaries of State, Commerce, and Energy to support the BTC oil pipeline as it demonstrates its commercial viability." Quoted from National Energy Policy Development Group, *Reliable, Affordable, and Environmentally Sound Energy for America's Future*, 19.
48 Simon Clark, "BP's Caspian Pipeline Needs Greater Scrutiny," *Bloomberg News*, 6 February 2007.
49 Judy Dempsey, "Russia Signs Deal for Gas Pipeline Along Caspian Sea," *New York Times*, 21 December 2007.
50 It met as the Shanghai Five in 1996 (grouping China, Russia, Kazakhstan, Kyrgyzstan, and Tajikistan), and adopted the SCO name in 2001, when Uzbekistan joined.

51 Harpriye A. Juneja, *The Emergence of Russia as Potential Energy Superpower and Implications for US Energy Security in the 21st Century*, (Düsseldorf: Institute for International Affairs, January 2005).
52 William Tompson and Rudiger Ahrend, *Realizing the Oil Supply Potential of the CIS: The Impact of Institutions and Policies*, OECD Economics Department Working Papers, no. 484 (Paris: OECD, June 2006).
53 Leon Aron, *The YUKOS Affair, Russian Outlook*, no. 2 (Washington, DC: American Enterprise Institute for Public Policy Research, Fall 2003); Leon Aron, "Russia's Oil: Natural Abundance and Political Shortages," *Russian Outlook*, no. 2 (Washington, DC: American Enterprise Institute for Public Policy Research, Spring 2006). The US itself seems to have stayed on the sidelines of the great debate over Russian oil exports to Asia – whether to build the pipeline to China or to a sea port, and whether to build the pipeline at all. The US support for their Japanese ally in this debate has been distinctly lukewarm.
54 "Joint statement by President George W. Bush and President Vladimir V. Putin on the New US–Russian Energy Dialogue," 24 May 2002, www.whitehouse.gov/news/releases/2002/05/ 20020524–8.html (accessed 31 August 2008).
55 James Baker III Institute for Public Policy, *U.S.–Russia Commercial Energy Summit*.
56 Ibid., 11.
57 David G. Victor and Nadejda M. Victor, "Axis of Oil?," *Foreign Affairs* 82, no. 2 (2003): 47–61, at 47. They were wrong, however, about oil prices dropping, and wrong about Putin's inability to influence the oil sector. See also William Ratliff, *Russia's Oil in America's Future* (Stanford, CA: Hoover Press, 2003).
58 "Vice President's Remarks at the Vilnius Conference," Reval Hotel Lietuva, Vilnius, 4 May 2006, www.whitehouse.gov/news/releases/2006/05/20060504–1.html (accessed 31 August 2008).
59 Artur Blinov, "Moscow's Oil is the Chief Source of Threats to America," *Nezavisimaia gazeta*, 15 January 2007.
60 Peter Rutland, "Russia and the WTO: Deal, or No Deal?," in *Russia and the WTO: A Progress Report*, NBR Special Report, no. 12 (Seattle, WA: National Bureau of Asian Research, March 2007), 31–6.
61 Daniel Yergin, "China and America Need Not be Energy Rivals," *Financial Times*, 20 May 2007.
62 See for example Jonathan Elkind, *Building a Secure Energy Future: A Challenge for New Presidential Leadership*, Opportunity 08 Series (Washington, DC: Brooking Institution, August 2007), which concentrates on conservation as the new paradigm, with no mention of Russia or Central Asia.
63 The Brookings Institution, *The Russian Federation*, The Brookings Foreign Policy Studies Energy Security Series (Washington, DC: The Brookings Institution, October 2006), 2, www.3.brookings.edu/fp/research/energy/2006russia.pdf (accessed 31 August 2008).

10 Chinese perspectives on Russian oil and gas

Indra Øverland and Kyrre Elvenes Brækhus*

In this chapter, we examine the role of Russian oil and gas in the broader Chinese context, including the main actors and perspectives on the Chinese side of the relationship, the exigencies of China's economic geography and energy markets, and the broader geopolitical situation. We argue that there is a match between Russian natural resources and Chinese markets, and that long-term developments in world politics as well domestic developments in China and Russia constitute a foundation for extensive energy cooperation in the future. But there are numerous sources of tension in the bilateral relationship, particularly from the Chinese point of view. The most important are the slow speed at which Russia is proceeding in the development of new fields and pipeline construction, the unpredictability of Russian decision-making, latent rivalry in Central Asia, and attempts by Moscow to play off China and Japan against each other.

Beijing nevertheless views Moscow as a key partner, and as the only great power that is not in some way aligned against it. Moreover, Russian oil and gas can be brought to China overland, unlike Middle Eastern, African, or Latin American shipments. Russia's proximity means that its supplies carry a unique strategic significance for Beijing, which lacks a proper blue-water navy. China has regarded Russia as a strategic partner since the mid-1990s. It is possible, although far from certain, that Beijing may seek to employ as a vehicle for a firmer alliance the Shanghai Cooperation Organisation (SCO), which has sometimes been an empty multilateral shell, at times been a symbol of Chinese–Russian cooperation, and occasionally served as a platform for joint resistance to the increasing US influence in Central Asia. One reason for doing so would be to get stable and predictable access to Russian energy supplies.

The chapter is divided into three parts. The first part starts with a brief analysis of the history of Sino-Russian relations, and then evaluates China's national oil companies, the country's petroleum imports, and the place of Russian oil and gas in this picture. The second part of the chapter explores political, economic, and environmental challenges to the Chinese petroleum sector. The third part examines the implications of these challenges for Sino-Russian relations and for the rest of the world.

Overview

During the historical trajectory of Sino-Russian relations, relations have been tense for many of the last 200 years, interrupted by brief periods of close cooperation following the first and second Chinese revolutions in 1911 and 1949. Understanding the dynamics of the past relationship between the two countries is an important step in attempting to comprehend the prospects for future energy cooperation.

In 2004, more than 200 years of territorial disputes came to an end when Russian President Vladimir Putin made a three-day state visit to Beijing and Xian and signed treaties codifying the last stretch of the 3,645-km border between the two countries.[1] Relations between China and Russia can be traced back to the late Ming Dynasty (1368–1644), but the first diplomatic contact did not occur until the 1660s. These contacts were the result of a conflict over Amur Krai on the left bank of the Amur River, which was settled with the Treaty of Nerchinsk (1689). In the eighteenth century, during the Qing Dynasty, China gained control over Xinjiang, while Russia expanded into Kazakhstan at the beginning of the nineteenth century. The two empires met in what is today western Xinjiang and eastern Kazakhstan, and trade was legalized with the 1851 Treaty of Kulja.[2]

In 1921, Moscow began supporting the Kuomintang militarily, and instructed the Communist Party of China to formalize cooperation with the Nationalists. This was based on Lenin's rationale that China, having just emerged from a backward feudal society, was not yet ready for a Socialist revolution. The alliance between Moscow and the Kuomintang came to an end in 1926, when Chiang Kai-shek dismissed his Soviet advisors and purged Communist Party members from the government, setting the stage for the Chinese Civil War, which did not conclude until 1949 – though the Communists and the Kuomintang formed the United Front in 1937 to fight the Japanese invasion.

The 1950s was a decade of close cooperation between China and the Soviet Union, and Moscow provided equipment and expertise to modernize and industrialize China.[3] However, the support provided did not meet Chinese expectations, and Russian big-brother attitudes were an additional irritant. The process of de-Stalinization and Khrushchev's emphasis on the idea of "peaceful coexistence" between Communist and capitalist states added to Chinese frustration, while Moscow was alarmed by Beijing's radicalism, particularly the Great Leap Forward. These differences led to the re-emergence of a Sino-Soviet split by the late 1950s, and the nadir of the ensuing standoff was a bloody skirmish over Zhenbao Island on the Ussuri River that briefly threatened to become a real war in 1969.[4]

Mao's death in 1976 and China's subsequent decision in 1978 to discard any radical revolutionary agenda set the stage for gradually improved bilateral relations. Initially, Moscow was uncomfortable with China's gradual embrace of a market economy. Since the collapse of Communism in Russia, however, relations have improved rapidly. China's pragmatic policy of non-interference in other states has enabled Beijing to approach the collapse of Communism in the Soviet Union as an opportunity rather than a loss.[5] In 1992, Russian President Boris Yeltsin and Foreign Minister Andrei Kozyrev came to Beijing; later that year, Russian troops were withdrawn from Mongolia and 200,000 troops from the Russian Far East redeployed, which led Beijing to conclude that Russia had become less of a threat.[6] In 1993, Jiang Zemin was the first Chinese president to visit Russia since Mao Zedong, and between 1992 and 1999, Yeltsin and Jiang held seven summits. In 1996, China and Russia formalized a "strategic partnership."

For Yeltsin, strengthening ties with China was a way of fending off the nationalist and Communist forces that challenged him in domestic Russian politics. Closer ties with China could counterbalance the impression of involvement with the US.[7] At the same time, Sino-Russian trade trebled between 1991 and 1993, due to a combination of booming border trade and increased Chinese imports of Russian weaponry.[8]

As we have tried to show in this section, historically the relationship between the two states has been one of the meeting of two territorially-expanding empires, and has involved much tension. The list of territorial disagreements has, however, gradually been whittled down until the last section of the border was finalized in 2004. From a historical point of view, the prospects for energy cooperation have, therefore, never looked better than now. On the other hand, the historical disagreements and old grudges between the two countries could resurface in other forms.

China's petroleum supplies and Russia's role

Energy is a bottleneck for the unfolding Chinese boom.[9] Between 1980 and 2000, China quadrupled its GDP per capita while only doubling its energy consumption, a remarkable development.[10] Since 2000, the Chinese economy has continued its rapid growth trajectory, but overall energy consumption and oil imports have expanded almost twice as quickly as the rest of the economy.[11] Most of the new Chinese demand for oil is covered through increased imports, which have soared since China became a net importer in 1993.[12]

At 7.3 mbd, China is the world's second largest oil consumer behind only the US, which consumes 20.6 mbd, and ahead of Japan, which consumes 5.2 million barrels.[13] Around 40 percent of the growth in world oil demand between 2001 and 2005 was due to China, and China's consumption figure is projected to at least double to 13.4 mbd by 2025. If China's per capita consumption were equal to that of the US, the entire global output of oil would not be enough for China alone.[14] China is the world's fifth largest oil producer at 3.8 mbd, but production growth cannot keep up with demand. In January 2006, proven domestic reserves were estimated at about 18.3 billion barrels,[15] and the new Jidong Nanpu field discovered in Bohai Bay has added another one billion tons to China's reserves.[16] However, production is declining in Daqing in the northeast Heilongjiang province, and the potential for large new fields in the northwestern

Xinjiang province is limited. Oil in the South China Sea is difficult to extract because the borders have not been delineated, and this also applies to gas in the East China Sea near the Diaoyu/Senkaku Islands, where China has a dispute with Japan.

China is currently the world's third largest oil importer at 2.97 mbd.[17] The top suppliers include Saudi Arabia, Angola, and Iran (see Table 10.1). Russia, ranked number four, provided 11 percent of China's total crude oil imports in 2006, or 15.96 mt. This figure was up from 12.78 mt in 2005 and 1.76 mt in 2001.[18] The Chinese government is seeking to increase supplies of oil and gas in countries across the Middle East and Africa,[19] but believes that Russian supplies carry particular strategic significance because imports from other parts of the world are subject to major risks (which are discussed below).

Coal accounts for two-thirds of China's overall energy consumption and nearly 80 percent of its electricity.[20] China has vast supplies of coal, but coal is also China's biggest environmental problem, and for this reason the government is promoting the use of natural gas instead of coal. Natural gas constitutes only around 3 percent of the energy consumed in China, and the grid remains woefully underdeveloped, but the government aims to increase that proportion to 8 percent by 2010. Environmental concerns are therefore another driver for imports of hydrocarbons from Russia and other countries, and imports are expected to cover 40 percent of China's natural gas needs by 2025.[21]

Table 10.1 China's top 12 sources of crude oil, 2001–6 (thousands of tons)

	2001	2002	2003	2004	2005	2006	Percent of imports 2006
Saudi Arabia	8,778	11,390	15,176	17,244	22,179	23,872	16.4
Angola	3,799	5,705	10,102	16,208	17,463	23,452	16.2
Iran	10,847	10,630	12,389	13,237	14,272	16,774	11.6
Russia	1,766	3,030	5,255	10,777	12,776	15,966	11
Oman	8,140	8,046	9,277	16,348	10,835	13,183	9.1
Congo	642	1,047	3,389	4,773	5,535	5,419	3.7
Equatorial Guinea	2,146	1,780	1,460	3,485	3,839	5,267	3.6
Sudan	4,973	6,426	6,258	5,771	6,621	4,847	3.3
Yemen	2,287	2,262	6,997	4,912	6,976	4,543	3.1
Venezuela	56	–	444	334	1,928	4,203	2.9
Libya	250	–	129	1,339	2,259	3,385	2.3
UAE	650	–	864	1,344	2,568	3,044	2.1
OPEC total	27,156	27,810	34,169	41,795	52,578	58,298	40.9

Source: Tian Chunrong, "2006 nian zhongguo shiyou jinchukou zhuangkuang fenxi" [Analysis of China's Oil Import and Export in 2006], *Guoji Shiyou Jingji* [International Petroleum Economics], no. 3 (2007): 17.

Note
The 15,966,000 tons of oil imported from Russia by China in 2006 are equivalent to about 330,000 barrels of oil, according to Tian, "2006 nian zhongguo shiyou jinchukou zhuangkuang fenxi," 17.

Chinese petroleum actors

As in Russia, political control of the oil and gas sector is strong in China. China's petroleum industry has also undergone major reorganization in the past decade, and there are now three Chinese oil majors, all of which originated in the 1980s: China National Offshore Oil Corporation (CNOOC, founded 1982), the China Petroleum and Chemical Corporation (Sinopec, founded 1983), and the China National Petroleum Corporation (CNPC, founded 1988).

In the past, CNPC tended to focus on oil and gas exploration and production, while Sinopec was responsible for refining and distribution. While this pattern remains evident, the restructuring in the late 1990s has blurred it.[22] In 1998, the government reorganized CNPC and Sinopec to create two vertically integrated oil companies, but CNPC remains the country's dominant upstream company and Sinopec the main downstream company.[23] Between 2000 and 2002, CNPC, Sinopec, and CNOOC all carried out successful initial public offerings.[24] Beijing, however, retains control of large majority stakes in each of the three companies held through state-owned holding companies.

During the 1980s, the government maintained a two-tiered pricing system, forcing CNPC to supply industrial customers at a fraction of market prices. As a result, the company was starved for cash, resulting in limited exploration. Pricing was relaxed in 1993, vastly increasing CNPC's cash flow. The appointment of Zhou Yongkang, who favored foreign investments, as general manager in 1996 resulted in rapid overseas expansion. Since then, the views of top CNPC officials – who are still appointed by the Communist Party – have been decisive for China's foreign petroleum investments.[25]

CNPC is now the largest integrated oil company, with proven reserves of 3.7 billion barrels of oil and over 30 international exploration projects. It is dominant in the northern and western parts of the country, while Sinopec has its main operations in the south. CNOOC is responsible for offshore exploration and production, and accounts for approximately 15 percent of China's domestic crude oil production.[26]

The current structure of China's petroleum industry gives rise to a classical principal-agent problem. Officially, it is the owner (principal) – the Chinese state or Communist Party – that controls the petroleum companies (agents). In the case of a one-party state such as China, one might expect the principal's dominant role to be indisputable. In practice, in China as in many countries, the companies often have more coherent interests and are better at promoting them than the state is at advocating its interests. Furthermore, their interest consists of a continued focus on supply-side factors in China's energy sector.[27] Since resources inside China are limited, the emphasis on gaining more supplies results in a strong drive to gain access to resources abroad.

One important reason for the companies' relative strength is their information advantage: they know more about the petroleum sector than the state does, enabling them to set the agenda. The imbalance between companies and the state in the Chinese petroleum sector is further exacerbated by the fact that

China's Ministry of Energy was disbanded in 1993 and has not been replaced.[28] Instead, responsibility is split between the National Development and Reform Commission, the State Council, and state-controlled companies in various energy sectors. The State Energy Leading Group, led by Premier Wen Jiabao, carries out research on China's energy strategy and has attempted to coordinate the approach, but lacks the necessary clout and cannot substitute for a full ministry. However, the Chinese government is working to remedy the situation. At the First Plenary Session of the 11th National People's Congress in March 2008, the delegates decided to restructure the government by creating a National Energy Commission to take responsibility for energy strategy, security and development. Yet this falls short of creating the expected super-Ministry of Energy as the National Development and Reform Commission, the top planning agency, will continue to control the administration and regulation of the sector.[29]

Whether the new National Energy Commission will be successful at creating a more coordinated government policy remains thus doubtful, and it will certainly be difficult to reassert authority over companies like Petrochina, whose market capitalization was double that of Exxon when it first went public on the Shanghai stock exchange in November 2007, and whose CEO enjoys full ministerial status (along with the CEOs of China's other main petroleum corporations).

The resulting setup is ambiguous. On the one hand, China remains a one-party state with state-controlled oil companies. The Communist Party appoints the leaders of these companies, and they are unable to make any major moves without its consent, neither domestically nor abroad. On the other hand, through inverted principal-agent relations, the companies set the agenda and are the main drivers in China's energy policy.

Partial privatization and listing on foreign stock exchanges, as in China or Russia or Norway, are meant to provide extra external checks on the companies in addition to the state owner. But stock markets only control the performance of the companies according to petroleum sector logic. This logic is that increased demand must be met with expanded production at home or abroad (rather than energy efficiency or alternative energy sources). That is what China has been trying to do for the past decades, bringing its companies to knock on Russia's door.

Chinese debates on Russia and Russian energy

Broadly speaking, there are currently three main factions inside the Communist Party of China, one led by current President Hu Jintao and Premier Wen Jiabao with its power base in the Communist Youth League; the other by former president Jiang Zemin, called the Shanghai Gang; and the third by the sons and daughters of former senior officials and revolutionary heroes, known as the "princeling faction." Xi Jinping, the new governor of Shanghai and a member of the princeling faction, seems to have emerged as Hu Jintao's likely successor when he steps down at the 18th Party Congress in 2012. While Xi Jinping is acceptable to Hu Jintao, he would prefer his protégé Li Keqiang, governor of the northeast

Liaoning Province. Whereas Hu Jintao emphasizes the importance of a "harmonious society" and prioritizes the poor western regions and the countryside, the members of the Shanghai Gang prefer a more market-based approach to development and prioritize the cities and coastal regions. Crucially, however, all factions agree on the pre-eminence of the Communist Party and have strong realist instincts in foreign policy. They concur on what they see as the inevitability of China's rise, in a world that may continue to be dominated by the US for decades to come, and on the resulting need to further secure external energy supplies.[30]

Regarding Russia, there is some irritation over what Beijing views as Moscow's excessive emphasis on relations with the US, the EU, and Japan. More importantly, Beijing is concerned about the reliability of Russian oil and gas supplies at several levels. The most pressing concern is the slow speed at which Russia is developing fields and pipelines. In the 1990s, Beijing built close relations with Yukos, and in 2003, Yukos CEO Mikhail Khodorkovsky proposed a private pipeline to northeastern China. The Kremlin's reassertion of control over the energy sector meant that these plans were scrapped. Beijing concluded that this was a fait accompli and did not protest politically in any public way, but there was considerable irritation behind the scenes. Beijing pursues a doctrine of non-interference, and this approach served the bilateral relationship well, because it meant that the conflict was not allowed to escalate unnecessarily.[31] At the business level, however, there was considerable turbulence. At the end of 2004, CNPC sued Yukos, which had stopped deliveries of crude oil to China in September. Yukos had initially agreed to deliver 3.86 mt of crude oil to CNPC in 2004, but only 2.85 mt were actually provided. Negotiations on the resumption of crude deliveries failed, and thus CNPC went to court. The failure of Yukos to deliver was particularly frustrating since CNPC had paid the Russian rail company with its own cash to avoid disruptions. It was not until December that supplies of oil to China by rail were resumed.[32]

Since 2004, relations have improved, but Beijing remains uncomfortable with Moscow's indecisiveness. In 2004, following the Kremlin's reassertion of power over the petroleum industry, Japan appeared to emerge as the core partner for Russia in the construction of Siberian energy infrastructure. Tokyo was willing to guarantee financing, possibly in the range of $15 billion.[33] It was envisaged that the pipeline terminus would be just one day away by tanker from Japan. Putin had reasons to favor the Nakhodka pipeline, because Japan's deal promised greater net investment in Russia and because a pipeline to the Pacific would make Russia less dependent on China as a customer for its sales. Beijing was upset. Zhongnanhai, the headquarters of China's Communist Party, had hoped that Russia would reward it for staying out of internal matters by honoring previous agreements. Beijing subsequently intensified cooperation with Kazakhstan, and in 2006, a pipeline from Atasu in northern Kazakhstan to Alashankou in the northwestern Xinjiang Province was finished.[34]

China is currently trying to ensure that progress is made with regard to the construction of pipelines from Siberia to China. The pipeline to Nakhodka is yet to be built, and no final decision has yet been made as to whether it will be.

However, Russia appears to have decided to build a pipeline to Skovorodino only 70 km from the Chinese border and to include a spur to Daqing.[35] This was originally scheduled for completion in the second half of 2008, and designed to carry as much as 600,000 barrels a day.[36] However, progress appears to be slow. The construction of the pipeline to Skovorodino would strengthen relations between China and Russia, while simultaneously giving the Kremlin the option of extending the pipeline to Nakhodka, giving Russia leverage over both China and Japan. It does, however, raise the specter of rivalry between China and Japan, on which there is more below.

Projects for natural gas cooperation in the massive Kovykta field, and perhaps Sakhalin, are likely elements of future Chinese–Russian energy cooperation. In 2006, President Putin and Hu Jintao reportedly agreed on the construction of a pipeline from Kovykta to China and possibly South Korea, at an estimated cost of $12 billion.[37] Also in 2006, Putin made public the idea of the Altai Gas Pipeline, connecting the Urengoi and Nadym fields in western Siberia with Xinjiang. The Altai Pipeline would largely follow the path of existing pipelines, but would necessitate a new section crossing the Ukok Highland in Altai, which has been declared a World Heritage Site by UNESCO. However, no formal decision on these projects has been announced. Meanwhile, there have been significant increases in rail shipments of oil to China and a commitment to increase these further. Heilongjiang has been importing electricity from Russian hydroelectric power stations since 2004, and plans to import 18 billion kW hours by 2010.[38] Sales to China decrease Russia's dependence on the European market and partially strengthen the Russian argument that it can turn to others if Brussels does not accept Moscow's conditions, although it also remains clear to all that in the short to medium term, Russia is chained to its European-oriented infrastructure for the vast majority of its exports.[39]

Chinese worries about Russia's ability to deliver on its promises on energy cooperation are summed up in the Chinese expression "loud thunder, no rain" [gan dalei bu xiayu]. High-level Chinese representatives have expressed such worries to the Russians on several occasions in recent years. At a mini-summit with Putin in November 2004, Hu Jintao called for the Russians and Chinese to "materialize their consensus," summing up the challenge in four points: maintain high-level contacts, seriously implement agreements, increase efficiency in bilateral cooperation, and strengthen communication and consultation.[40] As far as the Chinese are concerned, these points still have not been fully realized.

Challenges

The preceding discussion can be summed up as follows: historically, China–Russia relations have been troubled, but final demarcation of the last leg of their shared border has stabilized the relationship and opened new opportunities for cooperation, including in the energy sector. China's booming economy has created a large market for Russian hydrocarbons, and various pipelines and other projects are planned to increase Russian supplies of oil and gas. However, achievements on the ground have not lived up to expectations, and the Chinese have been left waiting. In the next part of the chapter, we look in greater detail at some of the political, economic, and environmental challenges to Sino-Russian cooperation and then examine the broader regional and global contexts.

Political dimensions

Global demand for oil is growing at 2.4 percent per year, and China is responsible for 40 percent of this demand growth. At the same time the US, by far the world's largest energy consumer, imports around two-thirds of its oil. Even though the dollar is weak and oil is expensive, the US is the main factor that shapes the global demand context in which China must satisfy its needs, and the US is also China's main importing-country interlocutor on energy security issues. Much US commentary on Chinese external petroleum activities focuses on the notion that China is attempting to "lock in" oil as a part of a mercantilist strategy.[41] This state-centered approach is normally contrasted against US external energy policy, which has long been based on arguments about the importance of allowing market mechanisms to provide for global energy security.

For the Chinese, however, a market approach to petroleum resources is desirable. According to US statistics, the trade balance between China and the US in 2007 was $237 billion to China's advantage.[42] Buying oil on open global markets is less of a problem for China than it is for the US. Rather, for China, the challenge consists of non-market political factors, which are often associated with the US. As outlined above, China receives a large proportion of its oil imports from the Middle East and other unstable parts of the world. The Middle East as a whole supplies 45 percent of total imports, and China sources another 32 percent of its total petroleum imports from Africa.[43] The result is that China is dependent on open waterways, in particular the crucial straights of Hormuz, Malacca, and Lombok. These passages are susceptible to instability and/or piracy and could be cut off in the event of a crisis over Taiwan or another emergency. China largely lacks the naval capacity to defend its supplies, and developing and using that capacity would bring it into dangerous competition with the US.[44] Only 9 percent of the crude oil imported by China is carried by Chinese ships, and the country has only 18 very large crude carriers (VLCCs).[45]

Not only is China dependent on US military protection of its oil imports, the US is also destabilizing Chinese imports through the occupation of Iraq and the possibility of military action against Iran. The experiences of Chinese companies in Iraq illustrate China's vulnerability to non-market forces. In 1997, a consortium of Chinese oil companies signed a 22-year Production Sharing Agreement (PSA) with Iraq to develop half of the Al-Ahdab field, the country's second largest oil field, as soon as UN sanctions were lifted. CNPC was also negotiating over stakes in three other major Iraqi fields: Halfaya, Luhais, and Suba. The US invasion of Iraq made all of these efforts meaningless.[46]

Geography, in the form of the shared Sino-Russian border, therefore, helps form the Chinese perspectives on Russian oil and gas: China and Russia can trade directly without relying on open waterways and unreliable transit countries. Moreover, Russia is relatively stable compared to many of the Middle Eastern and African states from which China imports oil. However, China is not the only East Asian country interested in Russian oil and gas; Japan is another important contender, giving rise to an important triangular drama.

Whether Moscow favors Beijing or Tokyo in the construction of energy transport infrastructure in Siberia will have significant implications for the balance of power in East Asia. A Chinese victory would support China's claim to regional pre-eminence and strengthen the Russia–China axis; Japanese success would promote a more multi-polar structure in East Asia. The Kremlin's hesitation on the matter is one indication of the geopolitical implications of the choice, as well as the desire to maximize the price paid for its hydrocarbons.

Aiming to gain an advantage over Japan, China has nurtured close relations with Russia.[47] The two states began intelligence collaboration in the early 1990s, and have since expanded into military cooperation. In 2005, they conducted their first joint war games, and in the summer of 2007, China, Russia, and the Central Asian states carried out the joint military exercise *Peace Mission 2007* in Russia under the auspices of the SCO. From the Chinese point of view, these are trust-building exercises, and the key aim for Beijing is to dispel Russian fears about China's rise and make China a preferred partner for Russia. In the process of doing so, Beijing hopes to get access to stable Russian energy supplies without having to pay too much for them.

Central Asia is an arena of latent Sino-Russian rivalry, and Beijing seeks to manage the situation carefully to avoid conflict. The establishment of a US network of military bases across Central Asia as part of the "war on terrorism" has increased incentives for China and Russia to cooperate and put aside differences in the region.[48] For Beijing, oil and gas from Central Asia carries the same benefits as Russian energy, namely that it does not have to be transported along sea-routes that could be blocked off. It also allows China to circumvent Russia's slow-moving project development. A key foreign policy challenge for Beijing is, therefore, to increase its access to energy resources in the Central Asian states without offending Moscow. Simultaneously, the option of circumventing Russia and collaborating directly with the Central Asian states gives Beijing leverage over Moscow. Relevant developments include the completion of the first international pipeline carrying oil to China, which connects Kazakhstan and China, and a new pipeline connecting Turkmenistan and China, the construction of which began in 2007. The Kazakhstan–China pipeline is currently being extended to connect new fields and parts of the pipeline system in Kazakhstan. The Turkmenistan–China pipeline is slated for completion in 2009, with plans to carry 30 bcm of gas per year for 30 years.

Economic and environmental dimensions

The shared Sino-Russian border and the possibility of direct pipelines mean that Russian oil and gas supplies are crucial to alleviating Chinese worries about energy security. However, China's demography and economic geography complicate the situation.

China's population is highly concentrated, with over 90 percent living in one-third of the country – along the south-eastern seaboard and in the Sichuan, Shanghai, and Beijing areas.[49] Foreign direct investment (FDI), which in China correlates closely with the economic growth that drives China's soaring energy demand, is also concentrated in the southeastern coastal areas, in particular the province of Guangdong. In contrast, the provinces in central and western China, which are closest to Russia's oil and gas fields, are sparsely populated and receive little FDI.[50] This demographic picture poses a fundamental challenge to Chinese–Russian energy cooperation. It entails that Russian oil and gas must not only be transported across long distances within Russia to reach the Chinese border, but must in addition travel similar distances within China to reach its markets.

This situation is reinforced by the distribution of energy resources within China. The provinces that are most easily accessible for Russian oil and gas are also those that have the most resources of their own. At least 60 percent of China's massive coal reserves are located on the border between the three provinces of Inner Mongolia, Shanxi, and Shaanxi, in the northern part of the country.[51] The coal from southern China tends to contain more sulfur, rendering it unfit for many purposes.[52] One of the options for improving energy security is to increase the amount of synthetic petroleum products produced from coal – something that should be done where the coal is located. The Shenghua coal-to-liquids plant in Inner Mongolia is scheduled to start production in 2008, producing 60,000 bbl/d of diesel.[53] Again, more energy will be produced within China close to Russia. Much of the country's oil is also located in the northwest and north-central parts of the country, and most of current Chinese onshore petroleum surveying takes place in the provinces of Xinjiang, Gansu, and Inner Mongolia.[54] It has been estimated that Xinjiang alone holds 26 percent of China's oil reserves and 29 percent of its reserves of natural gas.[55]

These geographical realities mean that although there are many reasons why it is convenient for China and Russia to trade energy – including a long shared border, safe transportation, and political compatibility – distance is not one of them. In terms of proximity, Russian resources may not even have a significant advantage over Iranian supplies, which arrive by ship directly to the parts of the country that need them most. Most of China's energy demand is located far from the Russian border, and the sparsely populated and impoverished areas that border Russia are the country's most energy-rich and have limited need for Russian imports.

Nonetheless, Chinese actors continue to vie for Russian pipelines, and the main reason, as argued above, is China's need to diversify supplies in order to improve energy security. An important additional reason is that long pipelines may not be as expensive for China to build as they are for other countries, due to China's large, disciplined, and cheap labor force. An overview of cost breakdowns for eight onshore pipelines in the US built between 1980 and 2003 show that on average, the non-material expenses made up 69 percent of total pipeline construction costs (49 percent were labor costs, the remainder were costs related to right of way, compensation, engineering, supervision, surveying, administration, and overheads – all of which are also likely to be cheaper for Chinese companies than for international oil companies, or IOCs).[56] Obviously, IOCs employ local labor wherever they operate, helping bring down labor expenses for pipeline construction in low-income countries, but China still has a significant advantage.[57] Whenever possible, Chinese companies temporarily import their own labor, and in any case they are not under the same pressure as Western oil companies to uphold safety and environmental standards or to deal fairly with organized labor.[58]

Environmental aspects of China's energy consumption affect the scope for cooperation with Russia in several ways. Currently, the energy squeeze in China is fuelling the rapid expansion of coal-based energy sources.[59] But China, having emerged as the world's largest source of CO_2 emissions,[60] is likely to come under greater pressure to accept obligations under a future Kyoto II agreement. Such environmental constraints might further boost China's interest in Russian hydrocarbons, especially natural gas.

China is one of the world's largest markets for alternative fuel vehicles and the third largest ethanol producer in the world. Between 2005 and 2010, the aim was to double annual production of ethanol to 2 mt/y.[61] However, raw materials are in short supply, and domestic food prices rose sharply in 2007.[62] These economic factors led China to reconsider its policy, and at the beginning of 2008, it imposed export taxes of between 5 and 25 percent on grains.[63] In the long term, however, Russia, with its swathes of fertile but unused land, could be a major contributor of agricultural produce for China's biofuels sector. At the same time, China ambitiously seeks to build a financially viable renewable energy industry, in particular using wind, geothermal, and solar power, and is benefiting hugely from the United Nations Clean Development Mechanism, with 48.25 percent of the world's total registered Certified Emissions Reductions expected to come from China.[64] These improvements result in annual transfers of billions of renminbi to China, but have not made these forms of renewable energy financially viable in their own right yet. Until they are, large-scale implementation is unlikely in a country where the majority of the population is still relatively poor.

To the extent that the emphasis on external supplies over internal measures in current Chinese energy policy is related to the development of relatively independent Chinese oil companies, the slow progress in building pipelines and opening new fields strengthens arguments for the recentralization and re-politicization of the Chinese energy sector in order to promote energy efficiency and other domestic solutions to the country's worries. In the coming decade, China will continue to emphasize supply-side solutions, which means both greater imports and increased domestic production of oil and gas. However, the rapid expansion since 2000 is not sustainable, and there will, therefore, be a concurrent emphasis on developing demand-side solutions through greater energy efficiency.

Implications

China's rapidly growing need for energy will greatly strain its own resources and those of the entire planet. Accordingly, there will be implications for the country's relationship with Russia, the international system, and the environment, economy, and security. In the following section, we will analyze each of these in turn.

Implications for bilateral energy ties and the stability of regional/global energy markets

The Chinese Communist Party depends on economic growth for its political legitimacy. Energy supplies are one of the main bottlenecks in the Chinese economy, and therefore, a potential stumbling block for the party and its continuing ability to remain in power. Insofar as imports from Russia can alleviate the situation, they will be sought actively.

Lack of decisive action on the part of Russia is a major concern for China at three levels. The Russians are seen as slow and fickle about making decisions, unreliable at keeping verbal agreements, and, most worryingly, ineffective in the implementation of firm agreements. From Zhongnanhai's point of view, it is easy to interpret these failings as a consequence of the discontinuation of the one-party political structure in Russia, which reinforces the conclusion that China has chosen a better path than the one represented by Russian reforms.

Key Russian energy projects remain years away from delivering natural gas and oil efficiently by pipeline to China. Internal conflicts in the Russian energy sector and export strategies that are deliberately ambiguous as a part of bargaining processes are holding up supplies. In the long run, the significance of Russian delays depends on the extent of international oil supplies: if hydrocarbons are globally scarce, the Chinese will be happy if they ultimately manage to win over the Russians, regardless of the price and the irritation along the way; if oil and gas are not scarce in the medium to long term and prices come down, the Russians may regret having missed the opportunity to lock in vast Chinese markets. The current price of oil indicates that the market thinks the Russians are right, and the Chinese can be kept waiting.

In the shorter term, Russian inaction encourages the Chinese to make more efforts to acquire Caspian oil and gas. In Central Asia, however, China competes both with Russia and Western countries for influence and access. The construction of the first leg of the Kazakhstan–China pipeline is illustrative: China's first import pipeline is not from Russia, but from one of its former satellites. At least symbolically, a major opportunity for the development of Chinese–Russian energy cooperation has been missed. In the mid-2000s, half of the oil transported by the pipeline came from Russia – in the future, when Kashagan and other large Kazakh fields start producing, the Russian share may drop.[65] However, in one important respect, Russia may also benefit from this development: if Central Asian oil and gas is diverted to China, Russia can keep the lucrative West European market for itself.

Such a division of influence may also help explain the Sino-Russian condominium in Central Asia.

Implications for the international system

The development of close energy ties between China and Russia is leading to what may be characterized as the emerging institutionalization of the bilateral relationship through frequent meetings between the two sides. These bilateral ties are compatible with the pattern that can be seen in the SCO, but do not mean that either Beijing or Moscow is ready to give up any sovereignty anytime soon. Moreover, the Chinese tend to regard the Russians as backward in comparison with the US and Europe, and to some extent as compared to China. While Beijing is willing to trade with Russia to obtain natural resources and arms, the admiration for the developed West often found among Chinese of all social layers affects the bilateral relationship between Beijing and Moscow because it means that the notion of a Sino-Russian bloc with Russian energy as its backbone makes little sense from the Chinese point of view. China still broadly adheres to Deng Xiaoping's adage "To enhance confidence, decrease troubles, promote cooperation, and avoid confrontation" [zengjia xinren, jianshao mafan, fazhan hezuo, bugao duikang].[66] Patience and caution are considered to be more productive than coalition-building with Russia against the US.

However, Beijing and Moscow do have compatible views on separatism, radical Islam, terrorism, democratization, and stability. US commentators such as Peter Brookes of the Heritage Foundation contend that the Sino-Russian relationship undercuts US global interests "on an unprecedented scale."[67] In a previous article, we argued that shared world views and common material interests constitute the foundation for "strategic convergence" between China and Russia.[68] Energy is the most important factor driving this development, and despite the tensions in the relationship, it is conceivable that they may set aside their differences and build some sort of sustainable alliance.

However, the creation of a full-blown alliance is not the most likely outcome. The Moscow Carnegie Center's Dmitry Trenin is probably right to argue that a Sino-Russian alliance could occur only as a result of "exceptionally short-sighted and foolish policies on Washington's part."[69] China is not explicitly pro-Western, but neither is it definitively anti-Western, and integration into international institutions is high on Beijing's agenda. Western policymakers who are worried about the implications of Sino-Russian strategic convergence would do well to pursue a policy of engaging both Beijing and Moscow.

From an energy perspective, Japan and the EU have particularly strong interests in learning to work with China. Moscow has on several occasions sought to play off China and Japan and, to some extent, China and the EU against one another in an effort to extract better contractual conditions. If China, Japan, and the EU could learn to cooperate and coordinate when negotiating with Russia, they would significantly lessen Russia's clout. In light of the EU's failure to coordinate its own energy policy toward Russia, such extensive international synchronization

Chinese perspectives on Russian oil and gas 215

may seem unlikely, but if Russia continues to seek to extract concessions by playing parties against each other without letting any of them win, some sort of coordination may emerge. China–Japan relations have been on a positive track since Japanese Prime Minister Junichiro Koizumi, best known in China for his visits to the Yasukuni Shrine in Tokyo, where 12 convicted Class A war criminals are enshrined, stepped down in September 2006 to be replaced by Shinzo Abe. Following Abe's resignation in September 2007, the even more China-friendly Yasuo Fukuda was appointed. Even though Fukuda's administration only lasted for a year until his resignation on 1 September 2008, there now appears to be a consensus in Japan that unnecessary confrontation with China should be avoided.

The simultaneous demise of the Soviet Union and the rise of China fundamentally changed the dynamics in China–US relations. Washington stopped viewing China as an ally against Moscow, and began to see it as a potential rival. The US is wary of the Communist government in Beijing, and many senior actors in US politics are increasingly skeptical of authoritarian trends in Putin's Russia. Beijing, on the other hand, is more comfortable with a relatively stable authoritarian Russia than with what it saw as the chaos of the 1990s, and feels vindicated in its decision to put down the rebellion at Tiananmen Square in 1989. The consolidation of what Putin calls the "power vertical," i.e. centralization, has made Moscow a more compatible partner for Beijing.

Implications for the environment, the economy, and security

As far as global warming is concerned, it may be better if China were successful in obtaining as much Russian oil and gas as possible. Russia's relatively cleaner energy could reduce Chinese reliance on coal. If Europe, Japan, and the US miss out on Russian hydrocarbons as a result, they may be forced to search out energy solutions that are less damaging for the environment. In both cases, the climate benefits.

If China and Russia can build trust through energy cooperation, there are many areas into which collaboration may be extended. China is the world's largest consumer of steel, cement, and copper;[70] and while Russia and Central Asia currently account for only about 6 percent of China's total supply of raw material imports, their role is likely to change.[71] Russia has a strong position in the global supply of many strategic non-ferrous metals necessary for the type of industrial production that is at the core of China's strategy for continued economic growth. Another area where China and Russia may come to work together more closely is agriculture. China's arable land amounts to only 0.27 hectares per capita, which is less than 40 percent of the world average, and half the level in India.[72] As China becomes industrialized and urbanized, while the government is seeking to convert lower-quality arable lands into grasslands or forest to prevent desertification, arable land is becoming increasingly scarce.[73] Beijing, therefore, appears to acknowledge that it will have to import more food, and in this context Russia is a natural partner. Guo Binqi, for example, suggests that "Russia in the near future could become China's granary."[74] While Russia's cultivated land currently comprises only 7.17 percent of its territory,[75] 55 percent of the world's fertile black earth (*chernozem*) is located in Russia, and there is clearly much more that could be put to agricultural use.[76]

Russia benefits from China's economic rise because Chinese demand has led to higher prices in world markets for the raw materials that Russia exports, while Russians, like the rest of the world, benefit from purchasing cheap Chinese consumer goods. Because of income from its exports of raw materials, Russia had a current account surplus of almost $96 billion in 2006.[77] For this reason, Russia is less concerned about China's exporting power or the undervalued renminbi than many other states. China and Russia have acknowledged each other as market economies, and China was among the first to conclude WTO negotiations with Russia, in October 2004, indicating China's emphasis on building close trade relations with Russia. On the other hand, Russia does have profound concerns about the rise of China as a superpower and a potential competitor and threat in the Far East.

Conclusions

The basic energy relationship between the Chinese and the Russians is determined by the logic of "We need it, you've got it." Bilateral state-state cooperation provides long-term supply/market security for Sino-Russian trade in hydrocarbons, but global markets set the price. Cozy bilateral state-state cooperation with the Chinese may provide better cover and more opportunities for individual gain for Russian and Chinese officials, politicians, and oil company executives. Regardless of developments in domestic politics in the two countries, the fact remains that in the diplomatic relations between them and in world politics, resource-rich Russia will have many of the commodities that the Chinese need, and the Chinese will provide vast non-Western markets for Russia. The Chinese know that. Meanwhile, they are trying to get the best price possible.

If Sino-Russian energy cooperation is successful, there will be increased trust between Moscow and Beijing. However, the energy relationship may also become a source of tension between the two capitals, which could lead either party to seek to work more closely with the US and the EU. But both Russia and China lack significant allies, and China has strong incentives to avoid any confrontation with Moscow so as to avoid the interruption of supplies. Moscow and Beijing may have hoped that the Iraq War would change the Western alliance structures fundamentally, but such a disruption has not taken place. In this context, energy cooperation may lay the foundation for an institutionalization of the relationship, which could later spread to other areas. There is certainly no direct parallel, but it is worth remembering that the EU started as a coal and steel union. To prevent the international system from degenerating into a destabilizing great-power rivalry, the US and Europe must seek to manage a precarious and multifaceted balance by pushing Russia and China to reform, while acknowledging that pushing too hard could lead to alienation, and allowing Russia and China to rise while managing and integrating their power.

Notes

* This chapter builds on research sponsored by the research project "RUSSCASP – Russian and Caspian energy developments and their implications for Norway and Norwegian actors," financed by the PETROSAM program of the Research Council of Norway. The project is carried out with the Fridtjof Nansen Institute, the Norwegian Institute for International Affairs and Econ Pöyry as consortium partners with the participation of other institutions and researchers.

1. China and the Soviet Union/Russia had signed border agreements in 1991 and 1994, delimiting the eastern and western sections of their boundary line, leaving only two parcels of land in the eastern section to be resolved. In this case, the two disputed islands – Heixiazi Island (Bol'shoi Ussuriiskii Ostrov) and the adjoining Yinlong Island (Tarabarov Ostrov) at the confluence of the Heilongjiang (Amur) and Ussuri rivers – were divided into equal portions. Yu Bin, "China–Russia Relations: End of History? What's Next?," *Comparative Connections* 6, no. 4 (2005): 145–55, at 145.
2. In the latter half of the eighteenth century, following the two Opium Wars that Britain fought to get market access to the Chinese narcotics market, the Qing government grew increasingly weak. Russia used this opportunity to annex the left bank of the Amur River and eventually Outer Manchuria and Sakhalin (Outer Manchuria includes present-day Primorsky Krai, southern Khabarovsk Krai, the Jewish Autonomous Oblast, and Amur Oblast).
3. Niklas Norling, "China and Russia: Partners with Tensions," *Policy Perspectives* 4, no. 1 (2007): 33–48, at 33.
4. Yu, "China-Russia Relations," 145.
5. On the other hand, the collapse of Moscow-style Communism led Beijing to tighten control on internal dissent.
6. Herbert Ellison and Bruce Acker, *The New Russia and Asia: 1991–1995*, NBR Analysis 7/1 (Seattle, WA: The National Bureau of Asian Research, 1996), 10.
7. Norling, "China and Russia: Partners with Tensions," 33.
8. Ellison and Acker, *The New Russia and Asia*, 10.
9. China's economy is the fourth largest in the world, with a Gross Domestic Product (GDP) of $2.5 trillion; in terms of purchasing power parity (PPP), it is the second largest, with an output of $10.2 trillion. See: *CIA World Factbook 2007* (Washington, DC: Central Intelligence Agency, 2007), s.v. "China," https://www.cia.gov/library/publications/the-world-factbook/geos/ch.html (accessed 16 October 2007). China is set to overtake Germany as the third largest economy in the world in two or three years.
10. Jonathan Sinton et al., *Evaluation of China's Energy Strategy Options* (Berkeley: The China Sustainable Energy Program, 2005), 3.
11. Sinton et al., *Evaluation of China's Energy Strategy Options*, 1; Haider Khan, *China's Energy Dilemma*, CIRJE Discussion Paper F 385 (University of Denver, 2005), 3.
12. Sinton et al., *Evaluation of China's Energy Strategy Options*, 1, 13.
13. Japan has virtually no indigenous production and imports 5.1 mbd: Energy Information Administration (EIA), "Top World Oil Producers 2006," www.eia.doe.gov/emeu/cabs/topworldtables1_2.html (accessed 15 August 2007). Throughout this chapter, the data for China refers to mainland China, excluding Hong Kong and Taiwan, unless otherwise noted.
14. Atlantic Council of the United States and the China Institutes of Contemporary International Relations, *US–China Energy Security Cooperation Dialogue* (Beijing: Tsinghua University, 2007), 14.
15. EIA, *China: Country Analysis Brief* (Washington, DC: Department of Energy, Energy Information Administration, August 2006), 2.
16. Jidong Nanpu's reserves are estimated at about one billion tons or 7.35 billion barrels. Following the discovery, the market value of Petrochina overtook that of Gazprom

and BP, and it became the world's third largest oil company after Exxon Mobil and Royal Dutch Shell. Michelle Batchelor, "Petrochina Shares Jump After Bohai Bay Oil Discovery (Update 7)," *Bloomberg*, 4 May 2007.
17 Tian Chunrong, "2006 nian zhongguo shiyou jinchukou zhuangkuang fenxi" [Analysis of China's Oil Import and Export in 2006], *Guoji Shiyou Jingji* [International Petroleum Economics], no. 3 (2007): 17.
18 Ibid.
19 The Middle East as a whole supplies 47.2 percent of total imports. China sources 30.3 percent of its total petroleum imports from Africa.
20 Liu Xuecheng, *China's Energy Security and Its Grand Strategy*, The Stanley Foundation Policy Analysis Brief (Muscatine, IA: The Stanley Foundation, September 2006), www.stanleyfoundation.org/publications/pab/pab06chinasenergy.pdf (accessed 8 September 2008), 6.
21 Ibid., 3.
22 EIA, *China: Country Analysis Brief*, 2.
23 Khan, *China's Energy Dilemma*, 9.
24 CNPC and Sinopec listed 15 percent of their shares on the Hong Kong and New York stock exchanges in 2000; CNOOC held an IPO of a 27.5 percent stake in 2001. EIA, *China: Country Analysis Brief*, 2.
25 Kenneth Lieberthal and Michel Oksenberg, *Policy Making in China: Leaders, Structures and Processes* (Princeton: Princeton University Press, 1998).
26 EIA, *China: Country Analysis Brief*, 2.
27 Sinton et al., *Evaluation of China's Energy Strategy Options*, 4.
28 Ibid., 16.
29 Willy Lam, "Beijing Unveils Plan for Super-Ministries," *Jamestown Foundation China Brief* 8, no. 1 (2008): 2–5; Rowan Callick, "Beijing Opens Green Super-Ministry," *The Australian*, 13 March 2008, www.theaustralian.news.com.au/story/ 0,25197,23363624-25837,00.html (accessed 15 September 2008).
30 The Chinese leaders are nevertheless very careful in terms of how they frame China's expansion. In an effort to calm neighbors in Asia, Beijing launched the concept of "peaceful rise" in 2004. When the Chinese government became aware that some viewed the word "rise" as threatening, it was rephrased with the term "peaceful development."
31 A central tenet of China's foreign policy is that the country will not intervene in the domestic affairs of other states, and it is hardly imaginable that Chinese politicians would comment openly on the Yukos affair. However, Chinese scholars have expressed opinions – see, for example, You Fang, "Youkesi: liushui luohua chun quye" [Yukos: Swept Away], *Zhongguo shiyou shihua banyuekan* [China Oil and Petrochemical Fortnightly], no. 16 (2006): 24f.; Feng Yujun, "Laolao zhangwo zhanlue ziyuan kongzhiquan: Eluosi 'Youkesi shijian' pouxi" [Firm Strategy for Right of Control of Natural Resources: Analysis of Russia's "Yukos Incident"], *Guoji maoyi* [International Trade], no. 9 (2004): 32f.; Qu Wenyi, "Cong Youkesi shijian kan Pujing zhengfu dui guatou jingji de zhili" [What the Yukos Incident Says About the Putin's Government Economic Policies Towards Oligarchs], *Shijie jingji* [World Economics], no. 3 (2004): 34–7.
32 Yu, "China–Russia Relations," 148.
33 Lyle Goldstein and Vitaly Kozyrev, "China, Japan and the Scramble for Siberia," *Survival*, 48, no. 1 (2006): 163–78, at 170.
34 Relations between Beijing and Astana have since grown closer. In August 2007, China and Kazakhstan agreed to build pipelines to carry oil and gas from the Caspian Sea to Xinjiang (Isabel Gorst, "Kazakhstan and China Sign Pipelines Deal," *Financial Times*, 20 August 2007). This is regarded as a setback for the EU and US, which had encouraged Astana to export the gas to Western markets. Russia is also skeptical about the project because it wishes to retain control of Central Asian exports. On the other hand,

this development may also be positive for Russia, because it diverts Central Asian resources from the lucrative European markets to which Russia is already tied.
35 "CNPC are Satisfied With Starting of ESPO Pipeline Construction from Skovorodino," *Transneft News*, 30 May 2006, www.transneft.ru/press/Default.asp?LANG=EN&ATYPE=8&PG=7&ID=11039 (accessed 30 June 2006).
36 EIA, *China Energy Data, Statistics, and Analysis: Oil Gas, Electricity and Coal* (Washington, DC: Department of Energy, EIA, 2006), 5.
37 Ibid., 9f.
38 "China Imports Electricity from Russia," *People's Daily*, 5 May 2004; Yang Li, "Electricity Trade Flourishes", *Xinhua*, 23 March 2006.
39 Faith Birol, "China Presentation," *World Energy Outlook 2004* (Paris: International Energy Agency, 2004), 24.
40 Yu, "China–Russia Relations," 147f.
41 Liu, "China's Energy Security and Its Grand Strategy," 14.
42 US Census Bureau, Foreign Trade Statistics ("Trade with China: 2007"), www.census.gov/foreign-trade/balance/c5700.html#2007 (accessed 31 January 2008).
43 Tian, "2006 nian zhongguo shiyou jinchukou zhuangkuang fenxi," 15f.
44 China is considering the development of a blue-water fleet, but it would take years to build. China is also seeking to improve the security of African and Middle Eastern supplies, an important step being an agreement with Burma to develop the port of Sittwe in Arakan State in Western Burma and building a pipeline to connect the port with Kunming, capital of China's southwestern Yunnan province. However, the Chinese government is frustrated with the incompetence of Burma's military leaders, and the project appears to be at a standstill. Cf. William Boot, "Burma Port Project at Standstill, Say Visitors," *Irrawaddy*, 8 August 2007.
45 EIA, *China: Country Analysis Brief*, 6.
46 Khan, *China's Energy Dilemma*, 10.
47 Russia has been China's main source of arms since the end of the Cold War, and has accounted for 90 percent of the estimated 165 billion renminbi worth of arms sales to China from the states of the former Soviet Union since 1991, according to a Pentagon report from 2004. Moscow has sold Beijing advanced submarines, fighters, destroyers, and missiles as well as strategic aircraft for troop movement and air-to-air refueling. As the EU is unlikely to lift its 1989 arms embargo on China in the near future, and the US is determined not to do so, Russia seems set to continue as China's main source of arms.
48 As long as Washington maintains a military presence in Central Asia, Beijing, and Moscow are likely to find that they have more to gain by uniting in seeking restraint on US power than by seeking mutual confrontation. In a long-term perspective, in particular in the case of decreased US interest in Central Asia, it is possible that the area could become an arena for competition between Russia and China. The US does not seem intent on abandoning the region either, and is rather attempting to extend the energy corridor that already exists between Azerbaijan, Georgia, and Turkey to Turkmenistan and Kazakhstan, while also promoting the Turkmenistan–Afghanistan–Pakistan–India (TAPI) pipeline from Turkmenistan via Afghanistan to Pakistan and India. In this perspective, Chinese–Russian relations in Central Asia are likely to remain mostly congruous, united by the external threat that US influence can be seen as posing to Russian influence over, and Chinese access to, the Caspian Basin's vast natural gas deposits.
49 Gerard Heilig, *Sustainable and Rural Regional Development in China: Where Do We Stand?*, Interim Report IR-03–026 (Laxenburg: International Institute for Applied Systems Analysis, 2003), 5; Aprodicio Laquian, "People's Republic of China," in *Urbanization and Stability: Case Studies of Good Practice*, ed. Brian Roberts and Trevor Kanaley (Manila: ADB, 2006), 103.
50 Heilig, *Sustainable and Rural Regional Development in China*, 5; Laquian, "People's Republic of China," 114.

51 Sinton et al., *Evaluation of China's Energy Strategy Options*, 5.
52 EIA, *China: Country Analysis Brief*, 10.
53 Atlantic Council of the United States and the China Institutes of Contemporary International Relations, *US–China Energy Security Cooperation Dialogue*, 9; EIA, *China: Country Analysis Brief*, 11.
54 EIA, *China: Country Analysis Brief*, 4; 8.
55 Sinton et al., *Evaluation of China's Energy Strategy Options*, 5.
56 This calculation is based on data from "Data for Worldwide Construction Projects," *Oil and Gas Journal*, 8 September 2003.
57 At the height of the construction of the BTC, the project employed 22,000 people. David Woodward, *BP Azerbaijan Business Update* (Baku: BP, 21 December 2004); cf. Jonathan Elkind, "Economic Implications of the Baku–Tbilisi–Ceyhan Pipeline," in *The Baku–Tbilisi–Ceyhan Pipeline: Oil Window to the West*, ed. Frederick Starr and Svante Cornell (Washington, DC: SAIS, Johns Hopkins University, 2005).
58 For an overview of the environmental, landowner, and employment pressures on the builders of the BTC pipeline, see Mevlut Katik, "The Oil Flows Through the BTC Pipeline, but a Problem May Loom," *Eurasia Insight Reports*, 20 October 2007.
59 Sinton et al., *Evaluation of China's Energy Strategy Options*, 14.
60 "China Now No. 1 in CO_2 Emissions; USA in Second Position," *Netherlands Environmental Assessment Agency – News*, 19 June 2007, www.mnp.nl/en/dossiers/Climate-change/moreinfo/ Chinanowno1inCO2emissionsUSAinsecondposition.html (accessed 31 January 2008).
61 Sinton et al., *Evaluation of China's Energy Strategy Options*, 7f.
62 Figures are year-on-year (yoy) until November 2007: National Bureau of Statistics of China, *Consumer Price Index (CPI) by Region* (Beijing: National Bureau of Statistics of China, November 2007), www.stats.gov.cn/english/statisticaldata/monthlydata/t20080129_402460828.htm (accessed 31 January 2008).
63 Jamil Anderlini, "China Will Tax Grain Exporters," *Financial Times*, 30 December 2007.
64 Data from the United Nations Framework Convention on Climate Change ("Expecte Average Annual CERs from Registered Projects by Host Party") at http://cdm.unfccc.int/Statistics/Registration/AmountOfReductRegisteredProjPieChart.html (accessed 31 January 2008).
65 EIA, *China: Country Analysis Brief*, 6.
66 Quoted in Lu Zhongwei, "On China–US–Japan Relations: Comments on the Recent Exchange of Top-Level Visits," *Contemporary International Relations* 7, no. 12 (1997): 9.
67 Peter Brookes, "Sino-Russian Strategic Romance," *Military.com*, 27 March 2006.
68 Kyrre Elvenes Brækhus and Indra Øverland, "A Match Made in Heaven? Strategic Convergence between China and Russia," *China and Eurasia Forum Quarterly* 5, no. 2 (2007): 41–61.
69 Dmitry Trenin, "Russia Leaves the West," *Foreign Affairs* 85, no. 4 (2006): 87–96.
70 Wayne Morrison, *China's Economic Conditions*, CRS Brief for Congress (Congressional Research Service, The Library of Congress, 15 May 2006), 13, www.au.af.mil/au/awc/awcgate/crs/ib98014.pdf (accessed 5 September 2008).
71 Goldstein and Kozyrev, "China, Japan and the Scramble for Siberia", 167.
72 Liu Yingling, "Shrinking Arable Lands Jeopardizing China's Food Security," *Worldwatch Institute*, 18 April 2006, www.worldwatch.org/node/3912 (accessed 29 March 2007).
73 Between 1996 and 2005, China lost approximately eight million hectares or 6.6 percent of its arable land. Between 1999 and 2003, grain production dropped continuously; although the situation has since improved somewhat, China faces a shortfall of nearly 20 mt by 2010. Adding to the difficult situation, one-sixth of China's total arable lands are polluted by heavy metals. Xinjingbao (Beijing News), "Guotu

ziyuanbu baogao xianshi, zhongguo shi nian gengdi jianshao 1.2 yi mu" [Ministry of Land and Resources Reports China Lost 122 Million Hectares of Arable Land Over the Last Ten Years], *Xinhuanet*, 16 March 2006, http://news.xinhuanet.com/house/2006-03/16/content_4308627.htm (accessed 16 March 2006); "Shiyiwu' qijian: ruhe tianbu 1000 yi jin liangshi quekou" [The Eleventh Five-Year Plan: How to Fill Grain Shortfall of 20 Million Tons], *Zhongguo nongye wang* [China Agricultural Net], 29 March 2006, www.zgny.com.cn/ConsHtml/5/9/4/94082.html (accessed 31 March 2006).

74 Guo Bin Qi, "Zhong e nongye hezuo qianjing guangkuo" [The Prospects for China–Russia Agricultural Cooperation Are Broad], *Xiboliya yanjiu* [Siberian Studies], 30, no. 3 (2003): 25.

75 *CIA World Factbook 2007* (Washington, DC: Central Intelligence Agency, 2007), s.v. "Russia," https://www.cia.gov/cia/publications/factbook/geos/rs.html (accessed 29 March 2007).

76 "Rossiia prokormit milliard zelmian" [Russia Will Feed a Billion People], *Rossiya vybiraet* [Russia Chooses], 105, no. 23 (2001): 2.

77 Data from the Central Bank of the Russian Federation ("Balance of Payments of the Russian Federation for 2006"), www.cbr.ru/eng/statistics/credit_statistics/print.asp?file=bal_of_payments_06_e.htm (accessed 5 September 2008).

Part IV
Conclusion

11 Russia's energy power
Implications for Europe and for transatlantic cooperation

Andreas Wenger

The realignment of power that has gone hand in hand with globalization in recent years is partly attributable to shifts in the global energy system. Indeed, the most significant shift of economic power, namely that from the West to Asia, has been driven by well-functioning and stable energy markets. Access to affordable energy from abroad has become a critical factor for the peaceful rise of developing countries like China, which until recently have been energy self-sufficient. Consumers in those rising economies are now joining their Western counterparts in their demand for energy, causing a significant shift in the demand-dynamics of global energy markets.[1] At the same time, the power to define the rules of the energy markets has shifted from the consumers and from the international oil companies (IOCs) to the producers and their national oil companies (NOCs).[2] Russia, for one, has clearly benefited from the recent transformation of the global energy system, and its accumulation of energy wealth thanks to high oil prices in the past years has in part enabled Russia to revive its position as a Eurasian power to be reckoned with.

Energy is linked not only to global market dynamics; it also affects local and global political conflict and cooperation. Bad governance and structural barriers to economic innovation are commonplace in states that depend on the export of natural resources. Political violence in energy-rich states is closely linked to the negative effects of high rents from exports of natural resources. At the regional level, the often highly politicized management of pipeline infrastructures reinforces asymmetric power relationships between neighboring states. An exporting country's interest in gaining a bigger share of the market is often inseparable from its interest in achieving political dominance over a region. Moreover, the fact that many known energy resources are concentrated in the region stretching from the Middle East across the Caspian Sea to Western Siberia – a notoriously volatile region – also influences the ways in which global actors design their foreign policies for countries in this region. In other words, energy is closely linked to the evolution of local and regional conflicts.[3]

Changes in the global energy system are connected to an increase in global market players and are affecting political stability on the local and regional levels. The coming together of these two trends has placed energy security high on the global political agenda over the past few years. Some experts fear that, as a consequence, "resource wars" will emerge as a key threat to global security.[4] However, the geopolitical effects of energy politics are likely to remain limited for the following three reasons: first, consumers and producers have a common interest in the long-term stability of their energy relationships – while consumers rely on a secure supply, producers rely on a secure demand. Second, producers are likely to realize that any attempts to use their energy-derived power for political gain would be unlikely to succeed, and would also be likely to backfire and have unintended side-effects.[5] Third, since independence from the import of fossil fuels is an unrealistic goal at least in the mid-term, old and new consumers will continue to rely on the flow of affordable hydrocarbons and on the stability of the world energy market.

At the same time, producers and consumers can no longer separate their energy policies from their foreign and security policies. Both have to deal with the reality that in a globalized world, the patterns of energy production and consumption are tightly linked to the patterns of political conflict and cooperation. The scale of the global energy trade is rapidly growing, as is the need to protect the entire energy supply chain. Producers and consumers understand that the growing (inter-)dependencies within the energy system demand new efforts to increase its overall resilience. However, they also realize that their perceptions about what represents a fair price for energy and what role the state should play vis-à-vis markets are unlikely to converge soon. This means that the energy policy priorities of producers and consumers will at times clash with some of their other domestic and foreign policy priorities. In the context of tight markets and asymmetric security risks, securing the supply (respectively the demand) of energy has become an important foreign policy goal, often sustained by highly emotional public perceptions of a country's "energy security." The growing interconnection between energy issues and security issues will, therefore, at least for the mid term, remain a key challenge both for producers and consumers.

Energy politics will evolve in a wider strategic framework, which is influenced by values and interests that are unrelated to oil and gas. Despite the potential for conflict, energy represents a potentially powerful tool to promote cooperative behavior. The many common interests and mutual dependencies between energy consumers and producers point to the cooperative potential of energy as an element in the foreign relations between states. In fact, it seems that there is room for compromise and cooperation between the various actors, both at the level of states, where the trend toward renationalization clashes with traditional laissez-faire approaches, and at the level of private actors, where new patterns of cooperation between IOCs and NOCs might emerge.[6] In addition to international concerns about the limited supply of hydrocarbons – evident in today's highly politicized debate about peak oil[7] – tight markets and high prices are stimulating the search for new technologies and alternative energy markets. While the promotion of greater energy efficiency and moves to increase the share of renewable energy are primarily a challenge for domestic politics, both areas are wide open to international cooperation. Efforts to increase the types and uses of renewable energy are proliferating due to growing fears concerning global warming. More and better cooperation to increase energy efficiency and to develop renewable energy promises many economic opportunities and is increasingly seen as a precondition for the joint reduction of CO_2 emissions and for coping with global warming.[8]

Russia as a key factor in the transformation of the global energy system

Russia is among the leading global energy exporters, and this has an impact on the way that Russia engages the outside world. This chapter will look in particular at Russian–European relations and also seeks to understand how, if at all, Russian energy power affects transatlantic cooperation. How Russia defines its energy strategy has important repercussions for global energy security. Russia's massive energy wealth has helped the country to recover from its decline in the 1990s, to achieve some progress in its political stability, and to spread some of its newly acquired wealth to its growing middle class.[9] However, Russia's economic boom has also been associated with a more assertive Russian foreign policy, which has triggered fears in the West about the political effects of Europe's energy dependence on Russia and, more generally, about Moscow's ability to influence the global agenda. Slowly but steadily, Russia's frustration and disappointment with the West, and Western fatigue with and fear of Russia, have been growing. Since Russia repeatedly cut off its supply of energy to Lithuania, Ukraine, Belarus, and Georgia, the Western debate about Russia has taken an alarmist turn, and issues surrounding energy security have been increasingly coupled with highly public disagreements between Russia and key Western countries about missile defense, NATO enlargement, the status of Kosovo, and the secessionist conflicts in the Caucasus.

Still, the depiction of Russia as an aggressive energy superpower seems overstated, a view that is supported by the analyses in the first three chapters of this book of the role of energy in Russia's social, economic, and political development. Russia's prospects as an energy superpower may be less secure than many Russian and Western policymakers believe: the Russian economy has grown rapidly since the financial crisis of 1998, and Russia has become a financially robust state with no big foreign debt, but its very limited ability to innovate and diversify its non-energy economy in an internationally competitive way may well result in a mid-term economic slow-down. At the very least, Russia will remain vulnerable to fluctuating oil and gas prices.[10]

Moreover, the leading role of the state in Russia's economic development is not helpful to the country's capacity to keep energy production at a level sufficient to meet growing domestic and foreign demand. While the Russian renationalization process is less than complete, and the state seems to be aiming for majority ownership rather than for complete control of the energy sector, Russia's political elites have been unable to create a stable market environment with clear property rights that might stimulate long-term (foreign) investment and encourage the effective management and good governance of Russia's energy sector. Further, without a major increase in investments for exploration and new production, and without cooperation with foreign actors, Russia will simply not be in a position to maintain its current level of energy exports. Given the trajectory of Russia's domestic economic and political transformation, it seems realistic to assume that the West, and especially Europe, will eventually have to come to terms with a situation in which Russia is unable to meet their growing energy demand.[11]

When the West sets out to define its energy relationship with Russia, it will need to acknowledge Russia as a regional power with global ambitions, while at the same time taking into account Russia's fragile political and social state. Russia's ability to shape the global political agenda in a creative manner beyond its role as a veto power and as the regional hegemon on the post-Soviet space is likely to remain restricted. The Russian state and its political system are dominated by a small and highly fragmented political elite. Pervasive corruption links politics and business. As a consequence, the Russian state possesses only weak administrative capacity, and the Russian business elites are highly vulnerable to state pressure. Although Russia's macro-economic stabilization since 1998 has been impressive, its ability to diversify its economy, and its capacity for managing the negative effects of the huge oil and gas rents on its domestic political development, remain limited.[12] The same can be said of Russia's energy policies: While the state has attempted to formulate a long-term energy strategy, its energy politics remain dominated by short-term personal gains and by the interests of competing elites, rather than by the long-term interests of the Russian people.[13]

A central challenge: readjusting the European–Russian energy relationship

Recent public debate in the West about the impact of Russian energy-derived power on international affairs has been highly emotional. Although a series of European states have long-standing bilateral energy ties with Russia, the West in recent years has viewed Russia as an unreliable energy provider. This negative perception is based on Russia's repeated cut-offs of energy supply to various consumer states, rejection of market methods, and much more assertive energy diplomacy beyond the sphere of its traditional areas of activity – whether in Asia, North Africa, the Middle East, or Latin America. Washington, fearing the consequences of Europe's growing political dependence on Russia, accuses Moscow of misusing its energy wealth as a political tool. In Europe official reactions vary widely, from alarmist to accommodating positions. Overall, however, the public debate in Europe has been dominated by calls for energy interdependence, on the one hand, and for a drive for greater diversity in energy and energy supply, on the other.[14]

Russia feels unjustly punished for its actions which, according to Russian policymakers, make economic sense: refusing to continue to subsidize post-Soviet economies by supplying them with cheap energy and securing the energy supply to Europe by building new pipelines circumventing Ukraine and Belarus. Moscow has complained that Europe's talk of energy independence and its attempts at diversification undermine Russia's efforts to secure demand. In response, the Kremlin recast its energy policy rhetoric away from Europe and toward the East. Bit by bit, the energy relationship between the West and Russia has developed into an energy security dilemma, a situation in which both sides diversify away from each other, only to leave them in a worse position than before.[15]

Mutual interdependencies, limited diversification options

Given the geography and the political economy of the West in relation to Russia, it appears that Europe, and not the US, holds the key to the successful management of the West's energy relations with Russia. The Europeans look back on what so far had essentially been a mutually beneficial energy relationship between producer and consumer, stimulated by economic logic and based on a durable physical connection (pipelines). However, an energy policy that sustains the stability of the European–Russian energy framework into the future would have to recognize the existing interdependencies between the two, as well as the limited diversification options for both sides. Policymakers on both sides would, therefore, be wise to assess the current trends that are shaping global energy markets and, more specifically, the patterns of European–Russian energy relations in an informed and transparent way. In particular, the following four factors – discussed in the chapters of this book – come to mind:

1   Many European countries – some to a considerably greater degree than others – will remain dependent on Russian energy supplies in the medium to long term, given Russia's geographic proximity to Europe and also its large reserves. Although Russia's overall share of the European market will decline, Russia will remain Europe's single most important source of hydrocarbons. Furthermore, as individual European states have very different energy relations with and levels of dependence on Russia, the European energy debate at the national level will also be characterized by a lot of variation.[16]
2   Russia will remain dependent on Europe's energy demand for the mid to long term. Russia is locked into European pipelines, and thus its reorientation toward Asia will perforce be partial and gradual. The export revenues from Russia's energy flows to Europe will remain crucial to Russia's economic welfare and domestic stability, and Europe will remain the most important player in Russian trade. Consequently, Moscow will be careful not to weaken its relationship with Europe. While some Russian players are concerned about Russia's high level of dependence on European demand, others point to the advantages of dealing separately – bilaterally, rather than multilaterally – with European governments and companies.[17]
3   Europe's additional diversification options for stable, reliable, and sustainable energy flows are limited. On the one hand, Europe already has a relatively wide range of energy types, sources, and transit routes due to the high diversity of energy policies at the national level.[18] On the other hand, Russia

has been rather successful in capturing Caspian energy and in monopolizing European access to it. Although the Kremlin's unilateral military and diplomatic approach to the Georgian crisis in 2008 met with little support in the region, for countries like Kazakhstan and Turkmenistan, China may provide a diversification option that is less likely to damage their relationship with Russia.[19] From a European point of view, transit routes and supplies from the Caucasus, North Africa, and the Middle East are fraught with risks of their own, given the complexities of the political conflicts in these regions – a point driven home during the 2008 crisis in Georgia.[20]

4   Russia has been – and will continue to be – slow in developing alternative export infrastructures to Asia and beyond. Although the Kremlin perceives the development of East Siberia and the Russian Far East – regions troubled by huge demographic, social, economic, and political problems – as a critical factor in terms of domestic stability and territorial sovereignty, the country has to overcome big internal obstacles in terms of decision-making and strategic planning in order to develop these regions. It is technologically challenging and expensive to capture resources there, and access to foreign technology, managerial experience, and funding will remain vital to the development of Russia's eastern territories.[21] Nevertheless, the West should acknowledge that there is a natural match between Russian resources and Chinese markets, not unlike the link between Russia and Europe. Russian supplies are of strategic significance for Beijing because China has no independent capabilities to secure its energy imports via waterways. Strong domestic and international forces will push these two countries toward energy cooperation in the long term.[22]

The policy-making process as a limiting factor

The patterns of European–Russian energy relations will be shaped not only by existing interdependencies and by limited diversification options. Energy issues cannot be addressed in isolation from the broader framework of the foreign policy relations between Europe and Russia. Political perceptions linked to issues of status, power, and security will remain important determinants of energy policies. More specifically, the intricacies of the policymaking process on both sides will seriously limit the options for maneuver and compromise in European–Russian energy relations.

On the Russian side, it seems unlikely that Moscow will be able to meet its supply commitments to Europe and fully cover the expected growth of European demand. The real threat, from a European point of view, is not that the Kremlin will play political games with its hydrocarbon supplies to Europe, but that it is unlikely that Russian elites will be able to design policies that will help to overcome the projected supply shortages within a reasonable time frame, due to the negative effects of huge rents on the strategic and administrative capacities of the Russian state. Policies that limit the growth of domestic energy consumption (that is, increases in domestic energy prices) and stimulate domestic and foreign investment (that is, tax reduction and clear property rights) will take time and remain politically difficult to implement.[23]

On the European side, it seems unlikely that Europe will be able to speak any time soon with a unified voice in its energy relations with Russia. Efforts at the level of the European Union (EU) to create an internal energy market based on competition and common standards and to expand this model to Russia regularly conflict with the asymmetric energy dependencies of EU members on Russia and with their diverse energy and foreign policy interests. Although the EU has taken over an agenda-setting role in the fields of competition, environment, and technology, its individual member states remain responsible for energy security and for implementing national regulatory standards. The gap between the formulation of policies at the level of the EU and their inconsistent implementation at the national level makes it unlikely that internal market liberalization will move ahead quickly, and that Russia will feel compelled to ratify the Energy Charter Treaty.[24]

Internal and external elements of Europe's energy security

While the political impact of Russia's deliberate interruptions to the energy supply to some of its consumers in past years has not yet fully dissipated, European policymakers are beginning to realize that an uncoordinated drive for energy diversity in reaction to Russia's actions cannot substitute for a policy that acknowledges the real complexities of foreign relations between Russia, the EU, and EU member states. It would seem that the key challenge to a constructive and forward-looking European energy policy regarding Russia is whether or not a balance can be achieved between a push for a more coherent and comprehensive European energy security policy at the level of the EU and the necessary degree of flexibility and pragmatism at the national level of policy implementation. This would involve a trade-off between the pace of deregulation in internal EU markets and a more coherent energy policy for Russia. The aim should be to move toward a more regionalized pattern of European–Russian energy relations, which would be less than speaking with one voice, but a better state of affairs than the current combination of Russian unilateralism and European bilateralism.

European energy policy toward Russia should be embedded in a broader policy framework that integrates Europe's internal and external energy security. The starting point for an internal European energy policy should consist of the following three factors:

1 The EU and its member states should do their best to maximize the benefits of existing diversity at the sub-regional level and work hard toward a more coherent strategic plan to ensure energy security.
2 The EU and its member states should attempt to reduce their energy consumption through greater efficiency.
3 They should stimulate investment in renewable energies and new technologies.

Political support for such a strong internal response should not be built on alarmist calls for independence. Rather, policymakers should justify their policies based on environmental sustainability and the associated economic opportunities at the national level, and on the cooperative potential of such measures at the international level.

As regards the external elements of European energy security, the EU and its member states should not focus exclusively on relations with Russia. While Russia will unquestionably remain a key strategic energy partner for the foreseeable future, its role must be seen in the context of the already existing diversity in Europe's energy relations. From a broader foreign policy perspective, two considerations are especially important:

1 The Europeans should define their energy relations bearing in mind the whole supply chain. Energy relations are more than simple producer–consumer relationships. Transit states have an important role to play and should not be left out of the energy security equation. Interests linked to transit routes affect both the EU's internal energy relations – as new pipelines around Central Europe result in a loss of these states' transit leverage in their foreign relations with other EU member states as well as with Russia – and its external relations with countries such as Ukraine, Belarus, and Turkey. Thus, a comprehensive approach that takes into account the whole energy supply chain should guide European energy policy in general.[25]

2 The Europeans should define the role of energy in their broader foreign relations policies, and they should also ask themselves how their foreign policies can contribute to European energy security. The goal of better relationships along the whole supply chain can only be achieved if the EU and its member states enhance their general foreign policy profile in the Caucasus, the Caspian, the Middle East, and North Africa.[26] Moreover, such a broad approach would allow them to recognize trade-offs between different policy fields that might otherwise be overlooked. For instance, a close energy partnership between Russia and China may mean a reduction in the oil and gas supply for Europe, but it may simultaneously be good for the environment, because it could potentially reduce Chinese reliance on coal and would also force Western states to find alternative energy solutions.

Toward a new European–Russian energy relationship

European energy security demands that EU and its member states formulate, communicate, and implement a more robust energy partnership with Russia. There are six specific considerations that emerge from the internal and external factors that define Europe's energy security, and these should be considered by European policymakers when they define their energy policies for Russia.

1 European energy policies for Russia should not be reactive and should not be too narrowly focused on Russia as a single source of energy. The Europeans

should aim for a mutually beneficial energy partnership with Russia that emphasizes the existing diversification of energy sources and takes into account the whole supply chain, including the interests of transit states. Moreover, European policymakers should make it clear that they understand the importance of the link between the domestic and foreign elements of European–Russian energy relations. For example, rapidly growing domestic consumption in Russia may increase supply shortages in the energy flows to Europe. More transparency and better information with regard to both the domestic and foreign dimensions of Russian and European energy policies is a precondition for a stable energy partnership.

2 European energy policies for Russia should relax the market principle somewhat and not insist that Russia liberalize its internal gas market quickly. At the same time, the Europeans should stress that the emphasis on non-discriminatory market access is driven by their own internal market considerations, which are aimed at unbundling production. Moreover, accepting Gazprom's monopoly of the gas export infrastructure in Russia is not incompatible with restrictions on Gazprom's access to the downstream markets in Europe. In other words, reciprocity in energy relations means that access to European downstream markets should go hand in hand with the opening up of the monopolistic market structures in Russia to European investment.[27]

3 European energy policies should acknowledge the very different energy relations of individual EU member states with Russia and should move toward a more regionalized pattern of European–Russian energy relations, while recognizing the limits this entails with regard to the cohesion of policies at the EU level. The great variance in energy dependence on Russia and the very different historical legacies of bilateral relations of individual EU member countries with Russia demand pragmatism and flexibility in policy implementation. In terms of overall energy security in Europe, attempts by some Eastern European EU members to reduce their energy dependence on Russia may not necessarily be incompatible with the attempts by some big European states to establish an interdependent, long-term energy relationship with Russia.[28]

4 European energy policies for Russia should actively seek ways to share and transfer know-how and technologies in the fields of energy efficiency and alternative energy industries. European policymakers should work hard to convince Russian elites that this is the way ahead in light of the energy inefficiency of the Russian economy and of the inefficient domestic consumption patterns in Russia. Energy efficiency is less politicized than the oil and gas sector, which are considered to be of strategic significance by the Russian state, and there is growing interest in efficiency among the Russian elites. The International Energy Agency (IEA) estimates that in the area of gas production alone, the domestic loss due to gas flaring amounts to 60 bcm/y, which is four times the official figure provided by the Russian government.[29] Reducing domestic consumption through improved efficiency would serve global climate protection policies and free export potential to meet Russia's

supply commitments to Europe. Thus, the Europeans should encourage Russia to establish a regulatory framework that allows it to attract investments in emission reduction schemes.[30]

5   European energy policies should go beyond gas and oil exploration and exploitation to include electricity supply. Both Russia and Europe have experienced problems in the reliability and capacity of their grids in the past. Moreover, the ongoing liberalization and privatization in EU markets, combined with the unbundling of Russia's electricity monopoly, should make cooperation on an equal basis easier to establish than in the case of oil and gas.[31]

6   European energy policies should take into account the integrating role of business-to-business relationships. Foreign direct investment of Russian private companies abroad opens up avenues for the diversification of the Russian economy, whereas foreign direct investment in Russia increases competition in the domestic market. Foreign companies are needed in Russia to provide financing, technology, and management if Russia is to simultaneously meet its supply commitments to Europe, maintain control over Caspian energy flows, and emerge as a key energy player in the East Asia-Pacific region. However, the engagement of foreign companies in Russia depends on the ability of the Russian state to provide a stable regulatory framework, and this is clearly an area where progress has been slow. In the meantime, Western IOCs will have to learn to work as minority partners with big Russian NOCs. The best hope is that the smaller independent gas and oil providers, which have been responsible for most of the country's output growth in past years, may eventually pave the way toward more liberal conditions in Russia's energy market.[32]

US–European cooperation: global energy markets and regional conflict

Neither Russia nor European countries are likely to disengage quickly from their energy partnerships. Nevertheless, European (and Western) energy security depends not only on a stable energy policy framework with Russia: energy issues are, in fact, inextricably linked to the broader framework of the relationship between Russia and the West, including the US and Canada.[33] Thus, when Europe's energy security is analyzed as part of a broader framework, it becomes clear that US–European cooperation is essential to the successful management of the global economic and political consequences of Russia's energy-derived power.

A well-functioning transatlantic partnership between the US and Europe remains crucial to European energy security for two main reasons:

1   The US and Europe need to work together to redefine the global producer–consumer framework, to sustain the stability of global energy markets, and to find solutions to energy-related challenges such as global warming. In the recent past, the rise of new consumers in Asia, together

with the concentration of energy resources in politically volatile regions, undermined the stability of the traditional producer–consumer framework, which had been to a large degree based on an alliance between the US and Saudi Arabia. These changes meant also the end of the area of cheap oil and the need for the US and Europe to move toward a new producer–consumer framework. Moreover, the US and Europe should also acknowledge that, in the context of global warming, the current bias in favor of supply-driven energy policies – policies that focus on increasing the supply of energy as opposed to demand-driven policies that focus on reducing the consumption of energy – is no longer sustainable.[34]

2 US–European cooperation will remain essential in dealing with the energy-related global realignment of power and, more specifically, in the management of associated regional instability. Energy wealth, combined with energy nationalism, is bound to have some geopolitical effects, especially in the Caucasus, the Caspian, and the Middle East, where energy issues are coupled with local conflicts, on the one hand, and with the strategic interests of great powers, on the other.

Obviously, these are huge challenges for US–European cooperation, and it is fair to say that over the past years, Washington and its European partners have found themselves at loggerheads more often than not, especially with regard to their attempts to direct their energy policies on to a more sustainable path and in their dealings with regional conflicts in energy-rich countries. Many an observer in Europe has seen George W. Bush's government as part of the problem, rather than as the solution, in reference to the destabilizing effects on global energy markets of the Iraq intervention and of the US "war on terror." Conversely, many policymakers in Washington have considered as naïve the European view that Russia could be engaged in an energy and economic partnership and have accused the Europeans of reacting too gently to very real security-related disagreements with Russia.[35] It is therefore essential that Europe and the US define a more coherent strategy for engaging Russia and determine a workable division of responsibility, if they wish to establish a more constructive energy relationship with Russia.

Toward a new producer–consumer framework

Stable energy markets that are also environmentally sustainable can only be achieved through combined governance by the US and the EU and its member states. Energy security, economic growth, and environmental protection are interrelated, and the US and Europe need to work closely to engage other international stakeholders in the development of a comprehensive strategy for addressing these three issues coherently and comprehensively. The US will remain the key actor in the successful management of the supply side-related dynamics of global energy markets. European leadership, however, will gain in importance with regard to the demand side-related dynamics of a sustainable global energy policy. The US, the EU, and EU member states need to combine their strengths in order to define a new producer–consumer framework that allows the dynamics that govern both the supply side and the demand side of global energy markets to be addressed.

The aim of US energy policy was from the beginning to maintain the global supply of oil. A central pillar of the liberal US approach has been maintaining open access to waterways and to the Gulf, with its huge reserves and low extraction costs. The relationship between Saudi Arabia and the US traditionally played a key role in the stability of the global oil market. In return for US security guarantees, the Saudis provided the necessary excess capacity needed to stabilize the global market. Then, between the terror attacks of 11 September 2001 and the US invasion in Iraq in 2003, Washington tried to build an energy partnership with Russia in the hope of at least partially replacing Saudi Arabia's critical role as a swing producer. This was considered necessary as US–Saudi relations turned sour when it became apparent that 15 of the 19 terrorists involved in the 2001 attacks were Saudi citizens. Russia's president, Vladimir Putin, was quick to cooperate when the US set out to overthrow the Taliban regime and purge al-Qaida from strongholds in Afghanistan. However, US hopes of building up an alternative US–Russian energy reserve were short-lived. Instead, Putin renationalized the oil sector, destroying the private oil company Yukos in 2003. Soon after, the US invasion of Iraq put an end to a phase of closer foreign policy cooperation between Russia and the US.[36]

While US–Saudi relations are likely to remain crucial to the stability of the global oil market, Washington and its European partners would be well-advised to prepare to broaden the governance framework that stabilizes global oil markets. Oil prices have risen sharply and have become more volatile over the past year, due partly to a lack in spare capacity, the declining value of the US dollar, and increased speculative activity. The current oil market situation demands an increase in investment throughout the oil supply chain and more transparent and better regulated financial markets. These are challenges that require closer cooperation, both at the technical level of gathering and integrating data – provided, for example, by the IEA, the Organization of the Petroleum Exporting Countries (OPEC), and the International Energy Forum (IEF) – and at the political level, through increased dialog between key consumers and producers. Western governance efforts at the political level should acknowledge the globalization of the energy security system and increasingly engage China and India in the trade and investment networks governing the global energy system.[37]

European leadership in managing the demand side-related dynamics of global energy markets will gain in importance as the need to curb global warming increases. The West should acknowledge that the current patterns of global energy consumption and economic growth are unsustainable due to their environmental consequences. Western societies should lead by example and renew their commitment to energy efficiency and renewable energy industries. The European focus on reducing energy consumption and on investing in renewable energies reflects the strengths of the institutional set-up in Europe and exemplifies the willingness of the European polity to include sustainability in its energy policies. Europe should take the lead and involve Russia and China in energy efficiency and alternative energy industries. In fact, the general interest in reducing greenhouse gas emissions, and the economic benefits and opportunities associated with policies that promote efficiency and alternative energy production, call for intense international cooperation.[38]

With Russia, the Europeans will be able to push the case for reduced consumption in the framework of the European–Russian energy relationship. Some progress has already been achieved. Russia agreed to sign the Kyoto Protocol after the Europeans stopped insisting that Russia liberalize its internal gas market and after they agreed to support Russian entry in the World Trade Organization (WTO). In the case of China, however, the US has so far been the main interlocutor in energy issues. This meant that the focus of China's energy relationship with the West was primarily on supply side-related issues and on the associated debate over China's mercantilist approach versus the US market-oriented approach. Beijing feels dependent on open waterways protected by the US and exposed to the unpleasant effects of US policies in Iraq and Iran on the stability of the oil market. Washington, on the other hand, would need to change its current supply preferences in its national energy policies and would also need to sign up to the Kyoto process if it wants to re-balance its energy relationship with China toward more emphasis on less and cleaner consumption. In the meantime, a closer dialog between Europe and China on energy efficiency and renewable energy industries could offset at least some of Beijing's political worries.[39]

Finally, the US, the EU, and EU member states should combine their strengths and redefine the current energy governance framework to take into account the emergence of new consumers in Asia and the shift of power in favor of energy producers like Russia. At the technical level, the US and Europe need to push jointly for increased transparency and better information flows with regard to energy and financial markets. At the political level, the US and Europe should concentrate on finding new ways to achieve minimum coordination between old (for example, Japan) and new consumers (for example, China and India) in order to limit the potential for political maneuvering by the producers, be they the OPEC countries or Russia. Special consideration should be given to modernizing the IEA, broadening its portfolio, and opening it up toward new consumers in Asia and Latin America.[40] At the same time, old and new consumers should engage the producers and a broad range of public and private stakeholders in policies that aim at the protection of the entire energy supply chain.[41]

Hedging against political instability in producing countries and against the geopolitical fallout of Russia's energy power

Unlike Europe, Washington tends to view Russian energy resources as secondary to the larger strategic considerations related to the political independence of states along the Russian periphery and to competition in the Caspian region. Thus, since the days of the Cold War, US–Russian relations have been dominated by diplomatic and military concerns, while energy has played only a secondary role. Of course, the US does not import significant amounts of energy from Russia, and US trade and financial relations with Russia are also limited. Moreover, and as shown during the period of closer US–Russian energy cooperation between 2001 and 2003 mentioned above, the US does not see Russia as a market maker in the global oil business, and to this day, few US companies are involved in Russia.[42]

In fact, there is only limited scope for a direct US–Russian energy partnership. There are no infrastructure interdependencies and only a limited number of common economic interests, a situation that does little to suppress the clash between the liberal US vision of global energy governance and the state-driven approach of Russian energy policies. However, current alarmist rhetoric from Washington that links energy and geopolitics could spill over into US energy policies and aggravate the European–Russian energy security dilemma. Naturally, such a development is not in the interest of European and global energy security. Instead, Washington should accept that the EU and its member states are in a much better position to take the lead in defining the West's energy relations with Russia. Nevertheless, it will not be easy for the US to accept a secondary role in Western energy relations with Russia, because while Russia's newfound confidence in international affairs is based primarily on its booming energy business, it also reflects a decline in US capacity to exercise global leadership across a broad set of economic and security challenges.

The Europeans, conversely, may come to realize that they need to work closely with Washington to achieve the successful management of political instability in energy producing countries. The West has an interest in helping Middle Eastern and African producers to overcome their governance deficits (rentier state symptoms) and to cope with the structural weaknesses of their economies (Dutch disease symptoms).[43] But the long-term success of political and economic engagement of Western states in energy-rich countries depends on local acceptance – and this may often mean that energy-rich countries will need to accept gradual political reforms, while Western states help them to build a strong state, rather than achieving quick democratization that is opposed by local elites. Moreover, US–European cooperation to ensure the political stability of key producing countries would be possible only if the broader foreign policy approaches, and in particular the regional policies, of both the US and EU were more or less compatible. This is especially relevant with regard to the US "war on terror." Western states should resist the temptation of subordinating their policies and strategies that deal with regional conflicts to the seemingly more urgent task of fighting global terrorism.

The same logic applies to how the West deals with the fragility of Russian power. Russia's domestic stability is closely tied to functioning energy markets and stable energy prices. A recession in the US and the EU or a slow-down in China's growth could lead to a significant drop in energy prices. While this may have positive effects in that it would force Russian elites to reconsider greater openness of their energy sector and allow more investment, it could also threaten internal stability and increase authoritarianism. A coordinated and pragmatic

US–European approach in such a situation could tip the balance in one or the other direction.

US–European cooperation is also needed to hedge against the potentially negative geopolitical effects of China's growing dependence on foreign energy. While there is latent rivalry between Russia and China in the Caspian region, the rapidly growing Chinese demand for new energy markets sometimes also collides with Western policies and governance efforts in Africa and in the Middle East.[44] China does not make its cooperation conditional on good governance principles or on the protection of human rights, as shown in Beijing's bilateral energy deal with Tehran, which has been harshly criticized by Washington. Still, although China's energy foreign policy tends to undermine Western influence in Africa and the Middle East, its regional policies are based on pragmatism, and not on anti-Western ideology. China shares the West's concern for regional stability and open waterways, a fact that could be used to establish a joint US–European strategy for engaging China in the West's broader stability efforts in these regions.[45]

It will be more difficult for the US and Europe to agree on a joint approach to hedge against the unavoidable geopolitical fallout of Russia's new energy-related power in the post-Soviet space. In particular, in the Caucasus and Caspian regions, the energy and economic interests of all relevant outside actors – Russia, the US, Europe, and China – are closely linked to strategic considerations. The rush of Western companies to the Caspian during the 1990s was directly connected to US attempts to break the Russian monopoly over the region's energy exports, to isolate Iran, and to reduce Russia's influence. Although Azerbaijan and Georgia tied themselves to the West by building the BTC pipeline before Russia managed to reassert herself in the region, Russia is now in a good position to cut short the delivery of oil from Kazakhstan and Turkmenistan to the BTC and thus to undermine plans to expand BTC pipeline capacity. Further, Moscow's military and diplomatic unilateralism during the 2008 Georgian crisis came as a strong signal that Russia is aiming to dominate the Caucasus, both economically and politically. The West needs to acknowledge that the degree to which Western states and companies can expect to have access to Caspian resources will remain dependent not only on economic, but to a large extent also on geopolitical considerations.[46]

Russia's success in its drive for dominance in the post-Soviet space is exemplified by the strong dependence of countries such as Belarus, Ukraine, and Armenia on Russian energy imports. Given the fragility of the sovereignty and the domestic instability of these countries, the West would be well advised to exercise caution in moving ahead with the promise of NATO membership made to Ukraine and Georgia at the Bucharest summit in spring 2008. While NATO's relationship with Russia has remained largely symbolic, Moscow's opposition to the planned third round of NATO enlargement, which would bring the alliance into close proximity of a long stretch of Russia's western borders, is very real. Ukraine joining NATO would have major consequences for Russia and for its relationship with its Slavic neighbors, as well as for the European security architecture. Together with the controversy surrounding plans to move ahead with the US missile defense system in cooperation with Poland, these security-related disagreements could lead to a spiral of action and reaction that could in turn result in a serious deterioration of the relationship between the West and Russia. It will be essential for the US and Europe to consult closely on the issue of Ukraine's EU and NATO memberships and also to take Russia's concerns into account.[47]

Conclusion

The global energy system is in the midst of a major transformation, and Russia's energy power is a key factor in the process. New consumers in Asia have joined their Western counterparts in rapidly growing energy demand, and the producers, among them Russia, have gained considerable influence over global energy issues. Furthermore, since the changing dynamics of the global energy markets are closely intertwined with local and regional political conflicts and global reactions to these, global energy security has risen to the top of the international political agenda over the past few years.

Russia's newly acquired energy wealth has facilitated the shift toward a more assertive Russian foreign policy, which in turn has triggered fears in the West regarding the political effects of Europe's energy dependence on Russia. However, Russia's energy power may be less secure than many observers – both in Russia and in the West – believe, and if Russia does not reform and diversify, it could face an economic slow-down in the mid-term and be unable to meet the growing domestic and foreign energy demand.

When the West sets out to deal with Russia and its energy power in the next few years, it will need to acknowledge Russia as a regional power with global ambitions, while at the same time taking into account Russia's fragile political and social state. The real complexities of foreign relations between Russia and the West, and, more specifically, the multifaceted role that energy issues play within this framework, make it essential that Europe and the US define a more coherent set of policies aimed at Russia and establish a more constructive energy partnership with Russia.

The EU and its member states are in a much better position than the US to define the key parameters of the West's energy relationship with Russia, a fact that Washington would do well to acknowledge. Thus, when they move ahead, the Europeans should aim at developing a more robust energy partnership with Russia that better integrates the internal and external elements of European energy security; that acknowledges the existing dependencies and limited diversification options on both sides, taking into account the whole energy supply chain; that recognizes the very different energy relations of individual EU member states with Russia and the limits this entails with regard to the cohesion of policies at the EU level; and that goes beyond state-to-state relations and oil and gas exploration issues to include business-to-business relationships and the fields of energy efficiency, alternative energy industries, and electricity supply.

Conversely, while Washington should recognize Europe's lead in defining the West's energy relations with Russia, the Europeans should accept the fact that energy issues are inextricably linked to global market and environmental dynamics, on the one hand, and to the development of regional conflicts, on the other – all of which issues Europe would find it a lot easier to deal with in collaboration with the US. In fact, a functioning transatlantic partnership remains crucial to the West's aims of maintaining the stability of global energy markets, dealing effectively with the energy-related challenges of global warming, and adapting the current producer–consumer framework to the changing energy system. At the same time, US–European cooperation will remain an essential tool for hedging against political instability in producing countries and against the geopolitical fallout of Russian energy power at the regional level, especially in the Caucasus and the Caspian region.

The energy system represents one of the key links between global markets and local conflicts in a globalized world. The growing interconnection between energy and security demands better coordination between the energy policies and the foreign and security policies of Western states. Narrow national security strategies must be complemented by policies that focus on improving the human security of individuals in destabilized regions, on the one hand, and on improving the global security of the environment and the global (energy) market structures, on the other. Narrow energy policies – too often driven by growth coalitions and biased toward supply-side solutions – must be expanded to engage a global range of public and private stakeholders in an effort to maintain stable (energy) markets that are environmentally sustainable.

Notes

1 See, for example, International Energy Agency (IEA), *World Energy Outlook 2007: China and India Insights* (Paris: OECD/IEA, 2007); Adam E. Sieminski, "World Energy Futures," in *Energy and Security: Toward a New Foreign Policy Strategy*, ed. Jan H. Kalicki and David L. Goldwyn (Washington, DC: Johns Hopkins University Press, 2005).

2 See, for example, the case studies written for "The Role of National Oil Companies in International Energy Markets," a project jointly sponsored by the Japan Petroleum Energy Center and the James A. Baker III Institute for Public Policy, Rice University, Houston, March 2007, www.rice.edu/energy/publications/nocs.html (accessed 8 September 2008).

3 See, for example, Terry Lynn Karl, *The Paradox of Plenty: Oil Booms and Petro-States* (Berkeley: University of California Press, 1997); Ian Bannon and Paul Collier, *Natural Resources and Violent Conflict* (Washington, DC: World Bank, 2003).

4 See, for example, Susanne Peters, "Coercive Western Energy Security Strategies: 'Resource Wars' as a New Threat to Global Security," *Geopolitics* 9, no. 1 (2004): 187–212; Michael T. Klare, *Blood and Oil: The Dangers and Consequences of America's Growing Dependency on Imported Petroleum* (New York: Henry Holt, 2004).

5 In fact, the link between energy and politics is more pronounced in regional gas markets, where pipelines establish a physical link between different territorial sovereignties. Nevertheless, even disruptive action at export choke points, such as the straits of Hormuz or Malacca, is likely to result in short-term political effects rather than in a

long-term realignment of political power. On the limits of the utility of the Middle East energy weapon, see, for example, Bassam Fattouh, *How Secure Are Middle East Oil Supplies?*, Oxford Institute for Energy Studies Paper, WPM 33 (Oxford: Oxford Institute for Energy Studies, September 2007), www.oxfordenergy.org/pdfs/WPM33.pdf (accessed 8 September 2008); Dennis Blair and Kenneth Lieberthal, "Smooth Sailing: The World's Shipping Lanes Are Safe," *Foreign Affairs* 86, no. 3 (2007): 7–13; Caitlin Talmadge, "Closing Time: Assessing the Iranian Threat to the Strait of Hormus," *International Security*, 33, no. 1 (2008): 82–117.

6 See, for example, Valérie Marcel, *Investment in Middle East Oil: Who Needs Whom?*, Chatham House Reports (London: Chatham House, February 2006), www.chathamhouse.org.uk/files/3304_vmfeb06.pdf (accessed 8 September 2008).

7 For studies taking an alarmist view, see, for example, Kenneth S. Deffeyes, *Beyond Oil: The View from Hubbert's Peak* (New York: Hill and Wang, 2005); Richard Heinberg, *The Party's Over: Oil, War and the Fate of Industrial Societies*, revised and updated edition (Gabriola Island: New Society Publishers, 2005).

8 See, for example, Melanie A. Kenderdine and Ernest J. Moniz, "Technology Development and Energy Security," in Kalicki and Goldwyn, *Energy and Security*, 425–59; Kevin A. Baumert, "The Challenge of Climate Protection: Balancing Energy and Environment," in ibid., 485–508.

9 On the Russian energy situation, see, for example, David Lane, ed., *The Political Economy of Russian Oil* (Boulder: Rowman & Littlefield, 1999); John D. Grace, *Russian Oil Supply: Performance and Prospects* (Oxford: Oxford University Press, 2005); Jonathan Stern, *The Future of Russian Gas and Gazprom* (Oxford: Oxford University Press, 2005); Michael Ellman, ed., *Russia's Oil and Gas: Bonanza or Curse?* (London: Anthem Press, 2006).

10 See Chapter 2 in this volume. See also Shinichiro Tabata, ed., *Dependent on Oil and Gas: Russia's Integration into the World Economy* (Sapporo: Hokkaido University, 2006); Julian Cooper, "Can Russia Compete in the Global Economy?," *Eurasian Geography and Economics* 47, no. 4 (2006): 407–26.

11 See Chapters 2 and 4 in this volume. See also Alan Riley and Frank Umbach, "Out of Gas: Looming Russian Gas Deficits Demand Readjustment of European Energy Policy," *Internationale Politik – Global Edition* 8 (Spring 2007): 83–90.

12 See Chapter 3 in this volume. See also Andreas Wenger, Jeronim Perovic, and Robert W. Orttung, eds., *Russian Business Power: The Role of Russian Business in Foreign and Security Relations* (New York: Routledge, 2006); Michael McFaul and Kathryn Stoner-Weiss, "The Myth of the Authoritarian Model: How Putin's Crackdown Holds Russia Back," *Foreign Affairs* 87, no. 1 (2008): 68–84.

13 See Chapter 2 in this volume: Russia's energy strategy to 2020 dates from August 2003, and the successor strategy for the period to 2030 is work in process as of the time of writing: Ministry of Industry and Energy (Minpromenergo), *Energeticheskaia strategiia Rossii na period do 2020 goda*, approved as decree no. 1234-r by the Russian government on 28 August 2003, www.minprom.gov.ru/docs/strateg/1/ (accessed 13 December 2007); Minpromenergo, Institut energeticheskoi strategii, *Kontseptsiia energeticheskoi strategii Rossii na period do 2030g* (proekt) (Moscow: Minpromenergo, 2007).

14 For voices warning concerning the security dimension of Russian energy policies, see, for example, Keith C. Smith, *Security Implications of Russian Energy Policies*, CEPS Policy Brief, no. 90 (Brussels, Centre for European Policy Studies, January 2006), http://shop.ceps.eu/downfree.php?item_id=1293 (accessed 8 September 2008); Robert L. Larsson, *Russia's Energy Policy: Security Dimensions and Russia's Reliability as an Energy Supplier* (Stockholm: Swedish Defense Research Agency FOI, 2006).

15 See, for example, Andrew Monaghan, "Russia–EU Relations: An Emerging Energy Security Dilemma," *Pro et Contra* 10, nos 2–3 (2006), English version available at: www.carnegieendowment.org/files/EmergingDilemma1.pdf (accessed 8 September 2008).

16 See Chapters 5 and 8 in this volume.
17 See Chapters 2, 5, and 7 in this volume.
18 See, for example, Gawdat Bahgat, "Europe's Energy Security: Challenges and Opportunities," *International Affairs* 82, no. 5 (2006): 961–75.
19 See Chapter 6 in this volume. For background reading, see also Jeronim Perovic, "Russian Energy Companies in the Caspian and Central Eurasian Region: Expanding Southward," in Wenger, Perovic and Orttung, *Russian Business Power*, 88–113.
20 See, for example, Andrew Monaghan, *Russia and the Security of Europe's Energy Supplies: Security in Diversity?*, Special Series 07/01 (Swindon: Conflict Studies Research Centre, 2007), http://se2.isn.ch/serviceengine/FileContent?serviceID=10&fileid=E01719FD-5CEE-6B5D-EF48-181E39EDFC83&lng=en (accessed 8 September 2008).
21 See Chapter 7 in this volume. See also Nina Poussenkova, *The Wild, Wild East: East Siberia and the Far East – A New Petroleum Frontier?*, Economic and Energy Policy Working Paper, no. 4 (Moscow: Moscow Carnegie Center, 2007), www.carnegie.ru/en/pubs/workpapers/77259.htm (accessed 8 September 2008).
22 See, for example, Kyrre Elvenes Bræhkus and Indra Øverland, "A Match Made in Heaven? Strategic Convergence between China and Russia," *China and Eurasia Forum Quarterly* 5, no. 2 (2007): 41–61.
23 See Chapters 2, 3, and 4 in this volume.
24 See Chapters 5 and 8 in this volume. See also Sanam S. Haghighi, *Energy Security: The External Legal Relations of the European Union with Major Oil- and Gas-Supplying Countries* (Portland: Hart, 2007), especially 37–64; Janne Halland Matlary, *Energy Policy in the European Union* (London: Palgrave Macmillan, 1997).
25 See, for example, Monaghan, *Russia and the Security of Europe's Energy Supplies*.
26 See, for example, Aad Correlje and Coby van der Linde, "Energy Supply Security and Geopolitics: A European Perspective," *Energy Policy* 34, no. 5 (2006): 532–43.
27 See, for example, Andreas Heinrich, "Gazprom's Expansion Strategy in Europe and the Liberalization of EU Energy Markets," *Russian Analytical Digest*, no. 34 (February 2008): 8–15, www.res.ethz.ch/analysis/rad (accessed 8 September 2008).
28 See Chapter 8 in this volume. See also Pami Alto, ed., *The EU–Russian Energy Dialogue: Europe's Future Energy Security* (Aldershot: Ashgate, 2007).
29 IEA, *Optimising Russian Natural Gas: Reform and Climate Policy* (Paris: OECD/IEA, 2006), 141–66.
30 See, for example, Petra Opitz, "Energy Savings in Russia – Political Challenges and Economic Potential," *Russian Analytical Digest*, no. 23 (June 2007): 5–9, www.res.ethz.ch/analysis/rad (accessed 8 September 2008). On the issue of energy efficiency, see also the contributions in *Russian Analytical Digest*, no. 46 (September 2008).
31 See, for example, Susan Wengle, "Power Politics: Electricity Sector Reforms in Post-Soviet Russia," *Russian Analytical Digest*, no. 27 (September 2008): 6–9, www.res.ethz.ch/analysis/rad/ (accessed 8 September 2008); William Tompson, *Restructuring Russia's Electricity Sector: Towards Effective Competition or Faux Liberalization*, OECD Economics Department Working Paper, no. 4003 (Paris: OECD, 2004).
32 See, for example, Daniel Simmons and Isabel Murray, "Russian Gas: Will There Be Enough Investment?," *Russian Analytical Digest*, no. 27 (September 2007): 2–5, www.res.ethz.ch/analysis/rad/ (accessed 8 September 2008).
33 See, for example, Kalicki and Goldwyn, *Energy and Security*.
34 See, for example, Baumert, "The Challenge of Climate Protection."
35 See, for example, David M. Andrews, ed., *The Atlantic Alliance Under Stress: US–European Relations after Iraq* (Cambridge: Cambridge University Press, 2005); Daniel Möckli and Victor Mauer, eds., *European–American Relations and the Middle East from Suez to Iraq: A Strained Partnership* (London: Routledge, forthcoming 2009).

36 See Chapter 9 in this volume. See also William Ratliff, *Russia's Oil in America's Future* (Stanford: Hoover Press, 2003); David G. Victor and Nadejda M. Victor, "Axis of Oil?," *Foreign Affairs* 82, no. 2 (2003): 47–61; Daniel Yergin, *The Prize: The Epic Quest for Oil, Money and Power* (New York: The Free Press, 1993).
37 See, for example, Daniel Yergin, "Ensuring Energy Security," *Foreign Affairs* 85, no. 2 (2006): 69–82.
38 See, for example, Patrick Avato and Jonathan Coony, *Accelerating Clean Energy Technology Research, Development, and Deployment*, World Bank Working Paper, no. 138 (Washington, DC: The World Bank, 2008).
39 See Chapters 9 and 10 in this volume. See also Jonathan Sinton et al., *Evaluation of China's Energy Strategy Options* (Berkeley: The China Sustainable Energy Program, 2005), http://eetd.lbl.gov/ea/china/china_pubs-policy.html (accessed 8 September 2008); Liu Xuecheng, *China's Energy Security and Its Grand Strategy*, The Stanley Foundation Policy Analysis Brief (Muscatine: The Stanley Foundation, September 2006), www.stanleyfoundation.org/publications/pab/pab06chinasenergy.pdf (accessed 8 September 2008).
40 See, for example, William F. Martin and Evan M. Harrje, "The International Energy Agency," in Kalicki and Goldwyn, *Energy and Security*, 97–116; Joe Barnes and Amy Myers Jaffe, "The Persian Gulf and the Geopolitics of Oil," *Survival* 48, no. 1 (2006): 143–62.
41 See, for example, Yergin, "Ensuring Energy Security."
42 See Chapter 9 in this volume.
43 See Chapters 2 and 3 in this volume. See also Erika Weinthal and Pauline Jones Luong, "Combating the Resource Curse: An Alternative Solution to Managing Mineral Wealth," *Perspectives on Politics* 4, no. 1 (2006): 35–53; William Tompson, "A Frozen Venezuela? The 'Resource Curse' and Russian Politics," in *Russia's Oil: Bonanza or Curse?*, ed. Michael Ellman (London: Anthem, 2006), 189–212; Egil Matsen and Ragnar Torvik, "Optimal Dutch Disease," *Journal of Development Economics* 78, no. 2 (2005): 494–515; Benjamin Smith, "Oil Wealth and Regime Survival in the Developing World: 1960–1999," *American Journal of Political Science* 48, no. 2 (2004): 232–46.
44 See, for example, Stephen Blank, "China, Kazakh Energy, and Russia: An Unlikely Menage a Trois," *The China and Eurasia Forum Quarterly* 3, no. 3 (2005): 99–109.
45 See, for example, Jin Liangxiang, "Energy First: China in the Middle East," *Middle East Quarterly* XII, no. 2 (2005), www.meforum.org/article/694 (accessed 8 September 2008); Kenneth Lieberthal and Mikkal Herberg, "China's Search for Energy Security: Implications for U.S. Policy," in *NBR Analysis 17/1* (Seattle: The National Bureau of Asian Research, April 2006), 13–19, http://nbr.org/publications/analysis/pdf/vol.17no1.pdf (accessed 8 September 2008).
46 See Chapter 6 in this volume. For background reading, see Svante E. Cornell and Niklas Nilsson, eds, *Europe's Energy Security: Gazprom's Dominance and Caspian Supply Alternatives* (Stockholm and Washington, DC: The Central Asia – Caucasus Institute and Silk Road Studies Program, 2008), www.isdp.eu/files/publications/scornell/sc08europesenergy.pdf (accessed 8 September 2008).
47 See Chapter 6 in this volume. See also Margarita M. Balmaceda, *Energy Dependency, Politics and Corruption in the Former Soviet Union: Russia's Power, Oligarchs' Profits and Ukraine's Missing Energy Policy, 1995–2006* (London: Routledge, 2007); Jeronim Perovic, "Caucasus Crisis: Implications and Options for the West," *CSS Analyses in Security Policy* 3, no. 39 (2008), www.isn.ethz.ch/isn/Current-Affairs/Policy-Briefs/Detail/?lng=en&id=90955 (accessed 8 September 2008).

Index

Note: Numbers in **bold** refer to figures; numbers in *italic* refer to tables

Aalto, Pami 15
Abdullah, Crown Prince 193
Abramovitch, Roman 58, 137
ACG oil field 111, 112, 113, 115, 116, 190
Achimgaz 171
AIOC 115–16, 117, 129n12, 190
Alekperov, Vagit 111
Alekseeva, Liudmila 60
Algeria 98
Aliev, President Heidar 115, 190
Altai gas pipeline 140, 208
Amerada Hess oil company 116
Amoco 183
Angaro–Lensk gas field 135
Angarsk–Daqing pipeline 96
Angarsk–Nakhodka pipeline 148
Anti-Monopoly Commission 81
ARCO 183
Armenia 5
Asian market future 132
Atasu–Alashankou pipeline 120
Austria 91, 159
Austrian National Bank 8
authoritarianism 52
AvtoVAZ 32, 59
Azerbaijan 14, 110, 114, 115–17
Azerbaijan International Operating Company *see* AIOC
Azeri–Chirag–deepwater Guneshli *see* ACG oil field

Baku–Tbilisi–Ceyhan pipeline *see* BTC pipeline
Baltic Pipeline System (BPS) 98
Baltic States, diversification from Russia 166

Bank of Finland Institute for Economies in Transition *see* BOFIT
BASF 73
BASF Wintershall 170, 171
Belarus 5, 9, 93, 97, 227
Beltransgaz 93
Berdymukhammedov, President Gurbanguly 121, 123, 125
Berezovsky, Boris 58, 173
biomass 4
Blood and Oil (Klare) 188
Blue Stream pipeline 79, 96, 97, 110
Boeing 31, 32
BOFIT 28
Bogdanchikov, Sergei 127, 140, 147
Botas (Turkey) 98
BP 3, 4, 39, 71, 72–3, 76, 116, 146, 167, 174, 183, 185, 190; *see also* TNK-BP
Brækhus, Kyrre 17
Bratstvo pipeline 170, 174
British Gas 185
British Petroleum *see* BP
Browder, William 61
BTC pipeline 14, 110, 113, 116, 117, 121–2, 128, 191, 239
Bulgaria 91, 96–7, 127
Burgas-Alexandropolis pipeline 98
Bush, President George H.W. 188
Bush, President George W. 181, 189, 192, 235
business problems 145–7

CAC pipeline 120, 125
Cambridge Energy Research Associates 81
Carter Doctrine 188
Caspian Pipeline Consortium *see* CPC

246 Index

Caspian pipelines **113**
Caspian region 109–28
Center for the Russian Political Situation 54
Central Asia-Center pipeline *see* CAC
Central European Gas Hub 102
Centrica 98, 174
Chaiandinsk oil/gas field 145
challenges in Europe 96–9, 168–9
Chayandinsk gas field 139
Chemezov, Sergei 59
Cheney, Vice President Richard (Dick) 189–90, 194
Chevron 71, 116, 187, 190
China: Central Asia involvement 191–2; coal reserves 211; in Cold War era 3; dependency on Russia 213–14, 215; energy cost negotiations 148; energy imports 5, 96, 109, 110, 120, 123, 201, 203–4, 209–10, 213; environmental issues 210–12, 215–16; foreign relations 214–15, 218n31; historic relations with Russia 201, 202–3, 208; internal politics 206–7; oil companies 201, 205–6, 208; oil reserves 211; pollution 212; relations with Russia 15, 17, 140, 148, 201, 206–7, 208–10, 214–16; Russian arms supply 219n47; US trade 209; *see also* Shanghai Cooperation Organization
Chubais, Anatoly 43
Chufrin, Gennady 136
CIA and Soviet oil forecasts 2
CIS 89
civil liberties 7, 8, 12
Clean Energy Initiative 187
Clinton, President William (Bill) 183, 187, 188, 192
Closson, Stacy 13–14
CMEA 91
CNOOC 205
CNPC 120, 123, 140, 205
coal: Chinese 211; exports 5; production 31; reserves 3, 4; Russian consumption 6
coercion 57–63
Cold War era 1, 91–2, 181, 182, 202
Commonwealth of Independent States *see* CIS
conflict and energy 225–7
Conoco 183
ConocoPhillips 73, 183–4
contract of the century (BP and State Oil) 190
Cooper, Julian 29, 82

corruption 63–7
Council for Mutual Economic Assistance *see* CMEA
CPC pipeline 110, 126, 128, 187
Cyprus 186
Czech Republic 92
Czechoslovakia 91

Dauletabad gas field 111, 123
democracy 7, 8, 12, 52–6, 59–60, 70n54
Deripaska, Oleg 31
Devon oil company 116
domestic energy supply *38*
Druzhba oil pipeline 172
Druzhba–Adria project 98
Dutch disease 45

East Germany 91
East Siberia: development 15, 132, 151–2, 230; environmental challenges 144–5; finance 143; future issues 149–50; gas reserves 5–6; and Gazprom 138–41; infrastructure challenges 144–5; oil fields 39, 43; oil reserves 4; organizational challenges 144–5; potential 133–5; problems 135–6; production 134, *135*
East Siberia Pacific Ocean pipeline *see* ESPO
Eastern Gas Program 38, 42, 139–40, 146
eastern policy 136–8; *see also* East Siberia; Far East region
EC *see* Europe
economy (Russia): comparative economic development 24–5; economic dependence on oil/gas 23, 26–9; economic diversification 23, 29–33; economic performance 23, 24–6; energy sector prospects 23, 33–44; long-term economic prospects 24, 44–7
ECT 10, 46, 89, 91, 94, 160, 231
EEC: energy dependence on Russia 2, 89–91, 95–6, 102, 157–78, 229–30; energy policy 160; energy security 161–3, *169*
Ekho Moskvy 60
electricity: exports 5; power stations 39; production 4, 39
energy: cut off by Russia 227; and political conflict 225–7; potential 3–6; relations with EU 89–96, 157–78, 167, 232–4; resources and coercion 57–63; subsidies 61–3; supremacy 89; wealth and political system 53–7; *see also* coal; electricity; gas; oil

energy relationship EU/Russia 228–34
energy security 161–3, 169, 187, 211, 231–2
Energy and Security (Kalicki and Goldwyn) 189
Energy Strategies 4, 6, 33, 39–40, 134
Eni (Italy) 46, 100, 167, 182
E.ON Ruhrgas 46, 73, 91, 99, 100, 170
ESPO pipeline 96, 109, 138, 140, 141, 144, 145, 150
Estonia 93
EU: as coal importer 5; common energy policy 9, 15–16, 157–8, 161–3, 169, 175, 177–8, 231–2; Common Foreign and Security Policy (CFSP) 169; cooperation with US 234–41; debate on Russian energy 165, 166–8; energy relationship with Russia 228–37; enlargements 159; EU–Russian Summit (Sochi 2006) 94, 99; historical relations with Russia 159–61; internal tensions 157–8, 163, 175; Partnership and Cooperation Agreement with Russia *see* PCA; Russia energy conference (2008) 10; Russia Energy Dialogue 100; strategy documents 94
Europe: current energy situation 158–9; EC 4; EC Competition Directorate 46; *see also* EEC; EU; gas imports, Europe
European Energy Charter Treaty *see* ECT
European Investment Bank 94
Europort refinery (Rotterdam) 98
export tariffs 79
Extractive Industries Transparency Initiative 61
Exxon 184
ExxonMobil 71, 116, 147, 184, 187, 191

Far East region: development 15, 132, 151–2, 230; environmental challenges 144–5; finance 143; future issues 149–50; and Gazprom 138–41; infrastructure challenges 144–5; organizational challenges 144–5; potential 133–5; problems 135–6; production 134, *135*
Federal Anti-Monopoly Service 41
Federal Security Service *see* FSB
Federal Statistics Service 7
Federal Tariff Service 38, 81
Fedun, Leonid 43
Finland 46, 91, 92, 168
Finmeccanica 31
foreign direct investments (FDI) 186
foreign exchange reserves 8

foreign investment/ownership in Russia 30, 72–4, **73**
foreign policy 16, 149–52
foreign relations *see* individual countries
Fortnum/Neste 167, 168
Fradkov, Prime Minister Mikhail 146
France 91, 92
Freedom Support Act (US) 190
FSB 52, 57, 58–9, 74, 138
future policy 149–53

G8 presidency (2006) 99
Gaddy, Clifford G. 65–6
Gareev, General Makhmut 189
gas: dependence on **27**; development 17, 137; Eastern Siberia fields 10; exports from Russia 2, 4, 5, 89–91, *92*, 182; imports to Russia 96; pipelines 2, **5**, 42; prices 62; production 3, 12, 23, 27, **36**, 41, 95, 134, *135*, 181, 185; reserves 3, 4, 106n35, 114, 116, 118, *134*, 150; Russian consumption 6, 149; state nationalization 7, 62; supply restrictions 9; workforce 7; *see also* economy; energy; individual gas fields
gas imports, Europe 4, 42, 46, 89, *164*, 182; interdependence with Russia 98–9; as oil importer 1, 4, 42, 89, 230; relations with Russia 14, 46, 91–6, 103, 132, 167–78, 236–41; Russian dependence on Europe 96, 103, 160, 229; Russian future in energy market 99–103; Russian investment in 100; *see also* energy
Gasunie 170
Gaz de France 46, 99
Gazexport 95
Gazprom: China market 98; in eastern areas 138–41, 145–6; exports 9–10, 93, 95, 128, 170–1, 174, 177; gas imports 122–3; inefficiency 66; investment/development 31, 41, 100; joint ventures 73, 74; new markets 185; pipelines 9–10, 43, 93; price regulation 81, 82, 109, 123; production 42, 76; revenue 27, 28; as state monopoly 9–10, 46–7, 59–60, 78–9, 93
Gazpromneft 98, 101
GDP 6, 7, 9, **25**, 26, 27, 28, 29, 32, **38**, 45, 51, 89–90, 186
Georgia 110, 113, 194, 227
Germany 2, 5, 11, 15, 46, 92, 167, 170–1, 174, 175, 176; *see also* East Germany; West Germany

Getty Petroleum 184
global energy system 227–41
global warming 195
GNI 24, **25**
Goldwyn, David 189
Gorbachev, Mikhail 51, 182
Gore–Chernomyrdin commission 183
Greece 46, 92, 127
Green Stream pipeline (Libya) 98
Gref, German *64*
gross domestic profit *see* GDP
gross national income *see* GNI
Gusinsky, Vladimir 60
Gutseriev, Mikhail 65

Hanson, Philip 12, 56
Hermitage Capital 61
Hu Jintao, President 194
Hungary 91, 92
Huntington, Samuel 52
hydro power 4

Ickes, Barry W. 65–6
IEA 39, 90, 233, 236
IEF 236
IMF (International Monetary Fund) 183
Indem 61
independent group suppression 59–61
India 141
initial public offerings (IPOs) 30–1
Inpex oil company 116
instability and corruption 63–7
Institute of Energy Policy 61
Institute on Problems of Globalization 61
International Energy Agency *see* IEA
International Relations (IR) theory 161–3
International Trade Commission (US) 185
Iran 91, 121, 150
Iraq 173
Israel and OPEC 2
Italy 91, 92, 176
Itochu oil company 116
Ivanov, Deputy Prime Minister Sergei 57, 59
Ivanov, Viktor 57

Jackson–Vanik amendment 193
Japan 6, 15, 91, 96, 148–9, 188, 215

Kaczynski, President Lech 166
Kalicki, Jan 189
Karachaganak gas field 111, 119, 126, 127, 190
Kashagan oil field 127

Kazakhoil 187
Kazakhstan 5, 14, 37, 42, 96, 110, 114, 117–21, 124–6, 127, 182, 191
Kazakhstan–China pipeline 128
key players in Russia's east **139**
KGB 52, 57
Kharyaga project 184
Khodorkovsky, Mikhail 58, 61, 76, 77, 193, 194, 207
Khristenko, Energy Minister Viktor 10, *64*
Klare, Michael 188–9
Kleiner, Vadim 79
Kohl–Gorbachev re-unification deal 170
Kontorovich, Alexei 134, 143
Korea National Oil Corporation (KNOC) 141
Korpedzhe oil and gas field 121
Kosovo 192
Kovykta gas field 42, 54, 89, 96, 139, 174, 195
Kryshtanovskaya, Olga 57
Kudrin, Finance Minister Aleksei 26, *64*
Kuwait Petroleum International 98
Kyoto Protocol 188, 196
Kyrgyzstan 191, 194

Latvia 93
leadership, political/industrial 63–5, *64*
Lebedev, Platon 76, 77
Ledeneva, Alena 77
liberalizing product markets 80–2
Libya 98, 171
Lipton, David 183
Liquefied Natural Gas *see* LNG
Lithuania 92, 93, 98, 227
LNG 6, 42–3, 46, 90, 95, 100, 149, 185
LUKarco 187
Lukoil 31, 39, 43, 49n38, 71, 73, 76, 93, 98, 111, 112, 116, 117, 129n4, 183, 184
Luxembourg 186

Mažeikių Nafta oil refinery 93, 98, 163, 166, 167, 173
Medvedev, President Dmitry 57, *64*, 74, 82, 114, 127, 146
MEMR 120
Menatep 76
MERT 23, 28, 41, 137
metals: aluminum 31, 45; gold 45; nickel 31, 45; steel 45; titanium 32
MIC 32
Middle East competition 148, 150
military spending 1, 2
Miller, Aleksei 10, 78, 98

Milov, Vladimir 47, 61, 69n37
Ministry of Economic Development and Trade *see* MERT
Ministry of Industry and Energy (Minpromenergo) 23, 140
Ministry of Natural Resources (MNR) 135, 138
Mobil 184
MOL (Hungary) 102
Moldova 5
Mordashov, Aleksei 31

Nabucco pipeline 106n38, 114, 116, 123, 126, 127, 128
Nadym gas field 208
NAIRIT 32–3
Nanay, Julia 14
Nanotekhnologii 32
Naryshkin, Deputy Prime Minister Sergei 59, *64*
National Anti-Terrorism Committee 57
National Association of Development of IT *see* NAIRIT
NATO 89, 101, 192, 239
Nazarbaev, President Nursultan 119, 124
Negroponte, John 194
Nesterov, Valery 144
new markets 147–9
NGOs 60
1973 oil crisis 2, 181
Niyazov, President Saparmurat 112, 121, 123
Nord Stream gas pipeline 11, 42, 97, 166, 170, 172, 174, 185, 197
North Sea 173
Norway 13, 163, 167, 172
Novy Urengoi gas field 171
nuclear power, production 4, 39–40

oil: dependence on **27**; development 17, 137; effect on political system 7; exports from Russia 2, 4, 5, 6, **34**, 89–91, 182, 184; industry profits 79; market prices 6, 129n6, 189; pipelines **4**, 5, 42; production 3, 6, 12, 23, 27, **36**, 40, 63–4, 76, 95, 116, 123, 134, *135*, 181; refining capacity 80; reserves 3, 4, 114, 118, *134*; Russian consumption 6; state nationalization 7, 62, 71–2, 74–8, 78–9; workforce 7; world demand 188; world prices **55**; *see also* economy; energy; individual oil fields
Oil and Natural Gas Corporation (ONGC) 141

OMV (Austria) 102
OPEC: future supplies to Europe 95; and Israel 2; and 1973 oil crisis 2; production ceiling 112; Russian presence 193; and US 159
OPIC 187, 191
Orttung, Robert 12–13
Øverland, Indra 17
Overseas Private Investment Corporation *see* OPIC

Paris Club 1
Patrushev, Nikolai 57
PCA 91, 93
Permanent Council for Mutual Cooperation 94
PetroCanada 185
PGNiG 172
Pichugin, Alexei 76
PKN Orlen 98, 173
Pleines, Heiko 13
Poland 11, 15, 91, 171–3, 174
Polar Lights 183
political conflict and energy 225–7
political system 12–13, 53–7, **56**, 66–7
post-Partnership and Cooperation Agreement 100
Poussenkova, Nina 15
power stations 39–40
Priobskoe joint project 183
producer–consumer framework 235–7
Putin, President Vladimir: and Abramovitch 137; authoritarianism 52; central energy control 9, 54, 60, 62, 67, 72, 78, 112–13; and Chechnya 51; and China 202; diversification policy 32; and energy supremacy 89; and EU relations 94; and Far East investment 136; foreign investment policy 74; and Medvedev's election 57–8; nuclear program 39; power of 13; relations with US 16–17, 192, 194, 236; sees Russia as world power 82

railways 93, 144, 153n30
reciprocity (Russia/EU) 10, 165
regional mergers 137–8
repressive capacity 57–9
reputation as supplier 9
Rice, US Secretary Condoleezza 11, 20n36
Romania 46, 91
Rosatom 32
Rosneft 65, 75, 76, 98, 101, 138–41, 145–6, 195

Ross, Michael L. 56
Rostekhnologii 32
RosUkrEnergo (RUE) joint venture 122
Royal Dutch Shell 167, 184
Ruhrgas see E.ON Ruhrgas
RUSIA Petroleum 77
Russia: eastern policy 136–8; as energy superpower 227; European policy see Europe; future policy 149–53; and global energy system 227–8; see also Putin
Russia–EU energy conference (2008) 10
Russia–Europe confrontation 101
Russian energy, EU debate on 165
Russian Railways (RZD) 93, 144
Russneft 65
Rutland, Peter 16

Sakhalin Energy 41, 42
Sakhalin Island 6
Sakhalin oil fields 39, 41, 54, 72, 89, 139, 140, 147, 150, 184, 195
Sakhalinmorneftegas 140
Salah gas field (Algeria) 98
Saudi Arabia 3, 148, 184
Saudi-Aramco 148
Scanled gas pipeline 172
Schlumberger 39
Schröder, Chancellor Gerhard 11, 170
Schröder–Putin alliance 170
science, technology and communications statistics **30**
SCP pipeline 110, 113, 114
Sechin, Igor 57, 58, *64*
Serbia 96–7
Severstal 31
Shah Deniz pipeline 110, 111, 115, 127, 128n3
Shanghai Cooperation Organisation (SCO) 17, 191, 201
Shell 97, 195
Shkolov, Yevgeny *64*
Shtokman gas field 42, 185
Siberian gas fields 93
Sibneft oil company 39, 54, 58, 65, 75, 77, 101
SIBUR oil company 80, 83
Sidanko oil company 72, 183
Sieminsky, Adam 189
Silovyemashiny 31
Simonov, Konstantin 54
Sino-Soviet relations see China
Sinopec 205
Sobianin, Sergei *64*

SOCAR 116
Solana, Javier 165
South Caucasus Pipeline see SCP
South Korea 6, 15, 96, 140
South Stream pipeline 96–7, 106n37, 197
Soviet Military-Industrial Commission see MIC
Spain 46
Stabilization Fund (*stabfond*) 28, 63
state nationalization/ownership 7, 62, 71–2, 74–7, **75**, 78–9
State Oil Company of Azerbaijan 190, 191
Statoil 100, 116, 167, 190
StatoilHydro 185
Stern, Jonathan 164
Stiglitz, Joseph 72
strategic mistakes 142
Strategy Partnership Agreement 94
SUEK 41
Summers, Larry 183
superpower status 8–9
Supsa pipeline 121–2
Surgutneftegaz 76
Surkov, Vladislav *64*
sustainable development 7
Sweden 91

Talbott, Strobe 183
tanker limitations 160
TCO 116
TCP pipeline 42, 122, 123
Technological Centre for Information and Technology Exchange 94
Tengiz oil field 111, 119, 187, 190
TengizChevroil see TCO
Texaco 184, 187
Timan-Pechora oil field 39, 98, 183
TNK-BP 4, 39, 73, 76, 77, 106n34, 112, 139, 167, 183, 193, 195
Tokarev, Nikolai 58, 127
Total 100, 167, 185
TPAO 116
Trans-Caspian pipeline see TCP
Transit Protocol 46, 165
Transneft 58, 93, 98, 127
Trenin, Dmitry 136
Troll oil field 92
Tsygankov, Stanislav 10
Turkey 1, 5, 95, 110, 113
Turkmenistan 5, 14, 37, 42, 96, 109, 111, 114, 121–5, 151, 191
Tusk, Prime Minister Donald 172
Tyumen Oil Company see TNK-BP

UC Rusal 31
Udmurtneft 146
UK 15, 46, 98, 173–4, 176
Ukraine 5, 9, 78, 93, 97, 194, 195, 227, 239
UN Security Council membership 9
United Aircraft Company 32
United Aviation Corporation 59
United Kingdom *see* UK
United Nations Conference on Trade and Development (UNCTAD) 187
United Shipbuilding Company 59
United States of America *see* US
Urengoi gas field 208
Urengoi gas pipeline 2
US 1, 6, 10–11, 91; cooperation with EU 234–41; energy policy/strategy 16, 183, 188–90, 236; Freedom Support Act 190; imports from Russia 186; international influence 235; International Trade Commission 185; National Energy Strategy 188; new Russian partnership 192–5; oil embargo to Japan 188; and OPEC 159; Reagan administration 91; relations with Russia 16–17, 91–2, 132, 181–97, 236, 237–8; rivalry with Russia 190–2; Russian trade and investment 185–7, *186*; and Saudi Arabia 236; trade with China 209
US–Russian Strategic Energy Reserve 193
Uskova, Olga 32–3
Uzbekistan 5, 96, 191

Vankor 147

Varandei oil terminal 184
Ventspils oil terminal 93
Verbundnetz Gas 172
Verkhnechonsk gas field 140
Verkhnechonskneftgas 140
Vostok Energy joint venture 141
VSMPO-Avisma 31, 32
Vyakhirev, Rem 78, 112

Wenger, Andreas 17
West Germany 2, 91, 92, 159
Western Balkans 1, 5
White Stream pipeline 96, 106n36
Williams energy company 93
WINGAS 171
World Bank 7
World Trade Organization (WTO) 193, 195

Yamal Peninsula gas field 103
Yamal-Europe pipeline 97, 166, 172, 174
Yeltsin, Boris 51, 53, 54, 55, 63, 183, 187, 192, 203
Yom Kippur War 2, 159
Yuganskneftegaz 101, 141
Yukos oil company 39, 54, 58, 60–1, 63, 65, 72, 75, 76, 97, 98, 141, 145, 184, 193, 195, 207
Yurubchen field 143
Yuzhno Russkoye gas field 171

Zakaev, Akhmed 173
Zarubezhneft oil company 58
Zhenbao Island 202

Lightning Source UK Ltd.
Milton Keynes UK
UKOW030400020312

188145UK00003B/51/P